Agricultural Trade between China and the Greater Mekong Subregion Countries

The **ISEAS – Yusof Ishak Institute** (formerly Institute of Southeast Asian Studies) is an autonomous organization established in 1968. It is a regional centre dedicated to the study of socio-political, security, and economic trends and developments in Southeast Asia and its wider geostrategic and economic environment. The Institute's research programmes are grouped under Regional Economic Studies (RES), Regional Strategic and Political Studies (RSPS), and Regional Social and Cultural Studies (RSCS). The Institute is also home to the ASEAN Studies Centre (ASC), the Singapore APEC Study Centre and the Temasek History Research Centre (THRC).

ISEAS Publishing, an established academic press, has issued more than 2,000 books and journals. It is the largest scholarly publisher of research about Southeast Asia from within the region. ISEAS Publishing works with many other academic and trade publishers and distributors to disseminate important research and analyses from and about Southeast Asia to the rest of the world.

Agricultural Trade between China and the Greater Mekong Subregion Countries

A Value Chain Analysis

EDITED BY

JAYANT MENON

VATHANA ROTH

YUSOF ISHAK INSTITUTE

First published in Singapore in 2022 by
ISEAS Publishing
30 Heng Mui Keng Terrace
Singapore 119614
E-mail: publish@iseas.edu.sg
Website: http://bookshop.iseas.edu.sg

All rights reserved. No part of this publication may be reproduced, stored in a retrieval system, or transmitted in any form or by any means, electronic, mechanical, photocopying, recording or otherwise, without the prior permission of the ISEAS – Yusof Ishak Institute.

© 2022 ISEAS – Yusof Ishak Institute, Singapore.

The responsibility for facts and opinions in this publication rests exclusively with the authors and their interpretations do not necessarily reflect the views or the policy of the publisher or its supporters.

ISEAS Library Cataloguing-in-Publication Data

Name(s): Menon, Jayant, 1965–, editor. | Roth, Vathana, editor.
Title: Agricultural trade between China and the Greater Mekong Subregion countries : a value chain analysis / edited by Jayant Menon and Vathana Roth.
Description: Singapore : ISEAS-Yusof Ishak Institute, 2022. | Includes bibliographical references and index.
Identifiers: ISBN 9789815011128 (soft cover) | ISBN 9789815011135 (pdf) | ISBN 9789815011142 (epub)
Subjects: LCSH: Produce trade—Southeast Asia. | Produce trade—China. | Southeast Asia—Commerce—China. | China—Commerce—Southeast Asia.
Classification: LCC HD9016 A9A28

Cover design by Lee Meng Hui
Index compiled by Raffaie Nahar
Typeset by Superskill Graphics Pte Ltd
Printed in Singapore by Mainland Press Pte Ltd

CONTENTS

List of Tables	vii
List of Figures	x
List of Annexes	xiii
Foreword by Dr Eng Netra	xv
Preface	xvii
Acknowledgements	xx
Abbreviations and Acronyms	xxi
The Contributors	xxiii

1. Agricultural Trade between China and the Greater Mekong Subregion Countries: An Overview
   Jayant Menon — 1

2. Economic Structural Change in China and the Implications for Agricultural Trade in the Lancang-Mekong Region
   Hong Song, Lingyun Gao, Qingyi Su and Chengwei Zang — 22

3. Agricultural Exports from Thailand to China: A Value Chain Analysis of Cassava and Durian
   Punpreecha Bhuthong, Papatsara Rattanasimanon and Nuttaporn Udomkiattikul — 59

4. Agricultural Exports from Cambodia to China: A Value Chain Analysis of Cassava and Sugarcane
   Narith Roeun and Hokkheang Hiev — 108

5. Agricultural Exports from Laos to China:
   A Value Chain Analysis of Rice and Cavendish Banana   164
   Viengsavang Thipphavong, Thantavanh Manolom,
   Vanaxay Soukhaseum, Phouthaphone Southammavong and
   Somdeth Bodhisane

6. Agricultural Exports from Myanmar to China:
   A Value Chain Analysis of Maize   205
   Ngu Wah Win, Zaw Oo, Aung Htun and Zaw Min Naing

7. Agricultural Exports from Vietnam to China:
   A Value Chain Analysis of Dragon Fruit and Coffee   256
   Nguyen Thang, Pham Minh Thai, Vu Hoang Dat and
   Vu Thi Van Ngoc

Index   295

LIST OF TABLES

1.1	Growth and Structural Transformation in GMS Countries	2
1.2	Agriculture's Importance in GMS Countries	3
2.1	Contribution of Agriculture to Economic Growth, 1966–2018	26
2.2	Estimation of Surplus Rural Labour in China, 1978–2017	29
2.3	Consumption Structure and Variation in Trends in 2017	34
2.4	Import Values of Major Agricultural Products and Variation in Trend in 2017	35
2.5	Per Capita Import Growth of Some Agricultural Products, 2010–17	36
2.6	Per Capita Domestic Production Growth Rate of Some Agricultural Products, 2010–17	37
2.7	Revealed Comparative Advantage of Each Product Category	38
2.8	Total Projects and Number of Chinese Central Enterprise Projects in Lancang-Mekong Countries, 2004–15	41
2.9	Regional Distribution of China's Foreign Investment in 2017	42
2.10	Regional Distribution of China's Agricultural Outward Investments in 2017	43
2.11	Investment Trends in Primary Agricultural Products	44
2.12	China's Import-Export Trade by Region in 2017	45
2.13	Trade Value and Growth Rate of Lancang-Mekong Countries, 2009–17	46
2.14	China's Agricultural Trade with Lancang-Mekong Countries, 2015–18	47
2.15	Top Five Products with Largest Trade Value between China and Individual Lower Mekong Countries	52

3.1	Top Five Agricultural Product Exports by Value to China, 2017	61
3.2	Key Actors in the Durian and Cassava Value Chains	76
3.3	Summary of Challenges in the Durian and Cassava Value Chains	85
3.4	Summary of NTMs for Durian Export	95
3.5	Summary of NTMs for Cassava Imports	98
3.6	Summary of NTMs for Cassava Exports to China	99
4.1	Contribution of Agriculture to the National Economy	111
4.2	Top Fifteen Agricultural Exports from Cambodia to China, 2016	113
4.3	Number of Respondents for the Cassava and Sugarcane Value Chain Analyses	115
4.4	Cassava Production Costs in the Selected Provinces	125
4.5	Returns and Profit from Cassava Production for Farmers	127
4.6	Number of NTMs Affecting Different Trading Partners' Exports of the Four Products to China as of 2020	138
4.7	Number of NTMs by Code Imposed on the Selected Products as of 2020	141
5.1	Rice Production in Laos and Other GMS Countries	172
5.2	Aggregate Data on Rice Production in Laos, 2013–17	172
5.3	Costs and Benefits of Rice Value Chain at the Farm Gate	178
5.4	Costs and Benefits of the Rice Value Chain for Vanida Rice Mill	180
5.5	Costs and Benefits of Rice Value Chain at Exporter (Wholesaler) and Retailer Stage	181
5.6	Key Actors and Challenges in the Rice and Cavendish Banana Value Chains	190
6.1	Producer Survey Sampling Frame	215
6.2	Major Crop Areas in Myanmar	219
6.3	Historical Prices of Maize	221
6.4	Cultivated Areas and Production of Maize in the Districts of Shan State, 2017	222
6.5	Cost and Return Analysis for Average Farmer	231
6.6	Farmers' Decisions on Harvested Maize	236

List of Tables

6.7	NTMs Imposed by China on Maize (HS 1005) Imports from Myanmar	238
6.8	Discrepancies in Maize Trade Statistics between Myanmar and China	240
7.1	Contribution of Agriculture to the National Economy	260
7.2	Coffee Production in Vietnam, 2013–18	261
7.3	Vietnam's Total Coffee Exports to China, 2015–18	263
7.4	Coffee Exported through Lang Son and Lao Cai Border Gates and Ho Chi Minh City, 2017–19	263
7.5	Exports of Dragon Fruit via Lang Son, Lao Cai and Ha Giang, 2017–19	266
7.6	Summary of Qualitative Interviews	267

LIST OF FIGURES

2.1	Changes in the Proportion of Employment in Agriculture, Industry and Services in China, 1978–2018	27
2.2	China's Trade in Agricultural Products, 1998–2017	31
2.3	China's FDI, 2012–17	50
2.4	China's Outbound Direct Investment and Growth Rate, 2012–16	50
3.1	Durian Planted Area and Production in Thailand, 2004–18	62
3.2	Average Farm Gate Durian Prices in Thailand, 2004–18	63
3.3	Thailand's Cassava Harvested Area and Production, 1997–2019(f)	65
3.4	Destinations of Thailand's Cassava Exports, 1961–2015	67
3.5	Thailand's Cassava Exports to China, 1998–2018	68
3.6	Composition of Thailand's Cassava Exports to China, 2000–18	69
3.7	Conceptual Framework for Value Chain Analysis	72
3.8	Change in the Structure of the Fresh Durian Value Chain between 2008 and 2016	74
3.9	Thai Cassava Value Chain	75
3.10	The Role of the Packing House and the Relationships with Packing House Partners	79
3.11	The Route of Durian Products from Thailand to China	83
3.12	Transport Routes for Exporting Durian from Thailand to China	89
3.13	Map Showing Land Transport Routes for Exporting Durian from Thailand to China	90

List of Figures

4.1	Cambodia's Cassava Value Chain	119
4.2	Total Domestic Cassava Processing Capacity	123
4.3	Benefit Distribution Among Key Actors in Three Distribution Channels of the Cassava Value Chain	124
4.4	Cambodia's Sugarcane Value Chain	129
4.5	Cost in Various Stages of Cambodia's Sugarcane Value Chain	132
4.6	Income Distribution in the Sugarcane Value Chain	134
4.7	Profit Distribution Among All Actors in the Sugarcane Value Chain	135
4.8	The Number of Active NTMs by Category Imposed by China on Raw Materials and Processed Commodities	137
4.9	The Most Used NTMs by Code on China's Imports of the Four Commodities as of 2020	140
4.10	Additional NTMs Imposed by China on Selected Products, 2010–16	142
5.1	Rice Value Chain under Xuanye-Vanida Business Cooperation	176
5.2	Rice Value Chain under IDP Rice Mill	177
5.3	Porter's Value Chain Framework for Lao Cavendish Bananas	185
5.4	Cavendish Banana Value Chain Costs and Revenues in Northern Provinces	187
5.5	Factors Affecting the Business Environment of Cavendish Banana Plantations (n=12)	189
5.6	Export Procedure for Cavendish Bananas	193
6.1	Number of Notifying Countries and Number of (a) SPS and (b) TBT Notifications, 1995–2010	211
6.2	Harvested Areas of Major Crops as Shares of Total Cultivated Area, 2017	220
6.3	Population Distribution in Shan State	223
6.4	Maize Value Chain Map in Shan State	225
6.5	Sources of Maize Seed Planted by Farmers in Shan State	228
6.6	Cost of Production by Farm Size	229

6.7	Productivity among Farmers	230
6.8	Comparison of Myanmar's FOB Prices of Maize to Different Markets	241
7.1	Top Destinations for Vietnam's Coffee Exports	262
7.2	Export Value of Dragon Fruit, 2003–18	265
7.3	Distribution of Dragon Fruit Exports by Market Destination, 2014–18	266
7.4	Coffee Value Chain in Vietnam	270
7.5	Dragon Fruit Value Chain in Vietnam	275

LIST OF ANNEXES

4.1	List of Districts and Villages Selected for Field Data Collection	151
4.2	Global Cassava Value Chain	152
4.3	Governance Structure in Different Linkages Throughout the Sugarcane Value Chain	153
4.4	Sugarcane Cultivation Areas and Production in Cambodia, 1961–2019	154
4.5	Sugarcane Trade Value of Mekong-Lancang Countries, 2001–19	155
4.6	Sugarcane Export Value from GMS Countries to China, 2001–19	156
4.7	Computation of Value-Added Costs for Sugarcane from Production to the Border	157
4.8	Constraints in the Cassava Value Chain	158
4.9	Weaknesses and Strengths in Sugarcane Value Chain Upgrading Strategies	159
5.1	AQSIQ Moisture Standards for Imported Rice	199
5.2	China's Sanitary and Phytosanitary Measures	200
Appendix 6.1	Various Documentation and Procedural Requirements for Trade with China	247
Appendix 6.2	More Statistics on Trade between China and Myanmar	249

FOREWORD

The Greater Mekong Subregion (GMS), which encompasses five Southeast Asian countries—Cambodia, Laos, Myanmar, Thailand and Vietnam (CLMV-T)—and China, is one of the most dynamic subregions in Asia. Apart from progressive market-oriented reforms, countries in the GMS have pursued broader regional integration through various multilayer cooperation frameworks. These include ASEAN, ASEAN-China Free Trade Agreement, China's bilateral economic partnerships, the Regional Comprehensive Economic Partnership agreement and the Lancang-Mekong River Dialogue and Cooperation. While manufacturing trade and global value chain activities significantly benefit from these cooperation frameworks, agricultural trade especially between the CLMV-T and China is hindered by high barriers to trade in the form of tariff and non-tariff measures. Under these circumstances, *what are the key constraints and challenges facing agricultural exports from the CLMV-T? What do China's rapid structural change and development mean for agricultural trade within the subregion? How can the CLMV-T further integrate their agriculture and rural economies to tap into the colossal Chinese market?* Those are the main questions explored in this volume.

This volume consists of six country papers covering each of the GMS countries. The papers were prepared collaboratively by local experts from leading research institutions within the subregion. The first chapter examines the rapid structural transformation and evolving economic policy taking place in China and their implications for agricultural trade within the subregion. Chapters 2–6 cover the CLMV-T country case studies, which examine a range of traditional and non-traditional issues relating to agricultural exports. The studies adopt broadly consistent value chain analysis frameworks to analyse not only key constraints and challenges in agricultural value chains from domestic to export market but also identify the key constraints and relationships between actors along the entire value chains.

Overall, the rapidly growing demand for food consumption represents huge opportunities for agricultural exports for the CLMV-T. However, those countries continue to struggle to address some of the domestic constraints related to absorptive capacity, requisite skills and market diversification for agricultural production and export. They also face difficulties in resolving non-tariff measures (NTMs) at the export market, especially with regard to more complex trade procedures such as obtaining SPS certificates; delays at the border; and lack of publicly available information on relevant NTMs.

I am delighted to present this volume, which offers an insightful overview of some of the key developments in agricultural trade in the GMS. I am sure this work will prove to be an invaluable reference for policymakers, academics and practitioners who strive to work on promoting agricultural development and trade for inclusive economic growth and poverty reduction.

Dr Eng Netra,
Executive Director,
Cambodia Development Resource Institute (CDRI)

PREFACE

The economic prospects of Southeast Asia are increasingly intertwined with that of China and the interdependency is growing with time. This is particularly true for the riparian states of the Mekong region—Cambodia, Laos, Myanmar, Vietnam and Thailand (CLMV-T). Although market-oriented reforms over the past few decades in the CLMV countries, in particular, have driven structural transformation that has involved the share of agriculture in GDP falling in favour of industry and services, it remains an important sector for several reasons.

First, the shares of agriculture in GDP do not reflect their importance as a source of employment or potential for addressing poverty, inequality or inclusion. Even in 2018, the rural sector continued to employ more than half of the labour force in Laos and Myanmar, and a third in Cambodia and Vietnam. There is also growing evidence that shows that growth driven by commercial agriculture in developing countries can have a much greater impact on poverty reduction than that coming from other sectors. Overcoming barriers that stand in the way of increased agricultural exports from the Mekong region to important and growing markets such as China can play a critical role in achieving economic and social objectives.

These developmental opportunities and possibilities provided the motivation for the study reported on in this book. The approach taken involved detailed case studies of key agricultural export commodities in the CLMV-T countries destined primarily for the Chinese market. It is only through detailed case studies that specific impediments along the value chain can be identified, as well as the non-tariff barriers (NTBs) that interfere with cross-border trade. Often these impediments and NTBs are not unique to the particular cases being studied but can manifest in other products and areas. Addressing the impediments along the value chains or the NTBs at the border can often have benefits that extend beyond the particular product or sector. These reforms can therefore produce spillover effects that can result in much larger economy-wide benefits.

There are several key takeaways for policy arising from the study. The first is that the agricultural export sector must continue to play a critical role in the development process of the Mekong region, while these countries look to industrialize through greater engagement in global value chains in manufacturing, driven by foreign direct investment. The second relates to the need for diversification to support more balanced and sustainable growth, which reduces vulnerability to external shocks. The study highlights the fact that such risk-mitigating diversification can be pursued through various avenues.

While a lot of attention has been placed on intersectoral diversification, mostly involving the movement out of agriculture into manufacturing, intrasectoral diversification can be equally important in achieving the same ends. Here again, the focus has been on diversification within manufacturing, although there is an important albeit somewhat neglected role for diversification within agriculture that can reduce vulnerability to external shocks. Pursuing greater diversification within agriculture could address some of the concerns associated with export instability, common amongst commodity-dependent developing countries. The exposure to terms-of-trade shocks can be reduced by processing activities along the agricultural value chain because the prices of such processed commodities tend to be less volatile than the primary commodities themselves. The prices of processed commodities tend not to go through the same swings associated with the commodity cycle. Therefore, pursuing diversification within both agriculture and manufacturing can contribute to an overall risk-reduction strategy.

Apart from product concentration—whether it is in agriculture or manufacturing—there is also a need to reduce the concentration of export markets. It is undeniable that the huge potential presented by the Chinese market has been a major driving force in the development of export-oriented agricultural value chains. While China will continue to be an important market for agricultural exports from the region, there may be a need to diversify sources of demand so that the effects of country-specific or regional shocks can be mitigated. This is particularly important for countries that currently rely almost exclusively on the Chinese market for their export sales. Reducing such high levels of dependency on a single market could also decrease the risk that highly unequal bargaining positions could be exploited for unequal gains that can end up deterring trade.

If policies can be instituted to address the various impediments identified in this study that operate along the agricultural value chain as well as the myriad of tariff and non-tariff barriers that interfere with cross-border trade, then the social and economic benefits to the CLMV-T countries and China can be substantially increased.

Jayant Menon
ISEAS – Yusof Ishak Institute, Singapore

ACKNOWLEDGEMENTS

This book would not have been possible without financial support from the government of the People's Republic of China through the Lancang-Mekong Cooperation Special Fund under the Lancang-Mekong River Dialogue and Cooperation Framework. We would also like to extend our appreciation to Cambodia's Ministry of Foreign Affairs and International Cooperation for administrative and technical support throughout the project. Special thanks go to Dr Ouch Chandarany, who led the project at the inception stage, and to Dr Saing Chan Hang, Dr Ven Seyhah, Pon Dorina, Hiev Hokkheang and Ker Bopha who provided research support to the program.

Our sincere thanks go to all contributors for their hard work. Many hours of writing, reviewing and editing have gone into producing this edited volume. Technical advisors, especially Dr Ray Trewin, and several anonymous external reviewers were also instrumental in guiding the research project and improving its analytical quality. We would also like to thank Anna Cassandra Melendez for valuable research assistance and Susan Watkins for her excellent editing work.

We are grateful to the various household heads, owners/managers of firms, traders, exporters, policymakers and other actors in the value chain who spent their valuable time answering survey questions, and participating in focus group discussions and key informant interviews. This book would not have been possible without their participation.

Jayant Menon and Vathana Roth

ABBREVIATIONS AND ACRONYMS

ADB	Asian Development Bank
AEC	ASEAN Economic Community
AQSIQ	Administration of Quality Supervision, Inspection and Quarantine
ASEAN	Association of Southeast Asian Nations
CAF	Centre for Analysis and Forecasting
CASS	Chinese Academy of Social Sciences
CDRI	Cambodia Development Resource Institute
CESD	Centre for Economic and Social Development
CLMV-T	Cambodia, Lao, Myanmar, Vietnam and Thailand
CTIS	Cambodia Trade Integration Strategy
ERIIT	Economic Research Institute for Industry and Trade
ELC	economic land concession
EU	European Union
FAO	Food and Agriculture Organization of the United Nations
FDI	foreign direct investment
FOB	freight on board
FTA	free trade agreement
GACC	General Administration of Customs of China
GAP	good agricultural practice
GATT	General Agreement on Tariffs and Trade
GDP	gross domestic product
GMP	good manufacturing practice
GMS	Greater Mekong Subregion
IFAD	International Fund for Agricultural Development
IMF	International Monetary Fund

KHR	Khmer riel
LAK	Lao kip
LMC	Lancang-Mekong Cooperation
MFIs	Microfinance Institutions
MMK	Myanmar kyat
MoU	memorandum of understanding
NTBs	non-tariff barriers
NTMs	non-tariff measures
OECD	Organization for Economic Co-operation and Development
RCA	revealed comparative advantage
R&D	research and development
RMB/CNY	Renmimbi/Chinese yuan
SMEs	small and medium enterprises
SPS	sanitary and phytosanitary
TBT	technical barriers to trade
TDRI	Thailand Development Research Institute
THB	Thai baht
UNIDO	United Nations Industrial Development Organization
UNCTAD	United Nations Conference on Trade and Development
UNIDROIT	UN-International Institute for the Unification of Private Law
VASS	Vietnam Academy of Social Sciences
VAT	value added tax
VCA	value chain analysis
VND	Vietnamese dong
WDI	World Development Indicators
WTO	World Trade Organization

ABOUT THE CONTRIBUTORS

Jayant Menon is Senior Fellow at the ISEAS – Yusof Ishak Institute in Singapore, following his early retirement from ADB, where he was Lead Economist in the Office of the Chief Economist. He began work life as an academic in Australia, spending almost a decade at the Centre of Policy Studies at Monash University in Melbourne. He has also worked at the University of Melbourne, Victoria University, the American University in Washington, DC and the ADB Institute in Tokyo. He has served as a Board Director of the Cambodia Development Resource Institute, and on the Advisory Board of the University of Nottingham, Malaysia. He holds adjunct appointments with the Australian National University, University of Nottingham, UK and IDEAS, Malaysia.

Vathana Roth is Research Fellow and Director of the Centre for Development Economics and Trade, Cambodia Development Resource Institute. He received an MA in Economics (Economic Development and Policies) from Kobe University, Japan. His main research interests include: the nexus of economic growth, poverty and inequality; rural economic revitalization and financial inclusion; private sector development; and impact evaluation using microeconometric modelling.

Hong Song is Deputy Director General and Senior Fellow at the Institute of American Studies, Chinese Academy of Social Sciences. He obtained his PhD degree in Economics in 1997 from Nankai University and was also visiting scholar at Columbia University. His study focuses on trade, investment and development issues. One of the main focuses is the impacts of multinational enterprises on industrial development in developing countries, especially in China.

Lingyun Gao is Director of the Department of International Investment and Senior Fellow of the Institute of World Economics and Politics, Chinese Academy of Social Sciences. He obtained his PhD degree in Economics in 2008 from the Graduate School of the Chinese Academy of Social Sciences. His study focuses on international trade and investment issues. He has published in peer-reviewed journals, including *Economic Research Journal*.

Qingyi Su is Senior Fellow and Deputy Director of the Department of International Trade, Institute of World Economics and Politics, Chinese Academy of Social Sciences. He obtained his bachelor's degree in Mathematics from Shandong University, and master's and PhD degrees from the Graduate School of Chinese Academy of Social Sciences. His research field is theory and policy of international trade, focusing on global value chains, global trade governance, and China's foreign trade. He has published in peer-reviewed journals, including *Economic Research Journal*, and the SSCI journal *China & World Economy*.

Chengwei Zang is Assistant Professor at the Institute of World Economics and Politics, Chinese Academy of Social Sciences. His research field is international trade and international investment. He got his bachelor's and master's degrees in Economics, Shandong University and a PhD degree in Economics, Nankai University. He has published several papers in peer-reviewed journals, including *Journal of World Economy*, and the SSCI journal *China & World Economy*. He is also an editor of *The Yearbook of World Economy*.

Punpreecha Bhuthong is Senior Researcher in the International Economic Relations Program at Thailand Development Research Institute. He received a master's degree in economics from the University of Illinois at Urbana-Champaign. His research interests include International Trade, Global/Regional Economic Integration and Agricultural Economics.

Papatsara Rattanasimanon is a former researcher at the Thailand Development Research Institute. Currently, she works as an economist at the Industrial Business Research Division, Export-Import Bank of Thailand. She obtained her bachelor's degree in Economics from Thammasat University. Her research interests are international trade and industrial economics.

Nuttaporn Udomkiattikul is an Economist in the Monetary Policy Group at the Bank of Thailand, responsible for analysing the labour market in Thailand. She formerly worked as a researcher in the Science Technology Development Program at the Thailand Development Research Institute. She received a bachelor's degree in economics from Chulalongkorn University. Her research interests include international trade and labour markets.

Narith Roeun is Research Associate at the Centre for Development Economics and Trade, Cambodia Development Resource Institute. He holds an MA in Commerce (Agricultural) from Lincoln University, New Zealand. He is knowledgeable in value chain analysis. He has also worked for several value chain-related projects at the Cambodia-HARVEST programme (USAID Funded), FAO-UN, FFI, IVY and CEPA since 2009.

Hokkheang Hiev is working for the United Nations Development Programme, Cambodia. He was formerly a research assistant at the Centre for Development Economics and Trade, Cambodia Development Resource Institute. His research interests include digital economy, development economics and international trade. He holds a bachelor's degree in international economics from the Royal University of Phnom Penh, Cambodia.

Viengsavang Thipphavong is Deputy Director General at the Institute for Industry and Commerce (IIC), Ministry of Industry and Commerce, Laos. He supervises two research divisions in the IIC, namely, Trade Policy Research, and Industrial and Handicraft Policy Research. He has a Master of Development Economics (Advanced) from Queensland University, Australia and completed an advanced course on Training of Trainers on International Trade and Competitiveness, organized by the Estey Centre.

Thantavanh Manolom is Research Fellow and Director of the Industry and Handicraft Policy Research Division of the Institute for Industry and Commerce, Ministry of Industry and Commerce, Laos. She graduated with a Doctorate from the Development Sciences International Programme from Khon Kaen University which included a three-year exchange program in Australia. She has published in several areas of social-economic development and international trade.

Vanaxay Soukhaseum is Director of Trade and Economic Cooperation Division, Department of Planning and Cooperation of the Ministry of Industry and Commerce of Laos. He obtained a master's degree in Public Administration from Australian National University. He is currently in charge of cooperation on bilateral trade as well as regional and subregional trade and industry cooperation.

Phouthaphone Southammavong is Deputy Director of Trade Policy Research Division at the Institute for Industry and Commerce, Ministry of Industry and Commerce, Laos. She obtained a master's degree in economics from Hiroshima University, Japan. Her research interests include trade, investment, agribusiness development and technology innovation at the firm level.

Somdeth Bodhisane is Research Fellow at the Institute for Industry and Commerce, Ministry of Industry and Commerce, Laos. An experienced postdoctoral research fellow with demonstrable skills in data collection, and qualitative and quantitative research methodology, he has published in top-impact journals and several book chapters on health economics and trade policies. He is currently Visiting Lecturer at Chulalongkorn University.

Ngu Wah Win is Senior Policy Coordinator at the Centre for Economic and Social Development, responsible for policy uptake and advocacy. She holds a Master of Public Administration in Economic Policy Management from Columbia University, a Master of Economics from Chiang Mai University, and an MA in Statistics from the Yangon University of Economics. She is currently focusing on gender in development issues while pursuing her doctoral studies in development economics.

Zaw Oo is Executive Director of the Centre for Economic and Social Development, Myanmar. He has postgraduate degrees in international development, finance and banking from American University and Columbia University. He has been an adviser on economic policy to government institutions and international organizations in Myanmar. His main research interests include circular migration, structural transformation, and agriculture innovation.

Aung Htun is Senior Research Coordinator at the Center for Social and Economic Development, responsible for organizing large survey studies. He holds a Master of Development Studies and a Bachelor of Economics from the Yangon University of Economics. In the past, he worked for Myanmar's Commission of Inquiry on Sectarian Violence in Rakhine State, which led him to focus his research on political economy issues.

Zaw Min Naing is Research Associate at the Center for Economic and Social Development, responsible for agriculture value chain studies undertaken in partnership with several international organizations such as IFPRI, Michigan State University, FAO, IFAD and GIZ. He holds Master's and Bachelor's Degrees in Agriculture Science from the Yezin University of Agriculture. He is also interested in rights-based approaches in development, sustainable development and agriculture transformation.

Nguyen Thang is Director of the Centre for Analysis and Forecasting of the Vietnam Academy of Social Sciences. His areas of research interest and expertise include macroeconomics, trade, productivity, competitiveness, employment, poverty and social protection. He has rich experience in policy engagement with Vietnam's top leaders and senior policymakers on a wide range of topics including the Fourth Industrial Revolution, productivity, employment, poverty and inequality. He also has extensive experience working with international organizations including IDRC, the World Bank, UNDP, ILO and Oxfam. He received a PhD degree in Economics from the Moscow Institute of National Economy and an MSc in Economics from the London School of Economics and Political Science.

Pham Minh Thai is Principal Researcher at the Centre for Analysis and Forecasting, Vietnam Academy of Social Sciences. He obtained a PhD degree in Political Economics from Hanoi National University. His research focuses on the labour market and trade. He has extensive experience in both qualitative and quantitative research methods. He has published in Children & Society Journal and Children and Youth Services Review.

Vu Hoang Dat is Head of the Division of Development Issues, Centre for Analysis and Forecasting, Vietnam Academy of Social Sciences. He obtained a PhD degree in Economics from Paris Dauphine University, PSL. His research focuses on poverty, labour market and international trade. He has extensive experience working with international organizations such as the World Bank, UNDP, ILO as well as development research institutions of countries in the Greater Mekong Subregion.

Vu Thi Van Ngoc is Researcher at the Centre for Analysis and Forecasting, Vietnam Academy of Social Sciences. Her research focuses on the informal sector, agricultural economics and the labour market. She has extensive experience dealing with qualitative surveys, particularly focus group discussions and in-depth interviews.

1

AGRICULTURAL TRADE BETWEEN CHINA AND THE GREATER MEKONG SUBREGION COUNTRIES
An Overview

Jayant Menon

1.1 INTRODUCTION

The Greater Mekong Subregion (GMS) encompasses five Southeast Asian countries—Cambodia, Laos, Myanmar, Thailand and Vietnam—and China. These six countries had a total population of 1.6 billion in 2018.

More than two decades of market-oriented reforms and rapid economic growth have transformed the GMS into one of the most dynamic subregions in Asia. With the exception of Thailand, GMS countries have grown at an average annual rate of more than 7 per cent in the last twenty-five years, placing them among the ranks of high-growth economies. GDP per capita growth has likewise been impressive, averaging roughly 8 per cent in China and Myanmar, and over 5 per cent in Cambodia, Laos and Vietnam since 1995. Across all six countries of the GMS, the structure of the economy has shifted from agriculture to industry and services (Table 1.1). The GMS

TABLE 1.1
Growth and Structural Transformation in GMS Countries

Country	Average GDP Growth (Annual %)	Average GDP per Capita Growth (Annual %)	Sector Value Added (% of GDP) Agriculture / Industry / Services	
	1995–2018	1995–2018	1995	2018
China	9.1	8.4	19.6 / 46.8 / 33.7	7.2 / 40.7 / 52.2
Cambodia	7.7	5.7	47.7 / 14.3 / 34.2	22.0 / 32.3 / 39.5
Laos	7.0	5.2	42.2 / 18.8 / 40.9	15.7 / 31.5 / 41.6
Myanmar	9.4	8.4	42.2 / 57.2 / 9.7*	24.6 / 32.3 / 43.2
Thailand	3.5	2.8	9.1 / 37.5 / 53.4	8.1 / 35.0 / 56.9
Vietnam	6.7	5.5	27.2 / 28.8 / 44.1	14.7 / 34.2 / 41.1

Note: *Myanmar data are for 2000.
Source: World Bank World Development Indicators.

countries are at different stages of transitioning to commercial agriculture. Whereas Thailand, Vietnam and China already have large commercial agricultural sectors, Cambodia and Laos are well behind, with much lower levels of commercial agricultural activity.

While agriculture's share of the economy is declining across the subregion, the sector remains a critical one for growth and poverty reduction. Agriculture still accounted for nearly a quarter of GDP in Cambodia and Myanmar in 2018. With the exception of China, the majority of the population in GMS countries continues to live in rural areas. Agriculture also remains a major source of employment in GMS countries, accounting for between 27 per cent and 68 per cent of total employment in 2018. More importantly, poverty remains a largely rural phenomenon in GMS countries (Table 1.2).

Empirical studies underscore the importance of agriculture in reducing poverty. The World Bank (2007) estimates that growth driven by agriculture is between two to four times more effective at reducing poverty than other sectors. Using time-series and cross-section regression analysis covering twenty-five countries, Cervantes-Godoy and Dewbre (2010) confirm this finding by showing that although economic growth is an important contributor to poverty reduction, the sector mix of growth matters greatly, with growth in agricultural incomes being particularly important. Moreover, agriculture's linkages to manufacturing and services—through the processing, packaging and transport of agricultural products—create

TABLE 1.2
Agriculture's Importance in GMS Countries

Country	Rural Population (% of Total Population)	Employment in Agriculture (% of Total Employment)	Rural Poverty Headcount Ratio at National Poverty Lines (% of Rural Population)	Poverty Headcount Ratio at National Poverty Lines (% of Total Population)
China	40.8	26.6	7.2 (2014)	7.2 (2014)
Cambodia	76.6	30.1	20.8 (2012)	17.7 (2012)
Laos	65.0	67.7	28.6 (2012)	23.4 (2012)
Myanmar	69.4	49.7	N.A.	N.A.
Thailand	50.1	30.4	13.9 (2013)	10.9 (2013)
Vietnam	64.1	39.4	18.6 (2014)	13.5 (2014)

Note: N.A. = not available.
Source: World Bank World Development Indicators.

multiplier effects that contribute further to economic growth. For these reasons, agriculture remains a strategic priority for all GMS countries. The sector continues to figure prominently not only in national development plans but also in regional cooperation schemes in which GMS countries are participants.

1.1.1 Opportunities for Developing Agriculture in GMS Countries

Vast opportunities exist for GMS countries to grow and develop their agricultural sector. They are endowed with natural resources and climate conditions that are favourable for growing high-value agricultural products. Their strategic location also allows them to link up with major markets across Asia as well as Europe, through different transport corridors that already exist or are being built.

At the same time, several trends in the global market for agricultural products bode well for GMS countries. First, the demand for food is expected to grow by 15 per cent over the coming decade, with demand predominantly coming from regions with high population growth, specifically, Sub-Saharan Africa, South Asia, and the Middle East and North Africa (OECD and FAO 2019).

Second, increasing income and urbanization are changing dietary and consumption habits, with more and more consumers demanding access to foodstuffs that are safe, convenient and high quality. Niche markets for organic and ethically sourced food are likewise growing. These changes in consumption habits provide GMS countries with increasing opportunities to export higher value-added agricultural products instead of just raw materials, a shift that is critical for raising farmers' incomes.

Third, trade in agricultural products has been growing at a significant pace. The value of global food and agricultural raw materials exports has more than tripled since the beginning of the century, from about US$545 billion in 2000 to roughly US$1.8 trillion in 2018. Food and agricultural raw materials exports share of global merchandise exports increased from 5 per cent to 9 per cent during the same period. More promisingly, although exports of food and agricultural raw materials continue to be dominated by developed countries, the export share of developing countries has increased steadily over time, from 31.5 per cent in 2000 to almost 40 per cent in 2018. China is the biggest trading partner of Cambodia, Myanmar, Thailand and Vietnam, and the second biggest of Laos; and, except for Thailand, agriculture dominates this trade. In 2017, trade between China and the other five Mekong countries surpassed US$200 billion and has continued to grow.

Fourth, foreign direct investment (FDI) in the agriculture sector has been rising on the back of increasing food prices, changing and expanding consumer markets, and increasing demand for biofuels. In the case of food, beverages and tobacco, the FAO estimates that FDI to developing economies doubled between 2003–8 and 2009–14, from an annual average of US$7.4 billion to US$15.1 billion (Fiedler and Iafrate 2016). China is not only the biggest source of FDI in the GMS region, a significant portion goes towards promoting agricultural development and trade in the CLMV.

The growth of trade and FDI in agriculture has been underpinned by unilateral reforms as well as liberalization commitments taken under different bilateral, regional and multilateral agreements. Improvements in infrastructure and logistics have also played a huge role. The GMS countries themselves remain staunchly committed to efforts to liberalize trade and investments. All six GMS countries are members of the World Trade Organization (WTO) and are parties to multiple free trade agreements. Their inclusion in the ASEAN Economic Community (AEC) and their participation in subregional programmes such as the GMS Programme and the Lancang-Mekong Cooperation initiative also provide different avenues for increasing trade and investments and improving trade facilitation that can ultimately benefit the agricultural sector.

1.1.2 Objectives and Coverage of This Research Study

Whether or not GMS countries are able to take advantage of the growing opportunities mentioned above will of course depend on several complex domestic and external factors. This particular study examines two of these factors: the extent to which GMS countries are able to meaningfully participate in agricultural value chains (AVCs), and the extent to which they are able to meet non-tariff measures (NTMs) applied to agricultural exports.

The main objective of this research is to increase the efficiency of agricultural trade in a manner that contributes to improvements in rural development, poverty reduction, and inclusive and sustainable growth. The study limits the analysis to the export of selected agricultural products from the five GMS (hereafter referred to as CLMV-T) countries to China.

This volume consists of six country papers covering each of the GMS countries. The papers were prepared collaboratively by experts from leading research institutions within the subregion.

Several significant events have taken place either just before or after the completion of the papers included in this volume that could affect some of the analyses or conclusions. Two global events that are worthy of note are the US-China trade war and the outbreak of the coronavirus (COVID-19) pandemic. Both are having a significant influence on the region and beyond. There have also been national challenges, such as the political turmoil in Myanmar, and to a lesser extent in Thailand, and these events continue to evolve and affect the countries concerned as well as the region.

As of mid-2021, it is still unclear when these events will resolve themselves, and therefore what the full impacts of these shocks are likely to be. What is clear is that the impacts of the COVID-19 pandemic and curtailment measures being taken by countries covered in this volume and elsewhere are having major, wide-ranging economic and social effects. The impacts from the pandemic appear to be outweighing those of the US-China trade war, although it is becoming increasingly difficult to disentangle the effects of each. Needless to say, the coup in Myanmar is having devastating effects on the economy and society. The general conclusions and recommendations drawn from the analyses contained within this volume need to be interpreted cautiously, bearing in mind the still uncertain impact that the evolving COVID-19 pandemic and trade war, in particular, could have across countries.

The next chapter examines the structural changes taking place in China and their possible implications for agricultural trade within the subregion. The paper identifies a number of factors that bode well for agricultural exports. It also examines trends in NTMs imposed by China on agricultural imports.

Chapters 3–7 of this volume contain country case studies that examine a range of traditional and non-traditional exports from CLMV-T to China. The studies adopt broadly consistent frameworks for analysing the value chains of each of these products and identify the NTMs faced by these products both domestically and in the Chinese market.

The remaining sections of this overview summarize the main findings and recommendations from these country studies.

1.2 AGRICULTURAL TRADE WITHIN THE GMS: THE IMPORTANCE OF CHINA

Chapter 2 of this volume, prepared by the Institute of World Economics and Politics, Chinese Academy of Social Sciences, highlights the important role played by China in agricultural trade within the subregion. The chapter identifies several factors that are likely to increase trade between the GMS countries and China.

First, China's population is expected to peak and reach between 1.45 billion to 1.5 billion by around 2030. Population growth, along with changes in the population structure, increasing income, growing urbanization, and shifts in dietary structure, are expected to increase demand for fruits, vegetables, meat products, special grains and feed grain.

Second, China's domestic supply of agricultural products has been unable to keep up with growing demand. Given the current availability of arable land and present constraints on the domestic production system, China has already reached the limit of its food production capacity. As such, China's total import volume of agricultural products will continue to grow in the next ten years.

Third, in the context of revealed comparative advantage (RCA), China's comparative advantage lies in machinery and electronics, textile and other labour-intensive industries (where the RCA index is greater than

1). Agricultural products or agricultural-related products such as food, vegetables and livestock are at a comparative disadvantage. Moreover, the RCA index of some of China's agricultural products has been declining. China is, therefore, better off importing agricultural products from the CLMV-T that have a comparative advantage in these products.

Fourth, China's average tariff on agricultural products has dropped to 14.6 per cent, or about a quarter of the global average tariff on agricultural products. More recent policy pronouncements by Premier Li Keqiang suggest that the average rate of China's tariffs would drop to 7.5 per cent. Customs clearance will also be expedited further.

Fifth, the CLMV-T has become China's main destination for FDI in agriculture. Private enterprises from China have been particularly active investors. Between 2004 and 2015, private enterprises established by China accounted for around two-thirds of total enterprises in GMS countries (Panthamit and Chaiboonsri 2020). Moreover, non-agricultural enterprises such as CITIC Construction and the CGCOC Group have gradually become an important driver of agricultural FDI. Moving forward, it bears highlighting that China's 13th Five-Year Plan contains a commitment to "actively carry out overseas agricultural cooperative development, establish scaled overseas production, processing, storage and transportation bases, and cultivate internationally competitive agricultural multinational corporations." (Central Committee of the Communist Party of China 2019).

Finally, China has been actively pushing several initiatives that should further improve trade and investment linkages with the CLMV-T, through various multilayer cooperation frameworks such as the Lancang-Mekong River Dialogue and Cooperation, the China-ASEAN cooperation framework, the Belt and Road Initiative, China's bilateral economic partnerships, and its participation in the Regional Comprehensive Economic Partnership agreement. China's overseas development assistance has also been an important source of financing for the CLMV-T. All of these initiatives signal continued commitment on the part of China to strengthen economic relations with its neighbours.

1.3 AGRICULTURAL VALUE CHAINS IN GMS COUNTRIES: KEY ISSUES AND CHALLENGES

Understanding how AVCs work in GMS countries is important given the fundamental changes that are taking place in how agricultural products are produced, processed and distributed. Traditionally, the markets for agricultural products have been mainly governed by spot market transactions that involved a large number of small producers and retailers. This dependence on impersonal commodity markets has decreased over time. Instead, modern agricultural production, processing and distribution are now starting to resemble value chains in manufacturing, characterized by vertical integration and consolidation of the supply base (Henderson and Isaac 2017; Montalbano, Nenci and Salvatici 2015).

This trend towards greater integration is particularly strong in the case of food products. As an OECD and WTO (2013, p. 14) report notes:

> The same processes driving the emergence of global value chains in other sectors are also at work in the agrifood sector, notably technological change, transport and logistics innovation and the penetration of global agribusiness companies into local markets, through both direct contract relationships and investments. At the heart of this structural change is the "value chain". Changes in food retailing are leading to greater involvement of the private sector in agriculture and a focus on developing and improving agriculture value chains in terms of quality, productivity, efficiency, and depth. As consumer demands for safety, quality and convenience is growing, so is the pace of change in food markets leading to a more active and assertive role for the private sector.

Gaining access to these value chains can provide developing countries with stable markets for their agricultural products. However, specific firm-level constraints exacerbated by broader policy and institutional challenges can affect the ability of domestic actors to plug into these value chains. Moreover, with lead firms now having a bigger say in how agricultural products are produced, processed and distributed, concerns regarding governance and power relationships within AVCs have inevitably come to the fore.

Within this context, the country papers included in this study examine the main processes and key actors involved in value chains for selected commodities, with the intent of identifying the key constraints and relationships between actors along the entire value chain. The analyses seek to identify options not only for improving performance within the value chain but also for maximizing benefits for all the actors involved. The country papers also examine, with the available secondary data, various NTMs that agricultural exporters in the CLMV-T face when exporting the examined agricultural products to China.

The products covered in the country studies were selected based on their importance in the country's overall export basket, as well as the growing demand for those products in the Chinese market.

The Thai country study prepared by the Thailand Development Research Institute (TDRI) focuses on two important local products—cassava and durian. Thailand has been the world's largest exporter of cassava products and durian, and China is Thailand's major export destination for both products. Cassava chips—which are processed products but only to a limited degree—still make up the bulk of exports to China, but in recent years there has been a noticeable shift in demand towards native and modified starches, which are much higher value-added products. Durian exports to China have been steadily climbing. Differences in harvest seasons in the main planted areas in East and South Thailand allow Thailand to supply durian to the Chinese market throughout the whole year. Up until recently, Thailand was the only country allowed to export fresh durian to China, but it now faces competition from Malaysia.

The Cambodia study produced by the Cambodia Development Resource Institute (CDRI) also examines the value chain for cassava, and the value chain for sugar cane. Cassava is Cambodia's second-largest agricultural crop after rice, and Cambodia is the world's second-largest exporter of fresh tubers and dried chips after Thailand. Sugar production is mainly for supplying domestic demand; only 20 per cent of domestically produced sugar cane is exported. Final and semi-final sugar cane products are exported to three major destinations. In 2016, Vietnam accounted for the bulk with 75 per cent, followed by the EU with 20 per cent and China with 5 per cent.

The Laos country study, prepared by the Economic Research Institute for Industry and Trade (ERIIT), examines rice and Cavendish banana, two of six potential commercial crops that have received a significant amount of foreign investments from China in recent years. In 2018, China granted Laos an import quota for rice of 20,000 tonnes. Laos has a surplus of rice and can export to foreign markets, but it is still a relatively small player in the region. Cavendish banana production is solely for export. In terms of volume and value, Cavendish banana crops have become Laos' second-largest cash-crop export to China after rubber.

The country study for Myanmar, prepared by the Centre for Economic and Social Development (CESD), examines the maize value chain, focusing on production from southern Shan State. Myanmar's trade with China expanded rapidly during the period when economic sanctions by the US and EU were in place, from around the 1990s. China is now Myanmar's biggest trading partner, and agricultural commodities make up most of this trade. The study finds that producers need to improve quality standards and compliance with international regulations in order to increase their exports to China and other trading partners in order to diversify sources of demand.

The final country study on Vietnam, produced by the Centre for Analysis and Forecasting of the Vietnam Academy of Social Sciences (CAFVASS), examines the value chains for coffee and dragon fruit. Vietnam is the second-biggest coffee producer in the world after Brazil, and it is currently the leading exporter of dragon fruit. Although the bulk of Vietnam's coffee exports goes to the EU and the US, China's demand for Vietnamese coffee has been rising. The export value of coffee from Vietnam to China increased dramatically from US$90 million in 2014 to more than US$330 million in 2016. Vietnam was the largest supplier of coffee to the Chinese market in 2016. China is the largest market for Vietnam's dragon fruit both in terms of volume and value.

The country studies in this volume confirm previous research which finds that the degree of vertical coordination or integration in AVCs depends on the country context, the agricultural product, and the standards that must be met to be able to export the product (Montalbano, Nenci and Salvatici 2015; Swinnen 2015; Bamber et al. 2014). Both global experience and the analysis presented here suggest that vertical coordination or integration is more likely to take place in countries where land is available and labour is abundant, but capacities at other nodes of the chain are either weak or non-existent. It is also more likely to take place in the case of agricultural products such as vegetables or fruits, which are highly perishable and must meet more stringent quantity and quality standards related to processing, packaging or transporting fresh produce.

Some examples from the country case studies are worth citing. The Thailand and Cambodia studies show that in the case of cassava, the value chain continues to be dominated by smallholders, and the relationship between actors in the entire value chain still relies mainly on market-based governance structures. In Cambodia, there is a small portion of producers who use written contracts with operators or exporters, but this is because they are focused on the niche market for organic products. By contrast, the production of Cavendish banana in Laos has a high degree of vertical coordination. This is because the majority of Cavendish banana plantations are owned by Chinese investors in the form of a land concession from the government or contract farming under a 1+4 model, whereby the local farmers lease their property to investors, and the investors provide the rest.

The country case studies in this volume illustrate how AVCs focused on exports can help improve income opportunities for domestic producers and enterprises that are able to participate in these AVCs. The country case study for Laos, for instance, shows that a farmer growing rice for export to China can earn about US$231 per hectare, more than double the amount that could be earned from producing for the local market, which is about US$109 per hectare. Some rice collectors have also benefited from representing rice mills in collecting rice from scattered farmers in different villages. The same study notes that farmers welcome the income from land lease agreements for the production of Cavendish banana. Meanwhile, the Cambodia case study on sugar cane reports that AVCs have helped create jobs for locals who are hired on the production and processing sides.

The studies also show some of the benefits that can come from increasing vertical coordination and integration, Contract farming arrangements—such as the 2+3 and 1+4 arrangements for rice and Cavendish banana in Laos—allow countries to access foreign markets even if they do not yet have the full range of capabilities required to produce, store, transport and distribute a particular product. Such arrangements can also reduce information asymmetries that often arise between producers and buyers with regard to product characteristics. This gives producers a better chance of meeting strict standards that must be met in order to access final markets overseas (Montalbano, Nenci and Salvatici 2015; Swinnen 2015; Bamber et al. 2014).

At the same time, contract farming arrangements can provide domestic producers with access to technical and input support and other forms of farm assistance that allows them to overcome constraints on capital and know-how. Lead firms may also build linkages with logistics providers to transport raw material to processing plants and final markets. This is evident in the case of rice in Laos and sugar cane in Cambodia.

Finally, vertical coordination and integration can provide access to new types of production and help all actors in the chain upgrade towards higher value-added activities. The analysis of the sugar cane industry in Cambodia notes that, with lead firms playing a central role from raw material production to transport and trade, the industry has been significantly upgraded.

However, the country case studies also yield a number of findings which suggest that the broader impact of these AVCs on inclusive and sustainable growth may be limited. For instance:

(i) Lack of requisite skills may be preventing local workers from participating in higher-value activities. Although AVCs have helped create employment to a certain extent, in some cases local workers are still mainly engaged in manual or low-skilled tasks that are highly informal. This is evident in the case of sugar cane in Cambodia and Cavendish banana in Laos. In sugar cane, farmers are mainly hired as fieldworkers. However, labour is now being replaced by machines on the production side, and farm service providers are at risk of disappearing from the value chain. Moving forward, only a small number of labourers will be required for activities in farming and processing. In Cavendish banana, Chinese investors mostly employ Chinese nationals as plantation managers. Laotians are given small administrative jobs, with a monthly average income that is just slightly higher than the minimum wage (US$175 vs. US$128, respectively). Temporary labourers hired during harvesting season receive a daily wage of about US$7 to US$8. The prevalence of informality in these kinds of arrangements has important implications for poverty and vulnerability.

(ii) Lack of absorptive capacity may be preventing local enterprises from participating in or progressing to more sophisticated forms of participation within a modern AVC. At the same time, the shift from traditional to modern AVCs could result in some domestic participants disappearing from value chains. Domestic enterprises can also be crowded out by foreign enterprises if they lack sufficient competitiveness. These issues are evident in the case of durian from Thailand and rice from Laos. The structure for fresh durian's value chain has dramatically changed. In the traditional value chain, durian orchardists sold their harvest to local merchants and various partners. But the need to sort durian for export has shifted power from the intermediaries to the packing houses, which now collect and prepare durian primarily to meet standards for export to China. Increasingly, these packing houses are owned and run by Chinese entrepreneurs who are attracted by the profitability of durian. Meanwhile, in the case of rice from Laos, only two Chinese-owned rice millers are qualified to export rice to China. Local rice mills in Laos are typically small and do not have the time or resources to obtain the necessary certification needed to export rice to China.

(iii) Power and economic gains may be unequally distributed. Several country case studies in this volume identify the lack of bargaining power as a major problem for smallholders and small and medium enterprises in the agricultural sector. This problem could be exacerbated within vertically integrated AVCs where investors or lead firms dominate decision making. The gains from participation in vertically integrated AVCs may also be distributed unequally, with lead firms in vertically integrated AVCs tending to have higher mark-ups and profits.

(iv) Negative spillovers may arise, compromising long-term sustainability. In Laos, the government has announced a moratorium for granting any new land concessions for banana plantations given concerns about the long-term negative impacts of heavy chemical usage on the environment and the health of farmers.

(v) Increasing dependence on a single market. With the exception of Vietnamese coffee, which is exported to more markets and depends mainly on world market prices, the prices of other agricultural products covered in this study are heavily influenced by what happens in the Chinese market. One good example is cassava. China is estimated to account for more than two-thirds of global imports of cassava. However, exports from Cambodia and Thailand have been negatively affected by China's policy to auction government stockpiled maize, a substitute for cassava. This also affects exports of maize from Myanmar, most of which is destined for the Chinese market.

The findings above underscore the reality that the contribution of AVCs to broader development goals will require reforms in several policy areas. Nevertheless, the AVCs in the GMS countries studied in this volume have generally advanced further than might be expected given their overall level of development, and have significantly increased the incomes and improved the livelihoods of low-income households engaged in agriculture.

1.4 NON-TARIFF MEASURES ON AGRICULTURAL EXPORTS TO CHINA: TRENDS AND MAJOR CHALLENGES

One major challenge that can affect the competitiveness of agricultural exports from CLMV-T is the increasing application of NTMs on cross-border trade in agricultural goods. Analysis by the FAO (2017) reveals that:

- Countries apply some form of NTMs on imports of almost half of all agricultural products.
- NTMs are becoming more complex, affecting agrifood products in particular.
- On average, NTMs can contribute twice as much as tariffs to overall trade restrictiveness in high-income countries.
- The incidence of NTMs is higher on agricultural tariff lines than on manufactured products; and on agricultural exports from low-income countries, it is four times higher.
- NTMs for processed agricultural products can have a higher impact on trade than plain tariffs.

While NTMs are necessary to address legitimate concerns about food standards and safety, they can also be manipulated to act as barriers to trade that can disproportionately affect exports from developing countries.

As the studies in this volume reveal, the NTMs facing agricultural exports from the CLMV-T come in three forms. The most obvious form would be NTMs imposed by the importing country, which could take the form of technical barriers to trade (TBT) as well as sanitary and phytosanitary (SPS) requirements. NTMs highlighted in the studies include requirements for import registration, certification and traceability, inspection and quarantine, storage and transport conditions. Importers could also require shipments to pass through a specified port of customs in case of disease outbreaks.

The exporting country itself, however, can also impose NTMs in the form of export-related administrative requirements such as export permits or certificates of conformity, along with other documents to guarantee quality. For such countries as Thailand, which also imports fresh cassava tubers to supplement local production, local enterprises also need to contend with NTMs imposed by Thai regulators on the import side.

As the chapters in this volume show, all of the CLMV-T continue to struggle with the NTMs that are currently in place. The issues related to

NTMs include: (1) more complex trade procedures, especially with respect to obtaining SPS certificates; (2) delays at the borders; and (3) lack of publicly available information on relevant NTMs. Difficulty in complying with technical and product standards is also an issue. Technical capacity is the main challenge for conformity assessment and harmonized technical regulations in the least developed countries such as Laos and Myanmar that lack qualified testing laboratories, sufficient competence in accreditation bodies, and skilled professionals to implement post-market surveillance. Meanwhile, challenges at firm level include the lack of appropriate technology and capabilities to meet identified standards, as well as the lack of supporting professional organizations.

There are some welcome developments worth highlighting. The Cambodia country study notes that in terms of the export of processed and semi-processed cassava and sugar cane products, exporters have so far been able to comply with Chinese standards due to large investments in modern processing facilities. The Vietnam country case study also reports that Vietnam has the capacity to comply with regulations of markets such as Japan, South Korea, Europe and the US that currently have far more stringent requirements than China.

Moreover, the regression analysis presented in Chapter 2 suggests that the number of NTMs imposed by China has declined by an average of 0.047 per year over the recent past. The authors note that China actually began actively reducing NTMs even before its accession to the WTO and retained only those NTMs that are allowed by the WTO.

However, the country studies also highlight that although the number of NTMs imposed by China is declining, China seems to be tightening the enforcement of existing regulations. The Myanmar country study suggests that implementation of measures at border-crossing points can be somewhat arbitrary, leading to uncertainty that can result in price volatility. Given all the potential opportunities for increasing trade in agricultural products between China and the CLMV-T, ensuring that these developments do not create barriers to trade becomes increasingly important.

1.5 POLICY IMPLICATIONS AND RECOMMENDATIONS

The issues identified by the country case studies highlight the need for governments in the CLMV-T to sustain domestic reforms and pursue regional cooperation in several areas. Priorities for action plans and reforms include the following:

(1) Improving absorptive capacity and overall competitiveness
Sustained reforms at the national level will be necessary to address both firm-level constraints and broader policy and institutional challenges that continue to hinder absorptive capacity and overall competitiveness. These will include:

- *Investing in human capital to enhance skills, productivity, innovation and specialization along the entire value chain.* Agricultural extension services are needed to help producers improve production techniques and foster the adoption of new technologies and production standards. At the same time, strengthening the provision of and access to vocational training, tertiary education and lifelong learning will be critical to meet the demand for skilled labour at other nodes of the value chain. Although contract farming arrangements may include some elements of skills development, public provision will continue to be important given the public goods nature of agricultural extension services (FAO and OECD 2019).
- *Promoting producer associations and professional organizations.* Investments in human capital need to be complemented by efforts to promote producer associations and professional organizations in the agricultural sector. Global experience highlights the important role these institutions play in enhancing services provision, developing and delivering extension programmes, transferring knowledge and technology, and mitigating transaction costs. More importantly, they play a central role in strengthening the governance and inclusivity of AVCs by empowering their members to form common positions, play an advocacy role, and engage in negotiations with both state and private actors. These institutions are integral to overcoming constraints faced by smallholders and small and medium enterprises. However, although countries such as Thailand have taken steps to support the formation of such groups, the findings in this volume show that participation remains limited.
- *Strengthening the enabling environment for AVC development.* Reforms to improve the overall business environment should be accelerated to support the development of AVCs and strengthen the competitiveness of local enterprises. Both research by the FAO (2017) and the studies in this volume identify the following reform areas as particularly important: establishing efficient land markets and tenure systems;

enhancing access to rural and agricultural finance and risk management products; providing adequate infrastructure (particularly transport networks, storage facilities, irrigation systems, water and electricity supplies); improving customs administration; reducing red tape; and combating corruption.

(2) Improving the contracting environment for AVCs
Given the shift towards greater vertical coordination and the increasing popularity of contract farming, governments will need to review their domestic regulatory frameworks to ensure that the contracting environment for AVCs promotes arrangements that are not only profitable but also equitable and sustainable. This is a challenging but necessary task. As UNIDROIT, FAO and IFAD (2015) point out, relevant laws and regulations will include not just those specific to contracting in agriculture, but also general contract law, agricultural laws, commodity-specific legislation and supply chain legislation. Laws that may have an indirect effect on agricultural contracts, such as labour and environmental legislation, will also need to be considered. These frameworks need to be strengthened to address issues surrounding the governance of AVCs, the responsibilities of lead firms, the distribution of power and benefits within AVCs, and dispute settlement, among others.

There are a number of helpful resources that can help domestic regulators in the CLMV-T undertake this work. These include the 2015 Legal Guide on Contract Farming produced by UNIDROIT, FAO and IFAD; the Principles for Responsible Investments in Agriculture and Food Systems (CFS-RAI Principles) endorsed by the Committee on World Food Security in 2014; the Principles for Responsible Agricultural Investment developed by the FAO, IFAD, UNCTAD and the World Bank; and the OECD-FAO Guidance for Responsible Agricultural Supply Chains produced in 2016.

(3) Increasing local capacity to comply with non-tariff measures
On the policy side, The CLMV-T will need to accelerate efforts to reduce administrative barriers on the export side, align regulatory systems with the WTO agreements on SPS and TBT, and adopt regulatory frameworks that are harmonized with international guidelines or standards.

On the capacity side, governments will also need to strengthen efforts to invest in skills development and institution-building for testing procedures and conformity assessments. Public-private partnerships will be necessary to prioritize areas for assistance and promote awareness of NTMs imposed by major training partners. These partnerships can also be used to develop and deliver training programs that are tailored to address the specific capacity needs of multiple actors along the value chain.

Finally, in order to ease constraints on public testing facilities, governments may wish to consider accrediting third-party laboratories that can handle testing procedures and conformity assessments.

(4) Diversifying export markets and baskets
The analyses in this volume highlight the importance of China as a major market for agricultural exports from the CLMV-T. There is a risk of the CLMV-T becoming increasingly dependent on a relatively small range of products for which there is a growing demand in the Chinese market. The CLMV-T clearly need to diversify both their markets and products. One option highlighted in this volume is a shift towards markets that have a greater demand for premium agricultural products, such as organic and fair-trade agricultural products that create a higher value supply chain.

(5) Strengthening regional cooperation
As participants in several regional cooperation platforms, GMS countries have numerous opportunities to use regional cooperation to complement domestic reform efforts and address pressing policy issues. Joint efforts in three areas are particularly crucial:

- Increasing investments in cross-border transport and trade facilitation. Improving connectivity through investments in cross-border infrastructure remains a major priority for GMS countries. The GMS Regional Investment Framework 2022 estimates investment needs amounting to US$77.7 billion for transport projects in the pipeline. Another US$106 million will be needed to finance investments in transport and trade facilitation. Not all of these projects have identified sources of financing. China's Belt and Road Initiative opens up opportunities for increased investments in cross-border infrastructure. At the same time, ASEAN has been developing an initial rolling priority pipeline of ASEAN infrastructure projects that have been shortlisted by the World Bank to achieve the implementation of the

ASEAN Master Plan on Connectivity 2025. The pipeline should further help the CLMV-T prioritize projects and mobilize financing from both development partners and the private sector.
- Strengthening cooperation on trade facilitation and NTMs. Critical measures include improving the implementation of bilateral transport agreements and the Cross-Border Transport Agreement under the GMS Programme, and strengthening joint capacity building and harmonization of standards. The CLMV-T could take advantage of initiatives to improve and harmonize standards under the ASEAN Food Safety Network. The APEC's Food Safety Cooperation Forum and its public-private Partnership Training Institute Network may also provide additional avenues for capacity building. China and the CLMV-T may want to consider special agreements to reduce non-tariff barriers and increase import quotas for products of interest, in line with China's food security policies and strategies.
- Sustaining or initiating programmes specifically aimed at developing AVCs within the GMS. The GMS Programme has already adopted the Strategy for Promoting Safe and Environment-Friendly Agro-based Value Chains in the GMS and Siem Reap Action Plan 2018–22. The strategy aims to help the GMS become a leading global supplier of safe and environment-friendly agricultural products through four pillars: policies, infrastructure, knowledge and marketing.
- Meanwhile, contract farming is a key initiative under the Ayeyawady-Chao Phraya-Mekong Economic Cooperation Strategy. Moving forward, China has decided to set up pilot free trade zones in Guangxi and Yunnan in 2019; GMS countries may want to examine whether these pilot zones could be used to cluster agri-business investments and interventions.

Most of these challenges are long term in nature and addressing them will take time. Improving absorptive capacity, enhancing domestic skills, and diversifying export products and markets will not happen overnight, although countries should start working towards them as soon as possible. In the short run, efforts to improve regional cooperation can be more vigorously pursued. Also, the unequal distribution of economic gains across actors in the value chain, as highlighted in the Laos and Thailand country studies, should and could be addressed quickly so that they do not become constraints to the growth and upgrading of AVCs.

References

Bamber, Penny, Karina Fernandez-Stark, Gary Gereffi, and Andrew Guinn. 2014. *Connecting Local Producers in Developing Countries to Regional and Global Value Chains: Update*. OECD Trade Policy Paper No. 160. www.oecd.org/officialdocuments/publicdisplaydocumentpdf/?cote=TAD/TC/WP(2013)27/FINAL&docLanguage=En

Central Committee of the Communist Party of China. 2019. *13th Five-Year Plan for Economic and Social Development of the People's Republic of China (2016–2020)*. Beijing: Communist Party of China. https://en.ndrc.gov.cn/policyrelease_8233/201612/P020191101482242850325.pdf

Cervantes-Godoy, Dalila, and Joe Dewbre. 2010. *Economic Importance of Agriculture for Poverty Reduction*. OECD Food, Agriculture and Fisheries Working Papers No. 23. OECD Publishing. https://doi.org/10.1787/5kmmv9s20944-en

Committee on World Food Security. 2014. *Principles for Responsible Investments in Agriculture and Food Systems*. Rome: FAO. www.fao.org/3/a-au866e.pdf

FAO. 2017. "Non-tariff Measures in Agricultural Trade". Trade Policy Briefs No. 26. www.fao.org/3/a-i8002e.pdf

FAO and OECD. 2019. *Background Notes on Sustainable, Productive and Resilient Agro-Food Systems: Value Chains, Human Capital, and the 2030 Agenda*. FAO: Rome.

Fiedler, Yannick, and Massimi Iafrate. 2016. *Trends in Foreign Direct Investment in Food, Beverages and Tobacco*. FAO Commodity and Trade Policy Research Working Paper No. 51. Rome: FAO.

Henderson Heath, and Alan G. Isaac. 2017. "Modern Value Chains and the Organization of Agrarian Production". *American Journal of Agricultural Economics* 99, no. 2: 379–400.

Montalbano, Pierluigi, Silvia Nenci, and Luca Salvatici. 2015. *Trade, Value Chains and Food Security*. Background paper prepared for "The State of Agricultural Commodity Markets 2015–16". Rome: FAO. www.fao.org/3/a-i5220e.pdf

OECD and FAO. 2016. *OECD-FAO Guidance for Responsible Agricultural Supply Chains*. https://doi.org/10.1787/9789264251052-en

OECD and FAO. 2019. *OECD-FAO Agricultural Outlook 2019–2028*. Rome: FAO. https://doi.org/10.1787/agr_outlook-2019-en

OECD and WTO. 2013. "Aid for Trade and Value Chains in Agrifood". www.wto.org/english/tratop_e/devel_e/a4t_e/global_review13prog_e/agrifood_47.pdf

Panthamit, Nisit, and Chukiat Chaiboonsri. 2020. "China's Outward Foreign Direct Investment in the Greater Mekong Subregion". *Journal of Economic Integration* 35, no. 1: 129–51.

Swinnen, Jo. 2015. "The State of Agricultural Commodity Markets IN DEPTH". Technical note prepared for "The State of Agricultural Commodity Markets 2015–16".

UNIDROIT, FAO, and IFAD. 2015. *UNIDROIT/FAO/IFAD Legal Guide on Contract Farming*. Rome: FAO.

Viinikainen, Teemu, and Carmen Bullón Caro. 2018. *Enabling Regulatory Frameworks for Contract Farming*. FAO Legislative Study 111. Rome: FAO. www.fao.org/3/I8595EN/i 8595en.pdf

World Bank. 2007. *World Development Report 2008: Agriculture for Development*. Washington, DC: World Bank.

2

ECONOMIC STRUCTURAL CHANGE IN CHINA AND THE IMPLICATIONS FOR AGRICULTURAL TRADE IN THE LANCANG-MEKONG REGION

Hong Song, Lingyun Gao, Qingyi Su and Chengwei Zang

2.1 INTRODUCTION

China's trade in agricultural goods depends essentially on three factors: demand, supply and the policies that affect them. Although China's agricultural exports and imports are primarily determined by the interaction of supply and demand, both trade and agricultural policies are also important. Even if a country has to import agricultural goods, the tariffs on those goods may be high because the government must also consider protecting domestic farmers.

Changes in population, urban-rural structure, and dietary habits are the fundamental variables affecting China's food demand. China's population is expected to peak by around 2030 at 1.45 billion to 1.5 billion, with more than 1 billion living in cities and an elderly population of about

500 million. As a result, the total consumption of main grains is expected to decline while the consumption of meat, eggs, milk, fruit, vegetables and special grains will grow.

From the domestic supply-side, China's current grain production capacity is 620 million tonnes, of which wheat straw- and rice straw-based rations account for about 390 million tonnes and corn-based feed for 230 million tonnes. According to current agricultural and arable land resource potential, production systems and technology management, China has reached its limit of food production capacity. Unless there is disruptive technology, it will be hard to envision and plan for a future of growth.

As for relevant policies, the Chinese government has introduced a food security policy of "ensuring basic self-sufficiency of grain and absolute security of staple food" (State Council Information Office of China 2019). The national food security strategy features self-sufficiency based on domestic grain production, guaranteed food production capacity, moderate imports, and technological support.

China's food security policy and strategy are unlikely to change in the short to medium term. Its imports of grains and staple foods will therefore remain low, but imports of other agricultural products, especially land-intensive agricultural goods, will increase significantly. China will still impose import tariff quotas on wheat, corn and rice, but will slash import tariffs on other grains and continue to eliminate non-tariff measures such as import quotas and licences for related agricultural products.

At present, research on China's agricultural products trade has focused on China's overall exports and imports, with less emphasis on China's agricultural economic and trade cooperation with specific countries, especially Lancang-Mekong countries. There is still a big gap between research and the objective of strengthening economic and trade cooperation among the countries of the Lancang-Mekong region. The goal of this paper is to provide a comprehensive review of the economic transformation and outlook in China and analyse the implications for agricultural trade cooperation between China and other Lancang-Mekong countries. Based on the analysis of agriculture's share of GDP and its changing role in China's overall economic structure, the paper makes reasonable predictions of China's agricultural product demand and Lancang-Mekong countries' agricultural trade potential. Based on these predictions, the paper provides policy recommendations for promoting China's trade in agricultural products in the Lancang-Mekong region.

The rest of the paper is organized as follows. Section 2.2 describes the research methodology and data. Section 2.3 presents an analysis of agricultural structural change within China, taking a future perspective by reflecting on the past. Section 2.4 gives an overview of economic and trade cooperation in the Lancang-Mekong region. Section 2.5 discusses the implications of the study and provides policy recommendations for enhancing agricultural trade between Lancang-Mekong countries. Section 2.6 concludes.

2.2 RESEARCH METHODOLOGY AND DATA

This research uses both quantitative and qualitative data and methods. Quantitative analysis includes descriptive statistics, comparative labour productivity inference (see Xu, Zhen and Su 2018; section 3.1.2 gives a detailed description of this method), and the construct of revealed comparative advantages (see Balassa 1965). These were used to study the past trends of variables, the problem of surplus labour, and patterns of trade, respectively. In order to forecast future trends in industrial structure and trade, a qualitative data analysis approach was adopted by integrating past trends, economic rules of economic development, and China's economic planning and policies.

The research is based on secondary data. Data were obtained from open databases such as the National Bureau of Statistics of China, World Integrated Trade Solution database and UN Comtrade database, as well as from academic reports such as the Report on Development of China's Outward Investment 2018 (MOC 2018).

2.3 ECONOMIC TRANSFORMATION IN CHINA'S AGRICULTURAL SECTOR: PRESENT AND FUTURE

Since implementing free-market reforms and opening up to foreign trade and investment in 1978, China has become one of the world's fastest-growing economies. Between 1978 and 2018, China's annual GDP growth averaged 9.5 per cent. Since 2012, economic growth has been significantly lower than the original 8 per cent mean trajectory. The Report of the 19th National Congress of the China Communist Party proposed a structural reform to shift the economy from high-speed growth to high-quality development. This indicates that the Chinese government is confident that the economy can tolerate slower growth. The main trend of China's economic growth can be summarized as the transition from an agricultural to a modern industrialized nation. Increased agricultural productivity stimulated rural labour transfer and industrialization. As more and more people moved to cities, China started to modernize. This is consistent with the development experience of other developing nations. The rest of this section focuses on economic transformation in China's agricultural sector.

2.3.1 Transformation of the Agricultural Sector

2.3.1.1 Reforms and Growth

China's reform and opening up started with rural reforms. With the rapid implementation of the contract accountability system, economic reform towards a free market economy began by reforming the price system for agricultural and sideline products, adjusting the rural industrial structure and developing township enterprises. These initial efforts ushered in a period of comprehensive agricultural development. China's agricultural and rural areas have since undergone profound change.

First, agriculture sector growth increased substantially. From 1952 to 1978, agricultural GDP grew at an average annual rate of only 2.2 per cent. From 1966 to 2018, average agricultural GDP growth was 4.5 per cent (last row of the first column in Table 2.1), more than double that before the reform.

Second, the output of land-intensive grain, cotton, oilseed and sugarcane increased significantly, solving the problem of obtaining enough food and clothing for city residents. For example, from 1966 to 2018, the average annual growth rates of cotton, oilseed and sugarcane were 3.3 per cent, 4.3 per cent and 4.4 per cent, respectively.

Third, the food consumption of urban and rural residents and the structure of food consumption improved. At the same time, population growth, income growth of urban and rural residents, and urbanization have placed higher demands on food consumption and consumption structure. For example, from 1966 to 2018, the average annual growth rates of meat and milk consumption were 5.2 per cent and 9.0 per cent, respectively. By the turn of the century, especially when the country needed to earn foreign exchange through agricultural exports, the demand

TABLE 2.1
Contribution of Agriculture to Economic Growth (per cent), 1966–2018

	Agriculture Growth Rate	Food Growth Rate	Cotton Growth Rate	Oilseed Growth Rate	Sugarcane Growth Rate	Meat Growth Rate	Milk Growth Rate
6th five-year period	8.3	3.6	12.2	16.6	19.2	10.1	17.1
7th five-year period	4.2	3.4	2.7	1.2	2.6	8.2	10.8
8th five-year period	4.1	0.9	2.8	7.0	3.1	13.0	6.8
9th five-year period	3.4	0.0	–0.8	5.8	1.3	3.1	7.7
10th five-year period	3.8	1.0	6.4	0.9	5.2	3.0	27.3
11th five-year period	4.4	2.9	1.3	0.9	4.5	2.9	2.0
12th five-year period	4.1	3.4	0.7	1.4	0.3	1.8	1.0
13th five-year period (2016 to present)	3.6	–0.1	1.4	0.5	–0.8	–0.9	–1.1
Annual average	4.5	1.9	3.3	4.3	4.4	5.2	9.0

for food from urban and rural residents could not have been fully met without rapid growth in domestic agricultural production and adjustment of the production structure. This underlines the importance of domestic agricultural production as the main source of meeting the growing demand for food in rural and urban China.

After China's accession to the World Trade Organization (WTO), its rapidly increasing participation in international trade in food and agricultural products brought about changes in the structure of domestic agricultural production and further improved the food consumption pattern of urban and rural residents. Since the reform and opening up, changes in the composition of China's agricultural imports and exports have given full play to the comparative advantages of China's agricultural products. On the one hand, net exports of relatively intensive agricultural products (such as grain, cotton, oilseed and sugarcane) are declining while net imports are rising. Yet at the same time, net exports of high-value relatively labour-intensive agricultural products (such as horticultural and aquatic products) are growing. Growth in agricultural trade along with a structural change in the agriculture sector has met the needs of domestic consumers and improved the consumption structure while optimizing comparative advantages in agriculture and securing efficient use of agricultural resources and sustainable agricultural development.

2.3.1.2 Agricultural Labour Transfer

The transfer of surplus labour from the agricultural sector to the industrial and service sectors and concomitant migration from rural to urban areas is necessary for industrialization, urbanization and agricultural modernization the world over. Since the reform and opening up, the higher birth rate, especially the rural birth rate, has enlarged the workforce. The resultant intense competition for agricultural resources has given rise to a marginal diminishing effect on agricultural productivity. Even as China's industry and service sectors are developing rapidly, rural employment is declining and non-agricultural employment increasing rapidly. With the declining proportion of agricultural employment and steadily increasing proportion of industrial employment, services became the main sector that absorbed new workers as well as those moving from agriculture and industry.

As Figure 2.1 shows, from the mid-1980s to 2000, industry's share of the total labour force remained at over 20 per cent. In 1994, service's share of workers surpassed that of industry for the first time, at 23 per cent. After China joined the WTO in 2001, service workers outnumbered farmers by as much as 35.7 per cent; and in 2017, service workers accounted

FIGURE 2.1
Changes in the Proportion of Employment in Agriculture, Industry and Services in China (per cent), 1978–2018

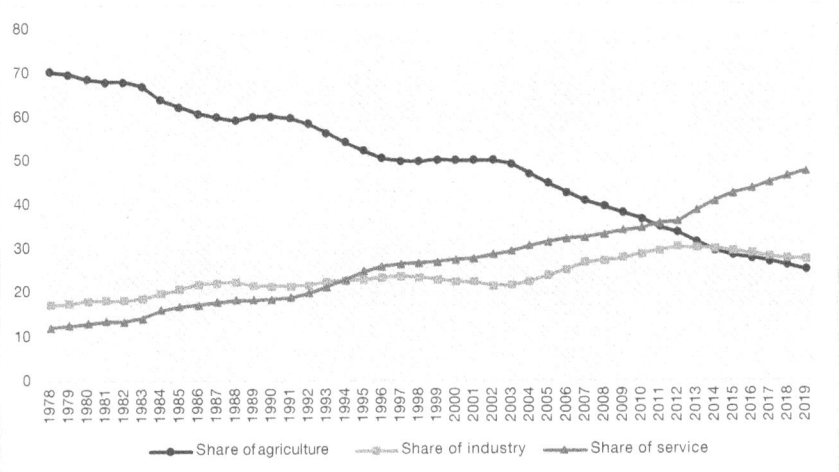

for 44.9 per cent of the total labour force. With the large transfer of labour from agriculture to industry and services, China has made efficient use of its abundant workforce.

The question of how much more surplus labour needs to be transferred in rural China remains, however. At present, academically recognized estimation methods mainly include international comparison, cultivated land labour ratio, average labour planting area inference, and comparative labour productivity inference. Different estimation methods have different angles and focus. Therefore, measurement results based on different methods will be quite different.

The current study uses the comparative labour productivity inference method proposed by Xu, Zhu and Su (2018). The design logic of this estimation method is clear and comprehensible, and the data can be easily obtained. For this method, we compare per capita agricultural labour productivity with average social labour productivity. We assume there is surplus agricultural labour when per capita productivity of agriculture is lower than average social labour productivity. Suppose the number of agricultural surplus labour in year t is LS_t, the number of social labour is A_t, the number of farmers is N_t, gross domestic product is G_g, gross agricultural product is G_n, and the ratio of gross agricultural product to GDP is b_t, the calculation formula is expressed as follows:

$$LS_t = N_t - \frac{G_n/N_t}{G_g/A_t} \times N_t = N_t - b_t \times A_t$$

China's surplus agricultural labour force increased between 1978 and 2003, peaked in 2003, and then declined year by year (Table 2.2). However, although China had already achieved a large transfer of labour from agriculture to industry and services, it still needed to transfer 145 million farmers by 2017. To adhere to the government's new domestic urbanization plan, usher in modernization and improve the "four comprehensive" strategies, China must vigorously advance the transfer of surplus agricultural labour to industry and services, foster new professional farmers and help more farmers settle in cities.

China is an upper-middle-income country on the brink of becoming a high-income country. In the process, the Chinese government has prioritized service sector development so that surplus labour will be properly placed. Enhancing the performance of the services sector by improving the output value and employment ratio reflects China's modernization.

TABLE 2.2
Estimation of Surplus Rural Labour in China, 1978–2017

Year	Farmers (10,000 people)	GDP (RMB100 million)	Agricultural GDP (RMB100 million)	Total Labour (10,000 people)	Agricultural Surplus Labour (10,000 people)
1978	28,318.0	3,593.0	927.8	40,152.0	17,949.8
1979	28,634.0	3,865.8	984.7	41,024.0	18,184.3
1980	29,122.0	4,168.6	970.1	42,361.0	19,263.9
1981	29,777.0	4,822.1	1,454.4	43,725.0	16,589.0
1982	30,859.0	5,257.0	1,622.1	45,295.0	16,882.8
1983	31,151.0	5,823.1	1,757.1	46,436.0	17,139.1
1984	30,868.0	6,707.8	1,983.5	48,197.0	16,616.1
1985	31,130.0	7,608.7	2,020.0	49,873.0	17,889.4
1986	31,254.0	8,289.6	2,087.1	51,282.0	18,342.6
1987	31,663.0	9,256.0	2,185.3	52,783.0	19,201.2
1988	32,249.0	10,294.7	2,240.8	54,334.0	20,422.4
1989	33,225.0	10,727.8	2,309.8	55,329.0	21,312.1
1990	38,914.2	11,148.3	2,479.0	64,749.0	24,516.2
1991	39,098.1	20,621.0	5,135.3	65,491.0	22,788.7
1992	38,698.9	23,554.3	5,374.1	66,152.0	23,605.8
1993	37,679.7	26,824.5	5,624.0	66,808.0	23,672.8
1994	36,628.1	30,321.5	5,845.9	67,455.0	23,622.9
1995	35,529.9	33,642.9	6,134.8	68,065.0	23,118.2
1996	34,819.8	36,981.2	6,444.0	68,950.0	22,805.2
1997	34,840.2	40,397.0	6,665.5	69,820.0	23,319.9
1998	35,177.2	43,566.6	6,894.3	70,637.0	23,999.1
1999	35,768.4	46,904.5	7,082.6	71,394.0	24,987.9
2000	36,042.5	50,886.7	7,247.5	72,085.0	25,775.8
2001	36,398.5	10,8639.2	15,105.6	72,797.0	26,276.5
2002	36,640.0	11,8561.9	15,513.5	73,280.0	27,051.5
2003	36,204.4	13,0463.2	15,881.4	73,736.0	27,228.4
2004	34,829.8	14,3657.8	16,851.0	74,264.0	26,118.7
2005	33,441.9	16,0027.0	17,706.0	74,647.0	25,182.6
2006	31,940.6	21,1147.7	22,843.7	74,978.0	23,828.9
2007	30,731.0	24,1195.8	23,648.6	75,321.0	23,345.9
2008	29,923.3	26,4472.8	24,867.9	75,564.0	22,818.2
2009	28,890.5	28,9329.9	25,863.3	75,828.0	22,112.2
2010	27,930.5	32,0102.6	26,962.7	76,105.0	21,520.1
2011	26,594.2	45,2429.9	41,006.9	76,420.0	19,667.7
2012	25,773.0	48,7976.2	42,839.8	76,704.0	19,039.1
2013	24,171.0	52,5835.4	44,473.5	76,977.0	17,660.5
2014	22,790.0	56,4194.4	46,277.5	77,253.0	16,453.4
2015	21,919.0	60,3212.1	48,084.2	77,451.0	15,745.1
2016	21,496.0	73,5355.0	62,863.8	77,603.0	14,861.9
2017	20,944.0	78,5770.0	65,332.3	77,640.0	14,488.7

Source: WIND Economic Database.

2.3.1.3 Agricultural Product Cooperation

Since the reform and opening up, China has continuously lowered its trade barriers and significantly opened up its market to agricultural product trade. Before, China had just over sixty agricultural trade partners. Now it has agricultural trade partners in almost all nations and regions. From re-entry into the General Agreement on Tariffs and Trade to multiple rounds of WTO accession negotiations, China began to align its foreign trade policies with international mainstream trade rules. In addition to tax rebates, China placed import tariff quotas on certain agricultural products and significantly lowered import tariffs on others.

Since joining the WTO, China's foreign trade rules and the trade rules and systems under the multilateral framework have been deeply integrated, and non-tariff measures such as import licensing and quantity restrictions have been abolished. Tariffs on agricultural products have been cut to 15.2 per cent, about one-quarter of the average tariffs for the world's agricultural products. In recent years, the diversification of China's foreign trade in agricultural products has accelerated. Seventeen free trade agreements have been signed with twenty-five countries including Chile, Pakistan, New Zealand and Singapore, as well as ASEAN member states. In addition, zero tariffs have been imposed on certain agricultural products. Introduced just five years ago, China's Belt and Road Initiative is accelerating both the formation of a new foreign trade pattern in agricultural products and the development of agricultural trade between China and Belt and Road countries and regions.

China has gradually emerged as a major power in agricultural trade. Consequently, its agricultural trade pattern has undergone significant changes. Apart from the continuous increase in the volume of agricultural trade, the trade deficit widened and became normal (Figure 2.2). First, China's agricultural product import and export volumes have grown steadily. Total trade value increased more than ninefold from US$20.37 billion in 1998 to US$188.88 billion in 2017, with an average annual growth rate of 13.0 per cent. Second, due to insufficient domestic factors of production, less cultivable and poor-quality land, there is an enormous gap between China's agricultural mechanization level and productivity and that of Europe and North America. Domestic supplies of land-intensive agricultural products such as soybeans and cotton fall short of demand. Due to growing external reliance, the import growth

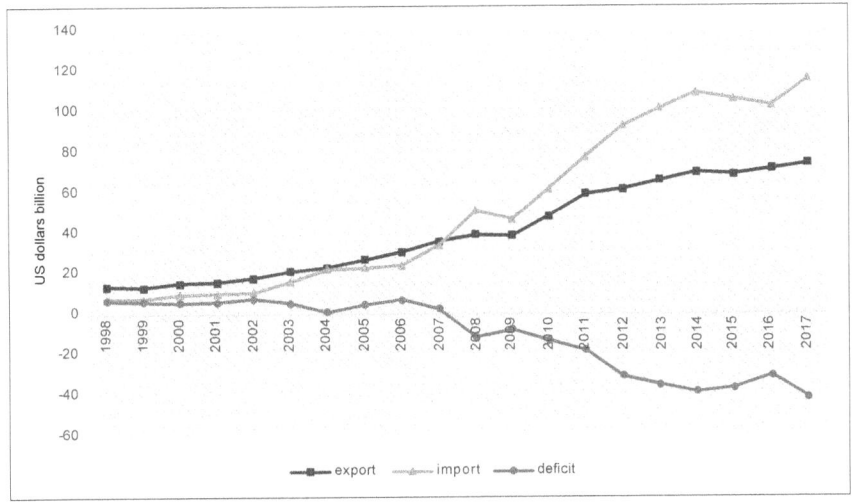

FIGURE 2.2
China's Trade in Agricultural Products, 1998–2017

Source: China Statistical Yearbook (NBS 2018),

rates in 2003 and 2004 were 52.2 per cent and 40.4 per cent, respectively. The corresponding export growth rates were only 18.7 per cent and 8.9 per cent. In 2008, agricultural trade turned negative and then the overall trade deficit continued to widen, reaching US$41.71 billion in 2017. Moreover, China's economic development, growing income per capita, and changes in dietary patterns have ushered in a third consumption upgrading. Demands for a good quality of life as well as better and more agricultural products and product varieties are constantly increasing. China's imports of agricultural products are therefore expected to increase consistently in the foreseeable future.

2.3.2 Future Direction of Agricultural Sector in the Next Decade

2.3.2.1 Economic Growth and Structural Changes

China's real GDP growth rate in 2018 was 6.6 per cent. GDP in the first quarter of 2019 increased by 6.4 per cent year-on-year. From 2009 to

2018, GDP growth slowed from 9.4 per cent to 6.6 per cent, a decrease of 2.8 percentage points.

The annual GDP growth rate target for 2019 is 6.0–6.5 per cent, according to the 2019 Government Work Report (State Council of China 2019). As set out in the 13th Five-Year Plan, the goal is to have doubled GDP growth in 2020 from 2010. China's real GDP growth in 2019 and 2020, therefore, needs to reach at least 6.1 per cent. At the time of writing, China's real GDP growth rates for 2019 and 2023 were forecast at 6.2 per cent and 5.6 per cent, respectively (International Monetary Fund 2018).

The authors contend that China's GDP will maintain moderate to high growth rates in the next decade, averaging 4–6 per cent. There are three main reasons for this. First, China's per capita GDP is still low, just close to US$10,000, lower than the global average and only one-sixth of that of the United States. There is vast growth potential. With similar per capita GDP, Japan and South Korea were able to maintain high growth rates. Second, China's technological and institutional capacities still have much room for improvement. China can benefit as a latecomer and speed up its reforms. In recent years, China's supply-side reforms have achieved positive initial results. With the comprehensive deepening of reforms and further expansion of openness, the environment for China's economic growth will be further improved. Third, the original factors that powered China's economic growth have not fundamentally changed. China's economic and social environment is stable, the basic economic system remains unchanged, and labour advantages still exist. With improving technical capabilities, infrastructure investment in high-speed rail and mobile Internet networks provides strong support for economic development.

At the same time, the growth of China's economy in the future will be affected by some unfavourable factors. First, at the higher economic development stage, economic growth may slow, returns to investment decrease, consumption growth decline and marginal returns of institutional reform decrease. Second, the Chinese economy faces several difficulties, including strengthening national independent innovation capacity, financing start-ups and expansion of private enterprises, especially small and micro enterprises, equating local governments' tax receipts and expenditures, risks in China's financial system, slowing population growth, and population ageing. In addition, protectionism and unilateralism have intensified, and escalating US-China trade friction has added to economic uncertainty.

As for structural changes in the future, we believe that both industrial structural change and demand-based structural change will have important impacts on agricultural trade. In terms of industrial structure, from 2009 to 2017, agriculture, industry and services all grew. However, their proportion changed: the value-added ratio of agriculture decreased from 9.6 per cent to 7.6 per cent, a decrease of 2 percentage points; that of industry from 46 per cent to 40.5 per cent, a decrease of 5.5 percentage points; and that of services increased from 44.4 per cent to 51.9 per cent, an increase of 7.5 percentage points. Thus, the transformation of China's industrial structure is in line with the general rule of industrial upgrading, and it is becoming more and more advanced. This trend is also consistent with the goal of the Chinese government's industrial upgrading. In the next few years, restrictions on agriculture imposed by natural conditions and consumer demand will narrow further and eventually stabilize. And the proportion of services will expand further.

In terms of demand structure, the contribution of China's final demand to GDP in 2017 was 57.6 per cent, that of investment demand was 33.8 per cent and that of net exports was 8.6 per cent. Since 2009, the contribution of investment demand has declined. The contributions of consumer demand and net exports have risen, which is also in line with the goals of the shift in government economic policy.

Table 2.3 provides data on consumer demand and expenditure in 2017. The largest expenditure category is food, tobacco and alcohol with a share of 29.33 per cent, 1.89 percentage points lower than in 2013. That is the biggest drop of any consumption category. The growth rate of food, tobacco and alcohol, which is also the slowest-growing consumer spending category, stood at 4.33 per cent in 2017. Residence is the second-largest expenditure category, with a growth rate of 9.64 per cent from 2013, representing a decrease of 0.27 percentage points. In terms of consumption growth, at a rate of 11.02 per cent, healthcare expenditure per capita grew faster than other expenditures, increasing from 6.90 per cent in 2013 to 7.92 per cent in 2017. Other supplies and services is the second fastest-growing consumption category, followed by residence, education, culture and entertainment, daily necessities and services, and traffic and communication. Food, tobacco and alcohol expenditure as well as clothing expenditure grew more slowly.

It is expected that future changes in the demand structure will conform to these trends. Analysis of consumer demand finds that Engel's coefficient[1]

TABLE 2.3
Consumption Structure and Variation in Trends in 2017

Consumption Category	Per capita Expenditure (RMB)	2017 Growth Rate (%)	2017 Share (%)	2013 Share (%)	Share Change (%)
Food, alcohol and tobacco	5.374	4.33	29.33	31.22	−1.89
Clothes	1.238	2.91	6.76	7.77	−1.01
Residence	4.107	9.64	22.41	22.68	−0.27
Daily necessities and services	1.121	7.38	6.12	6.10	0.02
Traffic and communication	2.499	6.89	13.64	12.31	1.33
Education, culture and entertainment	2.086	8.93	11.38	10.57	0.81
Healthcare	1.451	11.02	7.92	6.90	1.02
Other supplies and services	0.447	10.10	2.44	2.46	−0.02

Source: China Statistical Yearbook (NBS 2018).

for urban residents dropped from 36.5 per cent in 2009 to 36.3 per cent in 2017 while that for rural residents dropped from 41.0 per cent to 39.3 per cent. Because the demand for food by rural/urban residents declines along the income margin, the Engel coefficient of all residents will decline further in the next few years, though the decline for rural residents will be bigger than for urban residents.

In terms of population structure, the natural rate of population growth decreased from 4.87 per cent in 2009 to 3.81 per cent in 2017. Although the comprehensive two-child policy stimulated population growth in the short term, the effectiveness of the policy is not sustainable, and population growth will slow in the future. In terms of age composition, the proportion of the population aged 65 and above to the total population increased from 8.4 per cent in 2009 to 11.9 per cent in 2017. With the increase in life expectancy and weak population growth, the population ageing problem will be aggregated in the future.

In terms of urban and rural structure, the urbanization rate increased from 48 per cent in 2009 to 59 per cent in 2017. The urban population has surpassed the rural population. According to the 13th Five-Year Plan, the urbanization rate in 2020 is expected to reach 60 per cent, though this goal could be achieved ahead of time. Compared with the rates of urbanization in developed countries, China's urbanization rate still has much growth potential. It is expected to increase by as much as 10 percentage points over the next decade. The urban-rural gap will narrow further, and the urban-rural dual system will gradually diminish.

2.3.2.2 The Structure of Agricultural Trade

Table 2.4 shows the import values of major agricultural products in 2017. The import value of soybeans was relatively large, followed by cereals, edible plant oil, cotton, rice and wheat. Since 2009, the value of edible oil imports has declined and the values of other agricultural product imports have increased. Among them, imports of rice, grain and wheat rose quickly, while those of soybeans and sugar increased slowly.

In line with the characteristics of domestic agricultural production, the pattern of China's agricultural imports over the next decade should be determined by both supply and demand. Demand depends mainly on consumer demand for agricultural products and domestic production gaps. Supply depends mainly on domestic and foreign resource endowments and differences in comparative advantage arising out of technological differences. At the same time, agricultural trade is not entirely determined by market supply and demand but is also affected by policy and unexpected shocks.

We first analyse the supply-demand gaps. The total import volume of agricultural products is expected to continue growing in the next ten years. The main reason is that the population has not yet reached its peak. Gross national income has continued to increase, urbanization has continued to

TABLE 2.4
Import Values of Major Agricultural Products and Variation in Trend in 2017

Product	Value (US$ million)	Value Growth Rate	Ratio (%)	Ratio Growth Rate
Grain and grain powder	6,485.24	6.2213	0.3054	3.1149
Wheat	1,082.52	4.1263	0.0510	1.9211
Rice	1,860.00	7.6279	0.0876	3.9163
Soybeans	39,637.65	1.1098	1.8665	0.2022
Edible plant oil	4,530.56	−0.2315	0.2133	−0.5621
Sugar	1,078.48	1.8501	0.0508	0.6240
Cotton	2,189.77	0.0355	0.1031	−0.4099

Source: China Statistical Yearbook (NBS 2018).

increase, and demand for agricultural products has also increased. Despite China's fast-growing agricultural output, there are lingering output gaps as supply increases have failed to keep pace with the rapid development of domestic demand. Such gaps need to be covered by imports.

With growing per capita income and urbanization, the consumption demand for agricultural products increases year by year. The Engel coefficients of urban residents and rural residents slowly decrease and the production of agricultural products increases year by year. Given limited cultivable land, scarce water resources and ongoing large-scale transfer of labour from rural to urban areas, the proportion of agricultural output to total output decreases year by year and the gap between agricultural product consumption and domestic agricultural production widens. In addition, as the living standards of residents improve, better quality and more diverse agricultural products are demanded. Due to the constraints of domestic technology and resources, some of these new demands need to be met from increased imports.

Tables 2.5 and 2.6 respectively present the growth rates of per capita imports and per capita domestic production of some agricultural products. Although per capita domestic production of agricultural products is on an upward trend, the growth rate is lower. Per capita import volume is generally greater than the domestic production growth rate, though the growth rate is more volatile. It is expected that domestic agricultural product output will continue to grow slowly in the future, but the pace of growth will not be able to keep up with the widening domestic supply and demand gap. According to the statistics of the Rural Economic Research

TABLE 2.5
Per Capita Import Growth of Some Agricultural Products (per cent), 2010–17

Indicator	2010	2011	2012	2013	2014	2015	2016	2017
Grain and grain powder	80.4	–5.0	155.2	3.8	33.1	66.8	–33.2	15.8
Wheat	36.1	1.7	192.7	48.8	–46.1	–0.3	12.8	28.9
Rice	7.3	53.3	294.3	–4.6	13.0	30.3	4.8	12.6
Soybeans	28.2	–4.4	10.4	8.0	12.1	13.8	2.1	13.2
Edible plant oil	–16.2	–4.8	28.0	–4.6	–20.1	3.5	–18.7	3.8
Sugar	66.2	64.2	27.8	20.7	–23.8	38.3	–37.2	–25.6
Cotton	84.7	17.7	51.9	–19.5	–41.5	–39.8	–39.3	28.2

Source: China Statistical Yearbook (NBS 2018).

TABLE 2.6
Per Capita Domestic Production Growth Rate of Some Agricultural Products (per cent), 2010–17

Indicator	2010	2011	2012	2013	2014	2016	2017
Food	3.2	4.8	3.5	2.5	0.9	−0.6	−0.4
Cotton	−7.9	12.5	0.8	−5.3	−0.2	−10.9	6.3
Oilseed	0.1	1.3	1.8	−0.5	2.1	6.5	−4.8
Sugar	−2.7	3.8	7.1	1.5	−3.4	—	—
Fruit	4.4	5.9	5.1	3.8	3.6	—	—
Orchard fruits	4.6	8.9	6.7	—	—	—	—
Melon	4.3	1.3	2.5	—	—	—	—
Vegetables	4.8	3.9	3.8	—	—	—	—

Source: China Statistical Yearbook (NBS 2018).

Centre of the Ministry of Agriculture (Zhang et al. 2016), during the 13th Five-Year period from 2016 to 2020, China could become self-sufficient in rice and wheat. However, there is a supply and demand gap for quality wheat. Said gap for corn is 5 million tonnes, for soybeans 80 million tonnes, oilseed 5 million tonnes, cotton 2 million tonnes, sugar 4–5 million tonnes, pork 0.8–1 tonne, beef 0.3 million tonnes and dairy products 12 million tonnes. China is already basically self-sufficient in mutton.

At the same time, the structure of agricultural imports will change as agricultural production and consumption differ. First, with the increase in the disposable income of residents and the upgrading of consumption, the demand for food and grain has declined, while that for high-quality foods such as meat, eggs and milk and non-direct edible agricultural products has increased. This suggests that residents are paying more attention to the quality and diversification of agricultural products. Second, to improve food security, China needs a higher rate of food self-sufficiency, especially in rice and wheat, and needs to be basically self-sufficient in products such as corn. China-US trade friction has affected China's imports of agricultural products such as soybeans and rendered its imports of agricultural products more uncertain. This again underlines the important contribution of cereal grains to food security.

One way to measure trends in imports of agricultural products is to use the theory of comparative advantage. According to the basic principles of international economics, the division of inter-industry trade is determined by comparative advantage, so the degree and change of comparative advantage determine the pattern of trade in agricultural products. We adopt the revealed comparative advantage (RCA) index to measure the comparative advantage of each product category in 2017; the changing pattern of RCA since China's accession to the WTO in 2001 is also considered. The RCA index for all product categories (see Table 2.7) indicates that China's comparative advantage (RCA greater than 1) lies in machinery and electronics, textiles and other labour-intensive industries. Agricultural products and agriculture-related products such as food, vegetables and livestock are at a comparative disadvantage. The RCA index for agricultural products has also been declining, which means the situation of comparative disadvantage is also unlikely to change much in the future. According to the basic principles of international trade, China will continue to import agricultural products and trade labour-intensive products with other countries that have comparative advantages in agricultural products to achieve win-win results.

Natural endowment is an important source of comparative advantage, and agricultural production is highly dependent on natural conditions. The

TABLE 2.7
Revealed Comparative Advantage of Each Product Category

Product	RCA in 2017	RCA Change since 2001
Fuels	0.08	−0.12
Minerals	0.10	−0.47
Vegetables	0.21	−0.33
Transport	0.27	0.14
Livestock	0.28	−0.34
Food products	0.29	−0.20
Chemicals	0.48	0.10
Stone and glass	0.50	−0.27
Wood	0.64	0.10
Plastic or rubber	0.79	−0.02
Metals	0.93	0.13
Miscellaneous	1.42	−0.29
Machinery and electronics	1.95	0.79
Hides and skins	2.11	−2.24
Textiles and clothing	2.11	−0.72
Footwear	2.70	−3.73

Source: Calculated using World Integrated Trade Solution data.

difference in endowments between countries has an important impact on the comparative advantage of agricultural products, and that affects the trade structure of agricultural products. For example, China's geographical location determines that it has no comparative advantage in tropical and subtropical fruit production. Because of tensions between people and land, scarcity of cultivable land, limited water resources, and difficulty scaling up mechanized farming due to fragmented landholdings, China has no comparative advantage in land-intensive and resource-intensive agricultural products, and domestic production is low. China needs to give full play to its comparative advantages and enhance social benefits through trade. Of course, to ensure domestic grain security, it is necessary to guarantee self-sufficiency in grain, and sometimes it is impossible to fully abide by the principle of comparative advantage.

At the same time, agricultural imports are not completely determined by the market but are affected by policies and exogenous shocks. Consistent with national strategy, the government will guarantee basic food self-sufficiency and will also expand imports of certain emergency supplies in accordance with market fluctuations, such as the recent demand for pork. In addition, the international environment will also have an impact on agricultural product trade. For example, the phased results of the China-US trade negotiations will increase China's purchases of agricultural products from the United States. Countries with a similar agricultural structure to the United States will be negatively affected to some extent. However, short-term agreements will not affect long-term trade trends.

To sum up, China can be self-sufficient in basic food grains—wheat and rice. However, stronger emphasis should be placed on importing better and more agricultural products to meet higher consumer expectations. Due to insufficient domestic production, soybean imports are expected to increase. With domestic consumption upgrading and productivity constraints, imports of high-quality dairy products will rise. Due to domestic production cuts, cotton imports will increase. And international demand for sugar will slowly increase. Generally speaking, better quality and more diverse agricultural product imports are required. With the growth of industry and services, land and water resource constraints will become more evident. The comparative disadvantages of land-intensive and water-intensive agricultural products in China are more obvious. Import demands for such products will also increase accordingly.

2.4 CHINA'S ECONOMIC AND TRADE COOPERATION IN THE LANCANG-MEKONG REGION

2.4.1 Outward Foreign Direct Investment

The number of private enterprises has increased substantially and their foreign investments in agriculture have developed rapidly, forming the backbone of China's agricultural investment in the Lancang-Mekong region. From 2004 to 2015, of the 571 Chinese enterprises established in Lancang-Mekong countries, only 182 were state-owned enterprises, accounting for 31.9 per cent of total Chinese agricultural investment (Table 2.8). The number of private enterprises operating in the region was twice that of state-owned enterprises. At the same time, non-agricultural enterprises have also realized the development potential of agriculture and begun to deploy agricultural investments in Lancang-Mekong countries.

China has achieved remarkable growth in foreign investment in recent years. From 2002 to 2016, the average increase in foreign investment reached 35.8 per cent. In 2017, China strengthened the authenticity and compliance reviews of enterprises' foreign direct investment (FDI) and restricted irrational investment in some sectors. Foreign investment subsequently dropped by 19.3 per cent year on year. In 2018, China's overall net foreign investment was RMB859.14 billion, a year-on-year increase of 2.1 per cent. According to the 2017 investment results, China's largest foreign investment is in Asia, accounting for 69.52 per cent of total investment, followed by Europe (11.66 per cent), Latin America (8.89 per cent), North America (4.11 per cent), Oceania (3.23 per cent) and Africa (2.59 per cent). Compared with the same period in 2016, the proportion of investment in Asia barely changed and that in Europe and Africa grew. The proportions of investment in North America and Latin America are falling, mainly because the protectionist policies of the United States have curbed China's investment in North America. In order to exclude the impact of short-term policy fluctuations, the authors calculated the average growth rate of net foreign investment in 2009–17. The results show that the region with the fastest investment growth is North America (36.26 per cent), followed by Europe (33.03 per cent), Latin America (25.26 per cent), Africa (18.74 per cent), Oceania (14.56 per cent) and Asia (14.52 per cent). Details are given in Table 2.9.

The countries and regions with the highest growth in foreign investment are ASEAN (net foreign investment of US$14.12 billion, a

TABLE 2.8
Total Projects and Number of Chinese Central Enterprise Projects in Lancang-Mekong Countries, 2004–15

Year	Cambodia Total	Cambodia Number of Central Enterprises	Thailand Total	Thailand Number of Central Enterprises	Myanmar Total	Myanmar Number of Central Enterprises	Laos Total	Laos Number of Central Enterprises	Vietnam Total	Vietnam Number of Central Enterprises	Total Total	Total Number of Central Enterprises
2004	0	0	0	0	0	0	3	0	4	1	7	1
2005	1	0	2	0	0	0	3	0	7	1	13	1
2006	1	0	3	1	0	0	8	1	8	1	20	3
2007	0	2	0	2	1	1	10	1	9	2	20	8
2008	1	2	5	3	3	3	16	3	14	0	39	11
2009	5	0	6	4	5	6	19	2	13	2	48	14
2010	5	2	5	2	2	3	11	1	11	6	34	14
2011	12	4	7	4	3	7	11	2	12	6	45	23
2012	14	7	11	6	6	3	16	4	9	13	56	33
2013	19	5	8	4	4	7	17	5	10	2	58	23
2014	27	10	15	8	10	10	26	12	4	11	82	51
2015	39	0	16	0	30	0	44	0	20	1	149	1
Total	124	32	78	34	64	40	184	31	121	45	571	182

TABLE 2.9
Regional Distribution of China's Foreign Investment in 2017

Region	Net Foreign Investment		Proportion of Foreign Investment	
	Net Amount (US$10,000)	Growth Rate (Average over Years) (%)	Proportion (%)	Growth Rate (over Same Period in 2016) (%)
Asia	11,003,986	14.52	69.52	4.68
Africa	410,500	18.74	2.59	112.07
Europe	1,846,319	33.03	11.66	113.96
North America	649,827	36.26	4.11	−60.43
Oceania	510,539	14.56	3.23	21.39
Latin America	1,407,659	25.26	8.89	−35.93

Source: Report on Development of China's Outward Investment 2018 (MOC 2018).

year-on-year growth rate of 37.4 per cent), Russia (net foreign investment of US$1.55 billion, a year-on-year growth rate of 19.7 per cent), Europe (net foreign investment of US$10.27 billion, a year-on-year growth rate of 2.7 per cent), and Australia (net foreign investment of US$4.24 billion, a year-on-year growth rate of 1.3 per cent). Countries with declining FDI inflows include the United States (net foreign investment of US$6.43 billion, a year-on-year growth rate of −62.2 per cent) and Hong Kong (net foreign investment of US$91.15 billion, year-on-year growth rate of −20.2 per cent).

Thanks to the Belt and Road Initiative, China's total investment in the fifty-six countries along the Belt and Road in 2018 reached US$15.64 billion, a year-on-year increase of 8.9 per cent, far greater than the year-on-year growth rate of all investments, accounting for 13 per cent of total investments in that year. Main investment destinations include Singapore, Laos, Vietnam, Indonesia, Pakistan, Malaysia, Russia, Cambodia and Thailand.

Investment in agriculture in 2017 totalled US$2.51 billion, accounting for 1.6 per cent of total investment. Investment in industry totalled US$29.51 billion, accounting for 18.6 per cent of total investment. Investment in services totalled US$126.27 billion, accounting for 79.8 per cent of total investment. Therefore, investment in services dominates the foreign investment of Chinese enterprises, while investment in agriculture holds great potential for development.

According to data in the 2018 Report on Development of China's Outward Investment (MOC 2018), China's agricultural outward foreign investment in 2017 was US$2.25 billion. By region, investment in Asia accounted for 42.22 per cent, in Europe 31.56 per cent, in South America 13.33 per cent, and in Africa 6.67 per cent. Investments in Asia and Europe are sufficient while investments in South America and Africa have great development potential. China has different motives and objectives for its agricultural investments in different countries, as shown in Table 2.10. Investment in Asian countries is mainly geared towards resource utilization and risk aversion, that in European countries mainly focuses on market exploration and technology communication, and that in South America and Africa centres on resource utilization and market exploitation.

China's Ministry of Agriculture offers guidance and support for future foreign investment in agriculture. The idea is to give priority to China's neighbouring countries (in Southeast and Central Asia, and Russia), and then gradually extend investment to countries in other regions (Africa, South America, Oceania). Depending on agricultural foundation and development demand, investments in Lancang-Mekong countries are concentrated in rice, sugar, rubber and other tropical crops, those in central Asia and Mongolia focus on wheat and cotton, and those in Russia and the Far East focus on maize and soybeans (see Table 2.11).

TABLE 2.10
Regional Distribution of China's Agricultural Outward Investments in 2017

Name	Amount (US$100 million)	Ratio (%)	Purpose
Asia	9.5	42.22	Resource utilization and risk aversion
Europe	7.1	31.56	Market exploration and technology communication
South America	3.0	13.33	Resource utilization and market exploitation
Africa	1.5	6.67	Resource utilization and market exploitation
Rest of the world	1.4	6.22	
Total	22.5	100.00	

Source: Report on China's Outward Investment 2018 (MOC 2018).

TABLE 2.11
Investment Trends in Primary Agricultural Products

Region	Products with Significant Potential
Lancang-Mekong countries	Rice, sugar, rubber and other tropical crops
Central Asia and Mongolia	Wheat and cotton
Far East Russia	Maize and soybeans

Source: Report on China's Outward Investment 2018 (MOC 2018).

For the trends in China's foreign investment, the flow and stock of China's outward foreign investment have developed rapidly in recent years, but they are far from the peak and as such have great growth potential, especially considering the huge gap in outward FDI stock between China and the United States. As a result, China's foreign investment will continue to grow steadily in the future. With more stringent investment review policies and restrictions on irrational foreign investments in real estate, hotels, cinemas, entertainment and sports clubs, China's investment growth will ease in the future. However, the investment structure will be further optimized and investment quality greatly improved. Foreign investment will be deeply affected by investment policies. The US protectionist policy has significantly reduced China's investment in North America. The Belt and Road Initiative has significantly increased investment in countries along the route. If Sino-US economic and trade frictions continue to escalate, China's investment in the United States may be further reduced, and investment in countries along the Belt and Road will be an important investment growth point. At the industry level, according to the 13th Five-Year Plan, to drive agricultural modernization, the Chinese government "shall actively carry out overseas agricultural cooperative development, establish scaled overseas production, processing, storage and transportation bases, and cultivate internationally competitive agricultural multinational corporations". China's foreign investment mainly flows to services, but agriculture has much room for growth.

2.4.2 China's Agricultural Trade with Lancang-Mekong Countries

The total trade volume between China and the rest of the world from 2009 to 2017 grew rapidly. During that period, South America, Oceania and Africa experienced high growth rates, while Europe, Asia and North America had low growth rates. However, there is little difference in growth rates across these regions. The regions with higher growth rates are those with lower trade volumes, while the regions with lower growth rates are those with higher trade volumes. This indicates that China is actively exploring new international markets and diversifying its trading partners. Of total import and export volumes by region in 2017, Asia accounted for 52 per cent, followed by Europe (18 per cent), North America (15 per cent), South America (6 per cent), Africa (4 per cent) and Oceania (4 per cent). From 2009 to 2017, the change in the proportion of total trade volume in all regions was relatively slight; the largest change was in South America at 1.83 per cent, and the smallest was in Asia at –0.31 per cent. The proportion of total trade volumes in Asia and Europe dipped slightly, while in other regions it rose slightly. Details are given in Table 2.12. At the time of writing, the overall data for 2018 had not been announced. According to the data for the first three quarters of 2018 published by the Ministry of Commerce,[2] ranked by the proportion of total trade volume was Asia (51.40 per cent), Europe (18.50 per cent), North America (15.13 per cent), Latin America (6.66 per cent), Africa (4.40 per cent) and Oceania (3.42 per cent). Changes in rankings and proportions were not significant.

In the Lancang-Mekong region, Vietnam is China's largest trading partner in terms of trade volume, ranked 8th among all trading partners, followed by Thailand in 13th place (Table 2.13). Laos is China's smallest trading partner in terms of trade volume, ranking 85th among all China's

TABLE 2.12
China's Import-Export Trade by Region in 2017

Region	Total Trade Volume		Share of China's Total Trade	
	Amount (US$ million)	Growth Rate (%)	(%)	Growth Rate (%)
Asia	2,126,524.48	8.48	52	–0.31
Africa	170,644.77	9.96	4	0.40
Europe	756,106.75	8.23	18	–0.54
Latin America	258,590.12	11.49	6	1.83
North America	635,742.74	9.09	15	0.59
Oceania	159,158.77	12.82	4	3.15

Source: China Statistical Yearbook (NBS 2018).

TABLE 2.13
Trade Value and Growth Rate of Lancang-Mekong Countries, 2009–17

Country	Trade Volume		Trade Growth	
	Value (US$10,000)	Ranking	Growth Rate (%)	Ranking
Vietnam	12,199,187	8	25.11	45
Thailand	8,013,781	13	10.35	146
Myanmar	1,347,481	44	31.18	37
Cambodia	579,078	63	27.34	43
Laos	302,435	85	22.23	54

Source: China Statistical Yearbook (NBS 2018).

trading partners. The growth of Lancang-Mekong countries' combined trade with China ranges from 10.35 per cent to 31.18 per cent. Among all trading partners, China's trade with Lancang-Mekong countries is growing faster than with countries with similar trade volumes. Among them, trade with Myanmar is growing the fastest and trade with Thailand is growing the slowest.

As for agricultural products, the Lancang-Mekong region has excellent natural conditions, fertile land, relatively low labour costs, and superior agricultural resources. It is one of the most promising regions in Asia and the world and is the world's main grain, sugarcane and tropical crop-producing region. Thailand, Vietnam and Myanmar are the world's three most-celebrated agricultural commodity-producing countries. Thailand is the world's largest producer of natural rubber. Vietnam and Laos are major producers and exporters of coffee. And Cambodia is renowned for its rice production and rice exports.

In recent years, China and other Lancang-Mekong countries have actively applied for special cooperation funds to support the implementation of agricultural cooperation projects. Both sides actively seek agricultural cooperation opportunities to facilitate trade and expand trade scale and scope. As Table 2.14 shows, between 2015 and 2018, China's total agricultural exports to Myanmar, Cambodia, Laos and Vietnam grew on average by 19.3 per cent, 7.5 per cent, 37.6 per cent and 15.9 per cent, respectively; Thailand was an exception. In the same period, China's total agricultural imports from Myanmar, Cambodia, Laos, Thailand and Vietnam grew on average by 11.9 per cent, 22.6 per cent, 20.9 per cent, 6.0 per cent and 7.0 per cent, respectively. And again, except for 2016,

TABLE 2.14
China's Agricultural Trade with Lancang-Mekong Countries
(US$100 million), 2015–18

Country	2015		2016		2017		2018	
	Import	Export	Import	Export	Import	Export	Import	Export
Myanmar	1.7	3.2	1.7	3.7	1.9	4.6	2.4	5.4
Cambodia	1.1	0.5	1.1	0.4	1.3	0.4	2.0	0.6
Laos	1.1	0.3	1.2	0.3	1.2	0.2	1.9	0.6
Thailand	48.5	37.1	41.1	34.7	44.7	30.7	55.6	32.9
Vietnam	26.8	33.5	27.9	38.2	34.0	45.3	32.4	52.1
Total	79.2	74.6	73.0	77.3	83.1	81.2	94.2	91.6

China was in deficit because its agricultural imports from Lancang-Mekong countries were greater than its agricultural exports.

Lancang-Mekong countries are the main destinations for China's outward FDI and cooperation. All countries have made remarkable progress. Moreover, agricultural investments cover more and more items, including rice, beans, fisheries, livestock, fruit and vegetables, forestry and related services, and processing. This trend is the result of China's efforts to expand and deepen its opening-up and Lancang-Mekong countries' efforts to promote agricultural modernization and livelihood improvements.

In recent years, international trade has been shrinking due to the slowdown in global economic growth and the prevalence of unilateralism and trade protectionism. On 22 March 2018, the United States began to impose tariffs on certain Chinese products and provoke trade friction unilaterally. However, according to Sino-US trade data, the overall impact of trade friction has been small. In the first three quarters of 2018, the total value of China's imports from the United States was US$2.27 trillion, a year-on-year increase of 6.5 per cent. In the same period, the value of China's imports from the United States totalled US$798.13 billion, a year-on-year increase of 3.8 per cent. The underlying reason is that it takes time for trade policy to come into effect. And again, the United States has a huge demand for Chinese export products, and the Sino-US industrial chain is closely linked. However, in the long run, Sino-US trade friction may have profound impacts on both nations and even on the global economy and trade.

While the United States provoked trade friction with many countries and economic globalization suffered setbacks, China continued to press ahead with the Belt and Road Initiative and promoted smooth trade with Belt and Road countries. China held the first import fair and actively promoted imports. China has become an important force driving global trade development. In the first three quarters of 2018, the two-way trade between China and Belt and Road countries reached RMB6.08 trillion, a year-on-year increase of 13.2 per cent, 3.3 percentage points higher than China's overall trade growth rate. Such remarkable results reflect strong trade complementarity between China and Lancang-Mekong countries.

As China deepens its integration into the international community, its trading partners will become more diverse. However, the total trade volume will generally depend on the bilateral economic scale and trade costs (including tariffs, transport costs, geographical distance, institutional distance and cultural distance), while the Belt and Road Initiative has reduced trade costs and increased trade volume among Belt and Road countries. In addition, China actively builds multilateral and bilateral trade partnerships. Talks on the establishment of a China-Japan-South Korea Free Trade Zone and the completion of the Regional Comprehensive Economic Partnership between China and ASEAN will help promote trade between China and Lancang-Mekong countries. China and its trading partners are affected by trade frictions. For example, Sino-US trade friction continues to escalate, which will compromise Sino-US trade volume. Related products affected by trade friction may be transferred to other countries with comparative advantages.

2.5 IMPLICATIONS OF CHINA'S ECONOMIC STRUCTURAL CHANGE FOR THE LANCANG-MEKONG REGION

2.5.1 Opportunities

2.5.1.1 Increased Agricultural Trade and Investment

As China's per capita income and aggregate demand continue to grow, demands for various products will increase. At the same time, China's ability to produce and supply different products varies. When domestic production and supply of products falls behind demand, China has to import products to keep up with demand. Chinese President Xi Jinping, in his keynote speech at the opening ceremony of the 1st China International Import Expo on 5 November 2018, stated that China's imports of goods and services are expected to exceed US$30 trillion and US$10 trillion, respectively, in the next fifteen years. In other words, in the next fifteen years, China's average annual imports of goods in terms of value will be about US$2 trillion.

China's imports in 2018 amounted to US$2.14 trillion. As China's policy favours import expansion, and per capita income will increase continuously and steadily, the annual import volume will increase year by year (the import growth rate in 2018 was 15.8 per cent). Again, the annual import value of US$2 trillion is a conservative estimate. Under the circumstances, China will also import a large number of agricultural products (aggregate effect) every year. China's imports of agricultural products from Lancang-Mekong countries will also increase year by year. Especially in the face of Sino-US trade friction, China will make full use of the Belt and Road Initiative to enhance cooperation with Lancang-Mekong countries. China will import more products (including agricultural products) from Lancang-Mekong countries (proportional effect). Thus, the growth of agricultural product imports from Lancang-Mekong countries will accelerate.

China's total FDI in 2017 was US$131 billion, and the average annual growth rate of FDI over the previous five years was 3.24 per cent (Figure 2.3). However, China's outbound direct investment (ODI) grew much faster, with an average growth rate of 22.49 per cent over the five years to 2017 (Figure 2.4). In 2014, China's ODI surpassed FDI for the first time.

As Chinese enterprises are poised to reach out, China's annual FDI will reach US$200 billion. China now invests US$4.214 billion annually in Lancang-Mekong countries. Due to the labour cost advantage of Lancang-Mekong countries, the investment potential there is still huge. The main sectors that China will encourage investment in are agriculture and labour-intensive manufacturing. China's investment in the agricultural sectors of Lancang-Mekong countries will directly promote their agricultural development. China's investment in regional infrastructure, such as water conservancy and transport, will indirectly promote agricultural development. And its investment in manufacturing cooperation among Lancang-Mekong countries will indirectly promote agricultural development by promoting agricultural product processing and providing agricultural equipment.

FIGURE 2.3
China's FDI (US$ billion), 2012–17

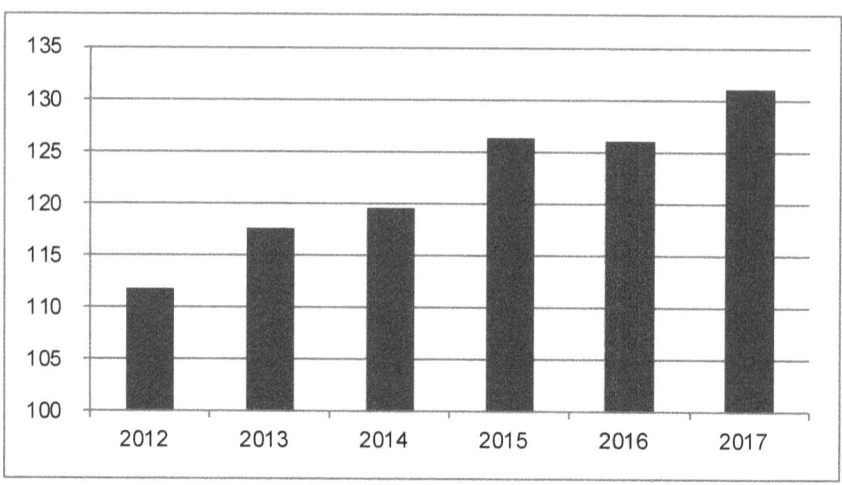

Source: China Statistical Yearbook (NBS 2018).

FIGURE 2.4
China's Outbound Direct Investment (US$ billion) and Growth Rate (%), 2012–16

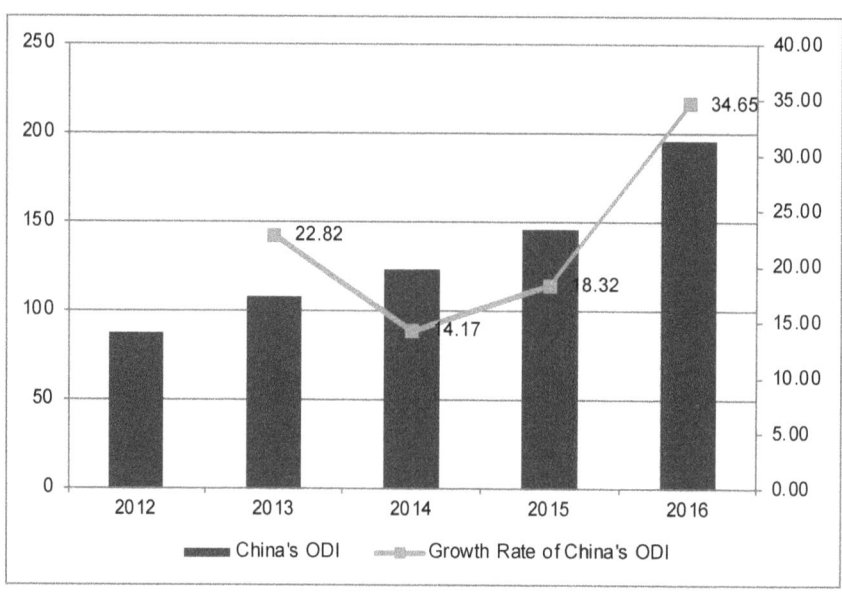

Source: China Statistical Yearbook (NBS 2018).

2.5.1.2 Complementarity of Agricultural Product Trade

Table 2.15 presents five products with the largest trade value between China and Lancang-Mekong countries. Although China and some Lancang-Mekong countries are competitors in some products, the relationship between China and Lancang-Mekong countries in agricultural product trade is mainly complementary. In terms of product intensiveness, China's advantageous products are mostly labour-intensive agricultural products, such as aquatic products; the advantageous products of Lancang-Mekong countries are land-intensive agricultural products such as rice. From the perspective of climate, much of China's territory lies in the temperate zone, and Lancang-Mekong countries lie in the tropics and subtropics. China mainly imports tropical products such as durian and cereals from Lancang-Mekong countries and mostly exports apples, pears, citrus fruits and grapes. Natural climate differences mean that some agricultural products mature at different times. These products include durian, dragon fruit, longan, bananas, watermelons, mangoes and vegetables, which have become the focus of intra-industry trade cooperation.

2.5.2 Challenges

2.5.2.1 Non-tariff Barriers

Free Trade Agreements (FTAs) between China and ASEAN countries have been established and upgraded, tariffs between China and ASEAN countries have been greatly reduced, and zero tariffs for most of the products imported from developing countries to China implemented. However, various non-tariff trade barriers between China and Lancang-Mekong countries still exist, such as tariff quotas, trade facilitation measures, technical trade barriers, and sanitary and phytosanitary measures.

China still retains the national tariff quota for rice imports and implements country-based and type licensing for fresh fruit imports; Lancang-Mekong countries also retain many protection and restriction measures for agriculture and agricultural product imports. In 2017, China's import quota for rice from Cambodia was only 200,000 tonnes, which was very limited. According to the Catalogue of Fresh Fruit Types and Export Countries/Regions that has been approved by China's Inspection and Quarantine (as of 9 April 2019), released by the General Administration of Quality Supervision, Inspection and Quarantine of China (General

TABLE 2.15
Top Five Products with Largest Trade Value between China and Individual Lower Mekong Countries

			Largest Export Value from China to Each LMC			Largest Import Value from Each LMC to China		
	HS Code	Products	Export Value (US$)	Share in China's Total Exports to Each LMC (%)	HS Code	Products	Import Value (US$)	Share in China's Total Imports from Each LMC (%)
Cambodia	52	Cotton	397,400,289	77.19	10	Cereals	73,814,942	67.00
	51	Wool, fine or coarse animal hair; horsehair yarn and woven fabric	78,812,004	15.31	7	Vegetables and certain roots and tubers; edible	15,482,476	14.05
	23	Food industries, residues and wastes thereof; prepared animal fodder	7,439,715	1.45	11	Products of the milling industry; malt, starches, inulin, wheat gluten	10,428,524	9.47
	24	Tobacco and manufactured tobacco substitutes	7,245,317	1.41	23	Food industries, residues and wastes thereof; prepared animal fodder	3,337,630	3.03
	11	Products of the milling industry; malt, starches, inulin, wheat gluten	6,404,577	1.24	3	Fish and crustaceans, molluscs and other aquatic invertebrates	2,459,656	2.23
Laos	24	Tobacco and manufactured tobacco substitutes	18,210,255	63.55	10	Cereals	69,481,006	59.01
	22	Beverages, spirits and vinegar	4,286,326	14.96	11	Products of the milling industry; malt, starches, inulin, wheat gluten	17,259,563	14.66
	52	Cotton	3,038,770	10.61	12	Oilseeds and oleaginous fruits; miscellaneous grains, seeds and fruit, industrial or medicinal plants; straw and fodder	13,505,783	11.47

Economic Structural Change in China

Country	#	Commodity	Value	%	#	Commodity	Value	%
	7	Vegetables and certain roots and tubers; edible	1,067,291	3.72	1	Animals; live	9,182,781	7.80
	20	Preparations of vegetables, fruit, nuts or other parts of plants	747,924	2.61	13	Lac; gums, resins and other vegetable saps and extracts	2,879,606	2.45
Myanmar	52	Cotton	169,964,535	30.34	10	Cereals	50,928,813	29.80
	8	Fruit and nuts, edible; peel of citrus fruit or melons	145,460,810	25.96	12	Oilseeds and oleaginous fruits; miscellaneous grains, seeds and fruit, industrial or medicinal plants; straw and fodder	49,236,585	28.81
	21	Miscellaneous edible preparations	53,320,265	9.52	3	Fish and crustaceans, molluscs and other aquatic invertebrates	27,918,129	16.34
	9	Coffee, tea, mate and spices	34,902,240	6.23	8	Fruit and nuts, edible; peel of citrus fruit or melons	19,042,372	11.14
	22	Beverages, spirits and vinegar	29,663,784	5.29	7	Vegetables and certain roots and tubers; edible	15,213,653	8.90
Thailand	8	Fruit and nuts, edible; peel of citrus fruit or melons	953,667,213	25.61	8	Fruit and nuts, edible; peel of citrus fruit or melons	1,153,256,891	27.50
	3	Fish and crustaceans, molluscs and other aquatic invertebrates	909,114,509	24.41	7	Vegetables and certain roots and tubers; edible	1,142,203,293	27.23
	7	Vegetables and certain roots and tubers; edible	447,117,267	12.01	11	Products of the milling industry; malt, starches, inulin, wheat gluten	565,464,557	13.48

continued on next page

TABLE 2.15 — cont'd

			Largest Export Value from China to Each LMC			Largest Import Value from Each LMC to China		
	HS Code	Products	Export Value (US$)	Share in China's Total Exports to Each LMC (%)	HS Code	Products	Import Value (US$)	Share in China's Total Imports from Each LMC (%)
Thailand	52	Cotton	231,194,516	6.21	10	Cereals	462,226,059	11.02
	20	Preparations of vegetables, fruit, nuts or other parts of plants	227,048,424	6.10	3	Fish and crustaceans, molluscs and other aquatic invertebrates	162,544,054	3.88
Vietnam	52	Cotton	1,694,559,636	29.66	52	Cotton	1,717,074,910	38.11
	7	Vegetables and certain roots and tubers; edible	1,583,740,479	27.72	10	Cereals	733,934,948	16.29
	8	Fruit and nuts, edible; peel of citrus fruit or melons	879,846,443	15.40	8	Fruit and nuts, edible; peel of citrus fruit or melons	638,409,323	14.17
	23	Food industries, residues and wastes thereof; prepared animal fodder	273,469,077	4.79	9	Coffee, tea, mate and spices	347,346,003	7.71
	51	Wool, fine or coarse animal hair; horsehair yarn and woven fabric	200,745,565	3.51	21	Miscellaneous edible preparations	238,233,890	5.29

Source: UN Comtrade.

Administration of Customs 2019), China's licensed fresh fruit imports from Lancang-Mekong countries include twenty-two varieties from Thailand, eight from Vietnam, eight from Myanmar, one from Laos and one from Cambodia.

2.5.2.2 Agricultural Product Trade Disparity

Agricultural product trade disparity between China and Lancang-Mekong countries is mainly reflected in two points: national disparities, and primary product dominance. At present, among Lancang-Mekong countries, Thailand and Vietnam are China's largest trading partners in terms of trade volume. China's trade volumes with Cambodia, Laos and Myanmar are too low. It is a great challenge to support the agricultural production capacity of Cambodia, Laos and Myanmar, attach importance to the development of products with comparative advantages and enhance their trade volume through Lancang-Mekong cooperation. Again, agricultural product trade between China and Lancang-Mekong countries is dominated by low value-added primary products. How to embrace high value-added agricultural products and by-products is a problem to be addressed.

2.5.2.3 Shortcomings in Supply of Agricultural Products

Lancang-Mekong countries boast abundant agricultural resources, superior natural conditions, sufficient labour force, large market potential, and good agricultural economic benefits. However, there are shortcomings such as outdated infrastructure and technology, lack of funds and talent, and private ownership of land. These vulnerabilities constrain agricultural production capacity. If they were to be eliminated, agricultural production and agricultural products trade in the Lancang-Mekong region would be more dynamic.

2.5.3 Policy Recommendations

2.5.3.1 Enhance Cooperation to Reduce Non-tariff Barriers

China and Lancang-Mekong countries may consider special agreements to reduce non-tariff barriers. Specifically, China can take the initiative to increase agricultural product quotas and expand market access for Lancang-Mekong countries' exports to China. Both sides can strengthen cooperation in trade facilitation measures, technical barriers, and sanitary and phytosanitary measures. In terms of trade facilitation, both sides may speed up the implementation of the Trade Facilitation Agreement under the WTO framework. In the areas of customs clearance, technical barriers, and sanitary and phytosanitary measures, special funds can be allocated for organizing training for of Lancang-Mekong countries. And again, funds may be provided for equipment and facilities. Lancang-Mekong countries also should promote the signing and bringing into force of the Regional Comprehensive Economic Partnership as soon as possible. Bringing the pact into force will greatly reduce the number of non-tariff barriers.

China can choose specific areas and agricultural goods for cooperation with the other five Lancang-Mekong countries. China decided to set up free trade pilot zones in Guangxi and Yunnan in 2019. In the construction of these zones, one important focus should be agricultural trade between China and other Lancang-Mekong countries. In addition, given China's food security policies and strategies, China can choose to reduce non-tariff barriers on key agricultural products such as tropical fruits and vegetables, and then vigorously promote imports of those products.

2.5.3.2 Improve Agricultural Supply

In China's experience, mobilizing the enthusiasm of farmers is a prerequisite for agricultural development. Lancang-Mekong countries need to formulate policies to support and incentivize farmers' enthusiasm for agricultural production. In addition, government guidance based on market rules and other agricultural support measures should be provided for agricultural development. Lancang-Mekong country governments should also invest a certain amount of resources in building agricultural infrastructure and increasing agricultural production capacity. Based on China's experience, agricultural development will accelerate industrial development. The development of agriculture is only a phased goal of national development. The next stage is the development of industry. Only industrial development can enhance a country's economic performance. Agricultural development can be supported through industrial development. And again, surplus agricultural labour can flow to industry.

2.5.3.3 Give Full Play to the Lancang-Mekong Cooperation Mechanism and the Belt and Road Initiative

Lancang-Mekong cooperation can complement the Belt and Road Initiative. First, connectivity advocated by the Belt and Road Initiative can support cooperation among Lancang-Mekong countries, thereby reducing transport costs. Second, Lancang-Mekong countries can strengthen communication, which will help prevent a vicious cycle of competition for agricultural products and enhance complementarity, create entire agricultural value chains, and ensure multidimensional integration of agricultural and manufacturing value chains through coordination and balancing. Third, Lancang-Mekong cooperation may be equipped with special agricultural insurance to enhance the ability of Lancang-Mekong countries to strengthen the resilience of their agricultural sectors to risks. The development of agricultural product trade cooperation is vulnerable to natural and international factors, and international commodity price fluctuations often affect the export of agricultural products from various countries. It is necessary to lower production risks for agricultural producers in Lancang-Mekong countries by setting up insurance schemes. Finally, Lancang-Mekong countries could consider establishing a cross-border e-commerce platform for the sale of agricultural products. This would greatly promote agricultural product trade among them.

2.6 CONCLUSION

This chapter has examined the economic structural changes occurring in China and has analysed its implications for China's agricultural trade with other countries in the Lancang-Mekong region. We believe that the trend of China's structural change and corresponding policies means there will be a large gap between its demand and supply of agricultural products. Lancang-Mekong countries can promote agricultural trade with China by taking advantage of their relative abundance of resources and production factors, such as land and labour.

China's economic structural change and the complementarity of agricultural products between China and Lancang-Mekong countries offer Lancang-Mekong countries great agricultural export opportunities. However, there are also great challenges, such as non-tariff barriers, agricultural trade disparities between China and Lancang-Mekong countries, and shortcomings in Lancang-Mekong countries' agricultural supply chains. To make full use of opportunities and overcome challenges, it is necessary to step up cooperation and reduce non-tariff barriers between China and Lancang-Mekong countries and improve the agriculture sector in Lancang-Mekong countries through supply chains.

Notes

1. Engel's coefficient measures the proportion of income spent on food. According to Engel's law, the Engel's coefficient decreases with total income rises.
2. See http://fangtan.customs.gov.cn/tabid/556/InterviewID/126/Default.aspx

References

Balassa, Bela. 1965. "Trade Liberalisation and Revealed Comparative Advantage". *The Manchester School* 33, no. 2: 99–123.

General Administration of Customs of China. 2019. *Catalogue of Fresh Fruit Types and Export Countries/Regions*. www.cccfna. org.cn/article/%D5%FE%B2%D F%B5%BC%BA%BD/28864.html

International Monetary Fund. 2018. *World Economic Outlook: Challenges to Steady Growth*. Washington, DC: International Monetary Fund.

MOC (Ministry of Commerce of China). 2018. *Report on Development of China's Outward Investment*. http://images.mofcom.gov.cn/fec/201901/20190128155348158.pdf

NBS (National Bureau of Statistics of China). 2018. *China Statistical Yearbook* (in Chinese). Beijing: China Statistics Press.

State Council Information Office of the People's Republic of China. 2019. "Food Security in China". www.gov.cn/zhengce/2019-10/14/content_5439410.htm

State Council of the People's Republic of China. 2019. "Government Work Report". www.gov.cn/guowuyuan/2019zfgzbg.htm

World Trade Organization. 2018. "Trade Policy Review: China". www.wto.org/eng lish/tratop_e/tpr_e/s375_e.pdf

Xu Xiaohua, Zhu Zhen, and Su Weifeng. 2018. "The Trend Forecast and Management of the Chinese Agricultural Surplus Labor Transfer during 2014–2030". *Management Review* 30, no. 1: 221–29.

Zhang Wenli, Shen Guiyin, Cao Hui, Xu Xuegao, and Wang Huimin. 2016. "The Consumption Trend, Influence and Countermeasures of China's Important Agricultural Products during the 13th Five-Year Plan Period". *Journal of Agricultural Economy* 37, no. 3: 11–17, 110.

3

AGRICULTURAL EXPORTS FROM THAILAND TO CHINA
A Value Chain Analysis of Cassava and Durian

Punpreecha Bhuthong, Papatsara Rattanasimanon and Nuttaporn Udomkiattikul

3.1 INTRODUCTION

China's dramatic transformation on both domestic and international fronts is redirecting not only its own but also the world economy. China's push to position itself as a key global economic leader and to strengthen its influence in Asia is increasingly visible through various cooperation schemes such as the Greater Mekong Subregion Programme, the ASEAN-China Free Trade Area and the Regional Comprehensive Economic Partnership. China has become the primary export destination as well as the biggest source of imports for many countries in the region. Importantly, China's growing purchasing power and sustained rapid expansion present vast opportunities for Thailand to expand its trade with China.

Indeed, Thailand's trade with China has grown markedly in the past two decades. The value of Thailand's exports to China increased from around US$1.7 billion in 1998 to almost US$30 billion in 2017, about 20 per cent of which was accounted for by agricultural exports. Further, the share of agricultural exports in total exports to China is the highest among major markets such as ASEAN, the European Union and the United States. Thailand's agricultural exports to China are concentrated in only a few products, however. In particular, exports of cassava and durian to China have grown steadily over the past years, which is why they were selected for value chain analysis.

Despite the rise in agricultural exports to China, Thai exporters still face various non-tariff measures (NTMs) from China. Thai jasmine rice exporters, for example, face quota restrictions and other sanitary and phytosanitary (SPS) requirements (Phanishsarn 2018). Longan exporters must also comply with SPS measures, which require longan growers to have at least good agricultural practices certification (Hasachoo and Kalaya 2013). While many NTMs are in place to protect human and animal health, some are seen as discriminatory measures to restrict trade. Understanding the NTMs facing actors in agricultural value chains is important for boosting agricultural exports to China.

This chapter analyses durian and cassava value chains in Thailand and identifies challenges for stakeholders at different stages of the chains. The study also reviews NTMs imposed by both Thailand and China on durian and cassava exports. Various types of information were collected from desk research as well as focus group discussions and key informant interviews.

The rest of the report is organized as follows. Section 3.2 provides an overview of durian and cassava production and trade. Section 3.3 describes the conceptual framework and the methodology. Section 3.4 presents and discusses the findings of the value chain analyses. Section 3.5 concludes with policy recommendations to improve value chain performance.

3.2 BACKGROUND

Agriculture remains a crucial cog in the engine driving the country forward. Top agricultural exports include cassava, rice, rubber, canned tuna, sugar, pineapple, chicken meat, fresh vegetables, durian and maize. Table 3.1 shows the top five products by value exported to China as of 2017, with

TABLE 3.1
Top Five Agricultural Product Exports by Value to China (per cent), 2017

Product	Export Share (%)	RCA
Cassava, fresh, chilled or dried	28.7	330.8
Cassava starch	14.0	215.6
Semi-milled rice	11.1	13.6
Fresh durian	5.8	128.1
Coconut Milk	5.0	2.9

Source: Foreign Trade Statistics 1998–2018 (Ministry of Commerce 2018).

the top three accounting for more than half of the total; cassava roots (fresh, chilled, dried) and cassava starch contributed the largest shares followed by semi-milled white rice and fresh durian.

3.2.1 Overview of Thailand's Durian Production and Trade

Over the last two decades, Thailand's durian planted area and production followed a flat U-shaped pattern, partly reflecting the ups and downs of farm gate prices and later durian's growing popularity as a luxury product. The durian planted area shrank by almost 27 per cent in the first half of this period, from 873,643 *rai*[1] in 2004 to 637,882 *rai* in 2012, as farmers switched to growing rubber, oil palm and other tropical fruit due to lower returns on durian (Figure 3.1). Many orchardists reportedly converted their durian groves to grow rubber trees.[2] Durian production consequently decreased, dropping to 509,381 tonnes in 2011, the lowest ever. Then, following an upturn in the farm gate price in 2012–13 (Figure 3.2), the durian planted area began to expand and by the end of 2018 had been restored to where it was in 2004 at 864,842 *rai*. Production gradually recovered as durian prices rose. By 2018, annual production had returned to 752,760 tonnes with the highest recorded average yield in a decade, at 1.1 tonne/*rai*.

Although durian can be grown throughout Thailand, the main durian plantations are concentrated in the east and the south. In 2018, durian production in the eastern region contributed 53.81 per cent to total production and that in the southern region 40.42 per cent. Among the top ten durian-producing provinces, Chanthaburi, Rayong and Trat in eastern Thailand and Chumphon in southern Thailand have the highest durian yields per *rai*.

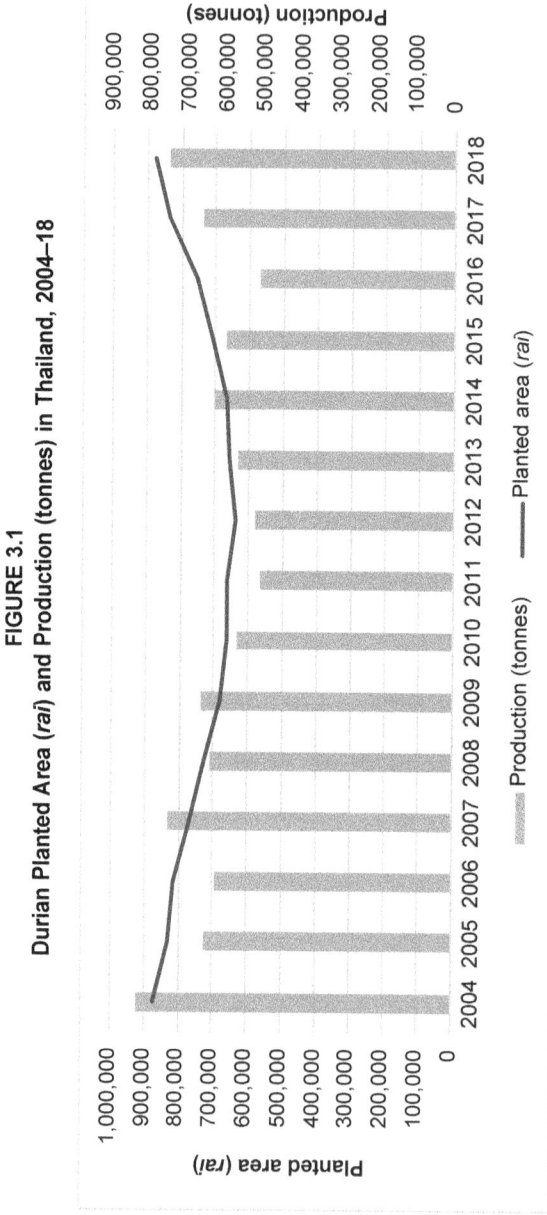

FIGURE 3.1
Durian Planted Area (*rai*) and Production (tonnes) in Thailand, 2004–18

Note: 1 *rai* = 1,600 m² or 0.16 ha.
Source: Agricultural Economic Information by Commodity (OAE 2019a).

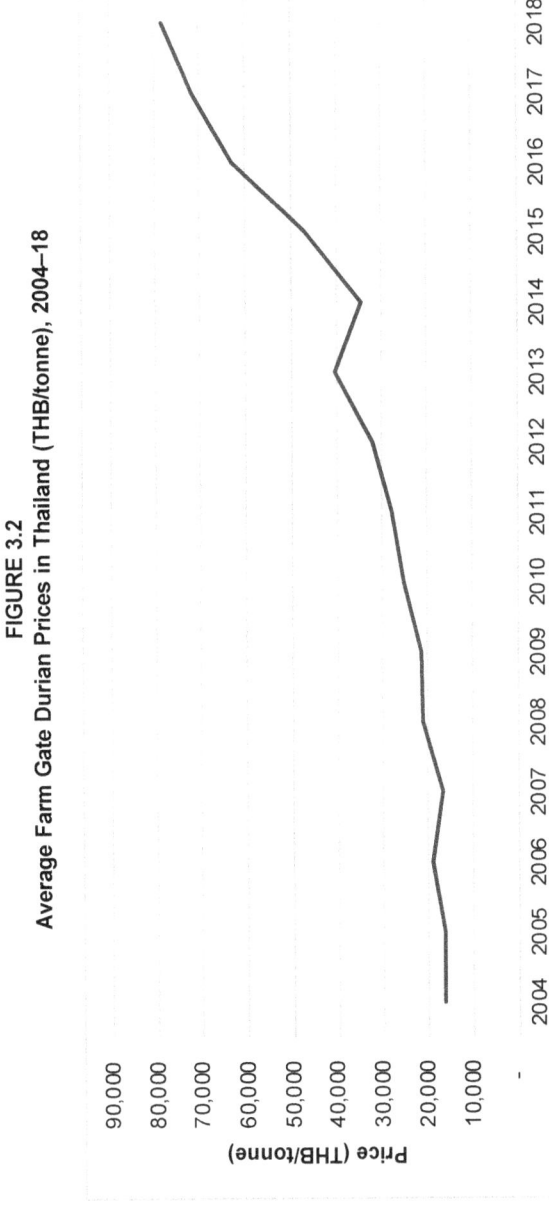

FIGURE 3.2
Average Farm Gate Durian Prices in Thailand (THB/tonne), 2004–18

Source: Agricultural Economic Information by Commodity (OAE 2019a).

Harvest seasons are completely different across regions. Generally, the durian harvest season lasts from March to June in the east, and from July to September in the south. Some farmers, however, have developed cultivation techniques for producing durian in the off-season. This means Thailand can supply durian to the market throughout the year.

As reported in interviews, more than 200 durian cultivars, whether native or hybrid, exist in Thailand. Yet only a few varieties are grown commercially, including Mon Thong, Chanee, Kradum, Kan Yao and Puang Manee. Mon Thong has come to dominate Thailand's durian production, accounting for 83.68 per cent of total production in 2018, as it has thick creamy flesh with smaller seeds and is less odorous than other varieties.

Durian can be processed in a variety of ways (e.g., frozen, freeze-dried and preserved). Moreover, it is increasingly being used as a key ingredient in food products such as ice cream, cake, milk tea and pizza, which have grown in popularity in East and Southeast Asia.

3.2.2 Overview of Thailand's Cassava Production and Trade

World production of cassava roots in 2017 stood at 291 million tonnes (FAO 2018). Nigeria is the world's largest producer of cassava, followed by the Congo, Thailand, Indonesia and Brazil. These five countries alone produce over half of the world's cassava. While it is the third-largest producer, Thailand is ranked as the world's largest cassava products exporter, contributing over 75 per cent of world cassava exports.

Cassava tolerates drought well and can grow in almost any kind of soil and almost anywhere. In Thailand, cassava production is concentrated in the northeastern region and the central region. The weather in southern Thailand is not suitable for cassava cultivation. Cassava is grown in fifty (out of seventy-seven) provinces, just seven of which accounted for over 50 per cent of total cassava production in 2018. Nakhon Ratchasima has the biggest cassava farming area and produces the most cassava tubers, accounting for 18.0 per cent of the total, followed by Kamphaeng Phet (7.9 per cent), Chaiyaphum (6.0 per cent), Ubon Ratchathani (5.2 per cent), Kanchanaburi (5.0 per cent), Sa Kaeo (4.0 per cent) and Nakhon Sawan (3.8 per cent).

Despite fluctuations, Thailand's cassava harvested area and production have increased over the past two decades. As Figure 3.3 shows, the estimated cassava area for 2018 was 8.3 million *rai* with an estimated production of

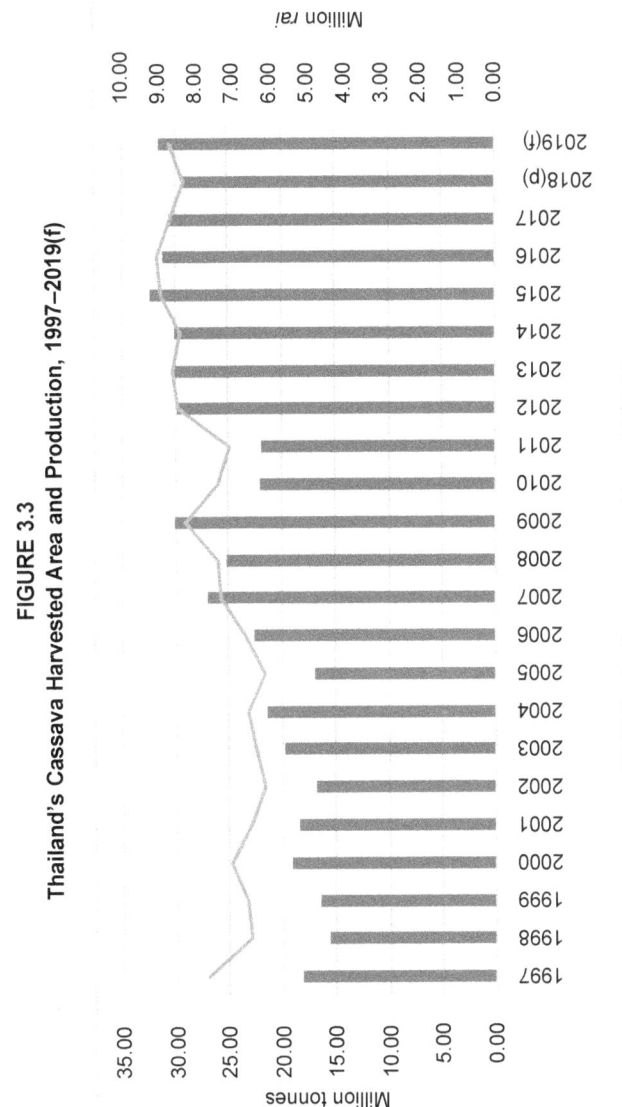

FIGURE 3.3
Thailand's Cassava Harvested Area and Production, 1997–2019(f)

Note: p – preliminary, f – forecast; 1 *rai* = 0.16 ha.
Source: Agricultural Statistics of Thailand (OAE 2019a).

29.37 million tonnes and, due to attractive prices, was expected to increase to 8.72 million *rai* in 2019 with an estimated production of 31.55 million tonnes (OAE 2019a).

The changes in Thailand's international trade in cassava can be seen clearly in Figure 3.4. For three decades Europe was the main destination for Thai cassava products, especially cassava pellets. But this started to change after a series of EU trade restrictions and policy reforms, particularly reforms of the Common Agricultural Policy. The consequent rapid decline in cassava exports to the EU from the mid-1990s almost caused the collapse of the Thai cassava pellet industry (Tijaja 2010) and forced Thailand to seek alternative markets. The cassava market quickly shifted to China, fuelled by increasing demand for cassava chips for use as animal feed and in ethanol production. China is now the world's largest importer of cassava and is the main destination of cassava products exported from Thailand.

In 2018, the value of cassava exports from Thailand amounted to US$3.1 billion. China accounted for 57.0 per cent of total cassava exports, followed by Japan (9.5 per cent), Indonesia (7.7 per cent) and Taiwan (4.6 per cent). The value of cassava exports to China increased gradually over the decade to 2008, rose quite steeply until 2014, fell abruptly in 2015 and then levelled out in 2016–18 (Figure 3.5). Behind the sudden slowdown in China's imports of cassava from Thailand (measured by value) is the lower price of corn, a result of China's policy to vastly reduce corn stocks across the country.

Looking at the composition of Thai cassava products exported to China (Figure 3.6), China's demand has been concentrated in cassava chips, a minimally processed product. However, in recent years, there has been a growing demand for native starch and modified starch, which are value-added products.

Despite the positive outlook for the Thai cassava industry, cassava farmers still face some risks which need to be addressed. These include low productivity due to poor farming practices, uncertain quality of raw materials whether produced domestically or imported from neighbouring countries, and high transport costs. Moreover, reliance on one major export destination exposes the entire Thai cassava value chain to uncertainties, while competitive pressure due to cassava industry development in neighbouring countries could depress cassava prices (Chuasuwan 2018).

Agricultural Exports from Thailand to China

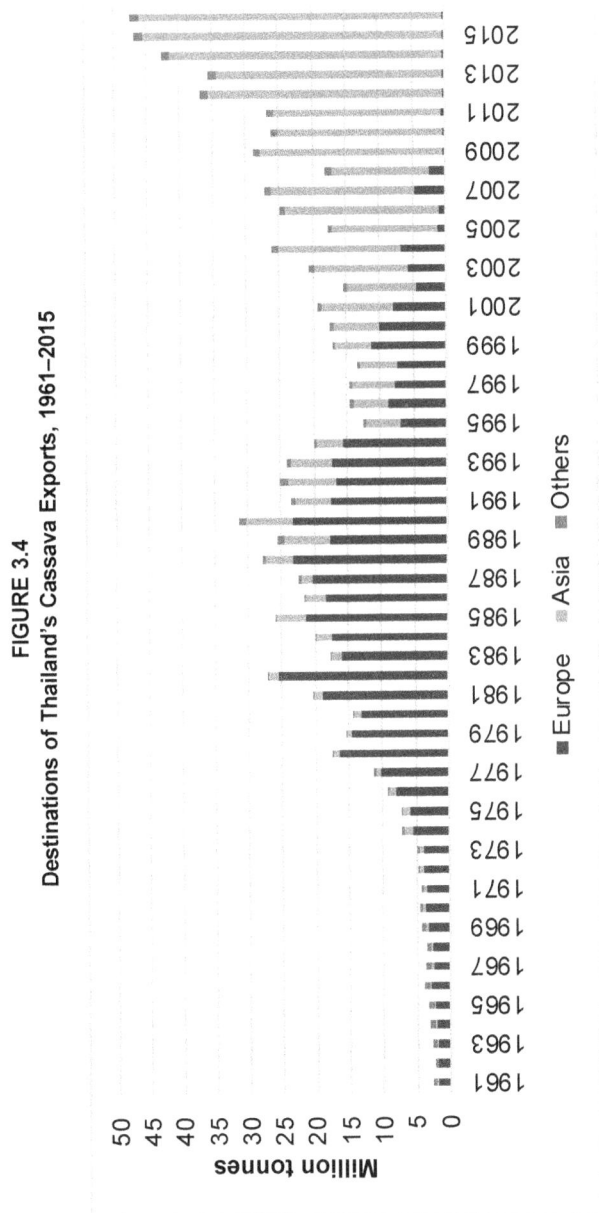

FIGURE 3.4
Destinations of Thailand's Cassava Exports, 1961–2015

Source: FAOSTAT Database (FAO 2018).

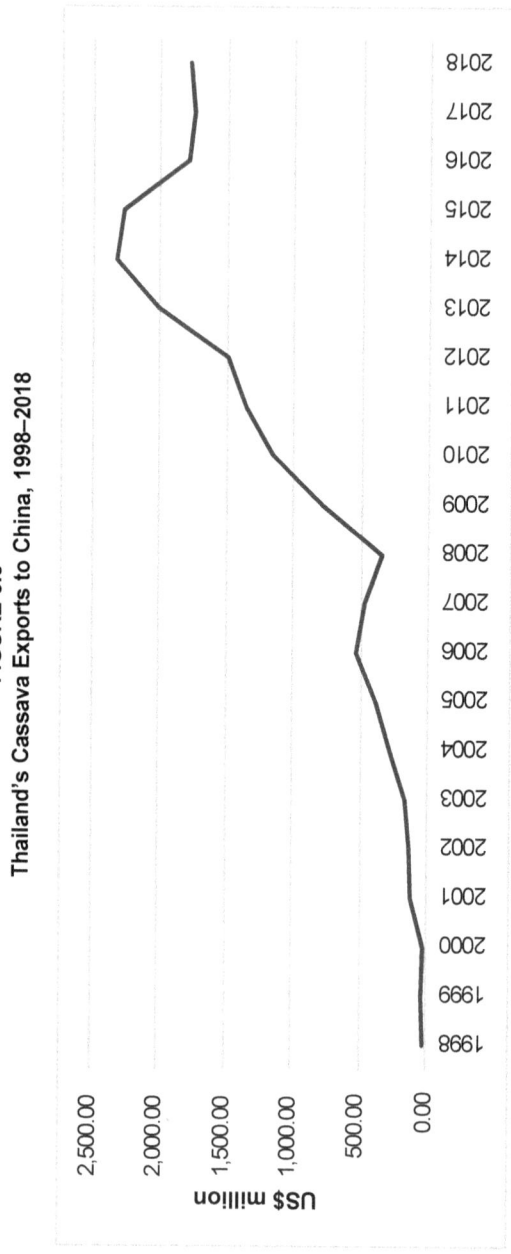

FIGURE 3.5
Thailand's Cassava Exports to China, 1998–2018

Source: Foreign Trade Statistics 1998–2018 (Ministry of Commerce 2018).

Agricultural Exports from Thailand to China

FIGURE 3.6
Composition of Thailand's Cassava Exports to China, 2000–18

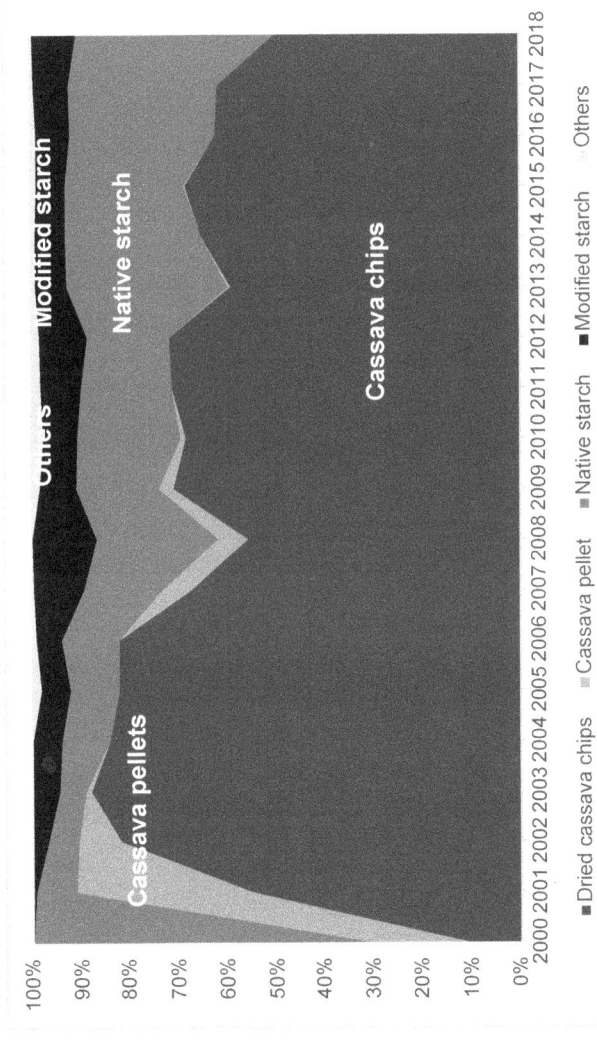

Source: Author's calculation using data from Foreign Trade Statistics 1998–2018 (Ministry of Commerce 2018).

Along with the rise in exports, the number of NTMs imposed by China increased during the period under investigation. SPS requirements are the most commonly used regulatory measure imposed on imports of Thai agricultural products, followed by technical barriers to trade (TBT) and quantity control. Specifically, in 2018, Thai agricultural exports to China were subject to seventy-six SPS, nineteen TBT and eleven quantity control measures (UNCTAD 2017).

NTMs aside, a review of the literature on agricultural exports to China identified a range of barriers affecting agricultural trade. Common issues include complicated import procedures and complex distribution channels (Taweesak 2014), to the extent that many Thai entrepreneurs have to rely on Chinese agents or distributors when selling products in China, which pushes up export costs. Another issue is the high rate of value-added tax charged on goods exported to China, ranging from 13 per cent to 17 per cent depending on the product. Now that China has emerged as a significant market for Thailand's agricultural exports, deepening understanding of the main barriers at all stages of the agricultural value chain is imperative to improving efficiency and boosting trade.

Several studies on the value chains of cassava and durian exist but few look at the overall aspects of value chains. Thitikan and Charoenchai (2007), for example, studied the logistics system for cassava products exported to China. They found that the export routes and modes of transport used vary depending on the nature of the product and customer needs (e.g., cassava chips transported in bulk due to lack of containers). The Thailand Development Research Institute (2009) compared the transport logistics (road vs rail) in Thailand for cassava and found that entrepreneurs prefer road haulage over rail freight because it is more flexible and because the railway infrastructure is in poor condition. Another study on logistics in fruit export value chains to China, using durian and mangosteen as case studies, found indirect constraints such as poor farming practices limiting crop productivity, uncertain product quality, poor inventory management, and logistics inefficiencies (OAE 2008). Overall, previous research often focused only on some aspects or on location-specific parts of value chains.

3.3 METHODOLOGY AND DATA

This section presents the conceptual framework, methodology and field survey data. This study follows the approach to value chain analysis adopted by the United Nations Industrial Development Organization (UNIDO 2009). In line with Porter's (1985) value chain model, UNIDO's approach gives precedence to the entire range of activities required to bring a product from the initial input-supply stage, through various stages of production, to its final market destination. However, the UNIDO approach puts more focus on value addition at each stage, therefore treating production as just one of several value-adding components of the chain. It also pays more attention to various auxiliary factors including enabling environment, coordinating institutions, and incentives. Key steps for the UNIDO approach are summarized below:

1. Mapping the value chain to understand the characteristics of the actors and their relationships;
2. Identifying the distribution of benefits among actors in the chain;
3. Defining upgrading needs within the chain by identifying constraints;
4. Emphasizing the role of governance.

Figure 3.7 depicts the conceptual framework for the study. The first step was to identify value chain actors and their relationships to map the structure of the value chains. The value chain environment was identified by looking at related institutions, regulations and support services along the value chains. Value chain analysis then identified key constraints and opportunities along the value chains.

The study uses a combination of descriptive statistics and qualitative methods to examine the selected value chains and the constraints behind the problems identified in the value chain analysis. Primary data was gathered from focus group discussions and in-depth interviews with various stakeholders along the value chains, including government officials, farmers, cooperatives, related associations and representatives from private firms. Secondary data was collected from a desk review of the literature and trade regulations obtained from government websites (e.g., National Bureau of Agricultural Commodity and Food Standards, and Office of Agricultural Economics) and non-government sources (e.g., Northeastern Tapioca Trade Association).

Secondary data is used for value chain mapping. Primary data collected from key informant interviews sheds light on the constraints and bottlenecks that affect overall value chain performance. The field survey was conducted mainly in March 2019 in Chanthaburi and Rayong

FIGURE 3.7
Conceptual Framework for Value Chain Analysis

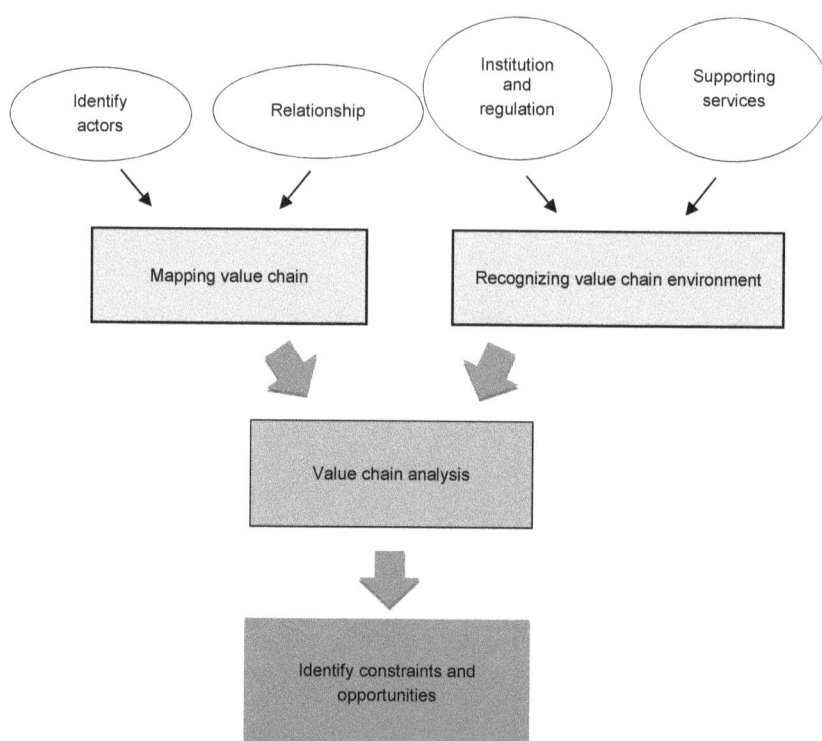

Source: Adapted from UNIDO (2009).

for the durian case study and in April 2019 in Nakhon Ratchasima for the cassava case study. These study sites were chosen because they constitute the largest production areas.

3.4 FINDINGS AND DISCUSSION

This section presents and discusses the key findings of our value chain analyses. It is divided into four main parts: (1) the structure of the durian and cassava value chains; (2) key value chain actors; (3) challenges faced by chain actors; and (4) non-tariff measures on exports to China.

3.4.1 The Structure of the Durian and Cassava Value Chains

First, we look at the evolution of the durian value chain in Thailand between 2006 and 2018. The structure of the fresh durian value chain has changed only slightly over time but the role of various stakeholders in the value chain has changed drastically (Figure 3.8). In 2006, domestic durian consumption predominated, and Thai intermediaries played a significant role in moving fresh durian through the value chain. Specifically, almost 85 per cent of orchard production went through intermediaries and much of the rest through packing houses (around 13 per cent), with processors and cooperatives buying negligible shares of total output. But the Thai market was not able to absorb all the durian produced, leading to excess supply and huge drops in durian prices.

The situation changed considerably when China began to increase its imports of fresh Thai durian. The roles of packing houses and intermediaries reversed. Packing houses became significant actors in the chain as a spate of Chinese entrepreneurs directly engaged in the Thai durian business. Eighty-five per cent of durian production now goes through packing houses, mostly as direct exports to China, and just over 3 per cent goes through intermediaries. Now that orchardists have more distribution channels, the role of intermediaries is much diminished, allowing orchardists greater bargaining power over prices. This is evident from the sharp rise in the price of durian from THB18.97 per kilogram (US$643.84 tonne) in 2006 to THB78.16 per kilogram (US$2,302.89 per tonne) in 2018.[3]

The shift towards production for export markets has changed domestic trading patterns. The ratio of domestic consumption to exports has also reversed, with export demand in 2018 amounting to around 72 per cent of total production from around 26 per cent in 2006. Some orchardists now sell durian directly to retailers, wholesalers and consumers, and some have embraced tourism by offering tours of their durian orchards. Durians are also properly graded, unlike before, to maintain high product quality and to ensure compliance with export regulations. Finally, e-commerce is now playing a big role in the durian distribution network.

The structure of the cassava value chain in Thailand, illustrated in Figure 3.9, has barely changed over the years. However, cassava value chain analysis can be very complicated given that cassava roots can be converted into numerous products—fresh food, processed roots, animal feed, starches for food and non-food industries, to name a few. For simplicity, this study

FIGURE 3.8
Change in the Structure of the Fresh Durian Value Chain between 2008 and 2016

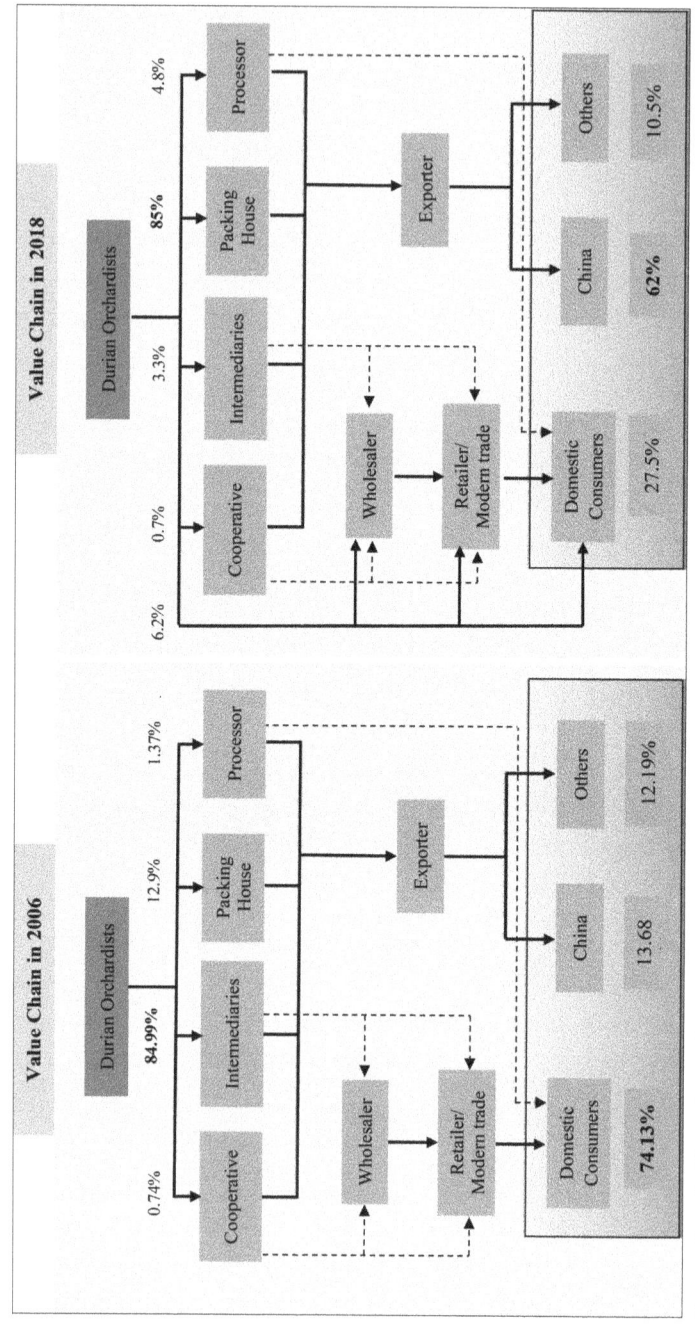

Source: Compiled by authors using data from Chanthaburi Provincial Agricultural Extension Office.

FIGURE 3.9
Thai Cassava Value Chain

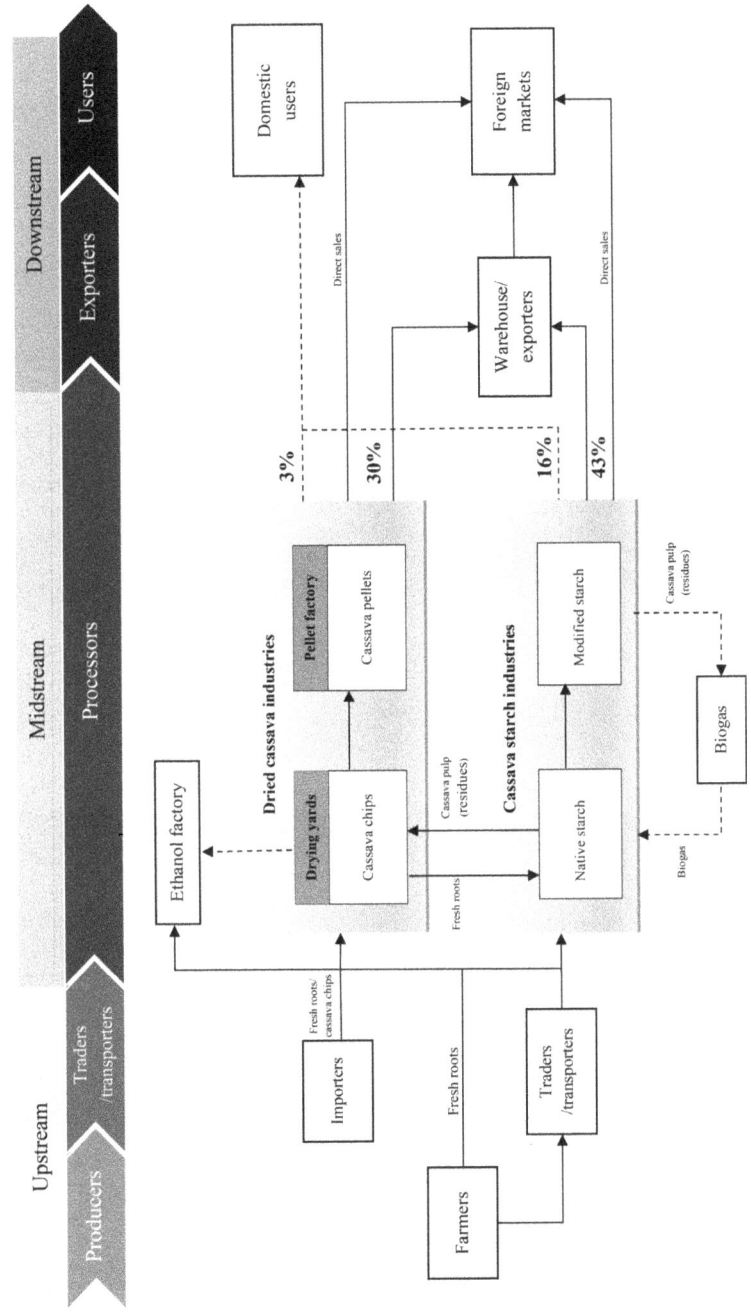

Source: Compiled by authors using data from Northeastern Tapioca Trade Association (2019), Chuasuwan (2018) and Piyachomkwan and Tanticharoen (2011).

focuses on the value chain of cassava products exported to China. In general, the cassava value chain in Thailand runs from cassava farmers, importers and traders in the upstream stage to cassava processors in the midstream stage and then to exporters and manufacturers in the downstream stage. In the midstream stage, cassava processing can be broadly categorized into two value chains: dried cassava and cassava starch.

3.4.2 Key Actors in the Durian and Cassava Value Chains

The main value chain actors can be generally categorized into three groups according to their position in the value chain. Agricultural value chains have three major stages: upstream, midstream and downstream. Table 3.2 summarizes the key actors involved in each stage of the value chains. The different activities of key actors at each stage reflect the different nature of the products (for more detail, see Bhuthong 2020). These activities are elaborated on in the following subsections.

TABLE 3.2
Key Actors in the Durian and Cassava Value Chains

Value Chain Stage	Durian Value Chain	Cassava Value Chain
Upstream	– Orchardists	– Farmers
		– Importers
Midstream	– Collectors	– Traders/transporters
	– Cooperatives	– Processors:
	– Intermediaries	– Drying yards
	– Packing houses	(cassava chip
	– Processors	makers)
		– Pellet factories
		– Starch factories
Downstream	– Exporters	– Exporters
	– Traders in domestic market	– Domestic users
	– Wholesalers	
	– Traditional retailers	
	– Modern traders	
	– Traders in the international Market	
	– Chinese importers	
	– Chinese distributors	

Source: Authors' preparation.

3.4.2.1 Upstream Activity

The upstream part of the value chain includes mostly farmers, or orchardists in the case of durian. Durian orchardists have several sales channels so they can choose the trading partners that offer the best price deal. The deal involves the usual commercial considerations such as the price, quantity and quality but also includes harvest and postharvest handling and operations. For example, orchardists may sell the entire crop for a lump sum and buyers must hire their own workers to carry out harvest and postharvest activities (i.e., grading, loading). The packing house is the main sales channel for orchardists, buying 85 per cent of total production. Some local orchardists join local cooperatives for collaborative farming. Small-scale and home orchardists mostly sell fresh durian directly to local collectors. Collectors deal with medium and large orchardists directly, either with a coemption, buying up the entire output of a durian orchard, or through forward contracting.

In the cassava value chain, the majority of farmers are small scale, with 494,618 households engaged in cassava farming in 2018 (OAE 2019a). About half of cassava farmers own land, 16 *rai* (25.6 hectares) on average, while the rest rent land. Because of their short shelf life, cassava roots should ideally be transported to cassava chip/pellet factories or starch factories on the day of harvest. Large-scale farmers, who have their own trucks, sell fresh roots directly to processors, either nearby drying yards, pellet factories or starch factories, whichever offers the better price. Small-scale farmers hire local transporters to deliver their produce to processors. The farmer pays for the transport costs to the processor, as agreed on beforehand. Starch factories tend to pay higher prices for cassava roots than drying yards because of the increasing demand for starch and strong competition among starch factories. In addition, starch factories measure the starch content in fresh roots on purchase, whereas drying yards usually pay suppliers a lump sum by weight.

Although Thailand is the world's third-largest cassava producer and cassava production in Thailand is rising consistently, demand for Thai cassava products is outstripping supply. This has put pressure on the domestic market, creating intense competition. In the past, Thailand imported only small amounts of cassava from neighbouring countries (Laos and Cambodia), mostly in the form of fresh roots and chips. But recently, cassava imports have increased rapidly to meet the ever-increasing demand.

In 2016, Thailand imported around 6 million tonnes of raw cassava and cassava products. Importers, which must be registered with the Ministry of Commerce, import cassava roots and cassava chips from neighbouring countries and sell them to processors and exporters of cassava chips.

3.4.2.2 Midstream Activity

The midstream portion of the value chain generally includes transporters, collectors and processors. In the durian value chain, packing houses are a key player as they collect and prepare durian for sale in the main market. At the packing house, durians are graded according to size and condition. Most fresh durians classed as grade A or B go to exporters (66 per cent), while lower grade durians either go to the domestic market (grade C) or processors (off-spec). About 27.5 per cent of all durian products, whether fresh or processed, go to domestic consumers, and the rest (72.5 per cent) are exported. China is the main export destination where most of the fruit is distributed through offline (brick-and-mortar) stores.

About 85 per cent of total durian production goes through packing houses. Interviews revealed that the number of packing houses in the major durian producing provinces has increased substantially and most of them belong to Chinese businesspeople. The packing houses are divided into three types according to exporting processes and ownership (Figure 3.10), as follows:

1. Thai packing houses that contract Chinese importers, hire freight forwarders and export durian products under their own brand (i.e., they are ODM [original design manufacturer] companies), and importers distribute the products in China. However, the packing houses must sell the products on consignment at a charge of 2 yuan/kg (THB9.78/kg).
2. Thai packing houses that fulfil Chinese orders and export durian products under importer brands (i.e., they are OEM [original equipment manufacturer] companies). Chinese entrepreneurs determine the quality, packaging and transport needs and the packing house receives a packing fee of THB5/kg. From our interviews, this type is the most popular because the packing house does not bear the risk and does not have to deal with any difficulties exporting agricultural products to China.

Agricultural Exports from Thailand to China

FIGURE 3.10
The Role of the Packing House and the Relationships with Packing House Partners

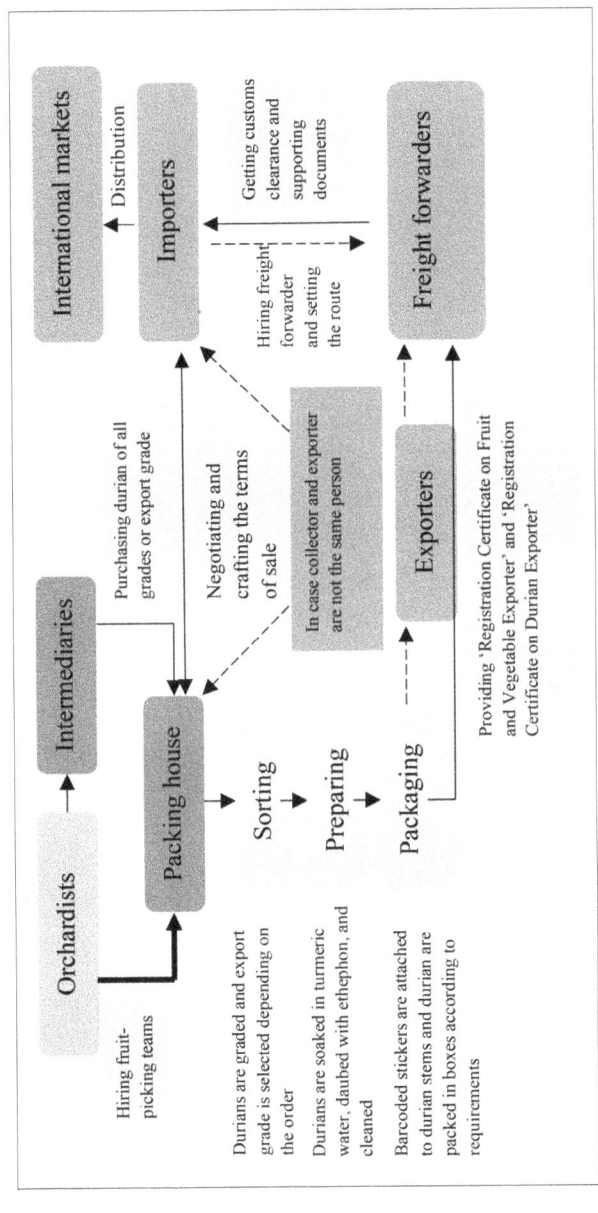

Source: Authors' compilation from interviews.

3. Chinese firms specialized in the trade of fruit that have expanded their business to Thailand to lower costs; they operate as collector, exporter and importer.

Traders/transporters in the cassava value chain are small to medium-sized businesses and usually run by farmers who own and use small trucks to earn additional income. Traders buy, collect, transport and sell products to processors, whereas transporters only provide transport services. Traders/transporters employ a small number of workers on a permanent basis as loaders and drivers. They play a vital role in areas with only a few processors as cassava roots must be transported long distances. They are also particularly important to processors when the supply of locally produced cassava is running low; processors rely on traders to acquire and supply them with cassava roots from distant areas (Arthey, Srisompun and Zimmer 2018).

Processors are key actors in the midstream part of the cassava value chain; they can be divided into two main industries: cassava drying and cassava starch manufacturing. All fresh roots are processed into either dried chips or starch to supply downstream industries. After harvesting, cassava roots are usually transported to processors within a day as fresh roots must be processed right away or no later than four days after harvest. The timing depends on the quantity of fresh roots received and production capacity, which is managed by processors.

Drying yards are usually small-scale businesses, often owned by farmers, and usually located near cassava growing areas. They basically consist of a cement yard, a simple chopping machine and a loader. Sometimes drying yards also act as traders, making a little profit by collecting roots and selling them to starch factories. Currently, about 2,753 drying yards are operating in Thailand. They typically hire workers on a permanent basis.

From the drying yard, cassava chips are transported in bulk to traders/exporters' warehouses for export, pellet factories and ethanol factories. The modes of transport are land and river. Cassava chips are mostly transported by truck to warehouses located near river ports on the Chao Praya (in Ayudhaya) and Bangprakong rivers. Cassava chips are then loaded in bulk onto pontoon boats and delivered to the marine port at Koh Si Chang Island, from where they are shipped to international markets via sea freight.

Given the competitiveness of fresh cassava root trade in Nakhon Ratchasima, most fresh roots go to starch factories where they fetch a better price. Drying yards in Nakhon Ratchasima have adapted by buying cassava residues from starch factories and sun-drying and then selling them to pellet factories.

Pellet factories have dwindled in number. There used to be over 200 such factories in Thailand. After the EU's agricultural policy reform, pellet production dropped significantly; now only fifty-one pellet factories are left, producing pellets for both export and domestic markets. Pellet factories usually purchase chips from drying yards. Due to fierce competition for fresh cassava roots with starch factories, some also purchase cassava leftover from drying yards.

Starch factories are usually medium- or large-scale enterprises. Like drying yards, they are usually located near cassava growing areas. With the increasing demand for starch, the number of factories has increased to almost 100. Most factories have a production capacity of 400–800 tonnes/day. The production of 1 kilogram of starch requires 4–5 tonnes of fresh roots. Large-scale starch factories are mostly located in the northeast and eastern regions.

Starch factories buy fresh roots from farmers and traders and usually set up a buying station in front of the factory. The purchase prices are announced and posted in front of the factory so that farmers and traders are informed and can compare prices. The announced price is usually set as the standard price for fresh roots with 25 per cent starch content. The fully loaded truck is weighed, unloaded and weighed empty to calculate the actual weight of the fresh roots, which are then measured for starch content. If the starch content is greater than 25 per cent, the factory will pay a higher price and vice versa. Cassava starch is transported by truck to downstream industries and exporters.

3.4.2.3 Downstream Activity

In the case of durian, an *exporter* refers to a person or a juristic person registered as a durian exporter with the Department of Agriculture (DOA). Most fresh durians are sold through this channel, accounting for 66 per cent of all production. Some exporters also own packing houses and others act as intermediaries between Thai packing houses and foreign importers.

Traders in the domestic market are the people who buy durian in the upstream or midstream stages of the value chain and sell to consumers, wholesalers, traditional retailers, modern traders and other stores in the downstream stage. However, it is rare to find this group operating in the off-season because almost all durians are exported to international markets.

Wholesalers mostly operate in fruit wholesale markets in the main durian-producing provinces or in Bangkok, for example, Thai Market and Four Corners Market. Those involved in the upstream or midstream stages sell discarded durians and some quality durians to wholesalers and sell other grades at the central fruit wholesale market for distribution to other provinces.

Traditional retailers include merchants in the wet market and street hawkers. Merchants usually buy durian from wholesalers. There are two types of street hawkers: orchardists and street vendors. The latter buy fruit from wholesalers. Some retailers also sell basic processed durian products such as durian chips, durian paste and durian-based snacks.

Modern traders include supermarkets (e.g., Tops, The Mall), hypermarkets (e.g., Big C, Tesco Lotus, Makro) and specialty stores. Most of them can sell high-quality durians throughout the year but set a higher price. However, an interviewee mentioned that modern traders have begun to expand their orders by adding medium-grade durians.

Other stores consist of restaurants and online stores. Restaurants usually order frozen durian pulp and durian paste for processing into various food products. Online traders are the orchardists and retailers who sell high-quality and premium durians through online platforms.

Traders in the international market are local intermediaries or China representative offices. These can be divided into importers, brick-and-mortar (offline) stores and online platforms. Most consumers buy durians from brick-and-mortar stores, but the share of online sales continues to grow.

Importers contract durian exporters and freight forwarders to prepare documents for customs clearance and to organize transport to Chinese markets. The transport route they choose depends on the product and destination market (Figure 3.11).

The best destination for fresh durian is the Jiang Nan Fresh Fruit and Vegetable Wholesale Market, the largest of its kind in China. Thai durians are therefore usually shipped via sea freight to Shenzhen and land freight to Nanning in southern China. Premium durians are usually

FIGURE 3.11
The Route of Durian Products from Thailand to China

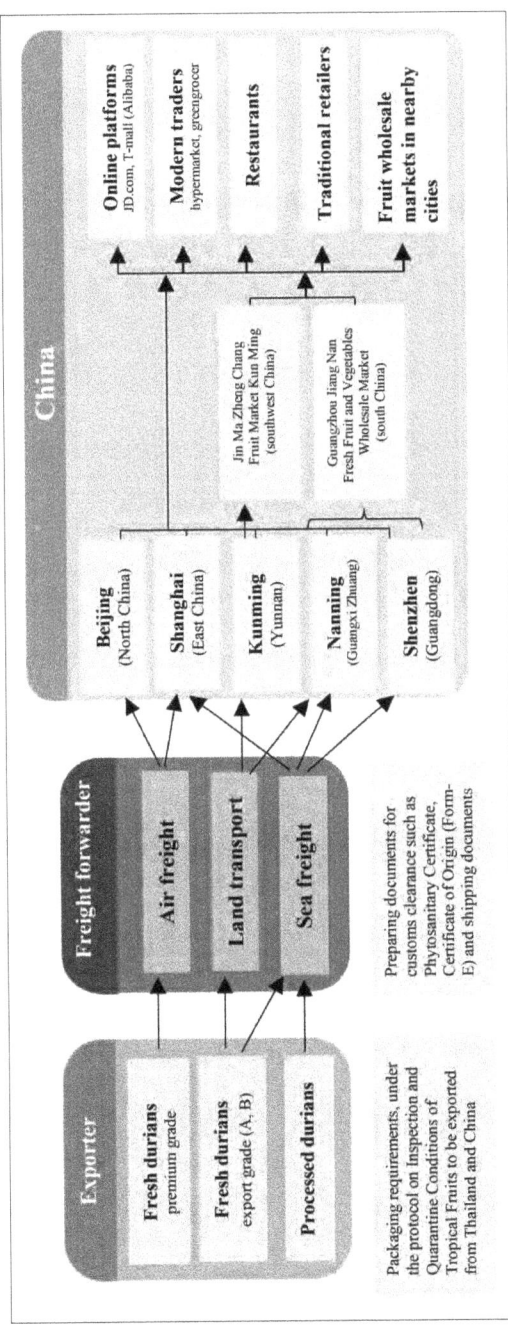

Source: Authors' preparation.

exported by air freight to reach consumers as soon as possible. Processed durian products are transported by sea freight due to low shipping costs and long product life.

Offline distribution channels include fruit wholesale markets, modern traders and restaurants. Central wholesale markets are the most important as wholesalers from other provinces travel to such markets to buy durians, which they then distribute to other traders such as traditional retailers and restaurants.

Modern traders sell fresh and processed durian. They buy fresh durians from wholesale markets and packing houses in Thailand. However, unlike in Thailand, specialty stores in China such as Pagoda, which is China's major greengrocer chain, have many branches across the country and play an important role. Moreover, foods that feature durian as a component such as durian pizza and durian ice cream are becoming increasingly popular in China.

Online platforms such as JD.com and T-mall have signed a memorandum of understanding (MOU) with packing houses and processors in Thailand to supply durian products. T-mall, for instance, signed an MOU with a Thai cooperative in 2018, though the agreement does not specify any practical terms.

In the case of cassava, *exporters* must be registered with the Department of Foreign Trade, Ministry of Commerce. Most processors are also exporters and export directly to end-users. Some processors use their own transport services to transport cassava products from the factory to the port of export but will outsource transport services during peak times.

Most cassava products are exported by sea. Processors/exporters hire shipping companies to undertake the export process including customs procedures. Sales contracts are mostly based on FOB terms, where exporters are responsible for transporting cassava products to the port of export and Chinese buyers are responsible for the transit operations from that point to destination.

Of the three modes of transport for cassava exports, two are multi-modal—road-water and road-rail. Road-water transport is mostly used for transporting cassava chips in bulk. Exporters usually have silos near Chao Praya River and deliver the goods by pontoon boat to Koh Si Chang where the goods are loaded onto a ship. Road-rail transport is rare. The third is transport by truck directly from factory to port. Cassava starch exporters are likely to use the first two modes of transport.

Domestic users in downstream industries can be broadly categorized into feed, food and non-food industries. Cassava chips go to animal feed factories, ethanol factories and citric acid factories. Pellets are used as animal feed. Native starch is used as raw material in food and non-food industries. Food industries include noodle, sago, bakery products and monosodium glutamate (seasoning powder) manufacturers. Non-food industries include paper mills and glue manufacturers. Modified starch is used as an additive in food and non-food industries. Food products include lysine (for animal feed) and sweeteners. Non-food products include fabrics and biodegradable plastics.

3.4.3 Challenges in the Durian and Cassava Value Chains

Challenges in the durian and cassava value chains are summarized in Table 3.3 and then elaborated on in the following sections.

3.4.3.1 Challenges in the Durian Value Chain

China's increasing demand for Thai durian coincided with its domination of Thailand's durian exports. This means that any problems or shocks

TABLE 3.3
Summary of Challenges in the Durian and Cassava Value Chains

	Durian Value Chain	Cassava Value Chain
Upstream	– Lack of strong association – Climate change adaptation – Inadequate financial management skills	– Lack of strong association – Low productivity farming – Lack of efficient mechanism to prevent disease epidemic – Persistent farm debt
Midstream	– Labour shortage – High cost of migrant workers – Low competitiveness of Thai entrepreneurs	– Insufficient supply to meet demand – Limited working capital – Logistics issues
Downstream	– Limited market access – High competition – Losses in transit	– Risk of single market dependence – Environmental impacts of transport

Source: Authors' preparation.

affecting trade between Thailand and China will reverberate along the entire Thai durian value chain. The bottlenecks and challenges facing the Thai durian industry at different stages of the value chain are outlined below.

3.4.3.1.1 Upstream Challenges
Inadequate financial management skills. Now that durian is a high-value agricultural product, finance is not a concern for most durian growers. That said, some small to medium-sized orchardists still need to take out loans to use as working capital every year at the beginning of the planting season. They receive sales income just once a year which, due to lack of financial management skills, can be a liability. Some orchardists often fail to allocate expenditure properly to repay loans, purchase new inputs and cover living expenses.

Adaptation and vulnerability to climate change. Durian is grown in the tropical climate of the highlands where rainfall is abundant and temperatures high. The trees bloom in the rainy season and bear fruit in the dry season, so durian in the eastern area is harvested from March to June and in the southern areas from July to September. However, in recent years, drought and heavy rains attributed to climate change have adversely affected durian production. Prolonged drought kills durian trees, reducing overall durian production. Heavy rain, especially during the flowering season, can have a negative impact on production, delay harvesting and cause insect and disease damage.

Lack of strong association. In the upstream part of the value chain is the Thai Durian Institute, which consists of a group of durian orchardists, but they do not have the power to negotiate with government agencies.

In particular, small-sized orchardists often have weak bargaining power, so they cannot profit from the highest prices during peak season. On the other hand, the Department of Agricultural Extension (DOAE) has launched a collaborative farming programme to group orchardists for product standardization, aiming to reduce their production costs and increase their bargaining power. However, this programme covers only 15 per cent of durian orchardists and most members of the group have been unsuccessful due to lack of cooperation. So, in 2019, representatives of the collaborative farming programme established a new group called the Confederation of Thai Durian Orchardists, which cooperates with the DOAE and the Office of the Prime Minister.

3.4.3.1.2 Midstream Challenges
Labour shortage. The workforce in this industry is inadequate as durian-related businesses are continuously growing and most activities require skilled labour. As a result, many workers have organized themselves into groups and offer subcontracting teams for specific activities and charge high rates for their services. Although most of them lack skills and experience, the stakeholders who face skilled labour shortages during the peak season, especially durian pickers, have little choice but to hire them.

High costs of hiring migrant workers. Hiring migrant workers is the best way to resolve the shortage of labour but compliance with labour law and regulatory requirements incurs high costs. Migrant workers can be divided into two categories: those with a passport and those with a border pass. Most stakeholders prefer to hire migrant workers with a border pass because they are in plentiful supply and hiring costs are lower, but they are restricted to seasonal work and cannot leave the border area. These workers, therefore, tend to be employed in packing houses and processing plants in the eastern region. Other stakeholders hire migrant workers with a passport; however, registering these migrant workers as legal workers costs THB20,000–25,000 per worker (US$640–800) and changing or adding a work location incurs extra cost.

Low competitiveness of Thai entrepreneurs. Chinese entrepreneurs have more influence than their Thai counterparts in the durian market. Chinese firms have gradually consolidated control over most of the packing house operations. They have rented empty packing houses and found nominees and OEMs through joint ventures, as foreign entrepreneurs are prohibited by law from operating agricultural businesses. When Chinese entrepreneurs with access to distribution channels and huge capital were able to deal with orchardists directly, Thai entrepreneurs could not compete and repositioned their companies to serve Chinese firms. A serious concern in the long run is that Chinese entrepreneurs could manipulate durian prices.

3.4.3.1.3 Downstream Challenges
Limited market access. The Chinese government requires an import licence and quarantine import permit for each type of fruit imported into China, and persons requesting such certification must register as a legal entity in China. Moreover, because Thai entrepreneurs cannot access the sales channels and credit system, which is the main form of payment in China,

they stand little chance of exporting durian products directly to the Chinese market. Instead, they have to sell goods on consignment through Chinese importers and pay commission. But doing so carries a high risk because they are unable to set the price and do not receive any payment until the transaction is complete. So, they supply Chinese importers instead.

Market competition is increasing. In the past, Thailand did not have any competitors because it was the only country allowed to export fresh durian to China. But now Malaysia can export frozen durian pulp and whole frozen durian to China, and the Malaysian government is in negotiations with the Chinese government to secure a deal to export fresh durians to China.

Transport logistics and losses. Spoilage during transit is a major concern. There are three main types of freight: land, sea and air. Air freight is the fastest but incurs the highest cost. Firms therefore usually use land or sea freight depending on the destination (Figure 3.12).

Sea freight. Durians are mostly shipped to China via sea freight, but the volume has decreased continuously. According to official records, the volume of durians shipped via Hong Kong decreased from 275,729 tonnes in 2016 to 180,874 tonnes in 2017. However, the volume of durian transported via sea is still higher than for road and air freight. Sea freight to China via Hong Kong poses two challenges: high transport costs and import/export regulations in Hong Kong. On the first point, durian shipments must be inspected by China Inspection Co., Ltd in Hong Kong before continuing to China by land transport or small boat. This incurs higher costs and takes longer than exporting to China directly. Regarding the second point, Chinese importers prefer durians that have been soaked in turmeric water. This process is done at the packing house to help preserve the durian shell and make it more appealing. Hong Kong import regulations, however, prohibit durians that have been soaked in turmeric water. Thai officials are now aware of the situation and urge durian exporters through this channel to follow the regulations.

Land transport. This is the most popular mode of transport because it is relatively cost- and time-efficient. There are three main overland routes for transporting goods to China: R3A, R9 and R12 (Figure 3.13). The protocol on inspection and quarantine between Thailand and China via

FIGURE 3.12
Transport Routes for Exporting Durian from Thailand to China

Channel	Thai customs	Third country	Destination	Delivery time (hour) and distance (km)	Cost (USD/freight)
R3A	Chiang Khong (Chiang Rai)	Laos	Mohan (Yunnan)	50 hours / 1,863 km	8,085
R9	Mukdahan	Laos and Vietnam	Youyi Guan (Guangxi Zhuang)	35 hours / 1,959 km	6,246
R12	Nakhon Phanom	Laos and Vietnam	Youyi Guan (Guangxi Zhuang)	30 hours / 1,694 km	5,716
Sea Freight	Laemchabang Port		Guangzhou (Guangdong)	220 hours / 1,863 km	2,652
Sea Freight	Laemchabang Port	Hong Kong	Shenzhen (Guangdong)	220 hours / 3,161 km	2,765
Sea Freight	Laemchabang Port		Nanning (Guangxi Zhuang)	190 hours / 1,694 km	2,166
Air Freight	Suvarnabhumi Airport		Guangzhou/ Shanghai/Beijing	4-6 hours (Transportation time)	39,150

Note: Delivery time and distance start in Bangkok and costs are per 40-foot container.
Source: Compiled by authors based on Thailand Institute of Scientific and Technological Research (2008), Centre for Applied Economics Research (2012), and Panichayakarn, Soratana, and Longsa (2017).

FIGURE 3.13
Map Showing Land Transport Routes for Exporting Durian from Thailand to China

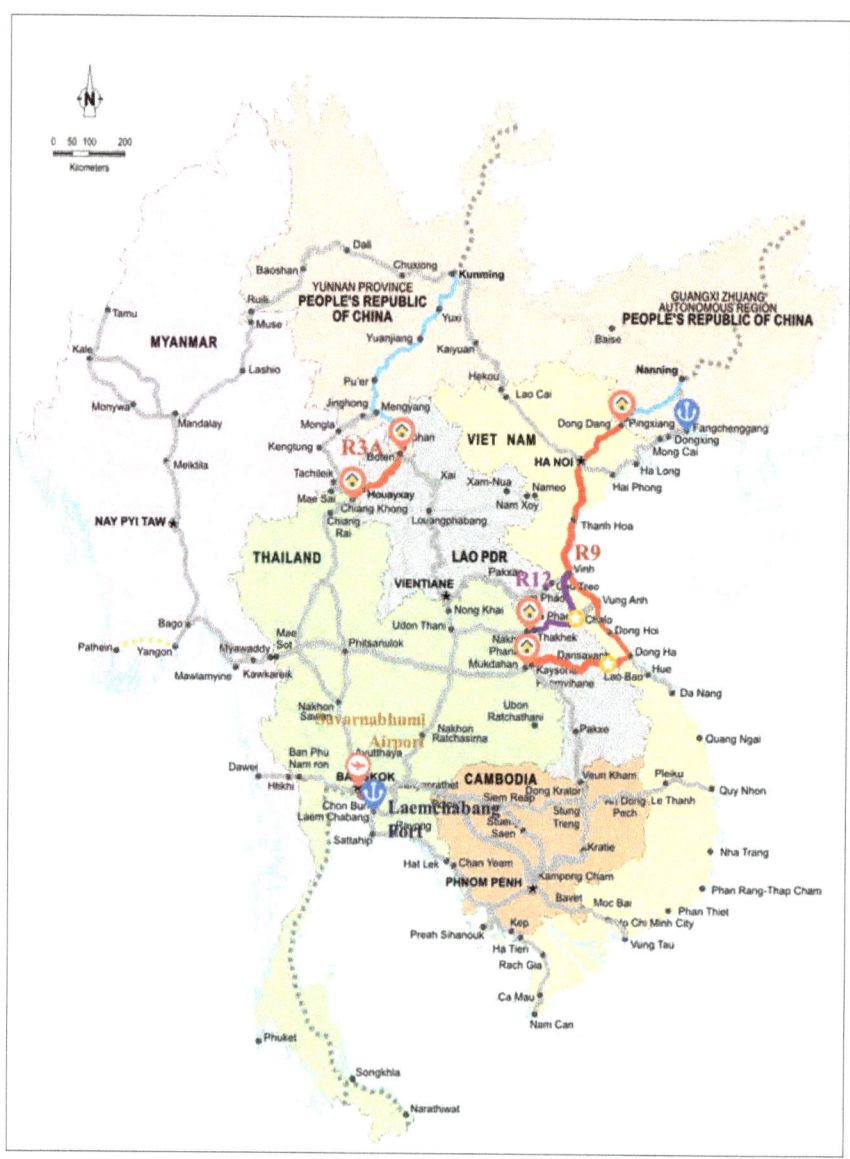

Source: Adapted from Asian Development Bank (2016).

a third country, and road infrastructure improvements under the GMS Cross-Border Transport Agreement (CBTA), are the key factors affecting the volume of durian exported by road. However, land transport faces three challenges:

- *Poor road conditions.* Even though many roads have been improved under the CBTA, road freight is still hindered by poor land transport infrastructure in Laos. Most Lao roads are narrow, uphill and unpaved, leading to slow-moving and delayed traffic in some areas, especially in the rainy season.
- *Thai trucks cannot enter all third countries.* Thai freight forwarders cannot transport durian to China directly because Thailand does not have a road transport agreement with Vietnam. Durian shipments must therefore be unloaded and reloaded onto Vietnamese trucks at the Laos-Vietnam border for transport to China. This incurs higher costs and takes time, especially if trucks have already been delayed by poor road conditions in Laos.
- *No protocol for using Route 12 in Laos.* This is the best route because it is the shortest and lowest cost, but there is no transport protocol for this route. Exporters therefore cannot export products via R12 to China, though some freight carriers use R12 for exporting goods to China via the grey channel.

Inefficient and insufficient customs administration. Durian exports must pass through two or three customs checks on the way to China. Interviews with freight forwarders highlighted problems at three border gates:

- *Laobao border gate.* Checking documents and containers takes a long time. Further, some officials at the border gate open containers which goes against protocol.[4]
- *Mohan border gate.* Facilities for changing containers are poor.
- *Youyiguan border gate.* Thai exporters are restricted by protocol to exporting durian through this gate when transporting products to South China via road. Logjams of container trucks are a common occurrence but were worse than usual at the time of study because of the increased strictness of inspections, unstable transborder transport system due to the switch from a manual to an automated freight system, and tightened control by the Vietnamese government. Logjams at the

border have several consequences: they can inflict damage and financial loss because the fruit ripens quickly and spoils easily, lowering the price; containers can be in short supply because trucks have been held up; and they can affect packing houses' purchase decisions.

3.4.3.2 Challenges in the Cassava Value Chain

3.4.3.2.1 Upstream Challenges

Low farm productivity. Cassava farm productivity in Thailand, despite some improvement since the development of new cultivars and adoption of better farming practices, is still low compared to other countries in the region. In 2017, Thailand's cassava productivity was around 20 tonnes/hectare, compared to Laos' at 32 tonnes/hectare and Cambodia's at almost 27 tonnes/hectare (FAO 2019).

The reason for the low average yield is that most farmers cultivate by experience and usually consult farm neighbours rather than experts or officials when a problem occurs. Many cassava farmers also lack a systematic cultivation plan. There is no data recording to improve farming efficiency. By nature, cassava is a drought-resistant crop that needs minimal care. Thus, farmers tend to pay scant attention to their plants, which can affect the quality of the roots. Most cassava planting areas have no irrigation system. As a result, most cultivation is rainfed. Although some farmers have started to use drip irrigation, they are still a minority. Climate change may affect future production if no action is taken. Energy-saving machines for harvesting are barely used. Although high-tech machines are available, most farmers do not invest in them. According to comments from stakeholders, farmers have always shouldered the highest risk compared to other stakeholders in the value chain. Adopting and investing in new technology means more risk for farmers, such as long-term debt; most farmers therefore stick with their usual practice to avoid those risks.

Lack of a well-managed farmers association. Unlike processors, farmers do not have a well-established association, hence their weak bargaining power. The government recently launched a programme called "Collaborative Farming" aiming to improve production efficiency and competitiveness by reducing production costs, increasing yields and aligning production with market demand. So far, only a few groups of cassava farmers have been successful.

Lack of an efficient mechanism to prevent disease epidemics. Disease epidemics can cause huge yield losses. Because there is no systematic mechanism to prevent such a catastrophe from happening, the government can only deal with disease outbreaks on a case-by-case basis. Crop breeders have so far been unable to develop new cultivars that are both highly productive and resilient to disease epidemics.

Financial issues for farmers. Farm debt is still a major bottleneck for farmers. Most farmers are caught up in a cycle of debt. They often take out state-funded loans from the Bank for Agriculture and Agricultural Cooperatives which they use to start their farms and pay for inputs. After selling their crop, farmers repay the loan with interest and are left with some profit, but not enough to invest in the next crop. The cycle goes on. Overall farmers' debt rose from THB2.4 trillion in 2016 to THB2.8 trillion in 2017, according to the National Statistical Office (2017 cited in Wipatayotin 2018).

3.4.3.2.2 Midstream Challenges
Insufficient supply to meet demand. The size of the harvested cassava area fluctuates depending on the cassava farm gate price in the previous year. When the price is low, farmers tend to allocate more land to grow crops that are more profitable such as maize and sugarcane, provided that the growing conditions are suitable. Meanwhile, cassava demand from processors continues to increase, resulting in stiff competition for locally grown cassava roots. Large-scale enterprises such as starch factories tend to have inherent advantages including more capital and leverage. Some factories have taken the initiative to support farmers by financing rent and inputs, in contractual exchange for the right to purchase cassava first-hand (Arthey, Srisompun and Zimmer 2018). In some highly competitive areas, drying yards perform additional work, alter their yards to other uses, or even go out of business. Cassava imports from neighbouring countries have somewhat relieved the situation. Yet, in recent years, cassava disease spread from these same countries. Strict measures were then implemented on cassava imports to protect domestic crops.

Logistics issues. Transport costs in Thailand remain high. The main mode of transport is land transport. Although rail transport has relatively lower unit costs, it is rarely used due to the poor state of railway infrastructure

(Prathanadee et al. 2009). This is reflected in the fact that 93 per cent of cassava was transported by land in 2013–15 (OAE 2018). Farmers, processors and exporters still prefer to use road transport because it is the most convenient and available mode of transport.

Transport constraints include a lack of farm-level coordination of cooperative transport arrangements, leading to transport inefficiency. The maximum allowable vehicle weight is 50.5 tonnes (including the weight of the truck) according to the Department of Highways. Without proper coordination for transport arrangements, some trucks transport far smaller loads or need to wait to be loaded. This adds to the transport costs of entrepreneurs.

Financing working capital needs   At peak harvest time, between December and March, processors need large amounts of capital to buy cassava roots from farmers, who usually only accept cash. The interviewed processors recommended that low-interest loans be made available to processors who could use cassava roots as a guarantee.

3.4.3.2.3 Downstream Challenges
Risk of dependency on a single market.   China is the main export destination for Thailand's cassava products, especially cassava chips. Almost all cassava chip exports go to China. Yet China has implemented policies that are unfavourable to Thailand's cassava exports, notably policy encouraging consumption of domestically grown corn and policy to expand cassava cultivation areas and invest in cassava processing plants in neighbouring countries (Chuasuwan 2018). In the long run, growing competition in the region coupled with a dependency on a single market could exert strong downward pressure on cassava prices, especially of low value-added products such as cassava chips.

Environmental issues.   For years, cassava exports have been transported from warehouses along the river to Si Chang Island and loaded onto seagoing cargo ships. This process creates a large amount of dust and some waste falls into the sea, threatening the marine environment. Some regulations have been implemented, but it is too soon to know if they can help solve these environmental problems.

3.4.4 Non-tariff Measures on Exports to China

3.4.4.1 Non-tariff Measures on Durian Exports

Exports of fresh Thai durian to China are subject to various NTMs, particularly SPS measures, both export-side NTMs which are regulated by Thai government agencies and issued under the Plant Quarantine Act BE 2507 (1964), and import-side measures specified by SPS-related regulations in China (Table 3.4).

For regulations imposed by Thailand, any person who wishes to export fresh durian must have two registrations: Fruit and Vegetable Exporter Registration, and Durian Exporter Registration. The registrations are valid for two years.

Growers, processors and packing houses exporting fresh fruit and vegetables must comply with national standards and obtain good agricultural practices (GAP) and good manufacturing practices (GMP)

TABLE 3.4
Summary of NTMs for Durian Export

NTMs Classified by UNCTAD 2018 Interim Version	NTM Type		Implementing Country
A. Sanitary and phytosanitary measures	A.15	Authorization for importing	China
	A.21	Tolerance limits for residues	
	A.41	Microbiological criteria	
	A.83	Certification requirement	
	A.84	Inspection and quarantine requirements	
	A.85	Traceability requirement	
P. Export-related measures	P.14	Export registration for technical reasons	Thailand
	P.15	Hygiene in production and post-production processes	
	P.17	Labelling and packaging requirements for durian	
	P.21	Export and import requirements to pass through specified port of customs	

Source: Authors' preparation.

certification. The GAP certificate is valid for three years and the GMP certificate (for exporters and packing houses) is valid for one year only and must be renewed annually.

Exporters must label durian boxes specifying the exporter's name and registration number, plant name, Thai quality classification, weight, and country of origin. They are also required to affix a barcode sticker on each durian stem stipulating the Q Mark, which contains the exporter's GMP code and the DOA's contact point for the purpose of traceability. Durian transported by land through third countries via the R3A or R9 highways[5] is subject to a special protocol.

For regulations imposed by China, any person importing durian must obtain an import licence and SPS certificate from the exporting country (Thailand). Any plant and plant products entering China must undergo inspection and quarantine by the Administration of Quality Supervision, Inspection and Quarantine (AQSIQ) to ensure those products are free from excessive harmful residues and the quarantine pests listed by China.

In addition, Thailand's Ministry of Agriculture and Cooperatives has a duty to submit to China's AQSIQ information lists on durian orchards, packing houses and exporters registered with the DOA, as well as a list of shipping companies. However, exporters not transporting goods via routes R3A and R9 are exempt from this requirement.

Over the past ten years, few durian orchardists placed importance on GAP certification because it was a voluntary measure, besides which they could sell their fruit without it due to high demand from China. In 2018, only around 14–15 per cent of durian orchardists had GAP certification, down from 40 per cent in an earlier period.[6] This is because some small-scale orchardists could not meet the standards required for GAP certification and others that passed the standards did not consider renewal important. Similarly, only 30 per cent of packing houses had GMP certification. And because around 50 per cent of newcomers' packing houses are rented and temporarily established at peak seasons, they did not bother to push for standards. Export regulations stipulate that all durian exporters must conform to GMP standards and that durian export labels should indicate the GMP certificate number. In practice, many exporters do not have their own GMP certification but use third-party GMP certification repeatedly for exports.

In 2018, the Chinese government reformed its internal organizational structure. Since the integration of AQSIQ, the agency in charge of import-export inspection and quarantine, with the General Administration of

Customs China (GACC), agricultural product inspections have become more stringent. Consequently, Thailand and China have agreed to exchange information on orchards and packing houses for selected fruits to raise the quality of fruit imports/exports between the two countries, to enhance traceability, and to be able to single out and suspend exports from non-compliant orchards and packing houses instead of pausing all exports.

As of July 2019, exporters of selected fruits to China, including durian, must comply with GAP and GMP standards. The packing house registration number must be included on every SPS certificate, every box, and every barcode label affixed to each durian stem to ensure traceability to the corresponding packing house and orchard. Consignments will be returned if these requirements are not met. The strictness is due to numerous detections of insect pests and residues that exceed the maximum levels specified by China.

In response, the Thai government introduced more strictness into inspections and urged all orchardists and packing houses to get GAP and GMP certification. Without these certificates, their durians cannot be exported to China and exporters risk being blacklisted.

Although the DOA has helped facilitate orchardists and entrepreneurs' access to GAP/GMP testing and certification, with limited resources and a limited number of certified inspection officers, the GAP/GMP compliance process has been proceeding slowly.

To ease the situation, the DOA plans to transfer all inspection services for GMP certification from the Office of Agricultural Research and Development to the private sector end of 2020. For GAP certification, there are already four private-sector inspection bodies to help out but the DOA has no immediate plans to transfer all inspection services to the private sector. It is estimated that inspection costs are going to rise to THB30,000–50,000 per GMP certificate. Even though the GMP certificate issued by private inspection bodies will be valid for three years, compared to the one-year validity of that issued by the DOA, DOA certification only costs around THB2,500 per certificate. Clearly, this raises concerns among packing houses over inspection costs charged by private sector inspection services, especially for small- to medium-sized packing houses.

3.4.4.2 Non-tariff Measures on Cassava Trade

NTMs on cassava trade can be divided into two groups: those imposed on imports of fresh cassava roots and processed products from neighbouring countries, and those imposed on cassava exports to China. The latter can also be divided into two types of NTMs: Thai export-related regulations and Chinese import-related regulations.

3.4.4.2.1 NTMs on Cassava Imports

Table 3.5 provides a summary of NTMs faced by cassava importers. Any person who wishes to import cassava or cassava products into Thailand must register as a cassava importer with the Department of Foreign Trade (DFT). The registration is valid for one year and must be renewed annually. Moreover, the importer must notify the DFT before importing any cassava products. Cassava importers are required to submit various certificates along with other documents. For fresh cassava roots, only certificates of origin and SPS are required. But for cassava by-products, a certificate of conformity is also needed. Upon receipt of fresh cassava or cassava products, importers must notify the Ministry of Commerce of import quantities within fourteen days of import. Imported cassava roots or cassava products must be stored in a specific warehouse that is not used to store domestic cassava products. Moreover, the movement of more than 10 tonnes of imported cassava roots or cassava products out of designated areas (mostly border provinces) must be approved by the Provincial Committee on the Price of Goods and Services. Due to recent plant disease epidemics in neighbouring countries, the DFT has added more regulations to prevent the spread of disease, aiming to tighten control

TABLE 3.5
Summary of NTMs for Cassava Imports

NTMs Classified by UNCTAD 2018 (Interim Version)	NTM type		Implementing Country
A. Sanitary and phytosanitary measures	A.15	Authorization requirement for importers for SPS reasons	
	A.64	Storage and transport conditions	
	A.83	Traceability requirement	Thailand
	A.854	Certification requirement	
C. Pre-shipment inspection and other formalities	C.3	Requirement to pass through specified port of customs	

Source: Authors' preparation.

over cassava imports by setting designated customs points and provinces that cassava can pass through.

Thailand imports cassava from neighbouring countries, in particular Cambodia and Laos, and re-exports it to profit from the difference between domestic and neighbouring countries' prices. Some are used as raw materials in processing factories. The problem of cassava smuggling in border areas persists. According to the interviews, about 2 to 4 million tonnes of cassava are smuggled yearly through informal channels from neighbouring countries. Many of these products are low quality and may not meet the standards set by the DOA and consequently cannot be approved for export to Thailand. Yet the price is usually lower than the domestic price, which persuades some businesses to support smuggling activities.

3.4.4.2.2 NTMs on Cassava Exports to China

Tariffs for all Thai cassava exports to China have been eliminated, but exports are still subject to various NTMs. The NTMs faced by exporters can be broadly divided into exported-related measures or regulations imposed by Thailand and import-related measures or regulations imposed by Chinese regulators (Table 3.6).

TABLE 3.6
Summary of NTMs for Cassava Exports to China

NTMs Classified by UNCTAD 2018 Interim Version	NTM Type		Implementing Country
A. Sanitary and phytosanitary measures	A.15	Authorization requirement for importers for SPS reasons	China
	A.21	Tolerance limits for residues	
	A.41	Microbiological criteria	
	A.83	Certification requirements	
	A.84	Inspection and quarantine requirements	
	A.85	Traceability requirements	
P. Export-related measures	P.14	Export registration for technical reasons	Thailand
	P.183	Certification required by exporting country	

Source: Authors' preparation.

For regulations imposed by Thailand, every cassava exporter requires permission from the Ministry of Commerce. They need to be registered as a cassava exporter to be able to export. In the case of cassava starch exports, a certificate of conformity is required along with other documents to guarantee product quality.

For regulations imposed by China, the entry regulations of China's AQSIQ specify that importers must provide an original phytosanitary certificate issued by the exporting country when applying for an entry inspection. Any plant and plant products, including cassava, entering China must undergo inspection and quarantine by AQSIQ. For cassava products used for human food or animal feed, import authorization is required. In addition, AQSIQ asks exporting country governments to provide a list of certified cassava exporters for product traceability.

Most cassava exported to China is in the form of cassava chips, which is used as raw material in various industries including processed food, animal feed, alcohol and citric acid. Due to its various uses, interpretation of the product is unclear depending on the judgement of inspectors at the time of import. For example, cassava products intended for use in the non-food industry might be interpreted as food and consequently could be rejected for import. To help resolve this issue, GACC has called for more stringent food quality standards and also plans to set some new export requirements for cassava factories and exporters, including that they are registered and inspected by GACC.

Aware of the sensitivity of the situation, Thailand's Ministry of Agriculture and Cooperatives (MOAC) has come up with a solution, which is to establish a protocol between Thailand and China to create understanding and set some guidelines for cassava trade. At the time of writing, the protocol was being drafted and considered by both sides. One of the proposals from the Thai side is for MOAC to make a list of registered factories, storage facilities and exporters and submit it to GACC for reference. MOAC is to update the list every six months. In addition, there is also a proposal for pre-inspection of products before export. The inspection will vary according to product type and intended use. For instance, an inspection of lead and arsenic residues must be conducted on cassava products intended for human consumption or animal feed but is not required for cassava products intended for other industrial uses.

3.5 CONCLUSIONS AND POLICY IMPLICATIONS

The main objective of the value chain research was to identify potential areas for increasing the efficiency of agricultural trade between Thailand and China, in particular for Thai exports. This paper has analysed the durian and cassava value chains in Thailand and identified constraints for stakeholders at different stages of the chains. It has also reviewed the NTMs imposed by both Thailand and China on durian and cassava exports.

The durian value chain in Thailand has changed slightly due to soaring demand from China. Challenges for stakeholders are as follows: financial management, climate change adaptation, and lack of a strong growers' association in the upstream part; labour shortages, high cost of migrant workers, and weak competitiveness of Thai entrepreneurs in the midstream portion; and limited market access to China, spoilage during transport, inefficient and insufficient customs administration, and increasing market competition within the region in the downstream stage.

For the cassava value chain, challenges for stakeholders include: low farming productivity, lack of a well-managed farmers association, lack of an efficient mechanism to prevent and control plant disease epidemics, and persistent farm debt in the upstream stage; insufficient supply to meet demand, high logistics cost, and insufficient cashflow in the midstream part; and single market dependency and environmental issues in the downstream segment.

The study also summarized existing NTMs for durian and cassava exports to China and discussed the main compliance challenges. The findings from the durian value chain analysis indicate that new regulations regarding GAP/GMP requirements exert some pressure on orchardists and packing houses, though resource limitations and shortage of inspectors remain major challenges. Challenges in the cassava value chain include cassava smuggling from neighbouring countries and the imposition of far more stringent quality standards on products entering China.

Based on the analysis of challenges in the durian and cassava value chains, along with comments from stakeholders in the policy dialogue, the following recommendations merit consideration.

(1) Encourage Collaboration among Farmers/Orchardists
The main problem for small-scale farmers/orchardists is their weak bargaining power and lack of negotiation with the government. They can

overcome these problems by working collaboratively to purchase materials in bulk, standardize their products, share knowledge, consolidate their bargaining power, raise funds to develop their group, and acquire GAP certification.

The government has launched a collaborative farming programme, but participation has been low, and the programme has attracted only small-scale farmers/orchardists. One problem is that most farmers are habituated to working independently and making the most of their land to grow any crops for the highest profit, whether cassava, maize or sugarcane. The government might have to adjust and ensure that the current incentives for the collaborative farming project meet farmers' needs. Moreover, the project should replace the condition of participant farmers being from the same community with the condition that adjacent farming areas be consolidated to facilitate machinery sharing as well as information sharing.

Moreover, when launching policies or designing training to support orchardists, the government should support and inquire about the problems of all groups, such as collaborative farming groups, the Thai Durian Institute and the Confederation of Thai Durian Orchardists. In addition, the government should encourage orchardist groups to form one large group that is representative of all durian growers.

(2) Encourage Farmers/Orchardists to Adopt Production Technologies
Thailand recently adopted a new development model based on applying information and communications technology through precision farming to increase agricultural productivity. Government should encourage farmers to adopt precision agriculture technologies such as soil quality testing, drip irrigation, and AI technology to reduce labour costs. The most recent initiative is the smart farm project, which is being piloted for six crops including cassava, to study which intelligent agricultural technology would be suitable for the production process.

Most durian producers cannot use production technologies for growing, harvesting and packing. Even though some orchardists use crop-spraying drones as a pest control solution, the technology is too costly for most. However, orchardists can adopt some technologies for production planning such as soil quality monitoring, weather forecasting and peak bloom predictions that can help prevent diseases and manage the harvesting schedule. The government should develop a mobile application and encourage orchardists to use it. Moreover, orchardists and collectors could use a QR (quick response) code to access and have at hand information about harvesting dates, orchard location, quantity, and so on. This would also give consumers confidence and ease traceability.

(3) Find Alternative Markets to Lower the Risk of Overreliance on the Chinese Market

Both durian and cassava exports are too dependent on China as the largest import market. Any sudden shift in China's import policy could have significant impacts on Thai exporters. Thailand should learn from its experience of changes in EU agricultural policy which led to a massive contraction of demand for cassava. The Cassava Policy and Management Committee acknowledge the risk and are now focusing efforts on three mitigation missions: preserving the current market with China, restoring old markets such as the EU, and expanding into new markets such as Turkey, New Zealand, India, South Korea and the Philippines.

Fresh durian is very popular and in very high demand. The low value-added at the processing stage of the value chain offers little incentive for food processors. However, orchardists can increase value added by planting other cultivars that may not be as popular but appeal to profitable niche markets. Thus, to incentivize orchardists, the government should devise a marketing strategy, find new markets and promote durian products. Thai entrepreneurs have already started to export frozen durian pulp to China and premium durians to other markets such as Japan, South Korea and the United States. However, these relatively small markets cannot compensate for the potential loss of Thailand's share of the Chinese market. The government should find new markets that can absorb a lot of durians. The Indian market is the best choice due to the size of India's population and its proximity.

(4) Collaborate with Greater Mekong Subregion Countries to Improve Transport and Customs Systems

Transport is the most pressing concern in the durian value chain. When durians cannot be transported efficiently to the export destination, the entire value chain is affected. The main problems are road traffic and at logjams at border crossings, especially at the Youyiguan border gate. The Thai government should cooperate with GMS country governments to improve this situation, as follows:

- Push forward the protocol on inspection and quarantine between Thailand and China for transportation via a third country along Route 12. In fact, there should be a protocol that opens all transport routes for flexibility.
- Improve road conditions on routes 3A, R9 and R12.
- Collaborate with the Vietnamese government to speed up document processing and prohibit the opening of containers by Vietnamese customs officers.
- Allow Thai fruit exports to enter China through Dongxing border gate in order to reduce traffic at the Youyiguan border gate. The Chinese government must improve road conditions and infrastructure standards. It should also create a protocol of inspection and quarantine for fruit transported from Thailand via Route 8 to Dongxing border gate.
- Negotiate a road transport agreement with Vietnam or develop a GMS Cross-Border Transport Agreement (CBTA) for transporting durians to China via Thai trucks to eliminate the costly practice of changing trucks at the Vietnamese border and reduce truck turnaround time. Under the early harvest GMS CBTA, each country (except Cambodia) has a maximum annual quota of 500 GMS road transport permits that allow vehicles to pass through specified customs offices, but the number of permits is inadequate. Besides, the permit is more concerned about driving in other countries and overcoming language barriers in customs negotiations rather than efficiently transporting goods from origin to destination.

(5) Increase the Strictness of Durian Quality Through Organizing Packing Houses

Insect pests, chemical residues, failure to ripen, and misuse of GAP and GMP certificates are the important problems besetting the export of durian. In response, the Thai government should increase the strictness of quality standards for durian. The DOA has already imposed stricter requirements on phytosanitary certification. Inspections are now carried out at the packing house instead of at customs in order to verify the packing house's GMP certificate. Even so, durian quality is still not checked thoroughly because the inspections are done after the durians have been packed in boxes.

The DOA should oversee the operations of Chinese-run packing houses that do not have a GMP certificate to prevent price rigging and thereby increase the competitiveness of Thai packing houses. Moreover, it should encourage packing houses to display their GMP certificate and increase the price of GAP-certified durians that are sold from the front of their premises. This would stimulate orchardists to apply for GAP certification and harvest durian themselves, which, in turn, could reduce labour inefficiencies.

(6) Development of New High-Yielding and Disease Resistant Cultivars

Government should support research and development for new cultivars that deliver high yields and disease resistance. At the same time, the government should provide benefits in the form of in-kind assistance, such as the distribution of disease-free varieties, cash coupons to hire people to eliminate and destroy infected stems, and incentives for farmers to immediately notify authorities and prevent the spread of disease in a timely manner. In addition, a working group comprising government, academia, private sector and international agencies should be established to conduct surveys and continually monitor plant disease epidemics.

(7) Support Downstream Industry Using Cassava Products

Low value-added producers (i.e., cassava chip manufacturers) need to move themselves further up the value chain to hedge against stiff competition from cassava starch manufacturers and downward pressure on prices from China. Thailand should allocate more resources to the stage of the chain where value-added is higher. Meanwhile, to absorb raw materials, the government should develop value chain linkages for cassava chips by implementing policy support for downstream industries such as ethanol production and biomass for electricity generation.

Notes

1. 1 *rai* = 1,600 m^2 or 0.16 ha.
2. Interview with an official from Office of Agriculture-Chanthaburi and Rayong, March 2019.
3. World Bank THB: US$ exchange rate in 2018 was THB33.94 for US$1.
4. Protocol on the Inspection and Quarantine requirements for Thai Fruit Export from Thailand to China through Territories of Third Countries.
5. Route R3E or R3A is part of the North-South Economic Corridor linking the southern Chinese city of Kunming, passing through Laos to Chiang Khong in Thailand. Route R9 is part of the East-West Economic Corridor linking Mukdahan in Thailand, passing through Laos to Danang in Vietnam.

6. Interview with an official from Office of Agriculture-Chanthaburi and Rayong, March 2019.

References

Arthey, Tom, Orawan Srisompun, and Yelto Zimmer. 2018. *Cassava Production and Processing in Thailand: Report to FAO*. Rome: Food and Agriculture Organization. www.agribenchmark.org/fileadmin/Dateiablage/B-Cash-Crop/Reports/CassavaReport Final-181030.pdf

Asian Development Bank. 2016. *Review of Configuration of the Greater Mekong Subregion Economic Corridors*. Manila: ADB.

Bhuthong, Punpreecha. 2020. "Non-tariff Measures on Agricultural Trade between China and the Greater Mekong Sub-region Countries: Evidence on Thailand". Unpublished manuscript.

Centre for Applied Economics Research. 2012. *The Expansion of the Thai Fruit Market to the People's Republic of China under the Thailand-China Free Trade Area*. Bangkok: Office of Agricultural Economics.

Chuasuwan, Chetchuda. 2018. "Cassava Industry". *Thailand Industry Outlook 2018–20*. Bangkok: Krungsri Research.

FAO (Food and Agriculture Organization). 2018. FAOSTAT Database.

Hasachoo, Narat, and Phattaraporn Kalaya. 2013. *Competitiveness of Local Agriculture: The Case of Longan Fruit Trade between China and the North of Thailand*. IRASEC's Discussion Papers No. 15. https://www.irasec.com/documents/fichiers/91.pdf

Ministry of Commerce. 2018. *Foreign Trade Statistics 1998–2018*. http://tradereport.moc.go.th/TradeThai.aspx

National Bureau of Agricultural Commodity and Food Standards. 2020. "Durian Standards in Thailand". http://www.acfs.go.th

North Eastern Tapioca Trade Association. 2019. Map of Cassava Factories in Thailand.

OAE (Office of Agricultural Economics). 2018. "Agricultural Logistics and Supply Chain Development Master Plan 2017–2021". Bangkok.

———. 2019a. "Agricultural Economic Information by Commodity from 2004–2018". Bangkok.

———. 2019b. "Agricultural Statistics of Thailand". Bangkok.

Panichayakarn, Boonsup, Kullapa Soratana, and Nathathai Longsa. 2017. *Information Analysis and Distribution on the Utilization of Beibu Gulf Ports, Guangxi*. Nanning: Royal Thai Consulate-General.

Phanishsarn, Aksornsri. 2018. "Why Exporting Thai Jasmine Rice to China Is Not as Easy as You Think?". http://www.setthasarn.econ.tu.ac.th/blog/detail/13/

Piyachomkwan, Kuakoon, and Morakot Tanticharoen. 2011. "Cassava Industry in Thailand: Prospects". *Journal of the Royal Institute of Thailand* 3: 160–70.

Porter, Michael. 1985. *Competitive Advantage: Creating and Sustaining Superior Performance*. New York: Simon and Schuster.

Prathanadee, Parthana, Jirachai Buddhakulsomsiri, Chumpol Monthatipkul, and Charoenchai Khompatraporn. 2009. *Supply Chain and Logistics Management for Cassava Products in Thailand: Final Research Report*. Bangkok: Office of the Higher Education Commission.

Taweesak Theppitak. 2014. "Problems and Threats of Importers and Exporters in Trading with China after the Launch of FTA: Past and Present to Ways of Solving Problems for the Future". www.freightmaxad.com/magazine/?p=7173

Thailand Development Research Institute. 2009. *Analysis of Transportation Cost Structure and Logistics System Project*. Bangkok: TDRI.

Thailand Institute of Scientific and Technological Research. 2008. *Logistics and Supply Chain Management of Agricultural Products for Expanding the Export Market to Asian Countries in 2008*.

Thitikan, Chaipichit, and Khompatraporn Charoenchai. 2007. "Logistics System for Cassava Export to China under ASEAN-China Free Trade Agreement". Paper presented at Annual Academic Seminar on Logistics and Supply Chain Management No. 7, Department of Industrial Engineering, King Mongkut's University of Technology Thonburi, Thailand.

Tijaja, Julia. 2010. "China's Impact on Commodity Producing Economies: Lessons from the Cassava Value Chains in Thailand". Paper presented at the China Postgraduate Network (CPN) UK 3rd Annual Conference, Conference Proceedings, University of Oxford, UK, 8–9 April 2010.

UNCTAD (United Nations Conference on Trade and Development). 2017. "NTMs TRAINS researcher File". Global Database on Non-Tariff Measures. https://trains.unctad.org/forms/Analysis.aspx

———. 2018. "International Classification of Non-Tariff Measures: Interim 2018 Version". UNCTAD/DITC/TAB/2018_

UNIDO (United Nations Industrial Development Organization). 2009. *Agro-Value Chain Analysis and Development: The UNIDO Approach*. A Staff Working Paper. Vienna: UNIDO.

Wipatayotin, Apinya. 2018. "Finding Ways to Beat Farm Debt". *Bangkok Post*, 4 November 2018. www.bangkokpost.com/business/news/1569802/finding-ways-to-beat-farm-debt

4

AGRICULTURAL EXPORTS FROM CAMBODIA TO CHINA
A Value Chain Analysis of Cassava and Sugarcane

Narith Roeun and Hokkheang Hiev

4.1 INTRODUCTION

Cambodia resumed trade with China in 1989, after opening its economy to the region and the world by lifting export bans, privatizing public enterprises and allowing foreign direct investment (FDI) inflows. Chinese firms started to invest in Cambodia's textile and garment industry in 1993, after Cambodia held its first multiparty national elections in decades, aiming to tap into the country's trade preferential status (i.e., most favoured nation and generalized system of preference) and low labour costs. Trade flows between the two countries have since been partially facilitated by a gradual reduction in the tariff rates on tradeable commodities under the China-ASEAN Free Trade Agreement (FTA) signed in 2014. It was expected that all things being equal, there would be greater potential for Cambodia to expand its exports to China. However, bilateral trade between the two countries at the time mainly involved exports of intermediate inputs for textile and garment manufacturing from China to Cambodia. Although the magnitude of total trade has been small, Cambodia has run up a substantial trade deficit with China. Cambodia's imports from China grew exponentially to US$4,550.9 million in 2016, but export growth continued to lag at only US$609.3 million (IMF 2017). It is clear that Cambodia has not yet been able to seize the growing opportunities from the closer trade relationship. Given that China is the world's second-largest agricultural market and Cambodia is a predominantly agrarian society with strong agricultural comparative advantages, the two countries should have the potential for economic and trade cooperation in agricultural commodities.

Due to the considerable efforts made over the last three decades to improve agricultural production, Cambodia's agricultural exports have gained greater access to international markets. Cambodia's membership of ASEAN in 1999 and its accession to the World Trade Organization in 2004 heralded a new era of land reform in favour of agriculture, which became a milestone in the country's development. The government set out to incentivize corporate investments in industrial agriculture through the issuance of economic land concessions (ELCs). Foreign investors seized the opportunity to secure long-term leases on vast swathes of arable land for large-scale industrial monocropping. In tandem, to promote export-oriented value chains, the government passed several domestic trade policy reforms including the adoption of the Automated System for Customs Data and the Twelve-Point Action Plan for Trade Facilitation and Investment in preparation for a trade sector-wide approach.

Export promotion activities to stimulate exports of high-value agricultural commodities and processed foods are set out in Cambodia Industrial Development Policy 2015–25, which calls for agricultural products exported in the form of processed products to constitute an ambitious 12 per cent of total exports by 2025 (Council of Ministers 2015). In line with this, Cambodia Trade Integration Strategy 2019–23 identifies potential agricultural products in the national strategic export commodity list (MOC 2019). Nevertheless, it seems that an array of challenges remains unresolved. Institutional and market failures, for instance, frequently hurt economic actors at the micro level, particularly small-scale farmers. This situation seems in stark contrast to the policy support and institutional arrangements for agricultural cooperatives and contract farming schemes, and the inclusion of private sector actors in governance mechanisms.

Despite stronger domestic policy support and international market openness, in particular with China, Cambodia's agricultural export base remains limited and could be easily eroded. The consequent sluggish growth in agricultural exports underscores the importance of this study. Identifying and unblocking the bottlenecks that hinder Cambodia's readiness to accelerate its exports of agricultural products to new markets is now more crucial than ever.

4.2 BACKGROUND

The major domestic and foreign obstacles to export growth need to be well understood from the policy standpoint because agriculture is a mainstay of Cambodia's economy. Importantly, agriculture is the main source of livelihood and income for around 80 per cent of the country's population. The sector accounted for almost one-third of employment and contributed just over one-third of total value-added as of 2016 (Table 4.1). The latest estimate by the National Institute of Statistics (2019) put agriculture's share of value-added at 24.9 per cent in 2017. The sector also generated substantial foreign exchange earnings between 2007 and 2016. Furthermore, with tariff cuts under various framework agreements such as the ASEAN FTA, the ASEAN-China FTA and the World Trade Organization's General Agreement on Tariffs and Trade, there are growing opportunities for Cambodia to export agricultural products to not only China, but also to ASEAN member states, Europe and North America.

Many studies confirm a significant correlation between agricultural exports and economic growth in developing and small economies (Sturton 1992; Henneberry and Khan 1999; Daramola et al. 2007; Blein et al. 2008; Yifru 2015; Bala and Sudhakar 2017; Ahmed and Sallam 2018; Siaw et al. 2018; Osabhien et al. 2019). Increased export opportunities for Cambodian agricultural products, however, have coincided with a growing number of trade barriers arising from the increasing complexity and intensity of competition. Non-tariff measures (NTMs) in the forms of sanitary and phytosanitary (SPS) measures and technical barriers to trade (TBT) are frequently reported as challenges that small and developing economies have to address before entering modern global agricultural value chains (Ven 2015).

Looking at previous studies on Cambodia, Mille, Hap and Loeng (2016) used value chain analysis (VCA) to examine the performance of Cambodia's

TABLE 4.1
Contribution of Agriculture to the National Economy

Indicators	2000–5	2006–10	2011–16
GDP annual growth (%)	9.3	6.7	7.1
Agriculture value added annual growth (%)	4.3	5.1	1.8
Industry value added annual growth (%)	16.8	7.0	11.2
Services value added annual growth (%)	10.1	6.8	7.3
Value added			
% of agriculture value added	34.3	34.4	32.2
% of industry value added	25.6	25.2	27.2
% of services value added	40.1	40.5	40.6
Employment			
% of employment in agriculture	71.1	66.2	32.7
% of employment in industry	10.0	11.4	25.2
% of employment in services	18.9	22.4	42.2
Agricultural exports (US$ million)	*2007–10*	*2011–13*	*2014–16*
World	49.7	263.9	467.8
China	5.2	15.9	78.4
ASEAN excluding Brunei and Myanmar	23.2	78.4	139.7
GMS (Laos, Thailand, Vietnam)	12.3	24.9	86.3
EU-25	18.3	76.3	127.1
North America	3.9	10.6	28.5

Note: Classification of agricultural products is based on the World Trade Organization's classification.
Sources: World Bank World Development Indicators (2018); Comtrade (2019).

fisheries sector in both domestic and international markets, finding that key actors including fishers, traders and exporters generated the least value-added. Kula, Turner and Sar (2015) used the VCA framework, supported by evidence-based elements (value chain mapping, governance structure, value-added, and bottleneck identification), for assessing the agricultural value chains of rice, horticulture and aquaculture. They identified several constraints in the rice value chain, namely low seed quality, low yields, opportunism, poor processing capacity, weak institutional arrangements and inefficient value-added activities. These findings confirmed the results of a similar analysis done as part of the Project for Agricultural Development and Economic Empowerment (EMC 2014), implemented in five provinces, which also used the four-element VCA framework to assess the value chains for eleven rural products: rice, chicken, duck, fish, frog, long bean, tomato, eggplant, cucumber, cassava and coconut. These studies provide some background to constraints along domestic value chains. The noteworthy research gap apparent in these studies is the lack of in-depth discussion on the links between domestic value chain performance and the export barriers imposed by importing countries.

Entry into global value chains requires lengthy, complex and massive investments in industries that have the most potential and in which would-be-participant countries have a comparative advantage. However, it is unclear how domestic supply chains would respond to such targeted investments because value chain literature providing a complete discussion on industries with potential for competitive advantage is scant. Moreover, few studies focus on potential agricultural exports from Cambodia to China, the world's largest agricultural importer. The present study intends to address this significant knowledge gap.

The aim of the study is twofold: to identify the key stakeholders involved at all stages of the agricultural supply chain and the interactions between them; and to shed light on the bottlenecks, NTMs in particular, hindering Cambodia's agricultural trade with China and the rest of the world. Specifically, the study sets out to investigate the following:

- *Agricultural value chains*—by identifying the main processes and key traders in the selected agricultural commodities and examining value chain constraints on Cambodia's export competitiveness.
- *Non-tariff measures*—by mapping at the aggregate level the extent to which NTMs are applied to Cambodia's agricultural trade with China.

4.3 DATA AND METHOD

4.3.1 Data

4.3.1.1 Selection of Two Agricultural Products

This subsection describes the identification of two Cambodian agricultural products exported to China based on the latest available data on the export value and highlights the evolution of China's import (demand) and Cambodia's production (supply) of those products.

According to the harmonized system (HS) 4-digit classification (Comtrade 2019), the composition of Cambodia's exports to China in 2016 mainly consisted of textiles and garments, electronics products and agricultural products. Among agricultural products at the HS 4-digit level, Cambodia predominantly exports rice and cassava starch to China, followed by cassava tubers, cane sugar and palm oil (Table 4.2). Rice has been the subject of much research, and policies are in place to promote rice production and export, although there is room for improvement. In contrast, relatively little research has been done on Cambodia's sugarcane production and sugar exports, on which China exacts a high tariff of 50 per cent. Moreover, when revealed comparative advantage (RCA)[1] is considered, in 2016, cassava and cane sugar had substantially larger RCAs than all other agricultural products except rice. Another consideration is the national goal to boost exports of processed agricultural products to at least 12 per cent of all exports by 2025 (Council of Ministers 2015). We, therefore, selected cassava and sugarcane as the two agricultural products for this study.

TABLE 4.2
Top Fifteen Agricultural Exports from Cambodia to China (US$ million), 2016

Rank	HS Code	Product	Export (US$ m)	Tariff (%)	RCA
1	1006	Rice (semi- or wholly milled rice, and broken rice)	71.53	34	23.8
2	1108	Starch (manioc/cassava starch only)	10.58	0	6.8
3	0714	Cassava/manioc roots and tubers, ...	8.36	0	13.8
4	1701	Cane and beet sugar	2.08	50	2.2
5	1511	Palm oil and fractions	0.91	9	0.7
6	1805	Cocoa powder	0.75	0	0.5
7	0306	Crustaceans, whether in shell or not, live, fish, ...	0.56	0	0.0
8	0801	Coconuts, fresh or dried	0.21	0	0.1
9	1904	Prepared foods obtained from cereal products	0.18	0	0.1
10	1905	Bread, pastry, cakes, biscuits, ...	0.09	0	0.0
11	0804	Dates, figs, pineapples, avocados, guavas, mangoes and mangosteens, fresh or dried	0.08	0	0.1
12	2007	Jams, fruit jellies, marmalades, fruit or nut puree	0.06	0	0.0
13	1513	Coconut "copra", palm kernel or babassu oil and fractions	0.06	0	0.4
14	1902	Pasta, whether or not cooked or stuffed with meat	0.02	0	0.5
15	2402	Cigars, cheroots, cigarillos and cigarettes	0.02	25	1.3

Source: International Trade Centre Trade Map (Comtrade 2019).

4.3.1.2 Study Site Selection

Criteria for site selection included the current and potential production area and volume, and the active presence of key supply chain actors.

4.3.1.2.1 Cassava

Site selection for the cassava value chain analysis involved three steps. First, we visited provinces in east and west Cambodia known for growing high volumes of cassava. The field visits were made based on information collected from the literature review, secondary data from the Ministry of Agriculture, Forestry and Fisheries (MAFF) and the 2018 Commune Database, and consultations with MAFF officials and development partners (e.g., United Nations Development Programme). During the field visits, we met and consulted key actors and stakeholders including commune chiefs, cassava traders and hauliers. We also visited the main border gates for cross-border trade between Cambodia and Vietnam and Cambodia and Thailand. Second, after combining information from the literature review, secondary data sources and field visits, we selected Oddar Meanchey province in the west and Tboung Khmum province in the east and identified communes and districts within those provinces. Finally, in consultation with commune chiefs, commune councillors and representatives from the local provincial departments of MAFF, the target villages were selected. We also verified the information gathered from those consultations with the secondary data and field information. Moreover, officials from MAFF and the local provincial departments of MAFF joined our research team to collect data. According to the 2018 Commune Database (NIS 2018), the cassava cultivated areas in the two selected provinces constitute 60.9 per cent of Cambodia's total cassava cultivated area.

Tboung Khmum province is in eastern Cambodia and borders Vietnam. The total cassava cultivated area in Tboung Khmum accounts for 53.9 per cent (662,412 ha) of Cambodia's total cassava cultivated area and is the second-largest in the eastern provinces (NIS 2018). Data were mainly collected in Dambae district.

Oddar Meanchey province lies in the western part of Cambodia where it borders Thailand. Its cassava cultivated area accounts for 7.0 per cent (85,639 ha) of Cambodia's total cassava cultivated area (NIS 2018). Cassava production is characterized by a growing number of cassava producers following recent land clearance and migration from other provinces. Anlong Veng and Trapaeng Prasat districts were selected for the study.

TABLE 4.3
Number of Respondents for the Cassava and Sugarcane Value Chain Analyses

No.	Type of Respondents	No. of Respondents	
		Cassava	Sugarcane
1	Farmer	202	57
2	Trader	16	0
3	Farm contractor	3	4
4	Fertilizer/pesticide supplier	23	0
5	Processor and/or exporter	6	3
7	Transporter	6	4
8	Farm service provider	7	3

Source: Authors' preparation.

4.3.1.2.2 Sugarcane
Site selection for the sugarcane value chain analysis was done in two steps: a review of available secondary data, and snowball sampling (to gather information from one subject about another). Due to the limitations of secondary data, most of which was retrieved from newspaper reports, it was necessary for the research team to conduct a field visit before selecting the study sites (Table 4.3). The checklist for this included the current and potential production volume and the active presence of key value chain actors. Because some of the potential study sites suggested by secondary sources no longer existed, information about other possible sites was collected along the way. As a result, Kampong Speu and Preah Vihear provinces were selected for data collection.

4.3.2 Methodology

4.3.2.1 Conceptual Framework of Value Chain Analysis

Since Porter's (1985) pioneering work introducing the concept of the value chain, several and to some extent contending concepts of VCA have emerged. Value chain mapping, governance mechanisms, economic analysis (benefit distribution), and upgrading performance assessment are the four main analytic elements used to build insight into value chains (Kaplinsky and Morris 2001; Kaplinsky 2004; Taylor 2005; Trienekens 2011; Bellù 2013; Gereffi and Fernandez-Stark 2016). Summarized below, these elements respond to the first research objective—to identify the key stakeholders involved at all stages of the agricultural supply chains and the interactions between them.

Value chain mapping is derived from network theory in supply chain management and comprises the linkages that connect actors engaged in different activities along the entire value chain (Trienekens 2011; Gereffi and Fernandez-Stark 2016). The use of this tool can produce a deeper understanding of the actors involved in a particular chain and the interactions between them, as well as information flows and product flows (Kaplinsky and Morris 2001; Bellù 2013). In reality, however, relationships between supply chain actors are flexible and interchangeable. Also, whereas theory tends to suggest a simple and clear focus, the real world can be far messier (Kaplinsky and Morris 2001).

Identifying the key dynamics of governance structures, similarly to value chain mapping, is fundamental to gaining insight into relative power among chain actors (Gereffi and Fernandez-Stark 2016). Transactions can be driven by product and service suppliers (producer-driven chain) or by buyers and service users (buyer-driven chain) (Gereffi, Humphrey and Sturgeon 2005; Gereffi 1994). The literature describes two main governance structure typologies. One divides the governance structure into five levels: market, modular, relational, captive and hierarchical (Gereffi 1999; Gereffi and Fernandez-Stark 2016). The other (Williamson 1979) categorizes it into three levels based on three contract laws: market-based governance relying on classical contracting, trilateral governance using neoclassical contracting, and transaction-specific (vertical integration) governance depending on one of two contract types—obligational contracting (bilateral governance) or internal organization (unified governance). This study focuses on contractual and non-contractual relationships.

The economic analysis specifically detects how actors create value added at different stages of the value chain (Trienekens 2011). Such analysis can also illustrate how actors share incentives or how the value chain attracts various actors (Kaplinsky and Morris 2001). Although there are many discussions in the literature on this analytical part, there is no escape from the use of accounting data (i.e., costs, margins and revenues faced and received by actors from their effort and investment) to bring the chain alive (see Kaplinsksy and Morris 2001; Kaplinsky 2004; Taylor 2005; Trienekens 2011; Bellù 2013; Gereffi and Fernandez-Stark 2016). This study therefore simplifies this part, aiming to show the value of benefits shared among actors along the chain.

Assessment of upgrading opportunities within the value chains, using upgrading theory to identify constraints and promising strategies, captures firms' strengths and weaknesses (i.e., areas for improvement). Theories of upgrading are applied in the works of Humphrey and Schmitz (2000), Kaplinsky and Morris (2001), Fromm (2007), Mitchell, Coles and Keane (2009), Trienekens (2011) and Bamber et al. (2017). The present study examines the performance of the selected value chains based on four types of upgrading—product upgrading, process upgrading, functional upgrading and chain upgrading.

In addition, the capability to comply with the import requirements of destination countries is a significant concern for export-oriented value chains in developing countries. This suggests the importance of our investigation into the occurrence of beyond-border barriers to trade. The present study examines the magnitude of export barriers in the form of enforced NTMs and how they affect domestic value chain actors. Categories of NTMs, the number of specific NTMs in each category, when they came into force and the frequency of their use over time are the main variables used in this analysis. The differences between these variables applied to main exporters are also important to gain insight into competition in the market.

4.3.2.2 Empirical Method

The study took an exploratory approach using qualitative tools to address the research questions. First, we conducted desk research by reviewing existing studies on agricultural trade between China and Cambodia, value chain analyses of agricultural products, and firms' perspectives of the effect of NTMs on exports to China. Second, we used snowball sampling to identify and interview key actors involved in various activities along the value chains to (1) generate a generic value chain for each selected agricultural product, (2) understand governance structures within the value chains, and (3) obtain in-depth information on the economic costs and revenues of chain actors. Specifically, we conducted focus group discussions (FGDs) with farmers and in-depth key informant interviews (KIIs) with other key value chain actors. Last, to obtain information about the impact of NTMs on exports to China, we interviewed processors and exporters. A wide range of secondary data was also collected from official sources, especially the UNCTAD NTMs TRAINS database.

4.4 FINDINGS

4.4.1 Cassava Value Chain Mapping

Cassava is the second-largest agricultural crop after rice in Cambodia, and Cambodia is the world's second-largest exporter after Thailand of raw cassava in the form of fresh tubers and dried chips (MOC 2019). Most of the cassava produced in Cambodia is destined for export markets. Cambodia exports raw cassava in the form of fresh tubers and dried chips and semi-processed cassava in the form of native starch and modified starch. Figure 4.1 depicts product flows and interactions between actors along Cambodia's cassava value chain. Vietnam buys fresh tubers and dried chips, and Thailand buys mostly dried chips. Native starch is exported to China, the EU and others, and modified starch is exported to China only. Several key value chain actors are involved in supplying these different products to various destinations, from input sourcing (upstream) to product distribution (downstream).

On the input side, there are four main actors: microfinance institutions (MFIs), private lenders, input suppliers and labourers. These actors supply cassava farmers with different types of essential inputs. MFIs provide loans to finance cassava production, though farmers also obtain higher interest rate loans from private lenders, and some use their own capital. Farmers buy fertilizers and agrochemicals (e.g., herbicides) from depots near their homes and farms. The majority of farmers grow cassava on their own farmland, and a small minority rent farmland. At harvest time, farmers save cassava stems for the next season's planting. This means that transactions with seed suppliers are rare. Farmers hire labourers for planting, chemical spraying, harvesting and chopping. Notably, these input linkages are not mediated by any written contract. The relationships between actors in the entire value chain mainly rely on a market-based governance structure. Only a small proportion of producers who focus on the niche organic market use written contracts with operators/exporters. The transactions for all inputs, product distribution and export of conventional cassava use verbal agreements based on trade relationship, location and price negotiation.

Only one of the six cassava processing firms interviewed reported using raw materials grown by the firm itself. This implies that the majority of cassava for processing as well as for raw material export is produced by farmers.

Agricultural Exports from Cambodia to China

FIGURE 4.1
Cambodia's Cassava Value Chain

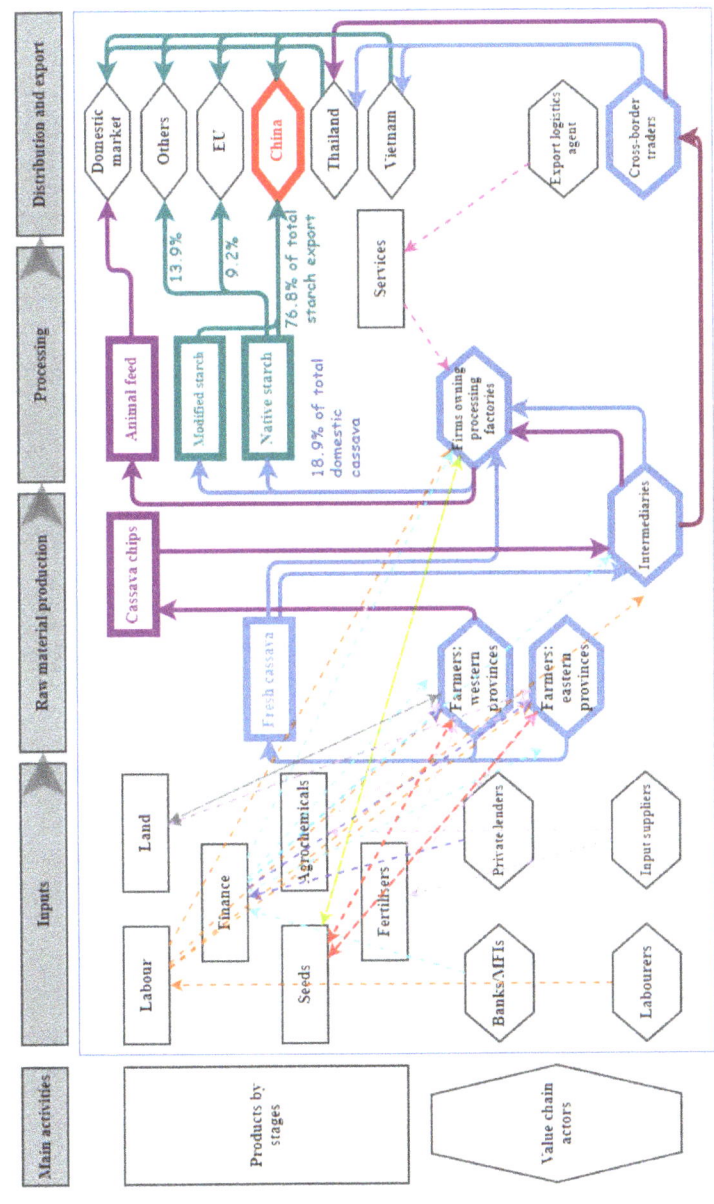

Note: The different colours used in this figure differentiate important flows in the value chain.
Source: Authors' compilation.

The trading of raw cassava takes various forms. Most farmers transport fresh tubers to an intermediary's collection point located in their or a nearby village. A small proportion of farmers chop and dry their cassava tubers beforehand. Another option is to transport and sell cassava directly to processing factories. Processing firms reported that farmers transport fresh tubers to factories up to 50 km from their farm. Farmers near the Cambodia-Thailand and Cambodia-Vietnam borders transport their fresh tubers to cross-border traders. Notably, Thai traders mostly buy dried chips whereas Vietnamese traders mostly buy fresh tubers.

There are several reasons influencing a farmer's decision to transport and sell fresh tubers to intermediaries in their or a nearby village. First, the decision is based on the farmer's relational transactions. From the farmer's position, the difference between the prices offered by different intermediaries is insignificant. Second, transporting fresh tubers further afield could push up the farmer's costs. Transport cost is proportional to the number of transactions and distance to market. This is because most farmers use tiller-pulled carts as a means of transport, which can carry a limited volume (less than 1 tonne) of fresh tubers. Third, in some harvest seasons, when the market price of cassava was really low, the situation of oligopsony or sometimes in worse seasons, monopsony, immediately occurred. Consequently, relatively few intermediaries have been willing to buy fresh tubers due to oversupply, inadequate storage space and facilities, high perishability, and price and quality uncertainties. Poor road conditions also influence farmers' selection of buyers.

A range of problems encountered by farmers regarding fresh tuber transactions at the harvest and post-harvest stages should also be discussed. The decision to harvest cassava tubers is influenced by two main factors: urgent need for money and extreme perishability. Based on information from FGDs, farmers need income from their cassava production to cover basic household expenses and to pay off loans. At least half of the participated cassava farmers had outstanding loans from various MFIs. Perishability is also a factor for cassava uprooting. Based on farmers' experience, the quality of mature cassava roots is highly susceptible to heavy rains, which typically coincide with the harvest season. Perishability is also a concern after harvest. This comprises various forms of degradation in tuber quality and weight loss. Most farmers therefore harvest cassava at the same time, which, coupled with the limited capacity of the domestic middle stream and downstream actors, creates a seasonal glut. Calculation using data from two sources—FAOSTAT (2019) and Cambodia Trade Integration Strategy (MOC 2019)—shows that domestic processing factories are able to absorb only 18.9 per cent of Cambodia's total cassava production. This situation pushes supply chain operations towards the dominant channel of raw materials export. In this sense, farmers face intense oligopsony in raw cassava transactions. Their bargaining power is low, forcing them to be price takers, implying that they are the most vulnerable actors in the chain. Various opportunistic behaviours by intermediaries seeking high profit margins were reported. An example of this is the use of inaccurate scales that favour the buyer to the detriment of the farmers who lose out.

Actors involved in the postharvest cassava chain also face challenges in their seasonal transactions. Intermediaries complained about the performance of their transacting partners including farmers and cross-border traders. In terms of linkages with farmers, the quality of fresh tubers is a serious concern. Intermediaries reported that farmers supply substandard products such as rotten and wet tubers contaminated with foreign matter (e.g., sand and soil) to increase the weight. When they fall prey to such practices and buy bad quality tubers, they make little or no profit as they must remove all damaged tubers and foreign matter before they can sell the cassava to actors further up the value chain. They encounter other problems in transactions with upstream actors, in particular cross-border traders. One issue is quality measurement. In transactions with Vietnamese cross-border traders, fresh tuber prices depend on starch density (locally known as DC), though this measure does not apply to transactions between local intermediaries and farmers. Apart from DC, the prices offered by cross-border traders also depend on the size of fresh tubers. Even if these two requirements are fulfilled, by the time intermediaries sell the product, the weight of the fresh tubers has usually depreciated by as much as 11 to 12 per cent. Such quality requirements limit the margin for intermediaries. Again, in an intense oligopsonistic situation, local intermediaries are also price takers with no bargaining power over price and quality.

Intermediaries face other constraints that can affect their margins. They need to store fresh tubers while waiting for market prices to increase. Sometimes they gain, sometimes they lose because there is a high level of price uncertainty in the cassava market. Wide price fluctuations can occur in a single day. Further, the weight of fresh tubers degrades with time and weather. Because of this, intermediaries do not always gain from the cassava business.

Regarding trade in native and modified starch, all processors use an export logistics agent to deal with all export procedures. This means after processing and packaging the products, processing factories simply pay export service fees to the agent, who then arranges for the products to be exported. Some processors use a service package which includes transport from factories to ports, and some arrange transport themselves.

According to data from Cambodia Trade Integration Strategy 2019–23 (MOC 2019) and our estimation based on information from KIIs, at the time of study, cassava processing plants were operating in nine provinces: Oddar Meanchey, Battambang, Pursat, Kampong Chhnang, Kampong Speu, Kandal, Kampong Cham, Tboung Khmum and Kratie (see Figure 4.2). The total annual processing capacity was around 499,000 tonnes of fresh tubers. Kratie had the highest processing capacity (27.1 per cent), followed by Battambang (15.6 per cent), Kandal (12.0 per cent), Pursat (10.0 per cent), Oddar Meanchey (10.0 per cent), Kampong Chhnang (10.0 per cent), Kampong Cham (10.0 per cent), Kampong Speu (6.0 per cent) and Tboung Khmum (1.6 per cent). In total, there were sixteen cassava processing factories (MOC 2019), four of which were Cambodian-owned. At the time of study, only thirteen of these factories were operating, including three Cambodian-owned firms. The combined production share of the latter was 22.9 per cent.

4.4.2 Economic Analysis of Cassava: Costs Faced by Farmers

Cassava production cost, calculated based on information collected from FGDs with cassava farmers, is KHR4.86 million (US$1,216.3) per ha for farmers in Oddar Meanchey province and KHR3.93 m (US$983.5) per ha for those in Tboung Khmum province, excluding loan interest (Table 4.4). This cost is about three times higher than that reported ten years ago by Hing and Thun (2009) for western Cambodia (US$464.8 per ha) and Tboung Khmum province (US$329.1 per ha). The difference between these results is due to the current study's inclusion of opportunity cost for land and additional postharvest costs.

Both current and previous findings show that cassava farmers in western Cambodia face higher production costs than those in the eastern

FIGURE 4.2
Total Domestic Cassava Processing Capacity (Tonnes Per Year of Raw Material)

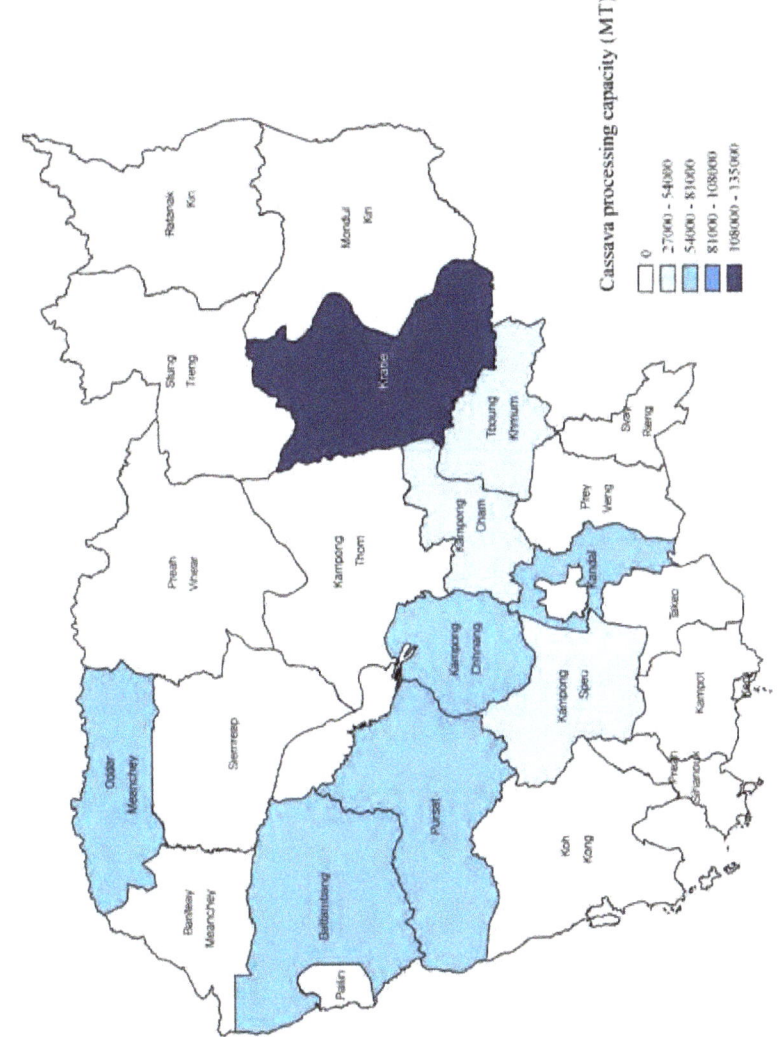

Source: Authors' computation using data from Cambodia Trade Integration Strategy 2019–23 (MOC 2019).

FIGURE 4.3
Benefit Distribution (US$ Per Tonne of Fresh Tubers) Among Key Actors in Three Distribution Channels of the Cassava Value Chain

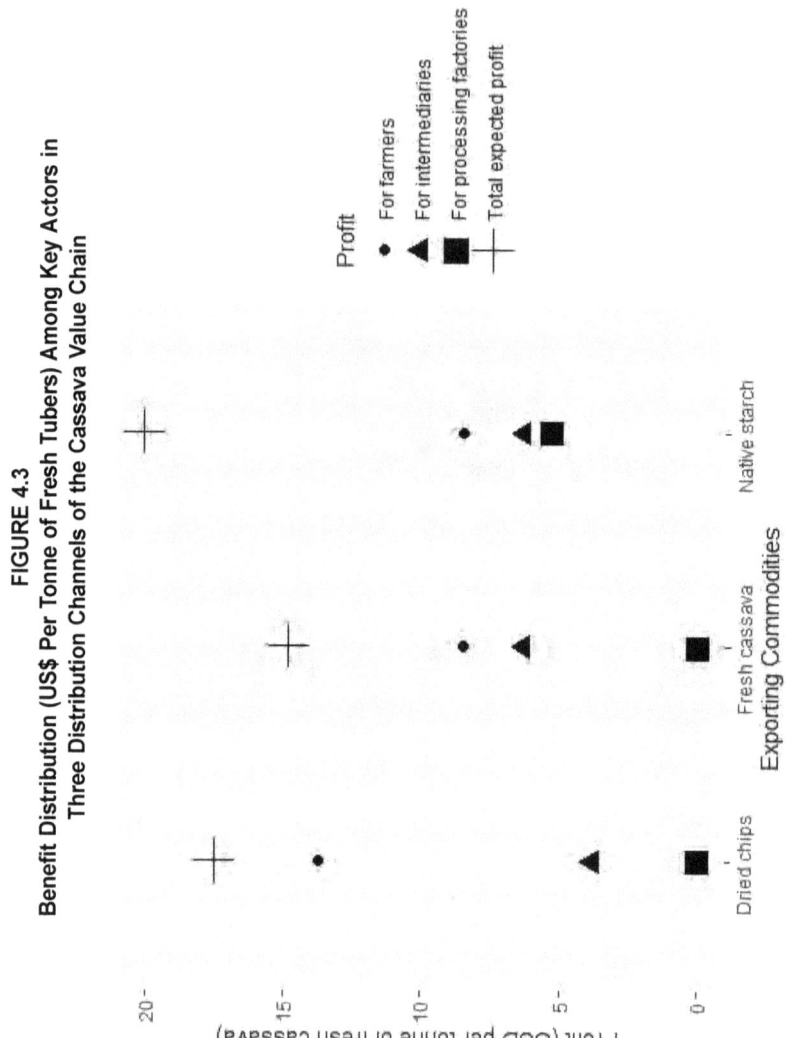

Source: Authors' compilation using primary data.

TABLE 4.4
Cassava Production Costs in the Selected Provinces

Activities		Tboung Khmum				Oddar Meanchey			
	Unit	Quantity	Unit Cost (US$/ha)	Total Cost (US$/ha)		Unit	Quantity	Unit Cost (US$/ha)	Total Cost (US$/ha)
A *Soil preparation*				485.0					372.5
1 Land rent	ha	1	375.0	375.0		ha	1	125.0	125.0
2 Bed raising	time/ha	2	25.0	50.0		time/ha	2	93.8	187.6
3 Fertilizer	bag/ha	2	30.0	60.0		bag/ha	2	30.0	60.0
B *Planting*				228.5					292.5
1 Stem for seed	bunch/ha	100	1.8	175.0		bunch/ha	150	1.5	225.0
2 Labour for planting	ha	1	50.0	50.0		ha	1	62.5	62.5
3 Hormone	bottle/ha	2	1.8	3.5		litre/ha	1	5.0	5.0
C *Maintenance*				95.0					92.5
1 Pesticide	bucket/ha	2	15.0	30.0		bucket/ha	2	13.8	27.5
2 Labour for pesticide spraying	person/ha	2	7.5	15.0		ha	1	15.0	15.0
3 Weeding	person/ha	10	5.0	50.0		person/ha	10	5.0	50.0
D *Harvest*				100.0					62.5
1 Uprooting (tractor)	ha	0	0	0		ha	1	62.5	62.5
2 Uprooting (labourers)	person/ha	20	5.0	100.0			0	0	0
E *Postharvest*				75.0					396.3
1 Labour for chopping/drying	tonne	—	0	0		tonne	11	20.0	220.0
2 Electricity/fuel	litre	—	0	0		litre	30	0.9	26.3
3 Transport	time	20	3.75	75.0		tonne	20	7.5	150.0
Total costs				983.5					1,216.4
Total costs plus loan interest (16.8% annually)				1,148.7					1,420.6

Source: Authors' computation based on primary data.

part. The main reason for this difference is higher postharvest costs in the former. Because Thailand restricts the import of fresh cassava, cross-border traders mainly buy dried cassava chips. Farmers who sell fresh tubers therefore face relatively low postharvest costs (see Table 4.4).

Table 4.5 shows the average return and profit among cassava farmers in Tboung Khmum and Oddar Meanchey provinces. Farmers in Tboung Khmum get US$93.8 per tonne for fresh tubers sold to Vietnamese traders, higher than the US$70.0 per tonne farmers in Oddar Meanchey get from selling fresh tubers to Thai traders. However, some farmers in Oddar Meanchey process cassava into dried chips, which fetches US$160.0 per tonne. Despite weight loss of 16 per cent, they can make over three times more profit from selling dried chips than farmers in Tboung Khmum province make from selling fresh tubers. This is also because cassava yields in Oddar Meanchey province are higher than in Tboung Khmum province. However, if loan interest is included, price uncertainty means that cassava farmers in both provinces are in danger of making a lower profit or even a loss.

Based on data from FGDs, KIIs and secondary sources, it is also important to look at the profit distribution among key actors in the chain. Three different cassava value chain distribution channels generate different value-added and different profitability, as shown in Figure 4.3. Because there are different outputs at different stages of the value chain engaged in by different actors, the profit for each channel is calculated in US dollars per tonne of fresh tubers, considered the farm-gate product in the upstream part of the chain. Thus, outputs of native starch and chips are converted into the volume of fresh tubers used to make those products. This computation intends to compare the profit generated by different actors and by different outputs (i.e., dried chips, fresh tubers and native starch).

At US$20.1, the export of processed cassava generates the largest total profit per tonne of fresh tubers compared to US$17.5 for dried chip export and US$14.8 for fresh tuber export. Among the three types of key actors in the three channels, farmers make a higher profit than intermediaries and processing factories, and they can generate more profit from the sale of dried chips. However, the accuracy of official data on the number of actors engaged in each channel is dubious, hindering estimation of the profit distribution on a macro scale, for example, the percentages of profit generated by farmers, intermediaries and processing factories as a whole

TABLE 4.5
Returns and Profit from Cassava Production for Farmers

Activities	Unit	Tboung Khmum				Oddar Meanchey			
		Quantity	Weight Loss (%)	Quantity Sold	Unit Rate (US$/t)	Total Revenue (US$/ha)	Quantity	Weight Loss (%)	Quantity Sold	Unit Rate (US$/t)	Total Revenue (US$/ha)

Activities	Unit	Quantity	Weight Loss (%)	Quantity Sold	Unit Rate (US$/t)	Total Revenue (US$/ha)	Quantity	Weight Loss (%)	Quantity Sold	Unit Rate (US$/t)	Total Revenue (US$/ha)
Sales											
Fresh roots	t/ha	14	16.0	11.8	93.8	1,103	20	16.0	16.8	70.0	1,176
Dried chips	t/ha	—	—	—	—	—	10	—	—	160.0	1,600
Total sale revenues						1,103					2,776
Loss on reduction rate for selling fresh roots						210					224
Profit before interest payment											
Fresh roots	ha					119					
Dried chips	ha										384

Source: Authors' computation based on primary data.

in Cambodia. Another important note is that even though farmers make more profit, as shown in Figure 4.3, because the profit is proportional to the volume of fresh tubers transacted, farmers as a whole do not make as much profit as other actor types. Farmers can make more profit from selling dried chips, but most of them sell fresh tubers. This constraint on profit maximization stems from limited land size, the number of production cycles per year and yield, which is possibly a function of growing techniques.

4.5 VALUE CHAIN ANALYSIS OF SUGARCANE

4.5.1 Value Chain Mapping

Based on trade data retrieved from Comtrade (2019) and collected from exporters, the major products produced and traded in the sugarcane value chain are white sugar, raw sugar and refined sugar, which share the same six-digit HS code (170111). Sugar processing concentration creates byproducts that are traded, such as molasses (HS 1703), biogas, waste products for making compost or mulch, and furnace ash for improving soil fertility.

The final sugar products are traded through two routes: 80 per cent goes to domestic markets (demand), and 20 per cent is exported. In 2016, final and semi-final sugarcane products were exported to three major destinations. Vietnam was the largest importer of Cambodian sugarcane products, accounting for 75 per cent of the total, followed by the EU at 20 per cent and China at only 5 per cent (Comtrade 2019).

The value chain of this industrial commodity has attracted participation from several types of actors, namely lead firms, financial institutions, input suppliers, inter-firms,[2] private-sector sugarcane producers, transporters, farm service providers (contractors) and labourers. Figure 4.4 depicts the interactions between these actors throughout the chain.

Because the industry requires large investments, smallholders' share of production is extremely small, at 0.30 per cent of the total sugarcane produced in Cambodia (ODC 2016). In addition, this small amount of raw material is not used in domestic processing plants but exported to processing factories in Vietnam.

Lead firms play dominant roles in domestic processing linkages, leading to a highly vertically integrated value chain. Owing to the government's economic land concession (ELC) policy, these firms have been granted long-

FIGURE 4.4
Cambodia's Sugarcane Value Chain

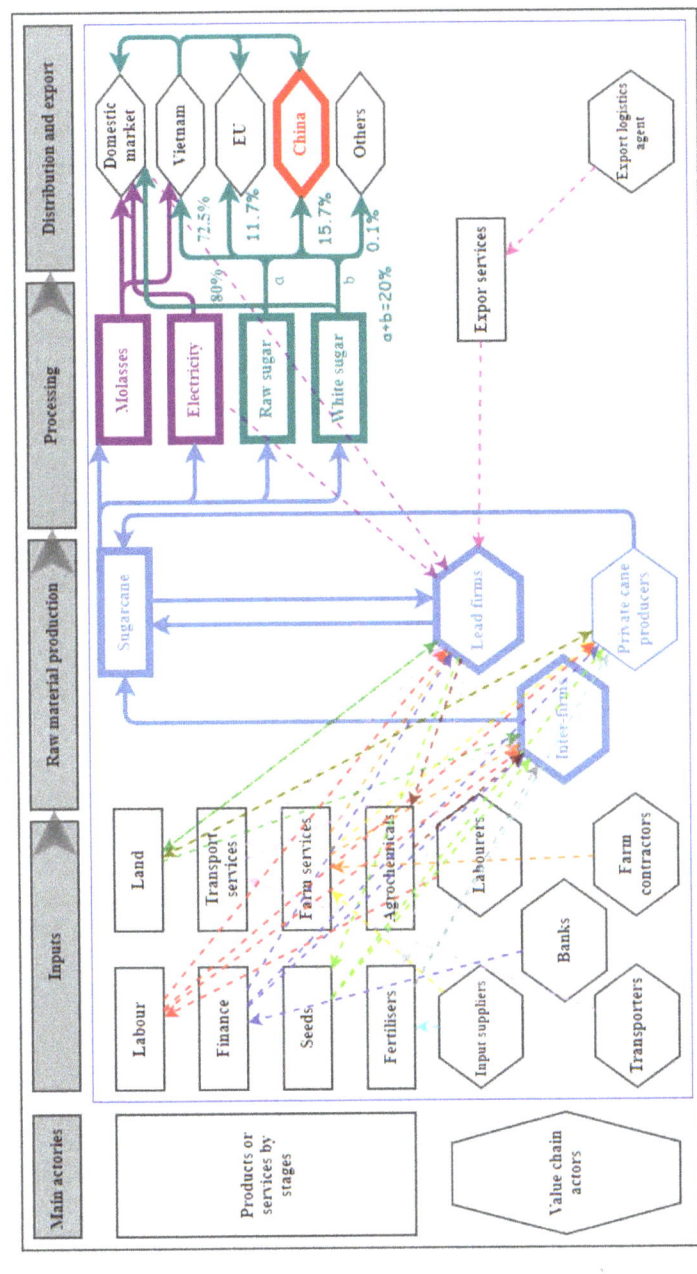

Note: The different colours used in this figure differentiate important flows in the value chain.
Source: Authors' work based on primary data and ITC TradeMap (2019).

term leases of up to seventy years on land for industrial-scale sugarcane production. Phnom Penh Sugar Co. Ltd, one of the three existing lead firms, leases a portion of ELC and supplies inputs on interest-free credit to several inter-firms to produce and supply sugarcane to its processing plants. The other lead firms, Rui Feng and Yellow Field International, not only lease ELCs but also buy raw material from various inter-firms which cultivate sugarcane on their private land or ELC. Another small percentage (0.7 per cent) of sugarcane is supplied to lead firms by private sector cane producers, who grow sugarcane on their own land with some technical support and inputs from lead firms. Lead firms also create linkages with hauliers engaged in transporting raw material from sugarcane plantations to processing plants and transporting final or semi-final products from processing factories. In relation to their raw material production, lead firms have a straightforward connection with input suppliers, who are the main input importers. Because of the increasing use of machines in sugarcane production, lead firms link directly with labourers in processing plants, mostly by providing full-time jobs. To cover the cost of their entire business operation, lead firms can obtain loans from both international and local banks.

Apart from the direct links between most actors and the lead firms, the sugarcane business entails several more linkages between other actors. In order to supply raw material to lead firms, inter-firms need to: (1) buy agrochemicals directly from input suppliers; (2) link with farm service providers to hire labour for sugarcane growing, maintenance and harvesting; (3) hire hauliers to transport sugarcane from plantation to processing plant; and (4) obtain loans from financial institutes to cover these costs. Notably, the computation based on information from lead firms shows that thirty-six inter-firms were involved in cultivating and harvesting sugarcane on a total area of about 30,000 ha in 2018. Private sugarcane producers growing sugarcane on various farm sizes ranging from 30 ha to 200 ha also require linkages with labourers for production activities and with hauliers for transporting raw material to processing factories. There were thirty-six private sugarcane producers operating in the study area covering a total area of 800 ha. Even though the scale of production is a lot smaller than that of inter-firms and lead firms, financial capital is crucial for private sugarcane producers, creating another linkage with financial institutes.

Although labourers' involvement in the chain has gradually become less important due to the shift towards mechanized production, the procurement of labourers is still coordinated by farm service providers as inter-firms barely use any modern farm equipment. However, this linkage is seasonal. If inter-firms start to invest in mechanized production (e.g., tractors), farm service providers will be at risk of disappearing from the chain, and only a relatively small number of labourers will be engaged in sugarcane farming and processing in the form of full-time workers.

Governance structures in the sugarcane value chain vary in different linkages. Only a few direct linkages to lead firms are through written contract: with the government for the granting of seventy-year ELCs, with international financial institutes and local banks for financial capital, with inter-firms and private cane producers for raw materials, with input suppliers for inputs (e.g. fertilizers and agro-chemicals), and with full-time workers. Lead firms do not use written contracts with other actors engaged in casual jobs (Figure 4.4).

The three main stages of the product flow (raw material production, processing, and sale or export) directly engage only four types of actors on a seasonal basis: cane producers,[3] hauliers, farm service providers and casual labourers. The frequency of these actors' involvement varies according to their importance for specific activities in each stage. In the stage of raw material[4] production, all actors are mainly involved in harvesting raw material for around four months from December to March. Lead firms use only full-time labourers on their plantations, while inter-firms and private cane producers still use casual labourers procured through farm service providers (contractors). It is the same for the other two activities: soil preparation and maintenance. In this sense, it is clear that raw material production relies on mechanization as lead firms dominate the production area. In terms of processing, one lead firm, Phnom Penh Sugar Co. Ltd, functions year-round, while Rui Feng and Yellow Field International process sugarcane in the harvest season only. Other actors besides full-time labourers are engaged in this stage. Regarding the stage of sale and export, it is a year-round activity for only lead firms.

4.5.2 Economic Analysis in Sugarcane Value Chain

Various costs arise in the four main stages of Cambodia's sugarcane value chain: raw material production, transport of raw material, processing, transport of final and semi-final products. As the computational results in Figure 4.5 indicate, 87 per cent of the value chain budget is concentrated in two main stages: raw material production (59 per cent) and raw material

FIGURE 4.5
Cost in Various Stages of Cambodia's Sugarcane Value Chain

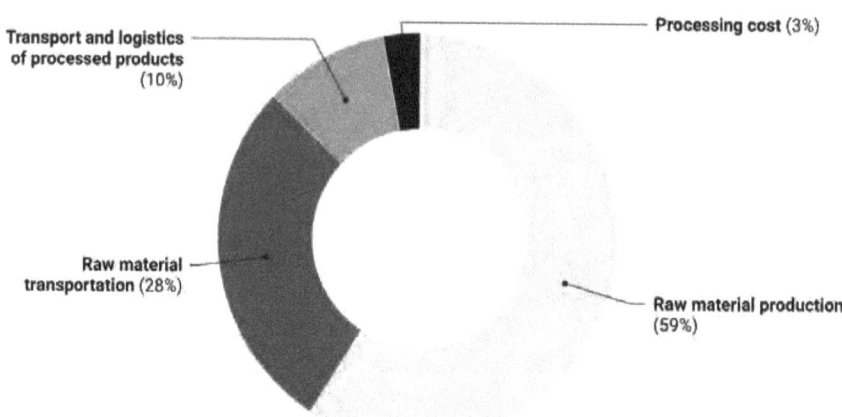

Source: Computational results based on primary data.

transport (28 per cent). The remaining 13 per cent is for the two downstream stages from processing factories to wholesale warehouses or ports.

Raw material production embeds five types of cost encompassing land fees, variable tradeable inputs,[5] fixed tradeable inputs, labour and loan interest.[6] Variable tradeable inputs impose the highest cost burden on sugarcane production. Input and labour costs amount to around US$1,400 per ha in the first year and decrease to US$900 per ha in the following years. Based on the data collected from KIIs, the average tradeable input cost (US$900 per ha) is seven times higher than the average labour cost (US$125 per ha). Fixed tradeable inputs, which are all the exported products, require a huge amount of investment at the beginning of the production cycle. However, when amortized over the fifteen-year depreciation period, the production cost of fixed tradeable inputs is lower than that of variable tradeable inputs. Land cost does not reflect the market value of this valuable production asset because the vast majority of sugarcane in Cambodia is produced in ELCs. Loan interest, given the capital investments procured from financial institutes, is included; at US$252 per ha per year, this is the second-highest cost in raw material production (see the detailed cost calculation in Annex 4.5).

Raw material transport refers to the transport of sugarcane from plantation to processing factory. This is a highly seasonal activity, mainly from December to mid-March, due to the seasonality of satisfactory sugar content. The average market value of transport is around US$9 per tonne (calculated based on information collected from KIIs with hauliers and firms' representatives). However, it can be lower or higher depending on the distance and complexity of products.

The production cost of 1 tonne of refined sugar is considerably low. Even so, processing plants require enormous amounts of investment by lead firms. The reason why this cost is low is because of the efficiency and long-term (up to fifty years) depreciation of factory equipment. Relying on the computational result, it takes only six minutes to process 1 ha of sugarcane (70 tonnes on average); the processing plant of Phnom Penh Sugar Co. Ltd, for instance, is capable of processing up to 18,000 tonnes of sugarcane or producing about 1,800 tonnes of refined sugar per day.

The transport and export logistics costs of cane sugar are about three times lower than that of raw material, at 10 per cent and 28 per cent, respectively, of the total cost. These costs are proportional to loading volume and distance. Notably, based on our interviews with processors and according to official data from the Ministry of Commerce (2019), transport and export logistics costs in Cambodia are a lot higher than in other large producing countries.

Revenue is distributed more or less to all actors in the chain. Based on various data sources including FGDs, KIIs and secondary sources (e.g., ITC 2019), it is possible to provide an estimation of income distribution on a macro scale. Income is proportional to the number of products transacted at an average price, and particular types of actors receive income from one or more actors depending on their role in the value chain. Downstream actors generate income from sales of processed or semi-processed goods to both domestic and international markets, and most upstream actors (direct and indirect) generate income from supplying raw materials, labour and local services. The government generates income from the value chain through taxes.

Profit distribution, then, is a function of income and total costs for the activities in which chain actors are engaged. Looking at the adjusted trade data in 2016 shown in Figures 4.6 and 4.7, the large investors holding stakes in lead firms are the main distributors gaining the largest share of gross revenue, followed by inter-firms and input suppliers, while private cane producers have the smallest revenue. The percentage of profit seems proportional to the amount of revenue generated by each actor; however, due to data confidentiality, it is impossible to separate the profits of lead firms, input suppliers and financial institutes. Figure 4.7 depicts how

FIGURE 4.6
Income Distribution in the Sugarcane Value Chain

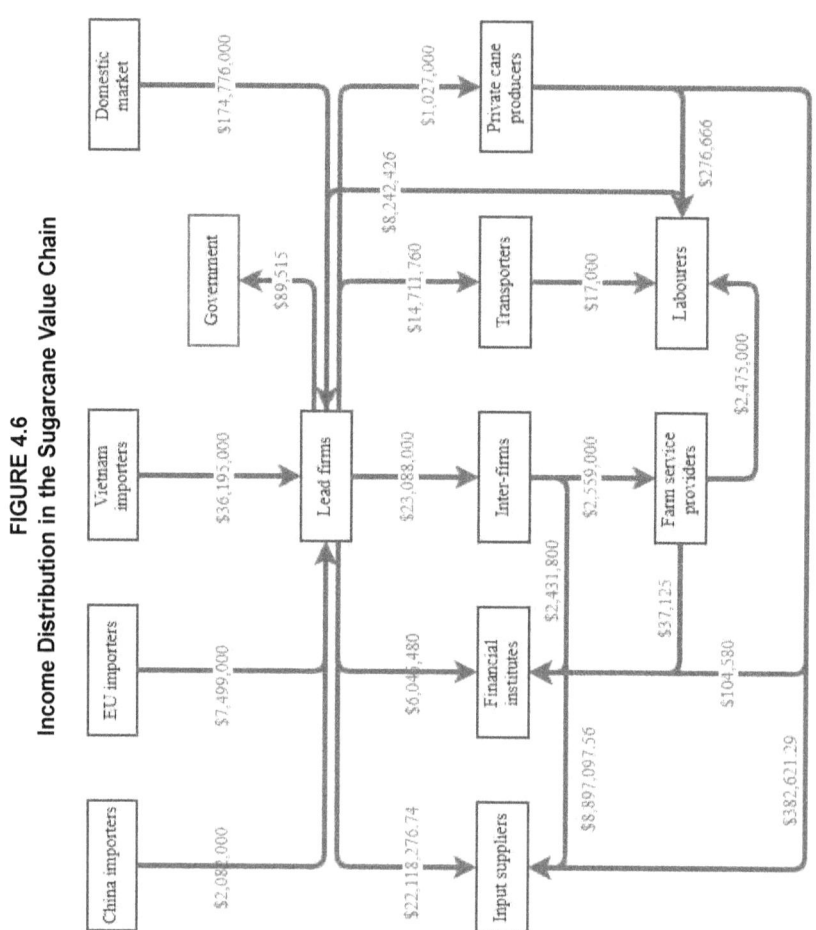

Source: Authors' computation.

FIGURE 4.7
Profit Distribution Among All Actors in the Sugarcane Value Chain (per cent)

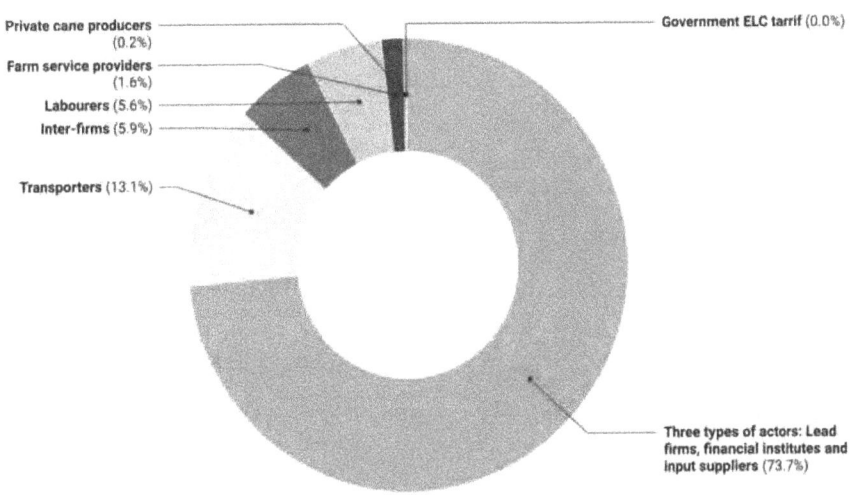

Source: Authors' computation.

these three types of large actors accumulate 73.7 per cent of the total profit generated by the entire sugarcane value chain. Because there is more than one transaction with multiple actors in the sugarcane business operation, the remaining 26.3 per cent is shared among six types of actors: hauliers (13.1 per cent), inter-firms (5.9 per cent), labourers (5.6 per cent), farm service providers (1.6 per cent), private cane producers (0.2 per cent) and the government (0.01 per cent). This result does not reflect the profit of individuals, but the types of actors. For instance, thirty-six inter-firms (see section 4.5.1) share 5.9 per cent of the total profit of the entire chain. These inter-firms receive more or less profit depending on the outputs they produce and the actual costs they face. Because of data constraints, this section does not look into micro-distribution among each specific type of actor.

4.6 NTMS IMPOSED BY CHINA ON THE IMPORT OF SELECTED COMMODITIES

According to the most recent UNCTAD data, China has imposed a total of 5,705 NTMs on imports from eight different groups of trading partners, and Cambodia features in all groups. By category, technical barriers to trade (TBT) constitute the largest proportion of total NTMs (69.3 per cent), followed by export-related measures (EXP) (12.1 per cent), sanitary and phytosanitary measures (SPS) (10.6 per cent), quality control measures (QC) (5.0 per cent), pre-shipment inspection (INSP) (1.2 per cent), other measures (OTH) (1.0 per cent) and price control measures (PC) (0.9 per cent). The following section describes the NTMs affecting Cambodia's exports to China of two processed products—cassava starch (HS110814) and cane sugar (HS170111), and two raw materials—cassava tubers (HS071410) and sugarcane (HS121293). This is followed by a focus on the perspectives of domestic value chain actors on the existing NTMs they face when exporting agricultural products to China.

4.6.1 NTMs Affecting Cambodia's Export of Selected Commodities to China

This subsection takes stock of the number and type of NTMs, to the extent possible, affecting Cambodia's exports to China of two processed commodities and their raw materials—cassava starch and cane sugar, and cassava tubers and sugarcane—throughout the three decades to 2016 (Figure 4.8), with particular attention to the abrupt increase in the use of NTMs between 2010 and 2016. The UNCTAD database characterizes all NTMs on these four commodities as multilateral, meaning they were imposed on China's other trading partners, not just Cambodia. Exporters face more NTMs, both in absolute number and categories, on the export of raw materials than on processed commodities. For the latter, they must comply with six categories, involving 100 NTMs for cassava starch and 91 NTMs for cane sugar. And for the former, exporters must comply with seven categories, involving 205 NTMs for cassava tubers and 167 NTMs for sugarcane (TRAINS 2015).

Disaggregating the data by NTM category, the number of TBT imposed by China on its imports of the four commodities from Cambodia increased dramatically in 2015, followed by a large increase in the use of SPS measures in 2016, not to mention the eleven SPS measures on sugarcane that appeared in 2011. At the time of writing, the number of NTMs on these commodities had remained unchanged since 2016. TBT measures were the most prolific, followed by SPS measures. Cambodia, unlike the countries listed individually in Table 4.6, is not subject to country-specific NTMs on

FIGURE 4.8
The Number of Active NTMs by Category Imposed by China on Raw Materials and Processed Commodities

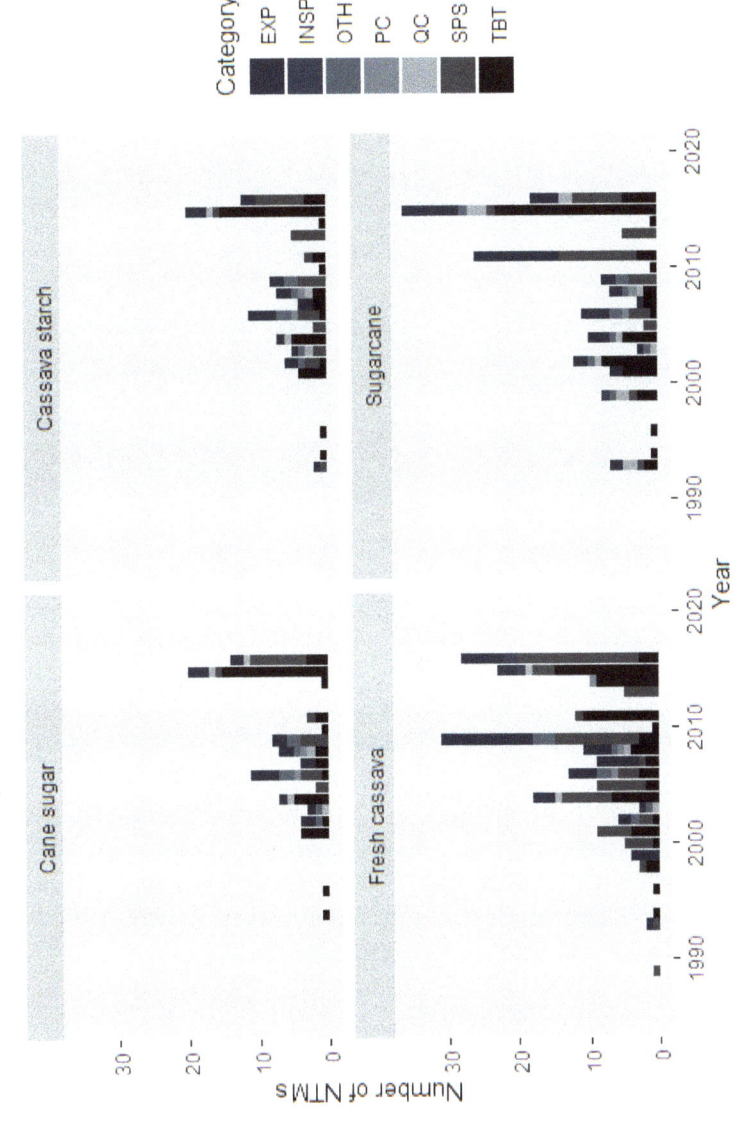

Source: Authors' computation based on UNCTAD database (https://trains.unctad.org/Forms/TableViewDetails.aspx?mode=modify).

TABLE 4.6
Number of NTMs Affecting Different Trading Partners' Exports of the Four Products to China as of 2020

China's Trading Partners	Number of NTMs Imposed by China on the Four Selected Commodities			
	Cane Sugar	Cassava Starch	Fresh Cassava	Sugarcane
All members	91	100	205	167
Belgium, Germany, Netherlands			2	
Taiwan				2
Ethiopia	3	3	3	3
European Union			1	
Germany, New Zealand			1	
Hong Kong			1	2
Macao				1
Ireland			1	
Japan	6	6	8	7
Madagascar			13	
Moldova	6	6	8	6
Myanmar			1	
Netherlands, New Zealand	1	1	1	1
Nigeria			9	
Philippines				1
Russian Federation			1	
South Africa	9	9	11	9

Note: "All members" refers to those exporting countries subject to China's multilateral NTMs only.
Source: Authors' compilation based on UNCTAD database (https://trains.unctad.org/).

exports of the four commodities to China, meaning Cambodian exporters face the minimum number of NTMs. Cambodia's rice exporters, however, must comply with twelve bilateral NTMs (ten SPS and two TBT measures), imposed since 2016, on China's imports of paddy rice (HS100610), milled rice (HS100630) and broken rice (HS100640).

The upward trend in the number of NTMs, especially the abrupt increase in TBT and SPS measures since 2011, especially in 2015 and 2016 (see Figure 4.8), suggests China is paying more attention to improving the quality of its agricultural imports. It would appear that China has shifted its focus from restricting the volume of agricultural imports to ensuring food safety, human and animal health, product quality and environmental protection. However, all exports to China of the selected commodities must comply with all NTM categories, not just TBT and SPS. Figure 4.9 shows the ten most used forms of NTMs affecting Cambodia's exports of the four products in 2020. This data is extracted from Table 4.7, which gives the number of NTMs applied, and Figure 4.10, which shows the increase in the number NTMs between 2010 and 2016, when China started tightening restrictions on its imports of the four commodities. At a glance, the same numbers and types of NTMs were imposed on both processed commodities (cassava starch and cane sugar), whereas raw materials (cassava tubers/chips and sugarcane) were mostly subject to different numbers of NTMs.

Among all NTMs, the most commonly used was B83, which in Chapter B of the UNCTAD NTM classification refers to import certification requirements for TBT reasons. B83 was applied fourteen times, affecting every export of sugarcane, but was used less often for fresh cassava (nine times), cassava starch (seven times) and cane sugar (seven times). B83 requirements mainly came into force between 2010 and 2020. They were imposed on sugarcane four times in 2015 and once in 2016; on fresh cassava once in 2011, once in 2014 and three times in 2015; on cassava starch three times in 2015; and on cane sugar three times in 2015.

P39, export restrictions not elsewhere specified (Chapter P on export-related measures), was the second most commonly used NTM on exports to China of fresh cassava (thirteen times), sugarcane (ten times), cassava starch (nine times) and cane sugar (nine times). The majority of P39 requirements came into force before 2010. This measure was most recently imposed in 2015 (once on each selected commodity) and 2016 (once on fresh cassava and once on sugarcane).

B31, labelling requirements for TBT reasons (Chapter B), similarly to P39, was applied to fresh cassava thirteen times, but less often to sugarcane (eight times), cassava starch (seven times) and cane sugar (seven times). Specifically, labelling requirements stipulate the type, colour and size of printing on packages and product labels and consumer information such as voltage, components, use instructions, and safety and security advice. The official language to be used is another criterion included in this measure.

E1, non-automatic import-licensing procedures other than authorizations under Chapter A on SPS and Chapter B on TBT, was the second most common NTM (thirteen times) restricting imports of sugarcane after three more impositions in 2015 and two more in 2016. There is no detailed

FIGURE 4.9
The Most Used NTMs by Code on China's Imports of the Four Commodities as of 2020

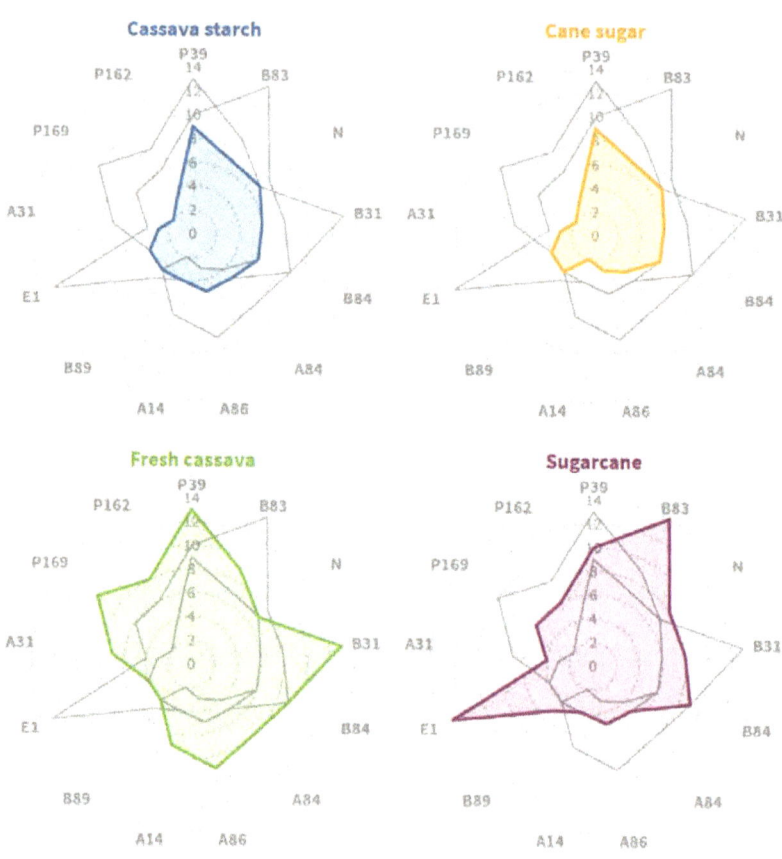

Source: Authors' compilation based on UNCTAD database (https://trains.unctad.org/)

TABLE 4.7
Number of NTMs by Code Imposed on the Selected Products as of 2020

Code	Product	Count
P39	Fresh cassava	13
P39	Cane sugar	9
P39	Sugarcane	10
P39	Cassava starch	9
B83	Cane sugar	7
B83	Sugarcane	14
B83	Cassava starch	7
B83	Fresh cassava	9
B31	Cane sugar	6
B31	Sugarcane	8
B31	Fresh cassava	13
B31	Cassava starch	6
B84	Fresh cassava	9
B84	Cane sugar	6
B84	Sugarcane	9
B84	Cassava starch	6
N	Cassava starch	7
N	Fresh cassava	7
N	Sugarcane	8
N	Cane sugar	7
E1	Cane sugar	4
E1	Sugarcane	13
E1	Cassava starch	4
E1	Fresh cassava	—
A84	Fresh cassava	8
A84	Cassava starch	—
A84	Cane sugar	4
A86	Sugarcane	5
A86	Fresh cassava	9
A86	Cassava starch	—
A86	Cane sugar	—
P162	Cane sugar	—
P162	Cassava starch	—
P162	Fresh cassava	8
P162	Sugarcane	6
P169	Sugarcane	6
P169	Fresh cassava	10
B89	Cane sugar	4
B89	Fresh cassava	5
B89	Sugarcane	5
A14	Cassava starch	4
A14	Fresh cassava	7
A14	Sugarcane	4
A31	Fresh cassava	7
A31	Cane sugar	—
A31	Cassava starch	—
B21	Fresh cassava	—
B21	Sugarcane	—
B21	Cane	—
B21	Cassava	—
A19	Fresh cassava	3
A19	Sugarcane	—
B851	Fresh cassava	3
B851	—	—
P14	Fresh	—
P15	Fresh cassava	3
P161	Fresh cassava	3
B7	Fresh cassava	7
B7	Cassava starch	—
B7	—	—
P163	—	—
P163	—	—
A64	Fresh cassava	4
A851	—	—
A851	—	—
B33	Fresh	—
B42	—	—
P33	Sugarcane	5
A83	Fresh cassava	7
A83	Sugarcane	—
A83	—	—
A33	Fresh cassava	—
A33	—	—
A33	—	—
A63	Fresh cassava	4
A89	—	—
F61	—	—
F61	—	—
F71	—	—
P19	Fresh	—
P31	—	—
B82	—	—
B82	Cane sugar	—
B22	Fresh cassava	—
B22	—	—
B22	—	—
B19	Sugarcane	3
B19	—	—
B19	—	—
P9	—	—
P9	—	—
B81	Fresh	—
B852	Fresh	—
P19	—	—
B82	Fresh	—
B82	—	—
B82	—	—
A21	Fresh	—
A15	Fresh	—
P13	Fresh	—
O	—	—
O	—	—
B6	B6	—
C4	—	—
C3	—	—
C3	—	—

Source: Authors' compilation based on UNCTAD database (https://trains.unctad.org/).

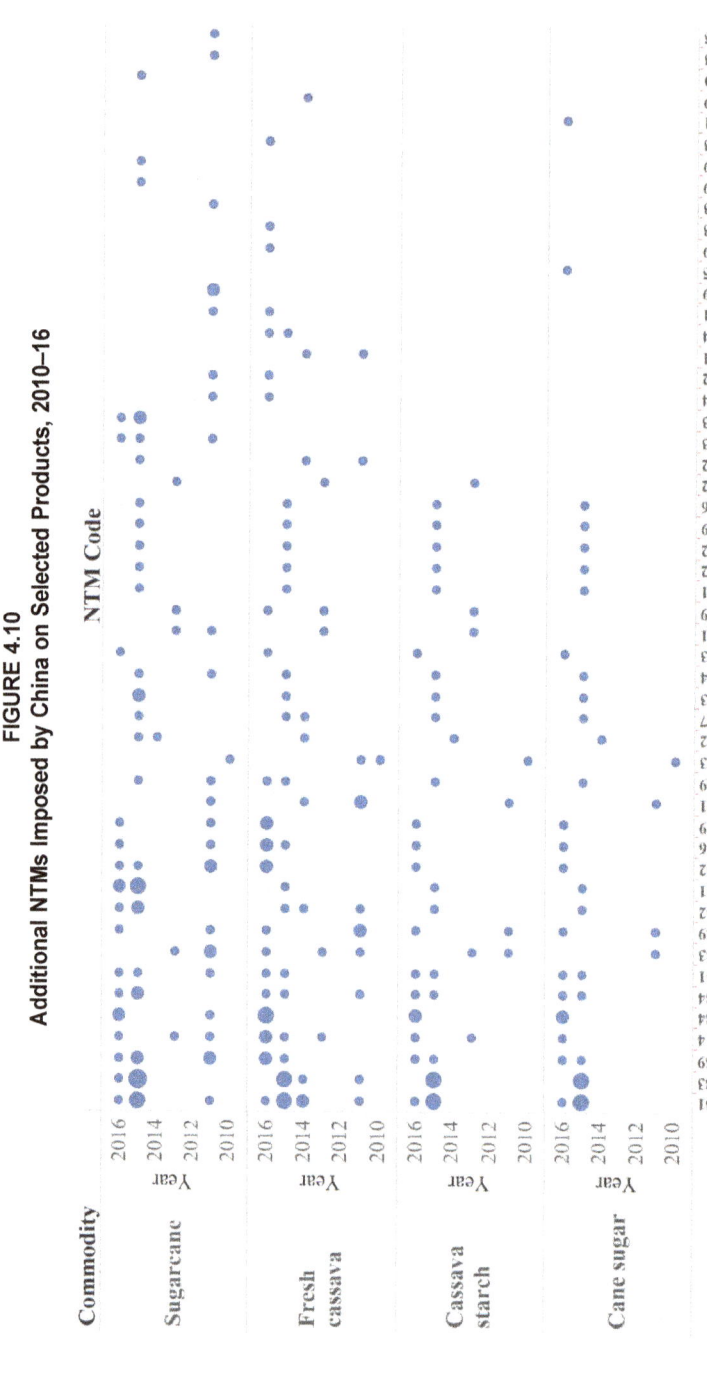

FIGURE 4.10
Additional NTMs Imposed by China on Selected Products, 2010–16

Notes: The largest dot represents 4 NTMs, while the smallest is 1. The number of NTMs remained unchanged as of 2020.
Source: Authors' compilation based on UNCTAD database (https://trains.unctad.org/).

structure under E1, which is a non-technical measure, in the dataset, meaning that this measure includes E11 (licensing for economic reasons) containing four measures and E12 (licensing for non-economic reasons) containing six measures. However, E1 measures were imposed only four times on both cassava starch and cane sugar but not on fresh cassava.

P169, conformity-assessment measures not elsewhere specified, was the most commonly used measure (ten times) on exports of fresh cassava, with one more imposition in 2015 and two more in 2016. This measure was also imposed on exports of sugarcane (six times), but not on cassava starch or cane sugar.

B84, inspection requirements by the importing country, was also in force, weighted more towards raw materials—fresh cassava (eight times) and sugarcane (eight times), though with a considerable number applied to processed commodities—cassava starch (six times) and cane sugar (six times). China has increased its imposition of this measure twice since 2010, with one more on each of cane sugar, cassava starch and fresh cassava and two on sugarcane in 2015 and one more on each commodity in 2016.

A86, quarantine requirements, also came into force in large number, with nine impositions on fresh cassava, five each on sugarcane and cassava starch and three on cane sugar. Since 2010, there have been seven more impositions of A86: one on cane sugar and one on cassava starch in 2016, two on sugarcane (one in 2011 and one in 2016), and three on fresh cassava (one in 2015 and two in 2016).

N, intellectual property rights in trade, came into force in large numbers before 2010, ranking it among the top ten most used NTMs. It is a broad measure with many sub-measures, including: N1 (eligibility and maintenance) covering patents, geographical indications, industrial designs, copyrights and trademarks; N2 (exhaustion) covering the conditions under which intellectual property rights can no longer be enforced, with rules for national, regional and international markets; and N3 (enforcement) covering border measures, civil remedies, criminal remedies and administrative remedies.

A84, inspection requirements, was used more on raw materials, with eight impositions on fresh cassava and five on sugarcane, but only three on each of the two processed products.

P162, requirements by the exporting country to conduct an inspection of the products before they can be exported excluding laboratory testing, mostly affected fresh cassava (eight times) and sugarcane (six times), followed by cassava starch (thrice) and cane sugar (thrice). There were four more impositions of this measure on sugarcane exports, two in 2011, one in 2015 and one in 2016, but only one more on each of the other three commodities in 2016.

A14, authorization requirements for SPS reasons, was mostly used on fresh cassava (seven times), followed by sugarcane (four times), cassava starch (four times) and cane sugar (twice). Four more impositions of this measure on fresh cassava came into force after 2010 (one in 2013, one in 2015 and two in 2016). Three of the four impositions on sugarcane came into force around the same time (one in 2011, one in 2013 and one in 2016), as did two of the four impositions on cassava starch (one in 2013 and one in 2016), with only one more on cane sugar in 2016.

A31, labelling requirements for food safety information that should be provided to the consumer, is also one the ten most prolific NTMs, most commonly affecting fresh cassava exporters (seven times), followed by sugarcane (four times) cassava starch (thrice) and cane sugar (thrice). Three (out of seven) impositions of this measure on cane sugar came into force in the last decade (2010–20), along with two (out of four) on fresh cassava and two (out of three) on the two processed commodities.

Although not as prolific, all other NTMs restricting exports of the four commodities to China must be complied with. For instance, A21 (tolerance limits for residues of or contamination by certain substances) and A64 (storage and transport conditions) are the banes of many small-scale actors wanting to enter the Chinese market. Therefore, it is worth looking at all categories of NTMs, not just the ones used most often. The coming into force of C3 (requirement to pass through the specified port of customs) and C4 (import monitoring, surveillance and automatic licensing measures) under Chapter C: Pre-shipment Inspection and Other Formalities, for instance, can create a considerable burden for exporters, especially from developing countries. Data shows that China applies C3 and C4 on its imports of raw materials (fresh cassava and sugarcane) only. Non-technical measures under Chapter F: Price Control Measures, which encompass F61 (custom inspection, processing and servicing fees), F69 (additional charges) and F71 (consumption taxes), can add to the cost of importing and exporting. Chapter O: Rules of Origin, only recently imposed in 2015 on the exports of fresh cassava to China in addition to the two existing impositions on sugarcane exports, is another barrier that induces procedural obstacles for exporters to overcome.

In sum, Cambodia faces the same number and type of NTMs as other exporting countries (i.e., its competitors) on exports of the four commodities to China; and is not subject to country-specific (bilateral) NTMs except for those on rice exports. It is therefore important to reflect on the performance of Cambodia's domestic value chains (supply side) to gain more insight into local perspectives on compliance with China's NTMs.

4.6.2 Perspectives of Domestic Value Chain Actors on Compliance with NTMs

NTMs represent a major barrier to the export of Cambodian agricultural products. Dao (2014) reported that exporters were finding it extremely difficult to comply with the SPS and TBT requirements imposed by trading partners. However, the level of difficulty in meeting these standards seems to have declined over time. A later study by Ven (2017) found that Cambodian processors and exporters of agricultural products were capable of meeting international standards. What most studies have found and recommended be improved are procedural obstacles related to export measures (ITC 2014; Ven 2015, 2017), suggesting the exporting side needs to be given greater attention. That said, the Ministry of Commerce (MOC 2019) recently asserted that SPS measures have deterrent effects on agricultural exports to China and suggested bilateral discussions. Our interviews with processors and exporters of processed and semi-processed cassava and sugarcane revealed a rather different picture, however. They are able to comply with all NTMs, but related procedural obstacles that can induce informal fees remain an unresolved and pressing issue.

The entry of large investors into Cambodia's sugarcane and cassava industries has positive effects on the compliance of production lines with NTMs imposed by buyers. This is largely because they make considerable investments in modern technologies and production facilities to boost productivity and product quality. As a result, they have been successful in exporting all types of processed and semi-processed products to international markets. None of the large exporters of native cassava starch and cane sugar reported experiencing export failure caused by quality and standards-related issues (e.g., SPS and TBT). To compete internationally, compliance with international requirements is obligatory for all exporting countries, not only Cambodia.

However, the study finds that only foreign-owned factories are exporting cassava and sugar to China. As well as the advantages gained from their enormous capital investment in technology in line with regulatory requirements and standards, they have experience in accessing Chinese markets. Indeed, they have linkages to China's main importers of native starch and raw cane sugar. However, compliance capability remains a limitation for new and potential market entrants, especially medium-sized and Cambodian-owned firms. To comply with NTMs, medium enterprises need substantial capital to invest in upgrading their processing operations. These barriers have already been foreseen.

Another considerable barrier for aspiring entrants to Chinese markets is that Cambodia's quality assurance system needs to be improved (MOC 2019). Inspection results and certification by local public bodies cannot ascertain the quality of export products because they have not been internationally accredited. The lack of knowledge and practical skills for using advanced analytical equipment also remains a key issue to be overcome.

Large processors have no great concerns about NTMs, but they do have concerns about domestic performance. Processors reported that even though the government has been reforming the customs regime aiming at improving and facilitating trade, high export costs still affect their competitiveness. Informal payments to public officials remain high. But, if they refuse to pay such fees, officers handling customs procedures will most likely create delays and complicate the process. Despite using export logistics agents to deal with the whole export process (from the processor's warehouse to the country of destination), export fees remain stubbornly high, at US$25 to US$55 per tonne (calculated based on data collected from processors). Based on Cambodian Trade Integration Strategy 2019–23 (MOC 2019), exporting goods from Cambodia takes longer and costs more than from Thailand and Vietnam, the two major neighbouring agricultural exporters. Total export cost in Cambodia, including border compliance and documentation, is 32.6 per cent higher than in Thailand and 9.7 per cent higher than in Vietnam. Lead time to export in Cambodia is 69.4 per cent longer than in Thailand and 41.7 per cent longer than in Vietnam.

Based on the face-to-face interviews, processors seem to place more importance on strengthening their competitiveness by reducing production costs and eliminating informal fees rather than petitioning for the removal of NTMs imposed by importing countries. It is reiterated that with large investments from leading investors, large processors are capable of complying with standards requirements. What they suggest would improve their competitiveness is the provision of a cheaper and more reliable electricity supply, better road conditions and connectivity to ports, and the elimination of informal fees through efficient controls at every stage of the clearance procedure. Notably, most of the processing firms exporting processed and semi-processed sugarcane and cassava products to China are owned by Chinese investors.

A constraint of the study relating to the effects of NTMs on other actors is the intensity of informal transactions in the selected products. What we can touch on in this discussion is the slow entry (almost non-existence) of domestic small- and medium-sized enterprises (SMEs) in particular industries. Inadequate financing capacity could be one of the main constraints limiting the market entry of SMEs. Access to funding is vital for aspiring firms to be able to make start-up investments in the processing sector and cover initial operating costs, including compliance with the increasing number of NTMs on international trade.

Another crucial aspect observed in the interviews, with the exception of foreign investors, is the low level of awareness of the importance of NTMs. As discussed in the value chain analysis section, the vast majority of growers (farmers) do not invest in improving the quality of crops; instead, they focus more on increasing crop yield and weight. As a result, they act as price takers with little to no bargaining power in the value chain, which is characterized by a loose governance structure and weak horizontal and vertical coordination. Weak horizontal coordination of small supply quantities from a large number of producers often leads to market failure, information asymmetry and oligopsony, and can become a chronic problem in agricultural product transactions. In such a situation, it seems that no extra incentives will induce smallholders to increase their investments in crop quality to meet export requirements, not in the face of household financial burden, inadequate information about quality assurance, high perishability of agricultural products, and opportunistic behaviour of main buyers favouring short-term self-interest rather than mutual benefit.

4.7 CONCLUSION

This value chain study investigates bottlenecks hindering Cambodian agricultural product exports to China by employing four elements: value chain mapping, governance structure identification, benefit distribution analysis and upgrading performance assessment. Beyond the understanding of domestic value chain performance, descriptive analysis of the non-tariff (NTMs) imposed by China, the importer, is also a core element of the study. Cassava and sugarcane were selected for study due to the volumes and revealed comparative advantages of exports to China.

The study finds that NTMs have indirect effects on the performance of domestic value chains, compounding a vicious cycle of problems facing vulnerable actors in the upstream parts of the value chains. The consequent absence of SMEs in cassava and sugarcane transactions limits the potential of diversifying from agricultural raw materials to high-value products. In turn, the vast majority of domestic processing factories are modern plants, financed in large part by massive inflows of capital from foreign private investors and oriented to supply the Chinese market. This implies that the capability to meet international regulatory and compliance export-import requirements for agrifood products requires a lot of capital, making investment in export-oriented agrifood processing an unattractive option for prospective small and medium investors. With the limited presence of these important actors in the value chain, the capacity of domestic processing plants to absorb locally produced raw materials, cassava in particular, is far lower than the seasonal supply from a large number of smallholders. Because smallholders cannot rely on selling at least part of their produce to domestic plants, they have become price takers in neighbouring countries' cross-border trade channels, wherein transactions are characterized by loose governance and a high level of opportunism. It is therefore reasonable to surmise that the recent increase in the number of NTMs has indirect effects on the agricultural value chains by concentrating upstream oligopsony power and inhibiting the entry of smaller firms downstream.

Appropriate increases in NTMs such as TBT and SPS measures are becoming common to protect producers facing fierce foreign competition and to satisfy consumer demand for safe, sustainable and environmentally friendly products. Exporting countries also use NTMs in this regard. The NTMs imposed by China on cassava and sugarcane, both raw materials and processed goods, are multilateral, applying equally to all exporters from all countries, and fewer in number than those imposed by many comparable OECD members (e.g., Australia, the EU and the US). This suggests that the readiness of domestic supply chains to comply with importing countries' requirements is imperative if chain actors are to reap the benefits of participating in global value chains.

This study concludes that to realize the optimum potential of promising agricultural export-driven industries in the long run, upgrading the performance of domestic value chains is more critical than minimizing the number of NTMs. Besides, the purpose of the majority of NTMs is regulatory cooperation, aiming to protect human, animal and plant life and safeguard the environment. Costs arising along domestic value chains, from farms to ports, need to be reduced. Also needed are efficient value chain mechanisms that can redress information asymmetries, increase competitiveness and minimize oligopsonistic distortions, and provide fair incentives to all actors. To achieve this, we propose two sets of recommendations, one for short- and medium-term and the other for long-term planning.

For the short and medium term:

- Motivate investment in export-oriented agricultural processing by reducing costs. Because compliance with strict regulatory and product quality standards is required for participation in global value chains, minimizing market entry costs, especially for domestic SMEs, is key. Interest rates and other tariffs (e.g., electricity, water, transport, customs fees) should be comparable with those in other producing/exporting countries (competitors). Providing technical assistance to help SMEs navigate regulatory requirements is also a must.
- Increase the bargaining power of domestic actors, especially small-scale farmers, by improving horizontal and vertical coordination within the value chains. Public sector actors can join forces in a national scheme to shorten value chains by expanding the scale and scope of collective works. Budgeting to support the purchase of raw materials, post-harvest storage facilities and improved road access are needed to manage the seasonal glut of highly perishable products from a large number of smallholders, and thereby avoid the loss of economic potential through informal cross-border trade.

In the long run:
- Promote harmonious business environment among value chain actors (producers, agricultural cooperatives and processing plants) to maintain commitment and trust.

- Improve basic physical infrastructure (road network, road quality, irrigation, electricity) for long-term competitiveness.
- Increase public spending on R&D in agriculture for higher productivity (e.g., high-yielding and disease-tolerant crop varieties, soil fertility stability, eco-friendly production practices). In the short term, diseconomies of scale can arise for a variety of reasons. Rather than view this as a constraint, R&D on high-value product differentiation and brand promotion should be considered one of the best long-term investments towards ensuring Cambodia's future economic growth and prosperity.
- Upgrade public quality assurance bodies as needed to achieve and retain international accreditation, promote best quality assurance practices, and gain international trust in Cambodian exports and exporters.
- Concentrate investment in strategic public-private partnership projects that can cover potential agricultural industries nationwide, instead of numerous small projects.

ANNEX 4.1
List of Districts and Villages Selected for Field Data Collection

Village	Commune	District	Province
Trapeang Pring	Trapeang Pring	Dambae	Tboung Khmum
Kampraeus	Trapeang Pring	Dambae	Tboung Khmum
Srae Kak	Trapeang Pring	Dambae	Tboung Khmum
Kouk Char	Kouk Srok	Dambae	Tboung Khmum
Kouk Srok	Kouk Srok	Dambae	Tboung Khmum
Tuol Proah	Seda	Dambae	Tboung Khmum
Trapaeng Thom	Lumtong	Anlong Veaeng	Oddar Meanchey
Chub Ta Mok	Lumtong	Anlong Veaeng	Oddar Meanchey
Toulsvay	Trapeang Tav	Anlong Veaeng	Oddar Meanchey
Trapeang Tav	Trapeang Tav	Anlong Veaeng	Oddar Meanchey
Toumnoub Akphivorth	Ou Svay	Trapeang Prasat	Oddar Meanchey
Ou Svay	Ou Svay	Trapeang Prasat	Oddar Meanchey
Thnal Kaeng	Trapeang Prasat	Trapeang Prasat	Oddar Meanchey
De Chor Akpiwat	Trapeang Prasat	Trapeang Prasat	Oddar Meanchey
Ou Chabtrei	Trapeang Prasat	Trapeang Prasat	Oddar Meanchey
Phluach	Trapeang Chor	Aural	Kampong Speu
Krang Tbaeng	Trapeang Chor	Aural	Kampong Speu
O Angkum	Amleang	Thpong	Kampong Speu
Pish	Amleang	Thpong	Kampong Speu
Toul Chhear Neang	Sangke Satob	Aural	Kampong Speu
Kreal Pong	Tasal	Aural	Kampong Speu
Chorm	Tasal	Aural	Kampong Speu

ANNEX 4.2
Global Cassava Value Chain

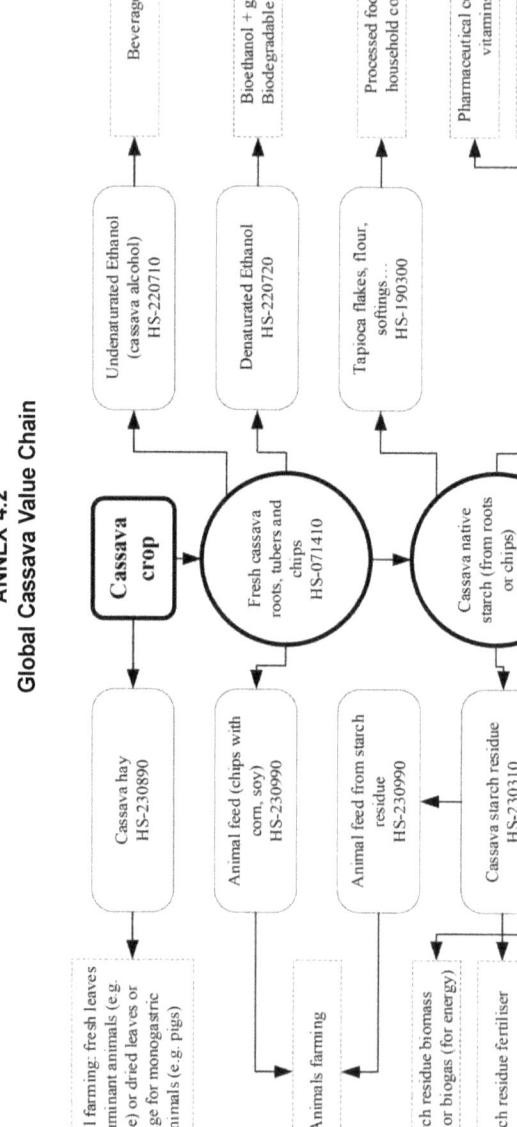

Source: Cambodia Trade Integration Strategy 2019-23 (MOC 2019).

ANNEX 4.3
Governance Structure in Different Linkages Throughout the Sugarcane Value Chain

Linkages	Type of Product/Service	Market Environment	Contractual Status	Frequency/Relationship Level	Level of Certainty	Level of Asset Specificity	Governance Structure
Government and lead firms	ELC	Monopoly (supplier-driven)	Written contract	Strong	>50 years High	High	Vertical integration (capital investment-based/bilateral)
Lead firms and inter-firms	Land Inputs Sugarcane	Oligopsony (buyer-driven)	Written contract	Strong	High	High	Vertical integration (bilateral)
Lead firms and financial institutes	Finance	Oligopoly	Written contract	Strong	High	High	Vertical integration (capital investment-based/bilateral)
Lead firms and input suppliers	Tradeable inputs	Oligopoly	Purchase order Invoice Clearance	Moderate	Moderate	Moderate	Market-based
Lead firms and private cane producers	Tradeable inputs Sugarcane	Oligopsony (buyer-driven)	Loose written contract	Moderate	Between moderate and low	Between moderate and low	Trilateral (contract)
Lead firms and transporters	Transport	Oligopoly	Verbal agreement	Low	Low	Between moderate and low	Market-based
Lead firms and labourers	Casual workers Full-time workers	Perfect competition Perfect competition	Loose written contract Contract	Moderate High	Low High	Low High	Market-based Vertical integration (unified structure)
Inter-firm and financial institutes	Finance	Oligopoly	Written contract	Strong	High	High	Vertical integration (capital investment-based/bilateral)
Inter-firms and input suppliers	Tradeable inputs	Oligopoly	Purchase order Invoice Clearance	Moderate	Moderate	Moderate	Market-based
Inter-firms and farm service providers	Farming service/ Labour supply	Oligopsony (buyer-driven)	Loose written contract	Between moderate and low	Low	Low	Market-based
Inter-firms and transporters	Transport	Oligopoly	Verbal agreement	Low	Low	Low	Market-based
Farm service providers and financial institutes	Finance	Oligopoly	Contract	Moderate	Moderate	Low	Trilateral
Farm service providers and casual labourers	Labour	Perfect competition	Verbal agreement	Low	Low	Low	Market-based

Source: Analytical results.

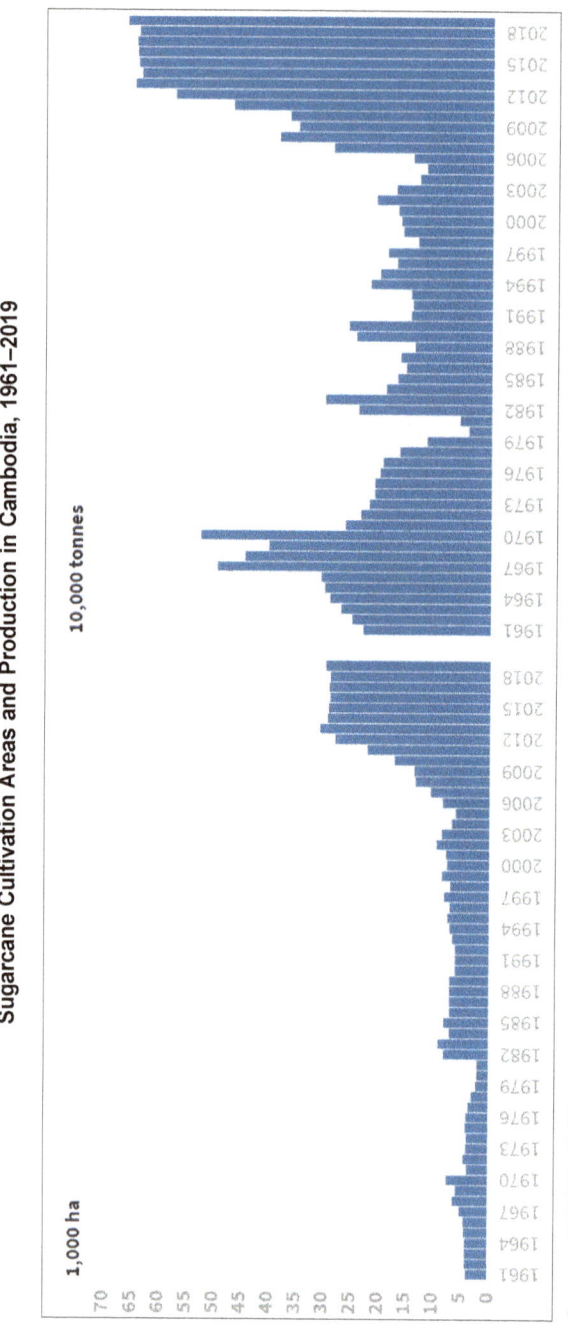

ANNEX 4.4
Sugarcane Cultivation Areas and Production in Cambodia, 1961–2019

Source: FAOSTAT (2019).

Agricultural Exports from Cambodia to China   155

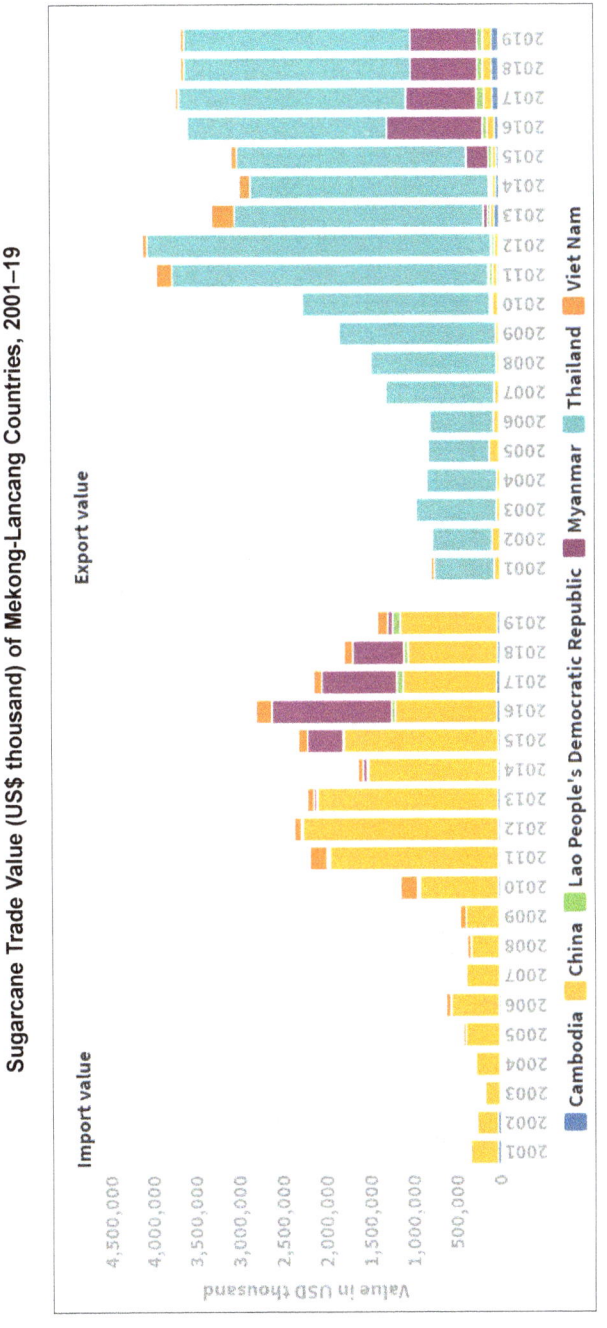

ANNEX 4.5
Sugarcane Trade Value (US$ thousand) of Mekong-Lancang Countries, 2001–19

Source: ITC TradeMap (2019).

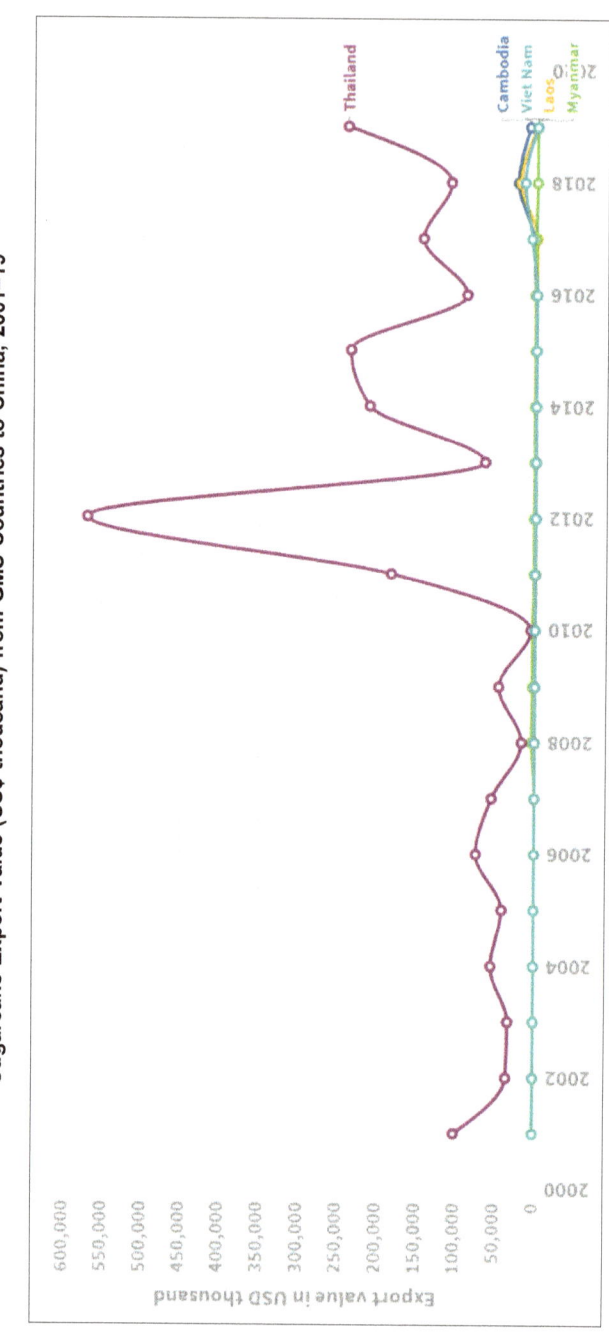

ANNEX 4.6
Sugarcane Export Value (US$ thousand) from GMS Countries to China, 2001–19

Source: ITC TradeMap (2019).

ANNEX 4.7
Computation of Value-Added Costs (US$) for Sugarcane from Production to the Border

Value-Added Activities	Unit	Period	Unit Cost	Total Cost	Remarks
1. Raw material production cost (US$/ha)				1,303.78	a+b+c+d+e
a. Land				5.00	ELC tax
b. Interest (US$/ha)	1.50%	12 months	1400	252.00	Average loan size is US$1,400/ha
c. Labour (US$/ha)				124.80	
d. Variable tradeable input cost (US$/ha)				900.20	
e. Fixed tradeable inputs cost (US$/ha)				21.78	15-year depreciation
2. Transport cost (US$/70 tonnes/ha)	70		9	630.00	
3. Processing cost (US$/70 tonnes/ha)				60.55	
f. Casual workers (US$/70 tonnes/ha)				4.42	
g. Full-time workers (US$/70 tonnes/ha)				20.60	
h. Office staff				1.48	
i. Supply cost (US$/70 tonnes/ha)				0.00	
j. Fixed equipment for processing plant (US$/70 tonnes/ha)				33.54	50-year depreciation
k. Interest for processing plant (US$/70 tonnes/ha)				0.50	
4. Total cost from raw material production to final product processing (US$/70 tonnes) = 1+2+3				1,994.33	
5. Total cost from raw material production to final product processing (US$/tonne) = #4/70				28.49	
6. Total cost per tonne of refined sugar (US$/tonne) = (1000 *#5)/100				284.90	
7. Transport cost from factory to wholesale warehouse (US$/tonne)				27.00	
8. Total cost from raw material production to final product export				311.90	

Note: Based on primary data, the average yield of sugarcane in Cambodia is 70 tonnes/ha.
Source: Computational results based on data collected from FGDs and KIIs and verified with data from secondary sources.

ANNEX 4.8
Constraints in the Cassava Value Chain

Upgrading	Weaknesses	Strengths
Products	• Farmers save stems from season to season • No prompt intervention from technical agencies to control the spread of disease • Highly volatile fresh tuber and chip prices • Low bulk density content because farmers harvest tubers too early • High production and transport costs • High supply uncertainty • Uncertain quality of farm inputs • Uncertain quality of raw material (fresh cassava)	• Scale of raw material production is large and growing (FAOSTAT) • Easy access to loans due to availability of MFIs • Yield is increasing and is the highest among all large producing countries in the Mekong-Lancang region (FAOSTAT)
Process	• High seasonality of raw material production • Opportunistic behaviours: farmers mix foreign matter into cassava; intermediaries use inaccurate scales • High electricity cost • Unreliable electricity supply • Limited number of domestic cassava processing factories induces surplus of raw material • Most processors have not been upgraded to generate electricity from cassava processing • Unsatisfactory quality of labourers for some processors	• Number of large-scale processors is increasing • Processing capacity is increasing • Large investors are adopting modern technology in processing plants
Function	• R&D has not fully engaged smallholders in practice • Small amount of collective work	
Value chain	• Cassava processing plants not yet widely linked to ethanol products • Switching cost is high for processors	• Cassava industry in Cambodia seems profitable

Source: Authors based on primary data and FAOSTAT database.

ANNEX 4.9
Weaknesses and Strengths in Sugarcane Value Chain Upgrading Strategies

Upgrading	Weaknesses (Areas For Upgrading)	Strengths
Products	• Input prices for raw material production and processing are higher than in other producing countries • Hard to scale up production because of production areas' reliance on ELC scheme • Cannot compete at scale in the international market • Land disputes frequently reported via social media may have negative effects on product reputation	• Ability to transform raw material into domestically produced final products • Yield comparable with that of other large producing countries • Loans readily accessible • Good quality inputs accessible by large investors • Able to produce valuable by-products (e.g., electricity, biogas, molasses) for domestic use and trade • Product quality has improved and reached international standards • Advantage from ELC policy: low land fee (ELC tax) and large production areas
Process	• Production is heavily seasonal • Jobs for local people are declining; only jobs for full-time workers are secured • Other large sugarcane producing countries have more experience in the industry	• Availability of labourers • Modern equipment and new technologies used in both raw material production and sugar mill refining • Shifting from labour-intensive to technology-intensive production to increase productivity
Function	• Limited R&D for the advancement of the industry in the long-run • Collective work to scale up supply not yet participated in by smallholders • High cost is a barrier to smallholders' market entrance • Technology flow to smallholders is also a cause for concern for scaling up production	• Value chain is functioning well at the current scale and with existing products due to large investment in modern technologies • Large investors have been repositioning their activities from the raw material value chain to the final products value chain (e.g., two sugarcane mills are in operation) • Value chain is highly vertically coordinated, driven by markets and large investors
Value chain	• Large percentage of value is generated from domestic supply	• Current value chain seems profitable

Source: Authors' analysis.

Notes

1. The revealed comparative advantage (RCA) index of country i for product j is often measured by the product's share in the country's exports in relation to its share in world trade: $RCA_{ij} = \dfrac{x_{ij}/X_{it}}{x_{wj}/X_{wt}}$, where x_{ij} and X_{wj} are the values of country i export of product j and world export of product j and x_{ij} and x_{wt} are the country's total exports and world total exports, respectively. A country has a comparative advantage in a product if its RCA is greater than 1, but it has a comparative disadvantage if its RCA is less than 1. The measure of RCA allows us to examine the probability that a country may expand its exports of that product.
2. Adopted from the work of Williamson (1979), the term "inter-firm" refers to those firms whose business is a part of a lead firm's business. For example, inter-firms in the sugarcane sector are those who use lead firms' land with a written contract to grow and supply sugarcane to their processing plants. They are highly vertically integrated.
3. Linked to the value chain map, there are three types of sugarcane producers: lead firms, inter-firms and private producers.
4. The term "raw material" in this case refers to sugarcane. In cassava value chains, the raw material refers to fresh cassava/cassava tubers/cassava roots/cassava chips.
5. Based on the work of Monke and Pearson (1989), who developed the Policy Analysis Matrix, cost is divided into two main categories: tradeable and non-tradeable (or non-tradeable factors and domestic factors). Tradeable inputs refer to products that have a world price (e.g., agrochemicals and agro-equipment), whereas non-tradeable inputs mainly focus on labour, capital (loan interest) and land.
6. Interest is included at various stages of the value chain in accordance with size of investment and loan.

References

Ahmed, Osama, and Walid Sallam. 2018. "Studying the Volatility Effect of Agricultural Exports on Agricultural Share of GDP: The Case of Egypt". *African Journal of Agricultural Research* 13, no. 8: 245–352. http://dx.doi.org/10.5897/AJAR2016.11 920

Bala, M. Lakshmi, and K. Sudhakar. 2017. "An Overview of Export Performance of Agricultural Products in India". *IOSR Journal of Business and Management* 19, no. 2: 1–5.

Bamber, Penny, Lukas Brun, Stacey Frederick, and Gary Gereffi. 2017. "Chapter 1: Global Value Chains and Economic Development". In *Korea in Global Value*

Chains: Pathways for Industrial Transformation, pp. 1–16. Durham: Duke Global Value Chains Centre.

Bellù, Lorenzo Giovanni. 2013. *Value Chain Analysis for Policy Making: Methodological Guidelines and Country Cases for Quantitative Approach*. EASYPol Series 129. Rome: FAO.

Blein, Roger, Bio Goura Soule, Benoit Faivre Dupaigre, and Borgui Yérima. 2008. *Agricultural Potential of West Africa (ECOWAS)*. https://www.fondation-farm.org/IMG/pdf/potentialites_rapport_ang_mp.pdf

Comtrade. 2019. UN Comtrade Database. https://comtrade.un.org/data/

Council of Ministers. 2015. *Cambodia Industrial Development Policy 2015–2015: Market Orientation and Enabling Environment for Industrial Development*. Phnom Penh: Royal Government of Cambodia.

Dao, Cambodochine. 2014. *Business Process Analysis: Export of Cassava and Maize in Cambodia*. https://unnext.unescap.org/sites/default/files/bpa-cam.pdf

Daramola, Abebiyi, Simeon Ehui, Emmanuel Ukeje, and John McIntire. 2007. "Agricultural Export Potential in Nigeria". https://www.csae.ox.ac.uk/materials/data/777/agricultural exportpotentialinnigeria.pdf

EMC (Emerging Markets Consulting). 2014. *Value Chain Mapping and Analysis: Land-Based Communities in Cambodia*. https://snv.org/cms/sites/default/files/explore/down load/p adee_value_chain_mapping_and_analysis.pdf

FAOSTAT. 2019. "Crops Data. "http://www.fao.org/faostat/en/#data/QC

Fromm, Ingrid. 2007. *Upgrading in Agricultural Value Chains: The Case of Small Producers in Honduras*. GIGA Working Paper No. 64. www.jstor.org/stable/resrep16502

Gereffi, Gary. 1994. "The Organization of Buyer-Driven Global Commodity Chains: How U.S. Retailers Shape Overseas Production Networks, Commodity Chains and Global Capitalism". In *Commodity Chains and Global Capitalism*, edited by Gary Gereffi and Miguel Korzenievicz, pp. 95–122. Westport, CT: Praeger.

———. 1999. "International Trade and Industrial Upgrading in the Apparel Commodity Chain". *Journal of International Economics* 48, no. 1: 37–70.

———, and Karina Fernandez-Stark. 2016. *Global Value Chain Analysis: A Primer*. 2nd ed. Durham: Duke Global Value Chains Centre.

———, John Humphrey, and Timothy Sturgeon. 2005. "The Governance of Global Value Chains". *Review of International Political Economy* 12, no. 1: 78–104.

Henneberry, Shida Rastegari, and Muhammad E. Khan. 1999. "An Analysis of the Linkage Between Agricultural Exports and Economic Growth in Pakistan". *Journal of International Food and Agribusiness Marketing* 10, no. 4: 13–29.

Hing Vutha, and Thun Vathana. 2009. *Agricultural Trade in the Greater Mekong Sub-region: The Case of Cassava and Rubber in Cambodia*. CDRI Working Paper Series No. 43. Phnom Penh: Cambodia Development Resource Institute.

Humphrey, John, and Hubert Schmitz. 2000. *Governance and Upgrading: Linking*

Industrial Cluster and Global Value Chain Research. IDS Working Paper 120. Brighton: Institute of Development Studies.

IMF (International Monetary Fund). 2017. "Exports and Imports by Areas and Countries". https://data.imf.org/?sk=9D6028D4-F14A-464C-A2F2-59B2CD424B85&sId=1409151240976

ITC (International Trade Centre). 2014. *Cambodia: Company Perspectives – An ITC Series on Non-Tariff Measures*. Geneva: ITC.

———. 2019. "Trade Map: Trade Statistics for International Business Development". https://www.trademap.org/Country_SelProductCountry_TS.aspx?nvpm=1%7c116%7c%7c%7c%7cTOTAL%7c%7c%7c%7c2%7c1%7c1%7c1%7c2%7c1%7c2%7c1%7c%7c1

Kaplinsky, Raphael. 2004. "Spreading the Gains from Globalization: What Can Be Learned from Value-Chain Analysis?". *Problems of Economic Transition* 47, no. 2: 74–115.

———, and Mike Morris. 2001. *A Handbook for Value Chain Research*. www.prism.uct.ac.za/papers/vchnov01.pdf

Kula, Olaf, Cheryl Turner, and Sanphirom Sar. 2015. "An Analysis of Three Commodity Value Chains in Cambodia: Rice, Horticulture and Aquaculture". PowerPoint presentation. http://avwebmaster.wpengine.com/wp-content/uploads/2016/05/LEO-Cambodia-Value-Chain-Assessment.pdf

Mille, Guillaume, Hap Navy, and Loeng Nob. 2016. *Economic Value of Fish in Cambodia and Value Added along the Trade Chain*. Phnom Penh: Inland Fisheries Research and Development Institute (Fisheries Administration) and WorldFish Cambodia.

Mitchell, Jonathan, Christopher Coles, and Jodie Keane. 2009. "Upgrading Along Value Chains: Strategies for Poverty Reduction in Latin America". Briefing Paper. www.odi.org/sites/odi.org.uk/files/odi-assets/publications-opinion-files/5654.pdf

MOC (Ministry of Commerce). 2019. *Cambodia Trade Integration Strategy 2019–2023*. www.moc.gov.kh/Portals/0/Docs/OfficialDocs/CTIS-20190725143301726.pdf

Monke, Eric A., and Scott R. Pearson. 1989. *The Policy Analysis Matrix for Agricultural Development*. London and Ithaca, NY: Cornell University Press.

National Institute of Statistics. 2018. Commune Database. Phnom Penh: Ministry of Planning.

———. 2019. "Methodology of National Accounts". https://www.nis.gov.kh/index.php/en/21-na

ODC (Open Development Cambodia). 2016. "Economic Land Concessions". https://opendev elopmentcambodia.net/profiles/economic-land-concessions/

Osabhien, R., D. Akinpelumi, O. Matthew, V. Okafor, E. Iku, T. Olawande, and U. Okorie. 2019. "Agricultural Exports and Economic Growth in Nigeria: An Econometric Analysis". *International Conference on Energy and Sustainable Environment*. http://doi.org/10.1088/1755-1315/331/1/012002

Porter, Michael E. 1985. *Competitive Advantage: Creating and Sustaining Superior Performance*. London; New York: Collier Macmillan.

Siaw, Anthony, Yuansheng Jiang, Robort. Becker Pickson, and Rahman Dunya. 2018. "Agricultural Exports and Economic Growth: A Disaggregated Analysis for Ghana". *Theoretical Economics Letters* 8: 2251–70. http://doi.org/10.4236/tel.2018.811147

Sturton, Mark. 1992. *Tonga: Development through Agricultural Exports*. Honolulu: University of Hawaii Press, and Pacific Islands Development Program, East-West Centre.

Taylor, David H. 2005. "Value Chain Analysis: An Approach to Supply Chain Improvement in Agri-food Chains". *International Journal of Physical Distribution and Logistics Management* 35, no. 10: 744–61.

Thai Tapioca Starch Association. 2019. "Weekly Tapioca Starch Price". http://www.thaitapio castarch.org/en/information/statistics/weekly_tapioca_starch_price

TRAINS. 2015 "Trains: Non-Tariff Measures (NTMs) Based on Official Regulations". https://trains.unctad.org/

Trienekens, Jacques H. 2011. "Agricultural Value Chains in Developing Countries: A Framework for Analysis". *International Food and Agribusiness Management Review* 14, no. 2: 51–82.

Ven Seyhah. 2015. "The Effects of Non-Tariff Measures on Cambodian Agricultural Exports: A Gravity Model". In *Trade Integration Within ASEAN: The Role of Non-Tariff Measures for Cambodia, The Lao People's Democratic Republic, Myanmar and Viet Nam*, pp. 211–34. Bangkok: United Nations Economic and Social Commission for Asia and the Pacific.

———. 2017. "Existing Non-Tariff Measures in Cambodia". *Cambodia Development Review* 21, no. 2: 1–7.

Williamson, Oliver E. 1979. "Transaction-Cost Economics: The Governance of Contractual Relations". *Journal of Law and Economics* 22, no. 2: 233–261.

World Bank. 2018. "Data Bank: World Development Indicators".

Yifru, Tigist. 2015. "Impact of Agricultural Exports on Economic Growth in Ethiopia: The Case of Coffee, Oilseed and Pulses". MSc thesis, Egerton University, Njoro, Kenya.

5

AGRICULTURAL EXPORTS FROM LAOS TO CHINA
A Value Chain Analysis of Rice and Cavendish Banana

Viengsavang Thipphavong, Thantavanh Manolom, Vanaxay Soukhaseum, Phouthaphone Southammavong and Somdeth Bodhisane

5.1 INTRODUCTION

Agriculture has been recognized as the foundation of the economic development of Laos since the New Economic Mechanism was introduced in 1986. To bring about a significant increase in agricultural production in a sustainable way, the Lao government recently adopted land zoning (at provincial and district levels) for agriculture. As a result, in tandem with the implementation of Agricultural Development Strategy 2016–25, agricultural land has been classified into three zones for specialization in large-scale production for export: plains, agricultural land not classified as plains, and arable land in mountain and plateau areas. The strategy also emphasizes the promotion of domestic and foreign investors in agricultural development, aiming to accelerate the transition from subsistence farming to commercial production of agricultural goods.

Agriculture is central to the Lao economy. The majority of the population live in rural areas where they depend on agriculture for their survival. Agriculture plays a crucial role in daily life, ensuring food and nutrition security and supporting livelihoods, employment and income generation. The promotion of commercial agriculture over the past decades has led to a significant shift in farming practices, from growing food (i.e., subsistence) crops only to cash (i.e., marketed) crops. More recently, growing cash crops for export has been encouraged in many parts of the country. Specifically, MOAF (2011) earmarked six cash crops with export potential and which Laos has comparative advantages in producing; they are rice, bananas, maize, coffee, cassava and sugarcane. The main motivation behind this export-driven strategy is twofold. Integration into regional markets facilitates participation in regional and global agricultural value chains, which is considered essential to boost agricultural productivity, which, in turn, is seen as vital to lift rural people out of poverty.

The six cash crops identified by MOAF grow well in many parts of the country, and large plantations have already been established. These commodities now dominate Laos' agricultural exports, with most exports going to countries in the Mekong region, notably China, Thailand and Vietnam. Combined, these three countries account for more than three-fourths of Laos' total agricultural trade in terms of volume. Several key factors have influenced Laos' deeper economic integration in the region. Transportation improvements, particularly better road connectivity, have directly enhanced access to regional markets in more populous countries (ADB 2018). For example, the upgrading of National Road No. 9, which links main towns in Laos to Thailand in the south and Vietnam in the east, is expected to release export opportunities offered by the rich farmlands of the Bolaven Plateau in southern Laos, where the climate is suitable for growing high-value cool-season vegetable crops. Recently, there has been a surge of large Chinese investments in crop plantations in Laos, particularly in Cavendish bananas, for export to China. Such speculation has largely been driven by China's Opium Replacement Programme, wherein cash crops grown in the northern provinces are eligible for unilateral trade preferences with China. This has opened the door for Lao agricultural products to enter value chains in China. Added to this, China is increasingly meeting its demand for agricultural products by participating in contract farming with investors and small-scale farmers in GMS countries, including Laos.

Although Laos can position many of its agricultural products in the value chains of regional trading partners, monoculture farming has clear disadvantages that should not be ignored. As production has increased to supply Chinese markets, many farmlands have been converted to large-scale plantations, for example, to grow banana and rubber trees. The concurrent adoption of intensive farming practices comes with adverse health and environmental implications. Degradation of farmland, declining soil fertility, deforestation and encroachment on forest reservations, and health risks to plantation workers, to name a few, are serious concerns stemming from greater investments in regional agricultural value chains.

The rest of the chapter is structured as follows. Section 5.2 presents brief background information about the study and the main steps involved in value chain analysis, including NTM-related issues that affect trade. Section 5.3 describes the data collection and research methods. Section 5.4 analyses the research findings. The chapter ends with a brief conclusion and policy implications.

5.2 BACKGROUND

Agricultural land in Laos is categorized into three main types: (1) flatland, (2) moderately sloping land with deep soil, and (3) natural grassland. Type (1) accounts for 2 million hectares and is suitable for growing rice, short life-cycle crops, and cash crops. Type (2) amounts to about 1.8 million hectares and is ideal for food crops such as rice, banana, maize, beans, green beans, fruit trees and industrial plantations. Type (3) is suitable for livestock (e.g., cattle and buffalo) farming and covers 0.65 million hectares.

Prior to market-oriented reforms, farmers mainly grew food crops on smallholdings to meet the needs of their families. Now, through the direct role of manufacturers in collecting and purchasing outputs from farmers, more and more smallholders and farmers are actively involved in growing cash crops for agribusinesses and agro-processing companies that offer a secure market and price. Farmers sell their outputs to trade arbitrators or directly to manufacturers depending on convenience and optimal price. Sugarcane, cassava and maize are examples of such manufacturing-pushed value chains. To ensure product quality and quantity, contract farming is often used as the coordination mechanism between farmers and businesses.

Over the past ten years, rice and Cavendish banana have become major agricultural exports to Chinese markets. Engagement in the agricultural value chains of these crops has been influenced by increased export demand resulting from the close bilateral trade ties between the two nations. The official rice import quotas granted to Laos by the Chinese government, and the recent surge of interest by Chinese investors in Cavendish banana plantations, have earmarked comprehensive commercialization of rice and banana production and marketing in Laos.

Although agricultural value chain development holds much promise, non-tariff measures (NTMs) hinder Laos from taking full advantage of the opportunities that integration into regional value chains offers. Various issues surrounding NTM compliance, commonly perceived as a significant trade barrier to Lao agribusinesses, deter access to foreign markets. In the absence of domestic laboratories or facilities capable of testing agricultural products, conformity with international standards and regulatory compliance is extremely challenging, especially where a food safety or other type of export certificate must be issued before shipping. Many Lao exporters, therefore, have no choice but to use the laboratory facilities of neighbouring countries, and quite often importing countries, for certifying product quality and safety. As a result of the higher costs incurred, small businesses tend to be left behind and fail to realize the full benefit of value chain participation. Rice and banana exports, even though they are prominent imports in China, are subject to pre-export quality certification. This issue alone has deterred many Lao agribusinesses from doing business with Chinese buyers in the value chain.

The development of Lao agricultural value chains has been consistent with the expansion of regional value chains; however, the stringent product quality regulations of importing countries have impeded market access. This situation underscores the importance of our in-depth country study. A critical turning point in agricultural value chain development in Laos came with an influx of foreign businesses, which played an essential part in farmers' engagement in agricultural value chains. Many crops are grown for domestic processing factories and many more are grown for foreign collectors or Lao businesses who are nominees of foreign buyers. Under these circumstances, Lao farmers are very often the first step in the value chain, trade arbitrators/collectors are the middle step, and factories/exporters are the last. Nonetheless, a value chain that involves overseas buyers is challenging due to NTM-related obstacles.

Despite the critical need to better integrate and position Lao exports in regional and global value chains, value chain studies in Laos are scant. Previous research efforts focused mostly on primary actors and their activities along the value chain up to and including domestic buyers, largely ignoring the chain segments beyond national borders. Rice value chain analyses in Laos, for instance, commonly focus on factors affecting production costs and constraints faced by farmers and businesses. Similarly, analyses of banana production in Laos focus on the costs and benefits for farmers of value chain participation and barely touch on cross-border value chain relationships. In addition, existing studies fail to meaningfully address food safety and quality issues related to importing countries' regulatory requirements and various certifications (i.e., NTMs) that affect Lao rice and banana exports (Hoppe et al. 2018; Setboonsarng 2008; Sacklokham 2009; Higashi 2015; NAFRI 2016).

As this review of the literature demonstrates, an agricultural value chain refers to the range of activities and set of stakeholders that bring an agricultural product from production in the field to final consumption, where at each stage value is added to the product. In value chain mapping, a vertical analysis serves to identify links between different types of business sectors. Value chain analysis by primary activities could include processing, labelling and packaging, storage, distribution and transport (FAO 2005). Value chain models are categorized into two groups, traditional and modern. In traditional models, smallholders are the starting point of agricultural value chain mapping, followed by the links between small farmers and traditional wholesale markets and then the links between wholesalers, retailers and processors. In contrast, modern value chain models are characterized by vertical coordination, supply-based consolidation, industrial processing practice, and product and process standardization (McCullough, Pingali and Stramoulis 2008).

A value chain map illustrates the linkages from field to end markets, including actor participation in value creation; the relationships between chain actors, productivity and competitiveness; constraints; and distribution of benefits and drawbacks (Achchuthan and Rajendran 2012). In general, an agricultural value chain is determined by intermediate and similar products comprising the activities of all firms involved in various stages of the chain such as production, storage, transport, processing, marketing and distribution.

Value chain analysis is a dynamic approach that examines how markets and industries respond to changes in domestic and international demand and supply for a commodity, technological advances in production and marketing, and developments in organizational models, institutional arrangements or management techniques. It also examines the effects of market trends, product innovation and changing consumer behaviour (Anandajayasekeram and Gebremedhin 2009).

Rice production is a mainstay of the Lao economy and rice is a staple of the Lao diet. A study of the Lao rice production value chain, published by the World Bank (Hoppe et al. 2018), identified input supply, production, assembly, processing, wholesaling and retailing as the critical stages in the chain. This study emphasized value chain analysis, broadly covering production, milling and marketing processes. Cavendish banana, on the other hand, was only introduced in the last decade, exclusively for export to China. Up until now, to the best of our knowledge, no study has been conducted to investigate the value chain of Cavendish bananas. That said, a comparable study by World Education (2016) assessed the role of value chain participation in supporting sustainable livelihood development for the poor through inclusive economic development. The study mapped the peanut and cassava value chains in a southern province using TOWS (threats, opportunities, weakness, and strengths) analysis and value chain score matrix. Another study (Manivong et al. 2016) related to banana production looked at the pathway and impact of the expansion of commercial banana production in the northern provinces of Laos. This study mainly assessed the economics of banana production.

Taking the above into consideration, the current study set out to deepen understanding of agricultural value chain development in Laos by examining the export of rice and Cavendish bananas to China. Furthermore, the study examines the impact of NTMs on Lao agribusinesses and exporters in China's segment of the rice and banana value chains. To achieve the research objectives, we used both primary and secondary data to understand (1) the nature of the rice and Cavendish banana value chains in Laos and (2) how NTMs affect the agribusinesses and exporters involved in Chinese value chains.

5.3 DATA AND METHOD

The study uses a combined qualitative and descriptive statistical approach. Data was gathered through a survey, which entailed in-depth interviews with government officials and representatives of businesses. Secondary data was obtained from the Lao Bureau of Statistics, Ministry of Industry and Commerce, Ministry of Planning and Investment, Ministry of Agriculture and Forestry, and the International Trade Centre.

Rice destined for export to China is processed in Laos by Chinese-owned Xuanye Company, which is supplied by two rice mills: Vanida rice mill (in Khammuan province) and Indochina Development Partners-Laos (in Champasak province). In-depth interviews were conducted with all three firms to understand in detail the rice export value chain to China. The data analysis methods used were largely adapted from the World Bank report *Commercialization of Rice and Vegetables Value Chains in Lao PDR: Status and Prospects* (Hoppe et al. 2018). Particular attention was paid to the analysis of the cost structure between consumers and farmers, which has been motivated by higher retail prices in Vientiane. Both quantitative and qualitative analytical approaches were used.

Behind the expansion of Cavendish banana plantations in northern Laos are fifteen large Chinese investment companies, some of which are possibly operating in more than one location. The initial plan was to interview representatives from fifteen plantations, each owned by a different company, but three companies were unable to participate in the study. As a result, the final sampling frame for the banana value chain analysis comprised twelve Chinese companies operating in the provinces of Bokeo, Luang Namtha, Oudomxay and Luang Prabang. These four provinces were selected because they are the top banana producing areas in northern Laos. Both in-depth interviews and a structured questionnaire were used to gather the required information. In-depth interviews were used to obtain information about policy recommendations, advantages and disadvantages of growing or investing in Cavendish bananas, and NTM-related problems. A structured questionnaire was used to collect information about costs related to value chain participation such as land acquisition, rent, wages and inputs, as well as pressing issues such as transportation and transit problems.

In mapping the Cavendish banana value chain, we applied the value chain analysis introduced by Michael E. Porter (1985 cited in IFM 2016).

Furthermore, to identify existing problems and challenges for value chain development and draw actionable policy recommendations, we used a TOWS matrix as a guiding framework. TOWS analysis was also used to recommend mini strategies with the greatest potential for proactive policymaking (strengths and opportunities) and strategic planning (weaknesses and opportunities) that can capitalize on opportunities and minimize threats (strengths and threats) and stay abreast of and adapt to changes (weaknesses and threats).

5.4 FINDINGS

5.4.1 Rice Value Chain

Rice Production

Rice is grown in all nineteen provinces of Laos, and rainfed lowland paddy is the dominant rice crop. Even in the north, where seven provinces are classed as mountainous, rainfed lowland paddy accounts for 56 per cent of total rice production. In the central and southern regions, rainfed lowland paddy accounts for 95 and 97 per cent of total rice production, respectively (MOAF 2018). As of 2017, the total rice harvested area was 963,754 hectares, annual rice production stood at 4,055,409 tonnes, and rice occupied just over 55 per cent of the total crop area (MOAF 2017). Overall, in the last five years, the harvested area has expanded and production increased by about 2.0 per cent. To an extent, this achievement reflects government efforts to increase rice production and thus achieve self-sufficiency in rice and produce a surplus for export. Laos has been self-sufficient in rice since 2000 and the surplus of rice that can be exported has increased over the last decade, leading to the emergence of more commercially oriented rice farmers (FAO 2019).

Although Laos produces a rice surplus and can therefore export rice, it is still a small player in the region. In comparison with Vietnam and Thailand, which are big players in the global rice trade, or even with the newly emerging rice exporting countries of Myanmar and Cambodia, Laos is lagging far behind. As Table 5.1 shows, in 2017/18, the annual rice production of these four major rice producers ranged from 10.6 million tonnes to 44.2 million tonnes compared to a meagre 4.2 million tonnes for Laos, with growth rates of 2.4 per cent to 3.2 per cent compared to 1.7 per cent for Laos.

TABLE 5.1
Rice Production (million tonnes) in Laos and Other GMS Countries

Country	2013–15 (Average)	2016	2018 (Forecast)	Percentage Change (2017/18)
Cambodia	9.3	10.0	10.6	2.6
Myanmar	28.1	28.6	30.4	3.2
Thailand	31.9	32.4	34.5	2.4
Vietnam	44.7	43.2	44.2	3.1
Laos	3.9	4.1	4.2	1.7

Source: Rice Market Monitor (FAO 2018).

TABLE 5.2
Aggregate Data on Rice Production in Laos, 2013–17

	2013	2014	2015	2016	2017	Average Growth (%)
Planted area (ha)	939,100	979,345	984,932	976,235	995,215	1.19
Harvested area (ha)	891,190	957,836	965,152	973,327	963,754	0.71
Production (tonne)	3,414,560	4,002,425	4,102,000	4,148,800	4,055,409	3.29
Yield (tonne/ha)	3.83	4.18	4.25	4.26	4.21	2.46

Source: Agriculture Statistical Report 2018 (MOAF 2018).

Lao rice farmers have small farms and rely on family labour. In the 2010/11 agricultural census, about 723,500 people or 11.3 per cent of the total population identified as rice farmers and 92 per cent of total rice fields were reportedly used for growing glutinous rice. Based on census data, on average, each rice farmer cultivates 1.4 hectares of paddy rice and household labour makes up 74 per cent of total paddy labour. Nonetheless, despite being a relatively small rice producer, Laos can become a net exporter of rice in the region. As Table 5.2 shows, between 2013 and 2017, per hectare rice yield increased by 2.46 per cent and rice production by 3.29 per cent.

Rice Value Chain Mapping

In general, Lao rice farmers operate independently and are unlikely to join a group or an association. They work in their own interests, growing and selling produce. Even though farmers enter into contracts with rice millers, rice cultivation is the sole responsibility of farmers. The real selling price is usually higher than the price pledge (minimum price) as in practice contractual parties rarely comply fully with the terms of the agreement. There were many complaints about contract breaches from both farmers and businesses, such as farmers' default on input credit, selling to outsiders for a higher price, businesses disappearing because of insolvency, and unfair terms of contract owing to farmers' weak negotiation skills or bargaining power (Setboonsarng, Leung and Stefan 2008; UNDP 2015; TKN 2012).

Similar to value chains for other cash crops, the rice value chain normally involves input supply, production, assembly, processing, wholesaling and retailing. Fertilizer and seed are the two main inputs for rice farmers in the growing season. Rice farmers usually obtain fertilizer from retailers or rice millers. Those without working capital can obtain fertilizer on credit from rice millers (they repay the loan in kind after harvest by deducting the cost of fertilizer from rice sold to the miller). Seed can be acquired from two sources—seed production groups and government seed research stations. Farmers typically replace their rice seed after the third generation or three years of planting saved seed. They are most likely to get hybrid or new generation seed from seed production groups given that government seed research stations can supply only a limited quantity of seed. Farmers usually repay the seed production groups in kind, in the following harvest season.

The second node of the rice value chain is paddy assembly, which is often performed by local collectors who buy rice directly from farmers and then sell and deliver it to rice mills. However, farmers in the vicinity of the mill are likely to supply the miller directly. The last node in the chain is occupied by wholesalers and retailers who sometimes serve similar functions. For example, a miller can function as a retailer by selling rice at the mill gate and also as a wholesaler by selling rice directly to big urban markets or even exporting rice to international markets.

5.4.2 Rice Export Value Chain to China

Lao rice has long been exported informally to neighbouring countries, with an estimated 300,000 tonnes of Lao rice crossing the borders annually to Vietnam, Thailand, China and other countries in the region (Xinhua 2017).

Until relatively recently, all rice exports were closely monitored by the Lao government in order to ensure sufficient food supply for the country. Since the ASEAN Trade in Goods Agreement entered into force in 2010 and Laos' accession to the World Trade Organization in 2013, restrictions on the import and export of rice have been relaxed, particularly after Laos received official rice import quotas from the Chinese government, starting in 2015. Now rice is subject to automatic export licence, which means the only requirement of export companies is that they declare to the Department of Import and Export the quantity of rice to be exported (Ministry of Industry and Commerce 2012).

Laos started exporting rice officially to China in 2015, exporting 42,000 tonnes of sticky rice and purple rice in 2016. In 2017, which marked the first exports under China's rice import quota of 8,000 tonnes, exports of rice to China almost doubled. China then increased the rice import quota to 20,000 tonnes in 2018 and 50,000 tonnes in 2019, which, albeit in a small way, supported Laos' ambition to increase annual rice production to 5 million tonnes by 2020 (*Globaltimes* 2016; *Vientiane Times* 2019). In 2018, with a market share of 2.4 per cent, Laos ranked fifth out of fourteen countries exporting rice to China (UN Comtrade 2018).

To date, only two companies in Laos are eligible to export rice directly to China under China's import quota. They are both foreign-owned, namely Xuanye Company (China) and Indo-China Development Partners (IDP) rice mill (France). Many rice mills in Laos are small and not up to international standards, not even for good manufacturing practice (GMP) certification. To be eligible to export rice to China, exporters/millers have to be certified by China's Administration of Quality Supervision, Inspection and Quarantine (AQSIQ)[1] and the General Administration of Customs of China (GACC).[2] However, it is not easy to acquire an AQSIQ licence as companies are required to be certified to the ISO 9001 standard[3] or equivalent such as good agricultural practice (GAP) certification (Quora 2015). Only three rice mills in Laos (Cheangsavang in Vientiane capital, IDP in Savannakhet, and Vanida in Khammoun) have GAP certification. To date, only IDP and Vanida meet the required standards and can export rice to China, either directly or by supplying a Chinese company (i.e., Xuanye).[4]

At the time of the study, Xuanye Company had received AQSIQ approval in 2015, IDP was in the process of applying, and Vanida had not yet started. Given the circumstances, it is reasonable to surmise that only one company qualified for rice export to China. However, to reach the export target under the import quota, Xuanye would help the IDP rice mill fill out the documents required for AQSIQ accreditation and had also signed a business contract with Vanida rice mill for the supply of milled rice. The following analysis of the Lao rice export value chain to China is therefore based largely on information and data collected from Vanida and IDP rice mills.

The value chains of rice exported to China depicted in Figures 5.1 and 5.2 are based on data collected from IDP, Vanida and Xuanye in 2019. To recap, in order to export food products to China legally, rice exporters have to conform to AQSIQ quality and food safety requirements. This means that the farmers who grow rice for Vanida and IDP have to comply with quality control measures; for instance, they must register the production area and their rice fields must undergo inspection. In addition, farmers are advised to use the seed supplied by Vanida and IDP, and they are expected to apply a certain level of chemical fertilizers as instructed by the millers. Therefore, rice exports generally go through a lengthy process from farmers to processors and then retailers at the destination market. The business cooperation between Xuanye and Vanida starts with farmers who buy all their inputs from local suppliers and grow rice for Vanida rice mill. More often than not, at the beginning of the harvest season, farmers sell paddy directly to Vanida rice mill; however, from mid-season onwards, rice collectors and Vanida rice mill usually go to the villages to buy any remaining paddy stocks. The processing stage is the sole responsibility of Vanida rice mill. Milled rice is sold to Xuanye company, which is authorized to export rice to China Oil and Foodstuffs Corporation (COFCO), China. Xuanye also organizes online selling to high-end customers. In the case of IDP, the processes are almost the same but IDP has sole responsibility for milling and exporting rice to COFCO and retail markets in China.

Economic Analysis of Rice Value Chains

Farmers

In principle, rice contract farming in Laos stipulates that smallholder farmers grow rice to supply rice millers under the 2+3 contract modality: the farmers supply land and labour, and the investor provides the capital, techniques and market. In practice, 2+3 contract farming between farmers and rice millers barely exists. This is because, historically, both parties

FIGURE 5.1
Rice Value Chain under Xuanye-Vanida Business Cooperation

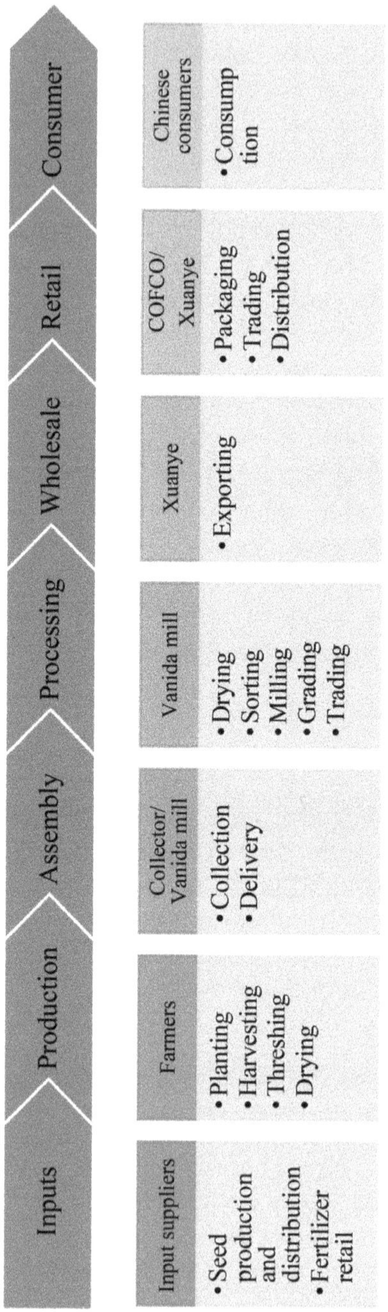

Inputs	Production	Assembly	Processing	Wholesale	Retail	Consumer
Input suppliers	Farmers	Collector/ Vanida mill	Vanida mill	Xuanye	COFCO/ Xuanye	Chinese consumers
• Seed production and distribution • Fertilizer retail	• Planting • Harvesting • Threshing • Drying	• Collection • Delivery	• Drying • Sorting • Milling • Grading • Trading	• Exporting	• Packaging • Trading • Distribution	• Consumption

Source: Estimated by authors using data from the field survey.

FIGURE 5.2
Rice Value Chain under IDP Rice Mill

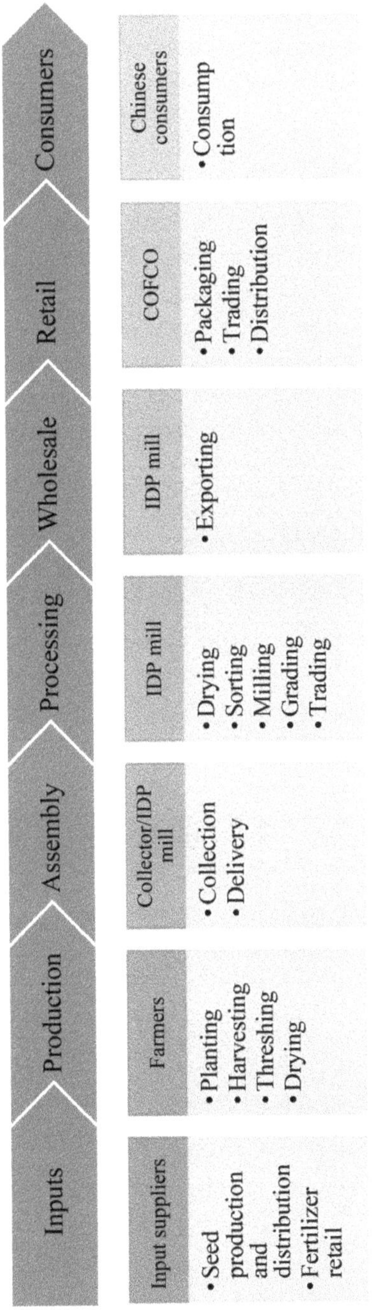

Stage	Actor	Activities
Inputs	Input suppliers	• Seed production and distribution • Fertilizer retail
Production	Farmers	• Planting • Harvesting • Threshing • Drying
Assembly	Collector/IDP mill	• Collection • Delivery
Processing	IDP mill	• Drying • Sorting • Milling • Grading • Trading
Wholesale	IDP mill	• Exporting
Retail	COFCO	• Packaging • Trading • Distribution
Consumers	Chinese consumers	• Consumption

Source: Estimated by authors using data from the field survey.

usually breach the terms and conditions of the contract. To deal with this issue and maintain the quantity of rice supplied, both Vanida and IDP use flexible contracts. For example, farmers can use rice seed and fertilizers from their stock or buy them on credit from the millers and can secure a good price (up to the current market price) for their rice outputs. Nonetheless, farmers have to bear the cost of all inputs and on-farm activities.

Land preparation, crop establishment and harvesting, which usually involve hiring labour for ploughing, crop maintenance and reaping, are the top three production costs (Table 5.3). Depreciation of equipment is mostly calculated for a two-wheeled tractor. Nutrition management includes fertilizers and weed control. After deducting costs, a farmer can earn about US$231 per hectare from growing rice for export to China. This is double the usual farm income from rice of about US$109 per hectare (Hoppe et al. 2018)

Vanida and IDP rice mills operate in different provinces. Vanida has strong ties with farmers in Khammoun province, where over 2,000 farm households are its main suppliers. IDP receives regular supplies of rice from 8,000 farm households in Savannakhet and Champasak provinces. Because of the large number of contract farmers, the rice millers frequently enlist assemblers and heads of farmer groups to collect paddy from contract farmers and then buy it from them at the current market price. The assemblers are local people either in the village or

TABLE 5.3
Costs and Benefits of Rice Value Chain at the Farm Gate (per hectare)

	LAK (thousand)	US$
Gross production costs	6,582.5	765.41
Land preparation	2,145	249.42
Crop establishment	1,137.5	132.27
Nutrition management	500	58.14
Harvest	2,000	232.56
Depreciation of equipment	800	93.02
Gross revenue (yield*price)	8,556	994.88
Farmer income (revenue minus costs)	1,973.5	229.48

Note: The farm gate price for paddy at the beginning of the 2018 harvest season was LAK2,139 (US$0.25) per kg. Average yield in the survey areas was 4 tonnes per ha. Exchange rate: LAK8,600 per US$1.
Source: Estimated by authors using data from the field survey.

nearby villages. According to Hoppe et al. (2018), assemblers employed by a rice mill as a representative for rice collection/consolidation can earn about LAK166 (US$0.02) per kg whereas freelance collectors can profit from price differences by selling paddy to rice mills for around LAK94.6 (US$0.011) per kg. Nonetheless, it seems that at the beginning of the harvest season, rice millers also go to the villages and buy paddy directly from farmers.

Rice Processing

Vanida rice mill signed a subcontract with Xuanye Company in 2018 to supply 250 tonnes of glutinous and generic rice. However, because of the heavy flooding that year, Vanida could only supply 18 tonnes of generic rice to Xuanye. All processes from buying paddy, drying, sorting, milling and grading are done by Vanida. Quality control requirements are stipulated in the contract: the moisture content of paddy should not exceed 14 per cent on the milling date and milled rice should not contain no more than 3 per cent broken kernels.

IDP rice mill follows such quality measures under GACC regulation. However, it was hard to obtain information from IDP about the cost of milling. The analysis of costs and benefits for rice mills therefore used estimated data collected from Vanida rice mill. Table 5.4 shows that Vanida rice mill can achieve revenue of US$441.81 per tonne by selling milled rice to Xuanye for US$0.96 per kg after deducting gross production costs (paddy, electricity and labour) of US$274.30 per tonne.

Exporting

Xuanye performs all the procedures required to export rice to China Oil and Foodstuffs Corporation (COFCO), which is one of China's state-owned food processing holding companies and the largest food processor in China. COFCO is also a major importer of rice from IDP rice mill. Freight costs and documentation fees are reported to be the main costs for both Xuanye and IDP. They both use Thai transport companies to ship rice through Laem-Chabang seaport in Thailand.

However, shipping rice (f.o.b.) from Laem-Chabang to China costs almost US$5 per tonne more than to other countries. Costs per shipment to China include purchasing rice, inland transport from Vientiane to

TABLE 5.4
Costs and Benefits of the Rice Value Chain for Vanida Rice Mill

	LAK (thousand)	US$
Gross production cost (per tonne)	5,190	274.30
Cost of paddy (farm gate price)	4,706	248.72
Electricity	180	20.93
Labour	40	4.65
Revenue (quantity milled rice*price)	3,799	441.81
Income of miller (per tonne)	1,440	167.51

Note: The price used for calculating revenue is based on the price that Xuanye offered Vanida mill in 2018, of about LAK8,260 (US$ 0.96)/kg.
*One tonne of paddy rice can produce 460 kg premium glutinous milled rice.
Source: Estimated by authors using data from Vanida rice mill

Laem-Chabang seaport, fumigation and quality inspection. Shipments also incur documentation fees, namely, sanitary and phytosanitary (SPS) certification, export licence issuance and origin certification. Nonetheless, after subtracting total shipment costs from total revenues, it was found that revenues from organic glutinous rice are higher than from fragrant rice (Table 5.5).

In China, Lao rice is repackaged to sell to Chinese supermarket customers or processed to make sweet rice flour. Based on information from the Department of Trade and Production Promotion of the Ministry of Industry and Commerce, the retail price of Lao rice in China ranges from CNY28 to CNY59 (US$4.17 to US$8.78) per kg, which is the price of medium to high-grade rice. However, the interview with IDP revealed that identical types of Thai rice sold on the Chinese market fetch US$30 to US$40 more per tonne than Lao rice.

Due to the unavailability of data on COFCO's retail prices of Lao rice in China, this study used price data from Xuanye Company, which is involved in both wholesale and retail value chains. Xuanye sells Lao rice, particularly in the form of gift sets of fragrant white rice and organic glutinous rice, to niche markets (high-end consumers) in China. The two types of organic rice fetch US$8.62 and US$7.13 per kg, respectively,[5] much higher than the average domestic price of US$1.16 per kg for non-organic generic rice.

TABLE 5.5
Costs and Benefits of Rice Value Chain at Exporter (Wholesaler) and Retailer Stage

	Export to China		Export to Other Countries	
	LAK	US$	LAK	US$
Shipment costs (per tonne)	6,138,760	713.81	6,097,410	709.00
Cost of rice	5,411,000	629.19	5,411,000	629.19
Transport to Thai seaport	661,600	76.93	661,600	76.93
Fumigation	49,620	5.77	24,810	2.88
Quality inspection by CCIC	16,540	1.92	—	—
Documentation fees (per set)	1,100,000	127.91	1,100,000	127.91
Sanitary and phytosanitary cert.	400,000	46.51	400,000	46.51
Export licence	200,000	23.26	200,000	23.26
Certificate of origin	500,000	58.14	500,000	58.14
Total cost (per tonne)	7,238,760	841.72	7,197,410	836.91
Revenue (per tonne)				
Organic glutinous	74,132,000	8,620.00	—	—
Fragrant white rice	61,318,000	7,130.00	—	—
Net profit (per tonne)				
Organic glutinous	66,893,240	7,778.28	—	—
Fragrant white rice	54,079,240	6,288.28	—	—

Note: The revenues are based on Xuanye Company's estimated income from online sales of organic glutinous rice at US$8.62/kg or US$8,620/t and fragrant rice at US$7.13/kg or US$7,130/t.

Source: Estimated by authors using data collected from IDP Mill and Xuanye Company.

5.4.3 Banana Value Chain

Cavendish Banana Production

Driven by agricultural land shortage in China, Chinese banana investors began streaming across the border to Laos in 2010. Most of them settled in the northern provinces to start growing Cavendish bananas. Villagers were happy with "the Chinese impact". From their perspective, Chinese investors brought a significant amount of money to the area and were ready to lease their land; the rent they offered was generous, and villagers were happy to accept it. They could earn more from renting their land to Chinese investors than from farming it themselves. During the 2015 harvest season, for example, banana plantation workers earned around US$10–US$20 a day, which equated to an average annual income of US$1,740 (Goh and Marshall 2017).

Chinese investors mostly operate in the provinces of Borkeo, Luang Prabang, Oudomxay and Phongsaly. In Phongsaly, twenty-three sub-companies, which come under the control of fifteen major companies/owners (BananaLink 2017), have invested in around 6,000 hectares of banana plantation. Hoang Anh Gia Lai Agriculture, a Vietnamese firm, has invested in Cavendish banana farming in Attapeu province in the southernmost part of Laos; 20 per cent of its outputs are exported to Vietnam and 80 per cent to China (via Vietnamese seaports) (Far Eastern Agriculture 2018). By 2016, Laos' total banana exports had reached 40,000 tonnes.

Exports of Cavendish bananas from the northern provinces increased tenfold during 2014–17 and accounted for nearly all fruits exported to China. The boom in Cavendish bananas has led to several problems, notably the drenching and pollution of fertile land with an array of agrochemicals. Despite the jobs and higher wages, banana investors bring to northern Laos, in 2019 the Lao government placed an investment moratorium on new banana plantations when it became known that the intensive use of agrochemicals was affecting workers' health and harming the environment (Khotpanya and Lipes 2019; Goh and Marshall 2017). Chinese investors were dissatisfied with the government's intervention and ban, stating that the chemical substances and fertilizers used were necessary and had not affected workers' health and wellbeing. The site manager of Jiangong Agriculture went as far as to say that without agribusiness investment, the place would be little more than a bare mountain.

A field study conducted by the Economic Research Institute for Industry and Trade (ERIIT 2017) found that most banana companies operate on economic land concessions granted by the Lao government and on rented farmland under long-term leases arranged directly with villagers. The leasing process is relatively simple: the contracts between Chinese investors and villagers are witnessed by the village chief and government officials, including representatives from the departments of Agriculture and Forestry, National Resources and Environment, and Planning and Investment. Cavendish banana plantations in the northern provinces are exclusively devoted to growing bananas for the Chinese market. As a result, without any compromise, all Cavendish bananas are exported to China.

Banana plantations in the northern provinces are wholly owned and operated by Chinese investors. Full-time Lao employees hold administrative positions; their monthly average income is approximately LAK1.5 million (US$175), higher than the minimum wage of LAK1.1 million (US$128) (Shira 2018). Temporary Lao plantation workers (employed in the harvest season) receive a daily wage of LAK60,000–70,000 (US$7–8). Plantations habitually hire workers from the same family and usually employ around three to four families (or six to eight workers) per hectare (each family usually consists of two adult workers). Plantation workers are paid piece rates of LAK350–380 (US$0.041–0.044) per kg of raw banana harvested and stacked in crates; this means their earnings largely depend on their stamina and speed.

Cavendish banana plantations on average produce approximately 40 tonnes of bananas per hectare. Average annual wage costs amount to LAK14.0–15.2 million (US$1,640–1,760) per hectare. This means that on average each plantation worker earns LAK1.8–1.9 million (US$203–220) per hectare per year. Cavendish banana production is relatively simple, labour-intensive and low tech; the main farming tools are hoes, shovels, rakes and wheelbarrows. Chinese investors supply seeds, chemical fertilizers, herbicides, pesticides and packaging materials, including a chemical dip to prolong ripening, plastic bags, foam-lined boxes and waxed boxes.

We had the opportunity to interview the director of Hoang Anh Gia Lai (HAGL) Group in Attapeu province, southern Laos. Similar to the situation in northern provinces, HAGL was granted a land concession by the government and local people have benefited from the jobs created. Lao workers make up 35 per cent of the total workforce on HAGL's plantation; during the harvesting season, they are paid an extra LAK300,000 (US$35) per tonne (Higashi 2015).

Cavendish Banana Chain Mapping, Key Actors and Export Process

Mapping of the Cavendish banana value chain was based on Porter's value chain framework, which consists of primary and supporting activities. As illustrated in Figure 5.3, primary activities cover inbound logistics, operations, outbound logistics, marketing and sales, and services, whereas support activities include plantation infrastructure, human resource management, technological development, and procurement. The final stage of Porter's value chain is the profit margin.

Because Cavendish bananas are produced solely for export, the primary value chain activities end with outbound logistics. Marketing, sales and services are under the control of Chinese importers. Inbound logistics (transporting banana plants, farming materials, chemical fertilizers, preservatives and packaging materials) are controlled by Chinese companies based in Laos.

Managerial positions in Chinese banana companies are mostly held by Chinese nationals, whereas all plantation workers and fruit packers are Lao. Outbound logistics are processed by two private companies, which operate in different geographical zones. LS Company operates in Luang Namtha, Oudomxay and Luang Prabang provinces, and Mangkone Trading, a Chinese-owned company, has a monopoly in Bokeo province. Both companies charge a flat rate for freight of LAK1.1 million (US$127) per 30-tonne truck. On human resource management, Chinese investors mostly employ Chinese nationals as plantation managers and Lao locals as administrators. Permanent workers' average monthly income is approximately LAK1.5 million (US$175) and temporary workers' average daily earnings are LAK60,000–70,000 (US$7–8), without any social insurance. Lao plantation workers are engaged in cutting, dipping, stacking and loading bananas during the harvesting period. For those activities, they are paid LAK350–380 (US$0.042–US$0.045) per kg of raw banana, amounting to an average yearly income of approximately LAK1.85 million (US$220).

There is little information about technological development in fruit crop production per se, let alone in the banana plantation industry, apart

FIGURE 5.3
Porter's Value Chain Framework for Lao Cavendish Bananas

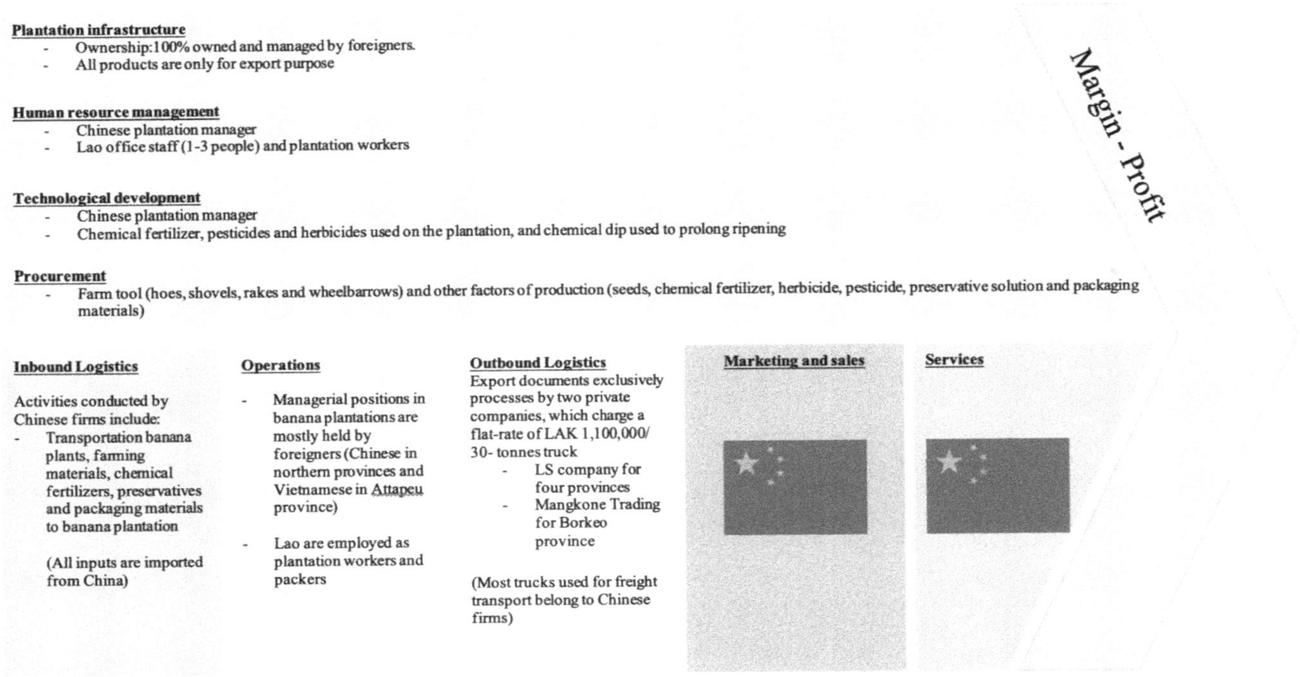

Margin - Profit

Plantation infrastructure
- Ownership:100% owned and managed by foreigners.
- All products are only for export purpose

Human resource management
- Chinese plantation manager
- Lao office staff (1-3 people) and plantation workers

Technological development
- Chinese plantation manager
- Chemical fertilizer, pesticides and herbicides used on the plantation, and chemical dip used to prolong ripening

Procurement
- Farm tool (hoes, shovels, rakes and wheelbarrows) and other factors of production (seeds, chemical fertilizer, herbicide, pesticide, preservative solution and packaging materials)

Inbound Logistics	Operations	Outbound Logistics	Marketing and sales	Services
Activities conducted by Chinese firms include: - Transportation banana plants, farming materials, chemical fertilizers, preservatives and packaging materials to banana plantation (All inputs are imported from China)	- Managerial positions in banana plantations are mostly held by foreigners (Chinese in northern provinces and Vietnamese in Attapeu province) - Lao are employed as plantation workers and packers	Export documents exclusively processes by two private companies, which charge a flat-rate of LAK 1,100,000/ 30- tonnes truck - LS company for four provinces - Mangkone Trading for Borkeo province (Most trucks used for freight transport belong to Chinese firms)		

Source: Authors' own work based on field survey.

from a 2018 IDE JETRO publication. Of particular relevance to the current study is Chapter 3, titled "Lao PDR's Fruit Production for Export: A Case Study of Watermelon in Luang Namtha Province" (Nolintha 2018), which mainly employs descriptive analysis to examine the status of fruit crop production in the face of increasing demand for agricultural produce from China. In Cavendish banana production, the most significant technologies relate to watering and irrigation systems, intensive agrochemical (fertilizers, pesticides, herbicides, rodenticides) use, and preservatives and specialist packaging to prolong ripening.

The procurement procedure is simple and easy to understand. Plantation managers are responsible for ordering farm materials, seeds and agrochemicals, and for managing the plantation workforce. The final part of the Porter value chain is the profit margin, which is the sum of revenue minus cost. It was not possible to estimate profit per hectare due to the unavailability of data on revenues and costs incurred in Cavendish banana marketing and distribution.

Figure 5.4 depicts the value chain for Cavendish bananas in northern Laos. There are roughly eight stages involving both Laos and China. Land concession costs depend on land specifications, starting from LAK13,000 (US$15) per hectare for government-owned land up to US$1,170 per hectare for privately owned and developed farmland. In stage 2, based on average annual productivity of 40 tonnes per hectare and the piece rate of LAK350–380 (US$0.041–0.044) per kg paid to plantation workers, the total wage cost for plantation workers is US$1,640–US$1,760 per hectare.

As mentioned earlier, each cultivated hectare requires three to four families (six to eight people) to work it. In stage 3, small plantations of 10 hectares reportedly employ only office staff at the rate of LAK18 million (US$2,090) a year and plantation workers at around LAK1.8 million (US$209) per hectare. On the other hand, it was also claimed that a massive 400-hectare plantation employs only three plantation/administration staff, giving total wage costs of LAK54 million (US$6,271) a year.

This study does not have much information about stages 4, 5 and 6, which fall into the China side via Chinese investors' employment of Chinese managers and control over inputs, inbound and outbound logistics. In stage 7, two Lao companies are in charge of processing export documents. They charge a processing fee of LAK1.1 million (US$128) per 30-tonne truck, giving a processing fee for 1 hectare or 40 tonnes of LAK1.5 million (US$170). However, in Bokeo province, this process is monopolized by

FIGURE 5.4
Cavendish Banana Value Chain Costs and Revenues in Northern Provinces

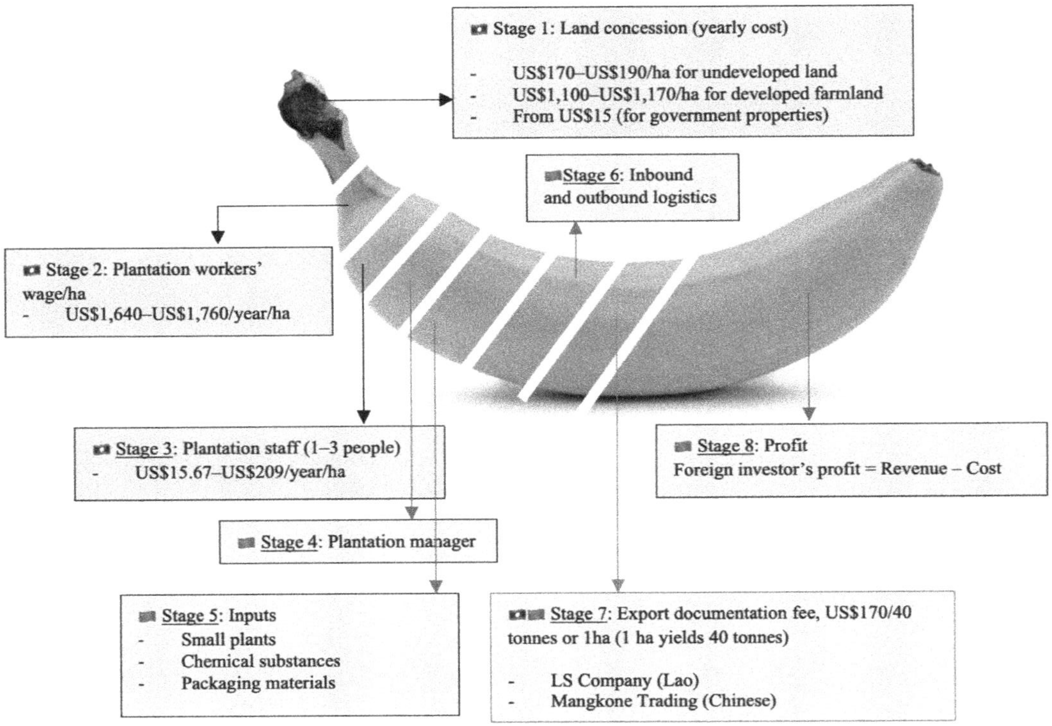

- **Stage 1**: Land concession (yearly cost)
  - US$170–US$190/ha for undeveloped land
  - US$1,100–US$1,170/ha for developed farmland
  - From US$15 (for government properties)

- **Stage 2**: Plantation workers' wage/ha
  - US$1,640–US$1,760/year/ha

- **Stage 3**: Plantation staff (1–3 people)
  - US$15.67–US$209/year/ha

- **Stage 4**: Plantation manager

- **Stage 5**: Inputs
  - Small plants
  - Chemical substances
  - Packaging materials

- **Stage 6**: Inbound and outbound logistics

- **Stage 7**: Export documentation fee, US$170/40 tonnes or 1ha (1 ha yields 40 tonnes)
  - LS Company (Lao)
  - Mangkone Trading (Chinese)

- **Stage 8**: Profit
  Foreign investor's profit = Revenue − Cost

Source: Authors' own work based on field survey.

Mangkone Trading, a Chinese company, which means that this source of revenue falls to the Chinese side. Stage 8 concerns profit and shows the profit estimation method for Cavendish banana exports. However, due to undisclosed information about revenues and production costs, we do not have enough information to calculate the exact profit per hectare. Still, we realize that the maximum or the best possible annual revenue on the Laos side is around US$3,309 per hectare (1,170 + 1,760 + 209 + 170).

Factors Affecting the Business Environment

Likert scale questions were used in the questionnaire to gain an understanding of the business environment. The questions covered complications in the business environment, licensing, starting an import/export business, importing of materials, and other factors that affect the business well-being of Cavendish banana plantations. Figure 5.5 shows that road transport is the most prominent factor: out of twelve respondents (plantation managers), eight reported that road transport has a very high impact on the business environment and nine said that transport costs and weak irrigation systems are problems for their plantations.

In contrast, all twelve respondents stated that workforce skills and experience, machinery imports and food safety have a low impact on the business environment. In addition, eight of them said that the supply-side price has very little influence on business in Laos. This empirical evidence supports the fact that there is plenty of room for value creation by improving the condition, quality and capacity of the road network in Laos; transport rules and regulations are not an issue for exporters because of the relative ease of inbound and outbound logistics.

Gaining access to farmland (through concessions) is not a problem for foreign investors. Indeed, making agricultural land available to foreign investors is supported by Lao government policy with a view to promoting land concessions as a means to enhance economic growth, develop and upgrade infrastructure, create new industries, exploit the full potential of its commodity exports, generate jobs and reduce poverty (LIWG 2018).

5.4.4 Challenges in the Rice and Cavendish Banana Value Chains

Key actors and challenges in the rice and Cavendish banana value chains are presented in Table 5.6.

Agricultural Exports from Laos to China 189

FIGURE 5.5
Factors Affecting the Business Environment of Cavendish Banana Plantations (n=12)

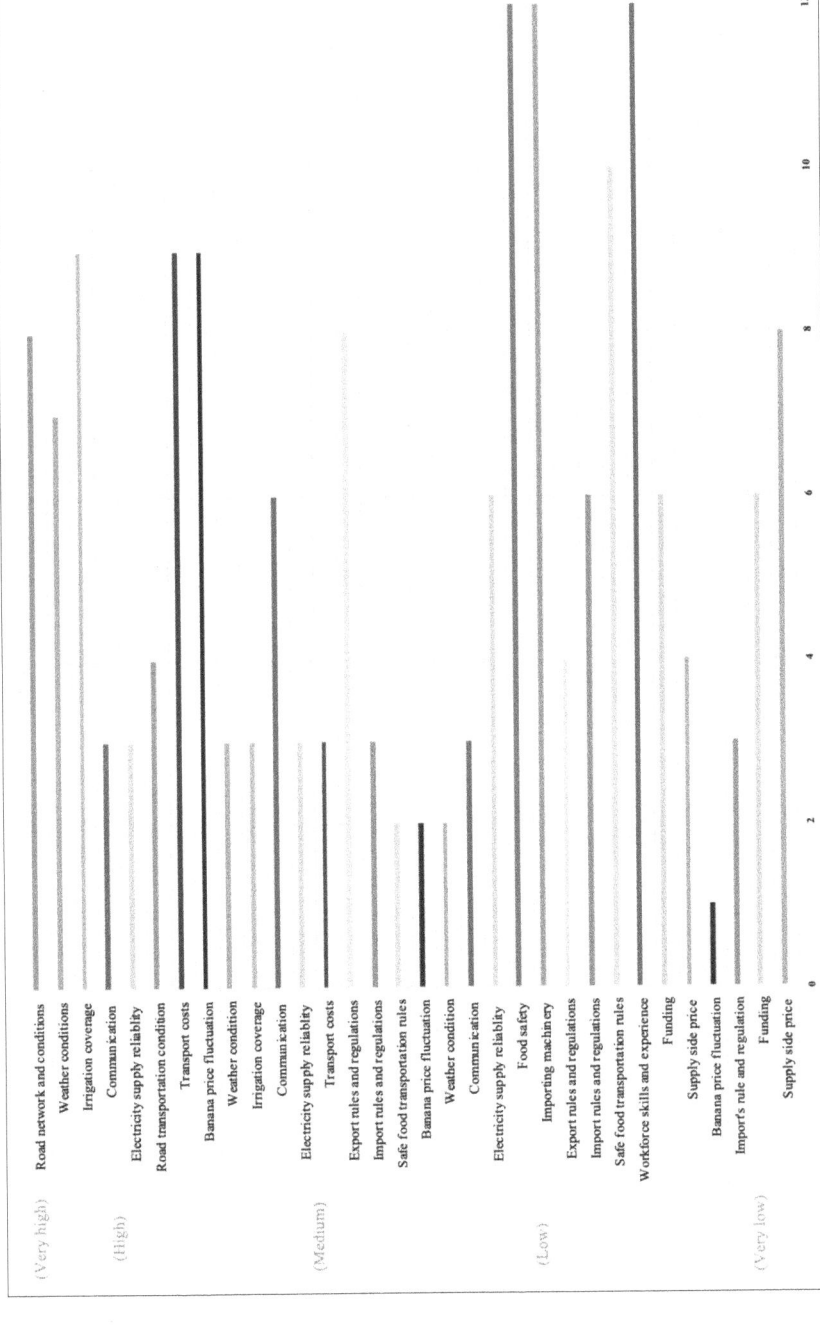

Source: Authors' own work based on field survey.

TABLE 5.6
Key Actors and Challenges in the Rice and Cavendish Banana Value Chains

	Crop Suppliers	Collectors and Processors	Exporters	Importers and Distributors
Rice				
Key actors	Local farmers (2+3 contract farming model).	IDP rice mill Vanida rice mill	IDP rice mill Xuanye company	COFCO
Challenging issues	Production losses due to natural disasters. Meeting quality standards for rice exports to China.	Meeting contract requirements for quality and quantity pledged to exporters/distributors	Freight and transport document costs. Getting export documents (e.g., SPS certificate, export licence, certificate of origin).	Seeking the right market for Lao rice. Difficulty competing in regional and global markets.
Cavendish bananas				
Key actors	Chinese investors own 15 plantations Chinese hired as managers. Lao hired as plantation workers and administrators.	Cutting, trimming, dipping and collecting are done at the farm	LS Company Mankone Trading	Various Chinese traders
Challenging issues	Plantation workers and land directly exposed to agrochemicals.	Occupational health issues caused by agrochemicals.	Meeting NTM quality compliance and conformity assessment requirements. Forging chain links with Chinese distributors.	Selecting the right distribution channel to compete with other rice exporting countries.

5.4.5 Non-tariff Measures

China's economic growth and share of global trade increased rapidly following its economic reforms and opening up beginning in 1978. In tandem with this dramatic economic development, China is paying greater attention to public health protection, environmental protection and food safety, or so it seems given the trend towards its increasing use of NTMs. Import and export companies have to comply with a wide range of requirements such as quality standards and measures as well as technical specifications and legislation. China's NTM-related regulations are set up under the auspices of twenty-nine different authorities, five of which account for just over 80 per cent of all NTMs; they are AQSIQ, Standardization Administration of China, Ministry of Agriculture, General Administration of Customs, and Ministry of Commerce. These authorities are responsible for administering SPS and technical barriers to trade (TBT) measures and checks. One of the most challenging issues is that there is no centralized source in China where NTM and trade-related standards, regulations and laws are readily available to the general public. Instead, the majority of this important information is narrowly publicized by implementation agencies, departments and ministries and therefore largely inaccessible (Li and Yu 2020).

Rice Value Chain

Although the Lao government openly promotes the export of rice to China under China's import quota, rice mills and export companies exporting rice to China need to ensure NTM compliance. Few rice mills can participate in the supply chain because their production and management systems are not certified. According to a statistical report by the Department of Industry and Handicraft (2017), Laos has thirteen large rice mills (out of 129 nationwide) and only three rice mills have good manufacturing practice (GMP) certification. Rice mills have to be GMP approved and certified before they can be considered eligible to export milled rice to China as AQSIQ has stringent safety and quality requirements (see Annex 5.1: AQSIQ Moisture Standards for Imported Rice). Conformity assessment related to SPS is especially strict and impedes the expansion of rice exports to China. Almost 90 per cent of rice mills in Laos are small and medium-sized and equipped with obsolete machinery; they cannot produce milled rice of good enough quality to comply with SPS export controls. A related obstacle is the lack of working capital, which constrains the ability of small and medium rice millers to control how rice is grown. As a result, poor paddy quality is often blamed for the low standard of milled rice, which impedes rice millers' participation in the rice export value chain to China.

Clearly, not all rice mills and businesses in Laos can export rice to China under the import quota. Rice is still listed as highly sensitive on the tariff reduction schedule between ASEAN and China. Semi-milled or wholly milled long-grain rice (HS10063010) is subject to tariffs of up to 50 per cent, making it difficult for rice exporters to access Chinese rice markets without the import quota. Laos was granted a rice import quota of 8,000 tonnes in 2017 and then 20,000 tonnes in 2018. Two companies currently ship rice to China under the quota system: however, only one company, Xuanye, is AQSIQ certified and able to comply with China's SPS measures. The process of applying for AQSIQ certification involves quality inspections at several production stages, from rice planting to processing, which is time-consuming and costly (see Annex 5.2: China's Sanitary and Phytosanitary Measures). This precludes many small and medium-sized rice millers from participating in the rice supply chain under China's import quota.

Cavendish Banana Value Chain

The export procedure for Cavendish bananas starts with plantation inspection by the exporter/investor and contract signing with villagers (Figure 5.6). Bananas are transported by logistics companies to Boten–Mohan international checkpoint (Higashi 2015). The shipping process involves four documents: (1) an export licence issued by the Provincial Department of Agriculture and Forestry to shipping agencies; (2) Lao customs payment; (3) quarantine inspection; and (4) release of goods. The shipping process is monopolized by two companies: Mangkone Trading and LS Company. Payment is finalized on the transfer of funds from the importer's bank to the exporter's bank (De et al. 2016).

Phytosanitary measures require fruit exporters to register (as an exporter to China) with AQSIQ. Cavendish banana consignments need to be further inspected by the China Certification and Inspection Company. Moreover, all food products need to comply with China's Food Safety Law, the documentation procedures for which involve the Ministry of Health,

FIGURE 5.6
Export Procedure for Cavendish Bananas

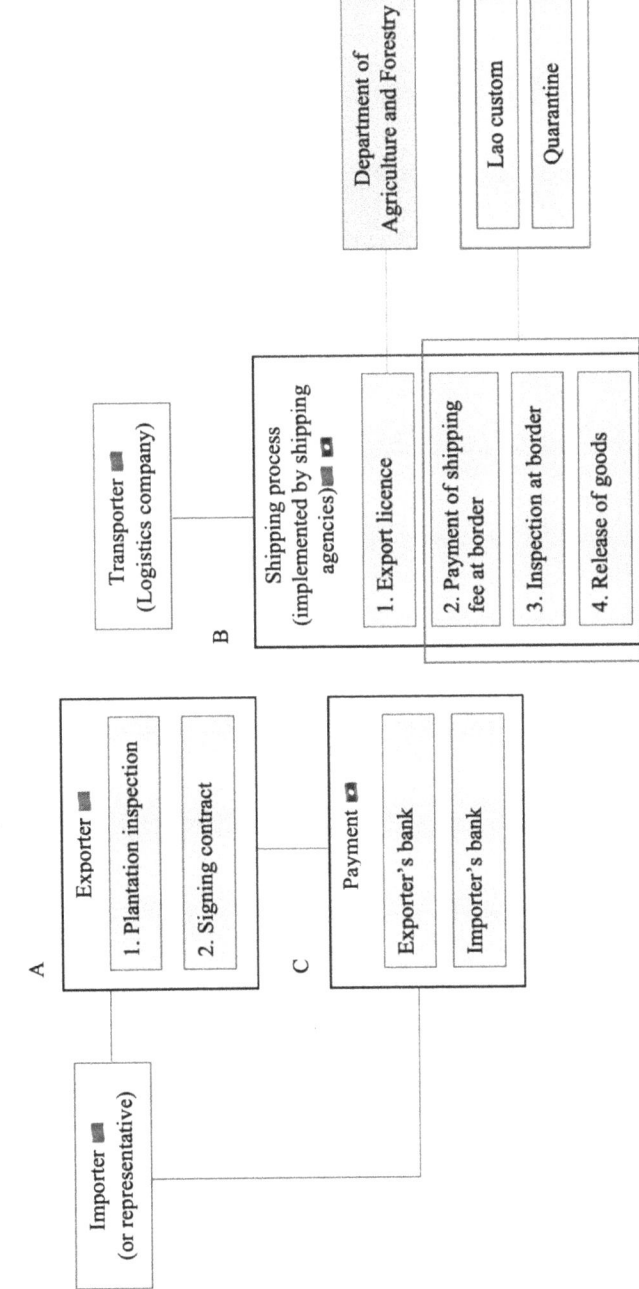

Source: Adapted from De et al. (2016).

AQSIQ, State Food and Drug Administration, and the State Administration for Industry and Commerce. To access the Chinese market, importers (mostly Chinese firms) need to obtain permission from China Inspection and Quarantine (DTF 2012; DITP 2010).

No clear export quotas or other NTMs for fruit products have been issued by the Chinese government. In December 2017, Lao and Chinese delegates reached an agreement on Lao banana exports to China.[6] Harvested bananas must meet Chinese standards and specifications if they are to enter Chinese markets. According to the bilateral agreement, exporters need to meet the following standards (Golnazarian 2018):

- Bananas should be harvested ten to eleven weeks after flowering; ripe bananas will be rejected.
- Exporters must meet China's phytosanitary regulations; contaminated bananas will be rejected.
- Shipments must be free of rhizomes, soil and leaves.
- Packaging facility location and chemical substances used must be declared.

The procedure for exporting Cavendish bananas to China is not straightforward. It is largely implemented by the Chinese side and due to NTMs and weak links with Chinese distribution channels is most likely inaccessible to Lao businesses. The NTMs imposed on agricultural products mostly prioritize food safety, environmental protection and biosecurity. Even so, regardless of the strict NTMs imposed by the Chinese government, Chinese-run Cavendish banana plantations in Laos make extensive use of herbicides and pesticides. The chemical residues have negative effects on the environment and are often cited as a cause of occupational ill health. In response, the Lao government has vowed to enforce its ban on granting land concessions for Cavendish banana plantations and penalize local people violating the rules (Khotpanya and Lipes 2019).

5.5 CONCLUSIONS AND POLICY IMPLICATIONS

This study demonstrates that commercialization in Laos' agricultural sector has paved the way for farmers and businesses to participate in agricultural export value chains. To analyse agricultural value chain development in Laos, rice and Cavendish bananas were chosen to examine how farmers, local businesses and exporters benefit from participating in the export value chains and the problems they face. The study finds that many rice farmers in Khammoun and Savannakhet provinces have participated in the rice export value chain since 2018, when the country received its first import quota from the Chinese government, and so far, more than 20,000 tonnes of rice per year have been officially exported to China. Participation in the rice export value chain under China's import quotas has brought substantial benefits to all actors along the chain. However, the profit margin varies among participants in each stage of the chain. Rice farmers and collectors have smaller profit margins than rice millers and exporters. The most profitable participants in the chain are exporters[7] who act as online retailers for high-end markets in China. The value chain of Cavendish bananas in the northern provinces has been greatly influenced by Chinese investments. Almost all Cavendish banana plantations are owned by Chinese investors in the form of land concessions from the government or land leased from local people based on the contract farming 1+4 model. The plantations employ workers from nearby villages. These plantation workers are paid a daily wage plus piece-rate pay.

Throughout the analysis, it is clear that two companies (Xuanye and IDP) play key roles in the rice value chain, from pre-sowing to harvesting, collecting and delivering paddy, and milling for export. Farmers are better off participating in rice exports to China than selling their rice locally. Local rice collectors also benefit from representing rice mills and collecting rice from farmers scattered in different villages. However, rice exporters, who act as online retailers for high-end markets, have benefited the most. The opposite is true for the Cavendish banana value chain: the benefits of value chain participation mostly accrue to Chinese investors, whereas the government and local people/businesses receive a relatively small share of the benefits in the form of land concession fees, wages and export documentation (i.e., freight forwarder) fees.

The study has identified several challenges associated with NTMs in both value chains. First, consistent quality and quantity are crucial for rice and fruit exports. NTMs have a striking influence on the Lao value chains of rice and bananas exported to China. China's stringent agricultural import regulations and quality standards under SPS measures are a major constraint on Lao exporters' formal exports of rice and Cavendish bananas to Chinese markets. It is difficult for Lao export companies, most of which are small enterprises with insufficient capital, to acquire certification from China's Administration of Quality Supervision, Inspection and Quarantine.

They also have to undergo preshipment screening by registering company information with the General Administration of Customs of China to smooth customs clearance for importers in China.

Based on the above-identified factors, this study sets out two sets of policy recommendations for consideration.

For Rice Production and Export

Becoming self-sufficient in rice and exporting surplus rice to China under China's import quotas are significant achievements. Yet there are some challenges and difficulties that need to be overcome through collective efforts for Laos to improve the quality and increase the quantity of its rice exports to China. To that end, the policy recommendations outlined below merit consideration:

- Collective efforts from the government and the business sector (rice mills/wholesalers) are required to strengthen farmer groups/clusters and rice mill collaboration by increasing investment in agricultural services to advise farmers throughout the production cycle so as to build trustworthy cooperation.
- High-quality paddy means high-quality milled rice. Specific measures are therefore needed to directly target the farmer groups involved in the supply chain of rice exported to China. In so doing, the government could pursue a two-pronged approach: promote public-private partnerships for providing the right technical assistance based on the quality control criteria stipulated by China in the early stages of rice farming; and ensure sufficient supplies of good-quality rice seed to improve the quality and quantity of rice produced.
- Rice mills disqualified from participating in the rice export chain to China are mostly small family-run businesses with obsolete machinery. They usually have difficulty accessing finance, which is a consequence of their low creditworthiness from the perspective of banking institutions. Government policy aimed at helping rice millers improve their business and management skills would enable them to approach banks for loans to modernize and increase the capacity of their rice mills.
- AQSIQ and GACC certification is the key factor determining eligibility to export rice to China. It falls on the government to provide sufficient

information about AQSIQ and GACC requirements to interested rice millers. In addition, the time-consuming bureaucratic internal procedures required for quality inspection from planting to rice milling should be streamlined.
- Transport costs, whether in-country transport or through a third country, are very high in the GMS. A more business-friendly approach could help reduce costs for hauliers and, in turn, for exporters/millers. First, police inspections of trucks carrying paddy and milled rice for export could be dropped. Second, burdensome approval procedures for the domestic transport of paddy/rice could be removed. And third, logistics cooperation between Laos and Thailand and between Laos and Vietnam could be strengthened under bilateral transport agreements and a Cross-Border Transport Agreement to increase cost efficiency for Lao rice exporters.

For Banana Production and Export

Due to Lao businesses' limited knowledge of sector-specific NTM barriers, export clearance processes are mostly done on China's side of the border. For Laos to gain the highest possible benefits from the production and export of Cavendish bananas, the following policy options are proposed:

- The Lao government should further promote banana production along with other agricultural products for export. To that end, the government needs to publicize export rules and regulations to improve investors' understanding of the export documentation process and reduce their reliance on shipping companies/agencies currently dominating this stage in the value chain.
- Industry organizations and trade associations should organize business-matching workshops with a focus on exporting agricultural products to China. Capacity-building projects to educate producers, wholesalers and exporters on how to conform with AQSIQ and GACC rules and regulations should be implemented. Strategies to improve business well-being should be developed.
- Rural and remote villages must be provided with road infrastructure capable of meeting the needs of inland exporters. Better road infrastructure would directly reduce transport times and costs, creating a comparative advantage for Lao exporters.

- Compliance with international health and safety standards on the use of agrochemicals and law on occupational health needs to be strengthened. Linked to this, the government needs to monitor workers' social insurance status to ensure that plantation workers have the protection of a reliable healthcare scheme.
- Premium agricultural products, including organic bananas and fair-trade products, should be paid more attention. They create higher value-added for local people without environmental harm and health hazards.
- Land concessions, despite the potential benefits to society, can have negative ecological impacts, as reported by several government bodies, academics and development agencies. The government needs to respond by supporting a proper contract farming scheme that ensures better benefits for farmers and plantation workers and, ultimately, the economy as a whole.

ANNEX 5.1
AQSIQ Moisture Standards for Imported Rice

	Items	Moisture Standard (Test Result)
1.	Moisture content	14.0% (13.70%)
2.	Whole kernels	95.0% (78.80%)
3.	Broken (3/4 basis)	3.0% (8–10%)
4.	Ratio	>2.0% (3.52%)
5.	Red and red streaked kernels	0.5% (0.12%)
6.	Yellow kernels	0.5% (0.20%)
7.	Chalky kernels	2.0% (1.84%)
8.	White glutinous rice	0.5% (0.16%)
9.	Damaged kernels	0.5% (0.28%)
10.	Paddy kernels	0.0%
11.	Live insects	0.0%
12.	Foreign matter	0.0%
13.	Purity	93.0%
14.	Average length of whole kernels	7.02mm

Source: Administration of Quality Supervision, Inspection and Quarantine.

ANNEX 5.2
China's Sanitary and Phytosanitary Measures

Measure	Commodity	Procedure	Implementation unit
Phytosanitary	Fruits	Register as an exporter to China* Provide required information on the packaging • Name of export company • Fruit type • Packing date • Destination • Exporting notes "Export to China" Ensure all fruits shipped to China are free of soil residues, leaves and insects	General Administration for Quality Supervision, Inspection and Quarantine (AQSIQ)/China Certification and Inspection
Food safety	All food	Ensure production processes comply with the Food Safety Law of China	Ministry of Health Ministry of Agriculture AQSIQ State Food and Drug Administration State Administration for Industry and Commerce
Food safety	Organic products	Organic food products are inspected by the China Organic Food Development Centre	China Organic Food Development Centre
QS mark	28 types of food products (including rice)	Products officially certified by the State Food and Drug Administration	State Food and Drug Administration under AQSIQ
Packaging, import and export	All food products and prepackaged food	Ensure information on packaging complies with Regulation on Management of Import-Export Food Labelling (under AQSIQ) Inspect packaging information, e.g., ingredients, nutrition, use instructions, country of origin (under CIQ)	AQSIQ China Inspection and Quarantine (CIQ)

Note: *Export companies must submit the following documents to register for AQSIQ certification: (1) type of product and quantity (along with flight/ship number), (2) bill of lading, (3) invoice, (4) packing list, (5) phytosanitary certificate, (6) certificate of origin. AQSIQ-related documents are submitted by exporters and CIQ-related documents are submitted by importers (China-based firms).
Sources: RYT9 (2010); DFT (2012).

Notes

1. Administration of Quality Supervision, Inspection and Quarantine (AQSIQ) is a Chinese government agency in charge of quality and standards control of imported products.
2. To pass through customs clearance at the Chinese border, exporters must obtain a registration number from the General Administration of Customs of China (GACC).
3. ISO 9001 is the international standard for factory quality management systems.
4. Information is from an interview with a representative of the Department of Trade Promotion, Ministry of Industry and Commerce, 12 February 2019.
5. Data on retail prices is from an interview with a managing director of Xuanye (Laos), Vientiane, August 2018. In China, most of Xuanye (Laos)'s rice is sold through Jingdong online store (https://landlao.jd.com).
6. For more information, see Annex 5.2: China's Sanitary and Phytosanitary Measures.
7. For preliminary illustrative purposes only as information about the delivery and operational costs of retailers in China was inaccessible.

References

Achchuthan, Sivapalan, and Kajananthan Rajendran. 2012. "A Study on Value Chain Analysis in Dairy Sector Kilinochchi District, Sri Lanka". *Global Journal of Management and Business Research* 12, no. 31: 1–13.

ADB (Asian Development Bank). 2018. *Agriculture, Natural Resources, and Rural Development Sector Assessment, Strategy, and Road Map: Lao People's Democratic Republic*. Manila: Asian Development Bank.

Anandajayasekeram, Ponniah, and Berhanu Gebremedhin. 2009. *Integrating Innovation Systems Perspective and Value Chain Analysis in Agricultural Research for Development: Implications and Challenges*. Improving Productivity and Market Success Working Paper 16. Nairobi: International Livestock Research Institute (ILRI).

BananaLink. 2017. "Chinese Banana Farms in Laos Halted for Using Hazardous Chemicals". www.bananalink.org.uk/chinese-banana-farms-laos-halted-using-hazardous-chemicals (accessed 1 April 2017).

De, Prabir, Thiphaphone Phetmany, Buakhai Phimmavong, Aliya Phommathan, Athith Pathoumvanh, Visay Sayyavongsa, Adisack Thongpathoum, and Thipphasone Inthachack. 2016. *Non-Tariff Measures (NTMs) Faced by Exporters of Lao PDR: A Field Survey Report*. Vientiane: Ministry of Industry and Commerce.

Department of Industry and Handicraft. 2017. *Statistical Industry Report*. Vientiane: Ministry of Industry and Commerce.

DFT (Department of Foreign Trade). 2012 *Sanitary and Phytosanitary Measures (SPS Report)*. Bangkok: DFT. http://taxclinic.mof.go.th/pdf/61A363ED 30FE_5C50_4F5F_82B571D 63716.pdf

DITP (Department of International Trade Promotion). 2010. "Xiamen Entry–Exit Inspection and Quarantine Bureau". https://www.ryt9.com/s/expd/994874

ERIIT. 2017. *Cost Structure of Banana Production in Southern Provinces*. Vientiane: Economic Research Institute for Industry and Trade (ERIIT) and Ministry of Industry and Commerce.

FAO (Food and Agriculture Organization). 2005. "Addressing Marketing and Processing Constraints that Inhibit Agrifood Exports. A Guide for Policy Analysts and Planners". *FAO Agricultural Services Bulletin* 60.

———. 2018. "Rice Market Monitor". www.fao.org/3/I9243EN /i9243en.pdf (accessed 18 April 2018).

———. 2019. "Laos at a Glance". http://www.fao.org/laos/fao-in-laos/laos-at-a-glance/en/

Far Eastern Agriculture. 2018. "Vietnamese Company to Expand Banana Farming for Export to China". Far Eastern Agriculture. www.fareasternagricultu re.com/ crops/agriculture/ vietnamese-company-to-expand-banana-farming-for-export-to-china (accessed 20 August 2018).

Globaltimes. 2016. "Laos to Increase Rice Exports to China". http://www.globaltimes. cn/content/1025503.shtml

Goh, Brenda, and Andrew Marshall. 2017. "Cash and Chemicals – for Laos, Chinese Banana Boom a Blessing and Curse". Reuters. https://www.reuters.com/ article/us-china-silkroad-laos/cash-and-chemicals-for-laos-chinese-banana-boom-a-blessing-and-curse-idUSKBN187334

Golnazarian, Sevan. 2018. "Laos Bananas Admitted to China's Allowable Imported Fruits List". Produce Report. https://www.producereport.com/article /laos-bananas-admitted-china's-allowable-imported-fruits-list (accessed 23 May 2018).

Higashi Satomi. 2015. *Impacts on Regional Land Use from Investment in Banana Contract Farming by Chinese Companies: Case Studies in Oudomxay Province, Northern Laos*. Mekong Watch.

Hoppe, Mombert, Sergiy Zorya, Anke Reichhuber, Kenekeo Sayarath, Wisambi Loundu, and Somchay Soulitham. 2018. *Commercialization of Rice and Vegetables Value Chains in Lao PDR: Status and Prospects* (in English). Washington, DC: World Bank.

IFM (Institute for Manufacturing). 2016. "Porter's Value Chain". University of Cambridge website. https://www.ifm.eng.cam.ac.uk/research/dstools/ value-chain-/

Khotpanya, Sidney, and Joshua Lipes. 2019. "Laos: Govt to Enforce Ban on New Banana Plantations Due to Overuse of Chemicals Reported to Cause Deaths and Illnesses". Business & Human Rights Resource Centre. https://www.

business-humanrights.org/en/laos-govt-to-enforce-ban-on-new-banana-plantations-due-to-overuse-of-chemicals-reported-to-cause-deaths-illnesses (accessed 18 May 2019).

Li Mingcong, and Yu Miaojie. 2020. "Non-Tariff Measures in China". In *Non-Tariff Measures in Australia, China, India, Japan, New Zealand and the Republic of Korea: Preliminary Findings*, edited by Denise Penello Rial and Muhammad Rizqy Anandhika, pp. 23–24. Jakarta: ERIA.

LIWG (Land Information Working Group). 2018. *Turning Land into Capital: A Review of Recent Research on Land Concessions for Investment in Lao PDR.Working Group on Land Issues*. Vientiane: Plan International Laos.

Manivong, Vongpaphane, Sengphachanh Sonethavixay, Piya Wonpit, and Isabelle Vagneron. 2016. "Fair Deal or Ordeal? Enquiry into the Sustainability of Commercial Banana Production in the Lao PDR". *Agri-Chains and Sustainable Development*. https://agritrop.cirad.fr/583059/1/P106.pdf

McCullough, Ellen, Prabhu L. Pingali, and Kostas G. Stramoulis. 2008. *The Transformation of Agri-Food Systems, Globalization, Supply Chains and Smallholder Farmers*. London; Sterling, VA: Food and Agriculture Organization of the United Nations and Earthscan.

Ministry of Industry and Commerce. 2012. Decision on the Procedures for Rice Import and Export in the Lao PDR No. 0452/MOIC. DIMEX. Vientiane: Ministry of Industry and Commerce.

MOAF (Ministry of Agriculture and Forestry). 2011. *Decree No. 1937*. Vientiane: MOAF.

———. 2017. *Agricultural Statistics*. Vientiane: MOAF.

———. 2018. *Laos' Agriculture Statistical Report 2018*. Vientiane: MOAF.

NAFRI (National Agriculture and Forestry Research Institute). 2016. "How Sustainable is Commercial Banana Production in Laos". Open Development Mekong. https://data.vietnam.opendevelopmentmekong.net/en/library_record/how-sustainable-is-commercial-banana-production-in-laos-2016

Nolintha, Vanthana. 2018. " Lao PDR's Fruit Production for Export: A Case Study of Watermelon in Luangnamtha Province". In *Impact of China's Increasing Demand for Agro Produce on Agricultural Production in the Mekong Region*, edited by Koji Kubo and Shozo Sakata, Ch. 3. Tokyo: IDE-JETRO.

Quora. 2015. "What is AQSIQ Certificate?". www.quora.com/What-is-AQSIQ-Certificate

RYT9. 2010. "Xiamen Entry-Exit Inspection and Quarantine Bureau". RYT. https://www.ryt9.com/s/expd/994874.

Sacklokham, Silinthone. 2009. "Rice-based Farming Systems in Lao PDR: Opportunities and Challenges for Food Security". Open Development Mekong. https://data.opendevelopme ntmekong.net/library_record/rice-based-farming-systems-in-lao-pdr-opportunities-and-challenges-for-food-security

Setboonsarng, Sununtar, PingSun Leung, and Adam Stefan. 2008. *Rice Contract*

Farming in Lao PDR:Moving from Subsistence to Commercial Agriculture. ADBI Discussion Paper 90. Tokyo: Asian Development Bank Institute. http://www.adbi.org/discussionpaper/2008 /02/25/2492.rice.contract.farming.in.lao.pdr/

Shira, Dezan. 2018. "Laos Increases Minimum Monthly Wage for the Third Time in Eight Years". ASEAN Briefing. https://www.aseanbriefing.com/news/2018/05/31/laos-increases-minimum-monthly-wage-third-time-eight-years.html (accessed 31 May 2018).

TKN (Trade Knowledge Network). 2012. " Business Models for Foreign Investment in Agriculture in Laos". https://europa.eu/capacity4dev/file/11999/download?token=4C CzV-U_

UN Comtrade. 2018. "Calculation based on HS1006 Rice Imported by China in 2018 ". UN Comtrade.

UNDP (United Nations Development Programme). 2015. *The Impact of Contract Farming on Poverty and Environment in Lao PDR*. Issue Brief.

Vientiane Times. 2019. "Laos Urges China to Increase Rice Import Quota to 50,000 Tonnes". 21 February 2019. www.vientianetimes.org.la/freeContent/ FreeConten Laos%2 u.php

World Education. 2016. *Value Chain Assessment Report – Lao Ngam: Assessment of Value Chains to Support Sustainable Livelihoods for the Poor through Inclusive Economic Development Lao Ngam District, Salavane Province*. http://53c5r2vuv7y1h7ipr2fx8kut-wpengine.netdna-ssl.com/wp-content/uploads/2014/10/World-Education-Value-Chain-Assessment-Lao-Ngam-2016.pdf

Xinhua. 2017. "Laos to Export More Rice to China: PM". Xinhua News Agency. www.xinhuanet.com/ /english/2017-01/15/c 135984 301.htm (accessed 15 January 2017).

6

AGRICULTURAL EXPORTS FROM MYANMAR TO CHINA
A Value Chain Analysis of Maize

Ngu Wah Win, Zaw Oo, Aung Htun and Zaw Min Naing

6.1 INTRODUCTION

Myanmar shares land borders with China, India, Laos and Thailand. Given this strategic location, the country plays an important role in facilitating trade between China and other Greater Mekong Subregion countries. Myanmar's trade with China expanded rapidly between the 1990s and the 2010s when the country was still subject to economic sanctions imposed by the United States and the European Union. In 1991–93, China's share of Myanmar's trade stood at 24.3 per cent compared to 10 per cent each for the United States and the European Union. At that time, Myanmar traded mostly within the ASEAN region, which accounted for 42.3 per cent of Myanmar's total trade. By 2011–13, China had become Myanmar's largest trading partner with a 39 per cent share of total trade, while ASEAN's share had fallen to just under 29 per cent, and the United States and the European Union each had just 3 per cent.

Although Myanmar continued to rely on natural gas as the main export commodity to Thailand and China, the share of agriculture trade with China rose rapidly in the last ten years. Myanmar's export portfolio with China mainly consists of raw and unprocessed agricultural products such as rice, beans and pulses, fruit and vegetables, maize, rubber and fishery products. About one-fifth of total agricultural exports are transported overland through cross-border trade to China, though a considerable share of this trade is informal. Here, informal trade refers to trade in processed or non-processed goods considered legal exports on the Myanmar side but illicit imports on the China side. This informal trade represents a massive loss of revenue for Myanmar in value-added and employment opportunities along agricultural value chains. The major bottlenecks behind such imbalance are created by the lack of national quality infrastructure at main border checkpoints and the dominance of informal trade highly susceptible to administrative border control measures. Added to this, the prevalence of non-tariff measures (NTMs) on the China side, and the lack of institutions and infrastructure to certify the quality of agricultural produce on the Myanmar side, are the underlying causes of this informal trade and its negative effects on smallholders.

Boosting agricultural trade is crucial for economic growth and poverty reduction in Myanmar. In 2018, agriculture contributed 25 per cent of total GDP, employed 49 per cent of the total labour force, and generated 20 per cent of total export revenues (World Bank 2018). The sector is dominated by smallholders practising traditional subsistence and labour-intensive farming. Agricultural productivity therefore remains very low. Lacklustre agricultural growth has held back wider economic growth and poverty reduction and pushed migration from rural areas to urban centres, both in Myanmar and neighbouring countries such as Thailand, Malaysia and China. Myanmar's agricultural export basket is relatively small. The main destinations for its agricultural exports are immediate neighbours such as China, Thailand and India, which process Myanmar's primary raw products into final food products and industrial goods for international markets. Yet such value-added activities (i.e., sorting, processing and packaging agricultural goods) have great potential in Myanmar, where a large share of the poor population live in rural areas and have a vocational understanding of agriculture.

At this juncture, natural resource extracts, such as natural gas and minerals, remain Myanmar's top export commodities to China. In 2017, natural gas topped the list of revenue-generating commodities. Among the top agricultural export commodities, we chose to focus on maize. Maize is Myanmar's third-largest agricultural export to China, accounting for over 95 per cent of the country's maize production, and exported mainly as raw and unprocessed food. Given that Myanmar's maize trade has long been reliant on China, the impact of Chinese NTMs on the domestic maize value chain can be clearly observed and analysed. While maize is grown countrywide, the largest maize cultivation area (62 per cent of the total) is in Shan State, the largest subnational administrative region among fourteen states and regions in Myanmar, which adjoins Yunnan province in southwest China. We therefore selected Shan State for our value chain analysis of maize.

This study analyses Myanmar's informal export of maize to China and its implications for domestic primary producers in terms of price instability and market uncertainty. Specifically, we aimed to extend previous research by providing an in-depth look at Myanmar's export of maize and linkages with Chinese markets to identify the challenges and opportunities of converting informal to formal trade, particularly the rise of NTMs and their trade effects. Maize value chain studies, similarly to many studies on the agricultural sector in Myanmar, have focused primarily on farm economics and production aspects of the value chain, from contract farming for a corporate agrofeed system (Woods 2015) to cropping characteristics and cultivar selection (Egashira and Than 2006). Scant attention has been paid to market access and opportunities for trade with China or other export destinations. This research contributes to filling that knowledge gap by focusing on downstream segments of the value chain and how upstream farmers must transform their production systems to meet export compliance requirements. In particular, this study traces the transmission channels of price and market shocks, such as China's border closures, and the consequences for primary producers or smallholders in Shan State, Myanmar.

6.2 BACKGROUND

6.2.1 Myanmar's Maize Exports to China

Trading relations between Myanmar and China have flourished over the last decade. Today, China is Myanmar's top trading partner and is increasingly dominating Myanmar's export basket. UN Comtrade data (2017 cited in Zhang and Chen 2019, p. 10) on the export destinations of Myanmar's agricultural products in 2016 illustrates the importance of China in many agricultural subsectors, where China's share represents 74 per cent of natural rubber, 80 per cent of dried fruit, 92 per cent of watermelon, 94 per cent of maize and almost 100 per cent of banana exports. Given the lack of product and market diversification, Myanmar's agricultural exports are highly susceptible to external shocks and changes in the trade policies and regulations of its trading partners, particularly China.

In 2017, Myanmar's total maize production was estimated at 2.2 million tonnes, of which 1 million tonnes was exported and the rest consumed domestically; maize production is an important component of the growing domestic livestock industry. Maize export volumes have increased rapidly since 2011–12 at an annual growth rate of 5 per cent. This mini-boom was to some extent spurred by China's softening of its self-sufficiency policy in response to greater demand in the feed industry, allowing border regions to import maize from neighbouring countries. This policy relaxation was short-lived, however. Just two years later, in 2019, Chinese authorities started reimposing stricter controls on informal cross-border maize imports. Although China still faces rising demand for maize imports and Myanmar is well positioned to supply its needs, China's trade policy uncertainty and tighter border control measures are negatively affecting the maize supply chain in Myanmar.

Meanwhile, Myanmar's prospects of exporting maize formally to China are very weak as most producers and traders cannot comply with the existing NTMs on maize exports. After decades of isolation, Myanmar struggled to facilitate international trade, particularly in agricultural commodities. Added to that, the challenges posed by NTMs, specifically sanitary and phytosanitary (SPS) measures and technical barriers to trade (TBT), have made it difficult for Myanmar traders to export agricultural commodities to China. "Ambiguity, inconsistency and discriminatory behaviour in both information and enforcement of SPS regulations" were found to be "most problematic" by the APEC Business Advisory Council (2016, p. 22). Under these circumstances, it is challenging for Myanmar exporters to obtain accurate and timely information about SPS regulations. Requirements are often spread across several agencies and regulations can change frequently and without warning, particularly with respect to labelling and packaging, product classification and testing requirements, slowing down certification and customs inspection processes.

Another significant limiting factor is China's "on-off" enforcement of trade policy measures on informal cross-border trade (Ramachandran 2020). Myanmar and China have a long history of small-scale cross-border trading in traditional agricultural products, livestock and other goods between peasants and merchants. More recently, this trade was semi-formalized through several bilateral agreements between district-level authorities on both sides of the border allowing local residents to barter their products. However, these arrangements have been exploited by traders attempting to evade formal trade. As a result, the last decade was marked by sharp increases in the volume and value of cross-border agriculture trade, most of which were not recorded in Chinese official statistics. The latest enforcement of trade restrictions and blocking of informal agriculture imports by Chinese border authorities triggered a chain reaction of unpredictable border demand and unpredictable border prices, hitting smallholders and producers in Myanmar the hardest. Conversely, when such rules are relaxed, Chinese buyers can exert considerable power over the buying price as they have ready access to regulatory information and advanced knowledge of border control measures.

Given the remarkable economic development and liberalization of trade coupled with the rapidly growing demand for food in China, the agricultural sector offers huge economic potential for Myanmar. However, even though China has significantly reduced its average tariffs on imports, exports to China are increasingly subject to NTMs particularly TBT and SPS measures. Meanwhile, "evidence from WTO disputes also shows a greater number of citations of the SPS and TBT agreements in cases involving agricultural products,"(WTO 2012) around the world, indicative of the global context of the increased use of stringent NTMs and their impact on China-Myanmar's agriculture trade.

The proliferation of NTMs in China has deep implications for Myanmar's formal agricultural exports, particularly in improving product quality to meet stringent regulatory standards, which increases production costs for Myanmar producers. Given that informal cross-border trade plays a significant role in Myanmar's agricultural trade, the impact is further compounded by the apparent see-saw nature of China's enforcement of these measures. Such inconsistency can be clearly observed at the Muse border crossing, through which the vast majority of Myanmar-China border trade passes. Weak law enforcement and loosely applied measures at the border have contributed to the price volatility of agricultural products, with serious implications for farmers in Myanmar.

6.2.2 NTMs in Agricultural Trade

UNCTAD (2019a, p. v) defines NTMs as "policy measures other than ordinary customs tariffs that can potentially have economic effect on international trade in goods, changing quantities traded, or prices or both". The proliferation of NTMs in international trade was highlighted as a pressing issue by Pascal Lamy, former Director-General of the World Trade Organization (WTO), in his farewell statement in 2013. Alluding to the shifting tides of international trade, he stressed that the move from traditional tariffs to "non-tariff barriers, which have gained enormous importance ... are becoming the main obstacle to trade" (WTO 2013). For developing countries, market mechanisms are becoming ever more complex and difficult to navigate, especially with the increase in the number of NTMs. Illustrated in Figure 6.1, the rising number of SPS and TBT notifications filed with the WTO between 1995 and 2010 highlights the increasing prevalence of NTMs. According to the SPS Information Management System database, WTO members have raised thirty-one specific trade concerns with respect to SPS measures applied by China (UNCTAD 2019b); however, being in China's neighbourhood and wanting to maintain good relations, Myanmar chose not to take this route.[1]

In the agricultural sector, the main NTMs deployed by governments around the world are SPS measures. Based on NTM data from thirty developing countries, the European Union and Japan, as of 2013, 71.3 per cent of live animals, 69.2 per cent of vegetable products and 57.0 per cent of processed food products were subject to at least one SPS notification, while 41.7 per cent of processed foods, 36.2 per cent of live animals and 31.7 per cent of vegetable products were subject to numerous TBT measures (UNCTAD 2013, p. 11). Empirical studies have found that developing countries are disproportionately affected by SPS measures due to challenges in instituting quality assurance and establishing laboratories that meet international accreditation standards in the face of limited access to scientific and technical expertise, finance and information (Jongwanich 2009; Henson and Loader 2001). Consequently, low-income countries are more likely than higher-income countries to be excluded from agricultural markets (Maskus, Otsuki, and Wilson 2005; Disdier, Fontagné, and Mimouni 2008). The overall effect leads to higher trading costs, with associated compliance costs (e.g., administrative procedures and processes) borne by the exporting country's government, as well as exporters and importers.

FIGURE 6.1
Number of Notifying Countries and Number of (a) SPS and (b) TBT Notifications, 1995–2010

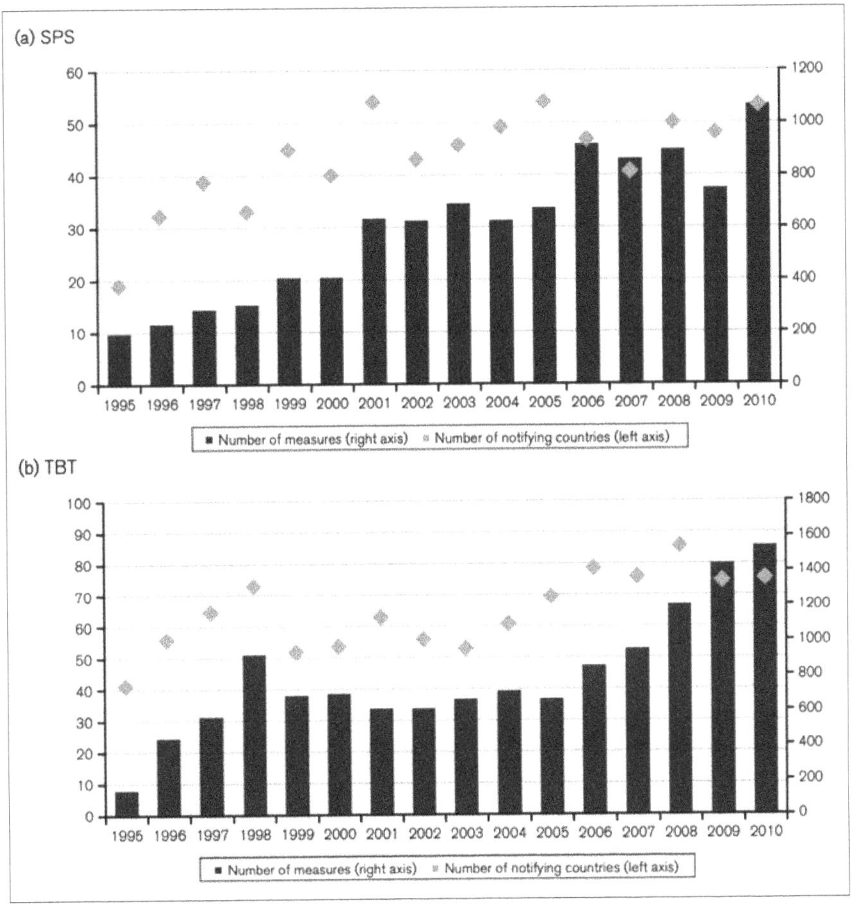

(a) SPS

(b) TBT

Source: World Trade Report 2012 (WTO 2012).

Researchers have used various methods to quantify the effect of NTMs, most commonly computing the ad-valorem equivalent (AVE) of each NTM type. Research studies based on AVEs have found NTMs to be almost twice as restrictive as traditional tariffs, and the level of trade restrictiveness for NTMs in agriculture to be 30 per cent higher than in manufacturing (Kee, Nicita, and Olarreaga 2009). A more recent study by Cadot and Gourdon

(2015) found that the AVE of NTMs is around 8.0 per cent and can be as high as 26.2 per cent, with the agricultural sector having the highest AVEs, contributed by SPS measures (around 12.9 per cent of the total 26.2 per cent) for live animals. Empirically, these results suggest that NTMs might be more trade distortionary than tariffs.

Despite the high compliance costs and distortionary effects of NTMs, it would be inaccurate to assume that these measures serve protectionist motives only and do not provide benefits to exporters/producers. Greater harmonization and mutual recognition of TBT and SPS measures between trading partners can have a positive effect on trade. Indeed, despite the increase in costs for compliance, SPS measures can benefit producers as they are forced to invest in product upgrading, enabling them to enter new agricultural markets. Case studies of Malawi's tobacco sector (Jaffee 2003) and Senegal's vegetable sector (Maertens and Swinnen 2009), and a global study of the complexity of TBT and SPS standards as they affect developing countries (Henson and Humphrey 2010), illustrate this point. Similarly, growing consumer demand for higher quality foods incentivizes producers to acquire certification. A case in point is the transformation of Cambodia from a small exporter of low-quality rice to a competitive exporter of high-quality rice in a relatively short time. This success story highlights the benefits of investments in product upgrading to meet the stringent food safety requirements of export destinations. From exporting just 12,600 tonnes of rice in 2009, Cambodia's rice exports increased 30 times to 378,850 tonnes by 2013, with more than half exported to the European Union (Aldaz-Carroll and Ly 2014).

6.2.3 Price Volatility in Agricultural Trade

The nature of agriculture means that most agricultural commodity markets are characterized by a high degree of inherent volatility. Three major market fundamentals contribute to price volatility: natural shocks such as pests and weather; relatively inelastic demand and supply, in the short run at least; and considerably long production times where supply cannot respond quickly to price changes in the short term (FAO and OECD 2011). A whole array of different factors underlies these fundamentals and could create short-term price shocks. Those factors include yields and stock levels, changing weather patterns, cycles in key markets, policy-driven developments, exchange rate and oil price fluctuations, changes in trade policies, and investment in agricultural production (Tothova 2011).

At the macroeconomic level, developing countries are often highly dependent on agricultural commodities for export revenues and are therefore vulnerable to acute price shocks. Significant downward pressure on prices can have an impact on the balance of payments, with cuts in investments due to market uncertainties, and even longer-term negative impacts on economic growth (FAO and OECD 2011). More importantly, in the context of Myanmar-China border trade, the microeconomic effects require further examination. For actors in the downstream and middle stream segments of the value chain, a sharp fall in price could cause significant losses in their productive investments. Typically, these actors include farmers who have already planted their crops and small-scale traders and collectors who lack access to credit to offset price falls. In the longer term, price volatility generates uncertainty in the agriculture sector and could lead to suboptimal investment decisions (FAO and OECD 2011).

The informality of border trade with China adds to price volatility, often causing huge and sudden price movements. Sporadic import bans and arrest of Chinese importers at the border create uncertainties for Myanmar producers and lower the quality of highly perishable products such as maize. A ban on informal maize trade at the border dampens demand, pushing down prices. Conversely, spikes in demand from China lead to immediate harvesting and maize of all qualities is transported across the border to China. The rush narrows the price differential between high-quality and low-quality maize, disincentivizing farmers and dryers from investing in postharvest drying and storage facilities. On top of that, when there is no demand, maize farmers cannot access affordable drying and storage facilities because grain drying capacity is mainly devoted to domestic corn feed mills throughout the postharvest season. Most farmers cannot afford to wait to capture higher prices; they, therefore, sell at lower prices, making lower profit margins.

Myanmar lacks the capacity to absorb domestic shocks in periods of high domestic price volatility. Poor access to technologies, weak infrastructure, high transport costs, and limited access to credit and insurance markets exacerbate the effects of high price volatility. Price transmission along supply chains means that consumers pay high prices for food products while primary producers such as farmers earn low farmgate prices and make small profit margins. Price volatility has historically been associated with the effects of climate change on production and the lack of postharvest infrastructure. However, price volatility in agricultural products has worsened since traditional farm sectors have engaged in trade with China, largely because of unpredictable demand and erratic border controls in China. Ultimately, agricultural commodity price volatility in Myanmar exports to China can have many negative effects, not only on the farmers who produce those commodities but also on Myanmar's agricultural production per se.

6.3 DATA AND METHOD

6.3.1 Data

The study uses both primary and secondary data to analyse Myanmar's informal and formal maize exports to China and map the NTMs imposed on them by China. The preliminary analysis of informal trade draws on secondary trade data from government departments and the UN Comtrade database.[2] Primary data was collected from a producer survey, focus group discussions and key informant interviews with farmers and traders in southern Shan State, the most concentrated area of maize cultivation and processing in the country.

6.3.1.1 Producer Survey

The producer survey was conducted in southern Shan State[3] between December 2019 and February 2020.[4] Eleven village tracts within four townships were targeted with the criterion that the maize cultivation area per village tract be greater than 300 acres. Information on maize cultivation areas was obtained from the Department of Agriculture, Ministry of Agriculture, Livestock and Irrigation (2018). Village tracts with maize cultivation areas of less than 300 acres were eliminated from the study. The survey collected information on farm production, postharvest storage, sales and trading from 555 maize farmers in the eleven selected village tracts, listed in Table 6.1.

6.3.1.2 Focus Group Discussions

Focus group discussions were conducted to consult key stakeholders along the value chain and identify bottlenecks in Myanmar's maize exports to China. The stakeholders were categorized into three groups, as follows:

TABLE 6.1
Producer Survey Sampling Frame

Township	Village Tract	Survey Respondents
Taunggyi	Mong Thaw (East)	60
Taunggyi	Bant Kway	49
Taunggyi	Than Te	60
Taunggyi	Kung Lon	56
Taunggyi	Kyauk Ni	46
Nyaung Shwe	Pont Mu	47
Pindaya	Mong Li	53
Pindaya	Inn Nge	46
Hsihseng	Par Law Per Kei	45
Hsihseng	Bang Yin	46
Hsihseng	Taung (East)	47
Total		555

- Producers/farmers: mainly in Taunggyi, Hsihseng and Nyaung Shwe townships in Taunggyi district; these townships have the largest maize cultivation areas in southern Shan State.
- Input suppliers/town traders: in Taunggyi, Yawk Sawk and Nyaung Shwe townships where major distributors are located.
- Processors/dryers: medium-sized dryers in Ayethaya Industrial Zone and Shwe Nyaung area, and small-scale village-level dryers in Nyaung Shwe township.

6.3.1.3 Key Informant Interviews

Key informant interviews were administered to research participants at local, district and national levels, as follows:

- Representatives from associations, local organizations and small- and medium-sized enterprises: Taunggyi-based Chamber of Commerce, a district branch of Myanmar Pulses Beans and Sesame Seeds Merchants Association, local NGOs, ethnic youth groups and cultural associations in PaO, Shan and Inntha communities, and other community-based organizations.
- Government representatives: Department of Agriculture, Department of Trade, Department of Consumer Affairs, Myanmar Investment

Commission, Department of Land Use Statistics, and Taunggyi University.

The research team also made efforts to visit Lashio, a major trading hub close to the China-Myanmar border, and consulted trade and border control authorities on the Myanmar side to understand the enforcement of NTMs that affect maize exports to China.

6.3.2 Methodology

Value chain analysis was performed to understand the impact of informal cross-border trade and NTMs on maize production, producers, traders, exporters and export trade in Myanmar. The first stage of value chain analysis involves mapping "actors connected along a chain producing, transforming, and bringing goods and services to end-consumers through a sequenced set of activities" (UNIDO 2011, p. 3) and "involved in the process of adding value to a specific crop or product" (Bernet, Thiele and Zschocke 2006, p. 159). The study followed the *filière* approach, developed to analyse the organization of agricultural production systems under the French colonial system, to understand how local production systems are linked to the processing industry and export trade. Economic analysis of smallholder maize production and how producers access final markets focused on price transmission from export trade and distributional dynamics along the supply chain (Durufle, Fabre and Yung 1988).

The *filière* approach helped us understand how cross-border trade could be managed differently to benefit the value chain actors supplying maize to China. As Kaplinsky and Morris (2001, p. 22) put it, "if they [producers] get it wrong, they are likely to enter a 'race to the bottom', that is a path of immiserising growth in which they are locked into ever-greater competition and reducing incomes". Myanmar's opening up and consequent trade boom fed through to increased activity along the entire supply chain; however, returns to this increased economic activity have fallen in recent years, suggesting lower chances of positive outcomes, particularly for producers. In this regard, the study also paid attention to the total export value and volume of maize exports to evaluate the long-term prospects for farmers' incomes and livelihoods. The essence of this approach is largely drawn from the framework used in *Making Value Chains Work Better for the Poor: A Toolbook for Practitioners of Value Chain Analysis* (M4P 2008).

We also used value chain analysis to examine the role of upgrading within the supply chain, with particular attention to improvements in the quality of maize, which could both enable traders to comply with NTMs and thereby participate in formal maize export to China and help producers achieve better prices. NTMs are instruments of commercial policy and as such are thought to constrain potential returns for smallholder farmers under prevailing conditions; however, they can also create important upgrading opportunities, which, with government intervention, could protect and benefit producers (Gereffi 1999). This study views the upgrading challenge from the wider perspective of creating an enabling environment in Myanmar to initiate process upgrading and functional reconfiguration of who does what in the chain as a whole (Gibbon 2001).

Trade data analysis used the multiple mirror technique to identify which side misclassifies products by commodity code and destination/origin (Hamanaka and Domingo 2012). It was expected that the recorded exports and imports on opposite sides of the bilateral trade (the mirror statistics) would be similar. The analysis identified two common inaccuracies concerning origin/destination and commodity codes that arise when products are wrongly classified by customs officers. The ultimate origin and destination of transhipments and re-exports can become confused, while commodities with similar characteristics (names and descriptions) can be misclassified. In this regard, we used a comparative research strategy to ascertain whether differences arise from the misclassification of cost, insurance and freight free-on-board factors and to identify other possible sources of data discrepancies.

6.4 FINDINGS

6.4.1 Overview of the Maize Value Chain in Myanmar

Maize is mostly cultivated in Shan State, which accounts for 80 per cent of total domestic maize production (Woods 2015), and where, unlike in other regions, maize is a main rainy season crop. Because of this, high moisture content at harvest can be problematic, affecting quality and price. Accurate weather forecasting at planting (start of rainy season) and harvesting (end of rainy season) times is therefore crucial for smallholders to manage crop production effectively. Maize is also produced in Bago and Magway regions and Nay Pyi Taw Territory in the Ayeyarwady River Basin and in irrigated areas, where it is grown as a winter season (November to February) crop, after the main rainy season rice crop, and harvested in February/March. The quality of maize grown in these areas is much better because dry season crops have a low moisture content.

As shown in Table 6.2, the maize cultivation area has increased steadily since 2011 while that of paddy has decreased. However, paddy remains the most important crop for Myanmar, accounting for 35 per cent of the total cultivation area in 2017 (Figure 6.2). That said, maize cultivation may have been underestimated due to the lack of farm records in remote border regions such as northern Shan State, where ongoing conflicts make such accounting impossible.

Despite price volatility and discrimination, maize is a profitable cash crop for smallholders in Shan State. As shown in Table 6.3, the price of maize increased sevenfold between 1995 and 2005, and nearly threefold over the following decade. Furthermore, farmers can cut production costs by letting the crop dry in the field, minimizing harvest and storage costs while waiting for the best price to make a profitable sale. Farmers sell their maize mostly to village and township collectors, who control the midstream segment of the value chain. Major feed millers such as Chaoroen Pokphand (CP), Japfa and Dehus, and local feed millers, have their own contractual arrangements with maize farmers. For instance, CP provides farmers with seed and those farmers supply CP with maize. Starting in 2010, Chinese buyers have been buying maize directly from farmers through collectors; since then, the market price has been determined by demand from China. Despite the promising long-term trend in maize demand from Chinese buyers, Myanmar farmers and traders have limited access to the Chinese market and are vulnerable to China's rather erratic border controls. This situation underlines the need for Myanmar stakeholders to pool their bargaining power to secure fair prices from Chinese buyers on a par with regional prices and China's domestic prices.

Demand from China has already changed the agricultural landscape of northern Shan State, which accounts for 60 per cent of total maize production in the region. According to a local maize trader, the cultivation area has expanded rapidly since 2011, after the liberalization of domestic trade and the promulgation of a new farm law in 2012 allowing crops such as maize, sugar, oil palm and rubber to be grown on large plantations. Nationwide, since the 1990s, the government has allocated 0.94 million ha (2.3 million acres) of vacant, fallow and virgin (VFV) land to 377 domestic companies, giving an average concession size of 2,497 ha, and

TABLE 6.2
Major Crop Areas in Myanmar (acres)

Year	Cereals			Oilseeds				Pulses	
	Paddy	Wheat	Maize	Groundnut (Rain)	Groundnut (Winter)	Sesame (Early)	Sesame (Late)	Matpe (Black Gram)	Pedisein (Green Gram)
2007–08	19,989,520	242,626	853,773	888,805	1,124,999	2,762,606	777,921	2,422,289	2,635,180
2008–09	20,001,012	246,438	877,549	907,876	1,178,288	2,876,298	809,847	2,441,363	2,566,509
2009–10	19,932,702	255,591	896,501	937,221	1,203,874	2,947,832	920,368	2,528,345	2,660,191
2010–11	19,884,840	250,748	962,295	950,729	1,216,675	2,875,277	880,606	2,606,642	2,770,519
2011–12	18,761,712	235,779	1,017,271	1,013,302	1,178,714	2,928,835	858,280	2,693,906	2,712,682
2012–13	17,893,424	245,809	1,042,395	1,059,368	1,193,024	2,790,979	897,975	2,737,213	2,685,521
2013–14	17,998,696	249,945	1,088,515	1,101,510	1,198,203	2,894,261	909,391	2,723,257	2,775,121
2014–15	17,722,355	243,603	1,134,308	1,136,499	1,209,688	2,703,308	917,368	2,712,047	2,899,154

Source: Annual Statistical Yearbook (2016).

FIGURE 6.2
Harvested Areas of Major Crops as Shares of Total Cultivated Area, 2017

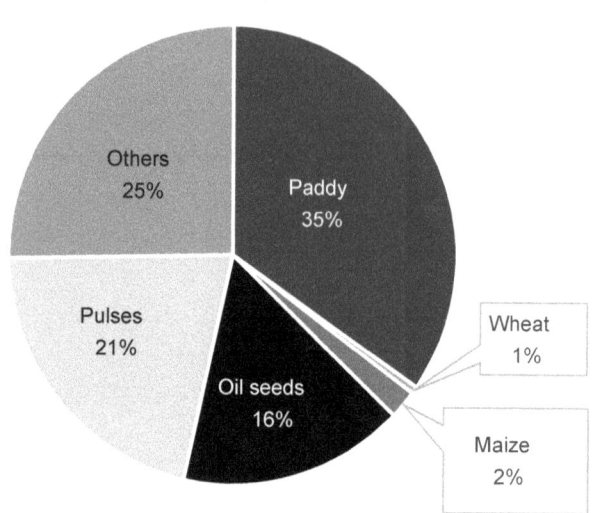

Source: Unpublished annual agricultural production statistics for 2017, Department of Agriculture, Ministry of Agriculture, Livestock and Irrigation (MOALI).

0.3 million ha (0.8 million acres) of forest land to 822 companies and individuals. Official data from the Ministry of Agriculture, Livestock and Irrigation (2018) indicates that the area of VFV granted as land concessions expanded by at least 0.2 million ha between 2010 and 2013. By far the largest land concessions are in Shan State; they are mainly being used to grow rubber, oil palm, rice and jatropha, followed by rice, sugarcane and cassava (Ministry of Agriculture and Irrigation 2014).[5] By this account, it would seem that maize production is overwhelmingly dominated by smallholders, and that is why it is crucial for the Myanmar government and its development partners to support smallholders.

According to the Department of Agricultural Statistics shown in Table 6.4, 55 per cent of the maize cultivated area in Shan State is located in the northern districts adjacent to the China-Myanmar border, 39 per cent in southern districts and 6 per cent in eastern districts. In southern Shan State, Taunggyi district, which covers Hopong, Hsihseng and Lawksawk townships, accounts for 80 per cent of the cultivated area. The population density here is three times higher than in northern Shan State

TABLE 6.3
Historical Prices of Maize (MMK per viss)

Crop	Unit	1995–96	2000–1	2005–6	2010–11	2011–12	2012–13	2013–14	2014–15	2015–16	2016–17
Grain	tonne	17,363	45,014	116,072	216,454	219,888	288,605	278,384	316,654	326,124	284,144
Cobs	100 cobs	350	710	3,300	3,600	7,800	11,500	6,600	9,600	11,200	13,400
Leaf sheath	tonne	12,444	36,743	139,999	311,111	171,500	183,750	183,750	183,750	n.a.	n.a.

Note: *Viss* is a Myanmar unit of measure for weight, equivalent to approx. 1.63 kg.
Source: Unpublished annual agricultural production statistics, Department of Agriculture, MOALI.

TABLE 6.4
Cultivated Areas and Production of Maize in the Districts of Shan State, 2017

District	Planted (acre)	Harvested (acre)	Productivity (basket)	Output (basket)	Output (tonne)
South Shan State	262,268	262,268	54.28	13,235,603	432,804
Taunggyi	191,519	191,519	53.70	10,284,309	336,297
Loilen	52,339	52,339	55.26	2,892,411	94,582
Langkho	18,410	18,410	57.52	1,058,883	34,625
North Shan State	370,585	370,405	73.93	27,385,779	895,515
Lashio	111,412	111,306	72.48	8,067,025	263,792
Muse	35,534	35,534	75.42	2,679,852	87,631
Kyaukme	184,453	184,453	75.18	13,867,392	453,464
Mongmit	875	875	59.09	51,706	1,691
Laukkaing	25,023	25,023	75.54	1,890,236	61,811
Hopang	11,974	11,900	62.53	744,089	24,332
Matman	1,314	683	125.15	85,479	2,795
East Shan State	36,694	36,694	59.95	2,199,690	71,930
Kengtung	21,267	21,267	57.87	1,230,720	40,245
Monghsat	7,554	7,554	52.69	398,035	13,016
Tachileik	7,873	7,873	72.52	570,935	18,670
Total	669,547	669,367	65.47	43,821,072	1,432,949

Source: Unpublished annual agricultural production statistics 2018, Department of Agriculture of Shan State.

(Figure 6.3), again pointing to the importance of supporting smallholders in southern Shan State as livelihood opportunities are shared among a larger population, predominantly poor households. However, there is a sharp difference in maize productivity between northern and southern districts: production in the former is 37 per cent higher than in the latter. During the survey, value chain stakeholders suggested that the effects of rain (both for planting and moisture control during the harvesting season) are more disruptive in southern districts than in northern districts. Again, this emphasizes the importance of timely and accurate weather forecasting for smallholders.

Another plausible explanation for the regional disparity in productivity is seed variety. Crops in northern Shan State are usually grown on large farms where companies use better quality seeds while smallholders in southern townships use only cheap and often non-certified varieties. Most farmers in southern Shan State use hybrid seeds produced by private sector

FIGURE 6.3
Population Distribution in Shan State

Note: The map shows the population density of townships from low density (light grey) to high density (darker grey). The circle indicates southern Shan State, the survey site, which has high population density as well as condensed farming of maize.
Source: Ministry of Agriculture and Irrigation (2014).

companies. CP has long been the leader in hybrid maize and accounts for approximately 55 per cent of Myanmar's seed market with annual seed sales growth of 1,500 tonnes. The widespread adoption of hybrid seeds has allowed maize yields to double, though they are still well below those in Vietnam and Thailand. In some areas, the crop is quite risky given the yield levels in relation to input costs. In general, the market availability of good-quality seeds and improved varieties at reasonable prices is extremely important to support the income of smallholders.

With increased production, Myanmar's maize export has increased dramatically since 2013–14; it surpassed 1 million tonnes in 2015 and has remained robust ever since. According to the United States Department of Agriculture (USDA 2018a), over 95 per cent of maize exports went to China through border trade. The rest went to Singapore, Malaysia, the Philippines, Vietnam, Taiwan and Hong Kong. In anticipation of greater demand from China, USDA also forecast that in the coming years Myanmar's maize exports will reach 1.5 million tonnes. Domestic demand for maize-based feed was also expected to increase by 2018–19 given the poultry sector growth of 15 per cent in 2016. However, an outbreak of Avian influenza in 2017 knocked sector growth down to only 5 per cent that year (USDA 2018b).

On the one hand, there is much potential to expand irrigated maize production in Shan State given its favourable agroclimatic conditions and proximity to China and the ability of large agribusinesses and foreign firms to exploit these advantages. On the other hand, smallholder farmers, typically engaged in rainfed production, face a mix of risks and challenges, notably unpredictable weather including a shift in rainfall patterns, limited market information, and weak bargaining power vis-à-vis large-scale traders or main buyers such as China. To help overcome these challenges, this value chain analysis aims to inform smallholder farmers about market prices and linkages both between actors at certain stages in the chain and within the entire chain, and to promote coordination and collaboration among them for sharing information and pooling their bargaining power for mutual economic benefit by linking with regional value chains.

6.4.2 Mapping the Value Chain Actors

This section analyses the position in the maize value chain of the three main chain actors in southern Shan State, namely producers, traders and processors. As shown in Figure 6.4, the maize value chain actors include primary producers (smallholders, large farmers, farmer-traders), collectors, traders, export market actors (Chinese buyers) and domestic market actors (feed mills, processing factories). Several different types of intermediaries

Agricultural Exports from Myanmar to China

FIGURE 6.4
Maize Value Chain Map in Shan State

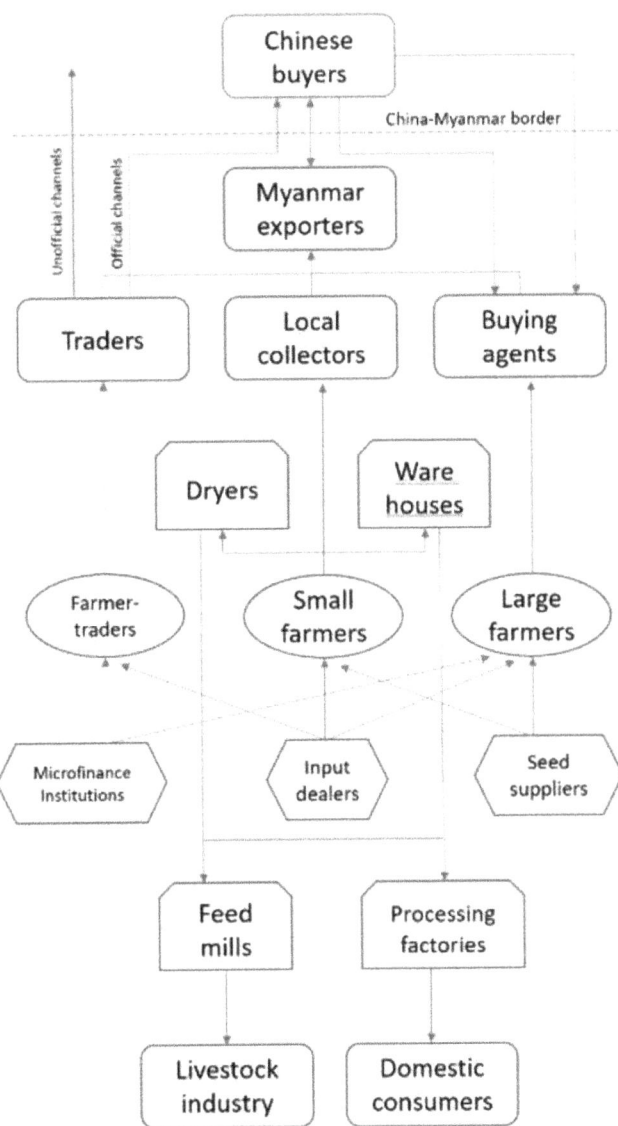

Source: Compiled by the authors.

operate in the two commodity flows, informally and formally, across the China-Myanmar border.

6.4.2.1 Producers

The majority of producers in the maize value chain are smallholders who grow maize on their traditionally owned farmlands. Farm size under this survey ranges from 3 acres to 50 acres. For this evaluation, we use the categorization of smallholder farmer (<5 acres), medium farmer (5–10 acres) and large farmer (>10 acres). Compared to smallholders, including maize farmers, in other regions, maize farmers in Shan State have larger landholdings. Indeed, in northern Shan State, Chinese investors are able to rent surplus land from farmers to grow maize. Even so, large farmers (who own more than 10 acres of land) represent not more than 10 per cent of the farmers in the study area. Although there is no systematic formation of farmer groups at the village level, these large farmers are traditionally viewed as leaders of farmer groups and/or their villages, where they often also work as collectors and input distributors.

Research participants were asked about sources of marketing and production information. Almost all farmers interviewed in the study area have mobile phones and access the farmer-to-farmer network. Some large farmers also use Facebook, Viber and other social media platforms to get information about market prices and plant diseases. Nonetheless, most farmers have limited knowledge about soil maintenance and still burn crop residues. Some farmers would like to access soil testing and extension information about how to use various types of fertilizers to condition the soil and improve yields.

In southern Shan State, maize is mainly cultivated from mid-May to late June/early July and harvested in September at the end of the rainy season. Farmers tend to leave their maize crops standing in the field to allow the cobs to dry before harvesting them. However, if farmers need to repay loans from input dealers or seed distributors, they have to sell their crops soon after the rains end. These early harvested crops usually fetch the lowest price due to high moisture content, though to some extent the price also depends on last season's price. Many farmers tend to keep their crops on the farm and sell them to collectors on site. Some large farmers recently purchased small dryers from China and have helped fellow farmers to dry their cobs before selling them to collectors and traders. However, because most of this equipment was imported informally across the border, the warranties may be invalid and spare parts unavailable.

Producers in Shan State have the advantage of cultivating maize in the rainy season and harvesting ahead of producers in the central dry zone. Because the demand for maize is year-round, farmers and traders in southern Shan State would like to have the right technology and facilities to dry and store cobs. Given that the summer maize produced in other regions cannot meet demand, having such postharvest facilities would add substantial value to the maize produced in Shan State.

A major concern of farmers in southern Shan State is seed quality and seed distributors' quality guarantee. They buy seeds, most of which is non-certified, from local seed distributors. In the event that seeds produce lower-than-expected yields, farmers have little or no recourse to compensation, leaving them bearing the brunt of crop losses and failures. That is why farmers are willing to buy or loan seeds from established firms such as CP, a leading distributor that imports seeds from Thailand. Indeed, 55 per cent of the surveyed maize farmers use CP-branded seeds. Until relatively recently, CP had a virtual monopoly over Myanmar's seed market, but now other seed companies such as Awba (Syngenta) and Golden Tiger, as well as unbranded seeds from China, have a combined 45 per cent share of the market (Figure 6.5).

The Myanmar government also produces and distributes local hybrid maize seeds, namely Yezin 3, 4, 5 and 6, through the Department of Agricultural Research based in Yezin. However, seed distribution seems to be confined to the central dry zone, which has similar agroclimatic conditions to Yezin. Instead, farmers mainly use non-certified hybrid varieties, particularly CP808, CP111, CP333, Thai 772 and Thai 515, procured by private-sector seed companies from Thailand via informal trade channels. The extremely low adoption rate of government-supplied seeds in Shan State has led to low levels of interaction between the government and farmers. More importantly, reliance on the informal seed market leaves farmers, especially smallholders, highly vulnerable to price manipulation and quality adulteration by seed suppliers, as well as the risk of being cheated by unscrupulous dealers selling fake or dud seeds. Farmers mostly rely on information from their peers when selecting the right maize variety for their farms. There was a case where a certain variety was unsuitable for the region and the soil, causing losses to farmers.

FIGURE 6.5
Sources of Maize Seed Planted by Farmers in Shan State

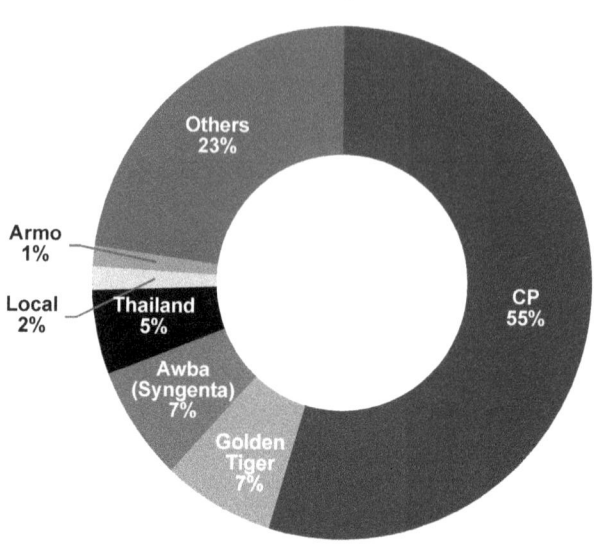

Source: Producer survey conducted between December 2019 and February 2020.

Most other farm inputs such as fertilizer and pesticides are imported, mainly from China and Thailand. Again, quality is an issue, largely due to the informality of imports. In addition, none of the packagings bears any instructions in Myanmar (Burmese) let alone its dialects. Most farmers therefore tend to buy such inputs from CP. Some input dealers take profitable advantage of the lack of information and advice and sell farmers input packages (seeds, fertilizer and pesticides) at higher prices. They can charge a premium because they get their supplies from established distributors such as CP. Farmers tend to listen to their peers before trying new brands or products, and normally stick to one brand known to give satisfactory results. One of the preferred local brands of compound fertilizer is Armo, distributed by a local firm called Diamond Star. Even so, cash-strapped smallholders tend to buy cheaper types of fertilizer, often imported from China.

In terms of production costs, smallholders seemed acutely cost-conscious and often managed costs at the expense of productivity (Figure 6.6). Given their lack of access to finance, they are unable to invest in adequate inputs

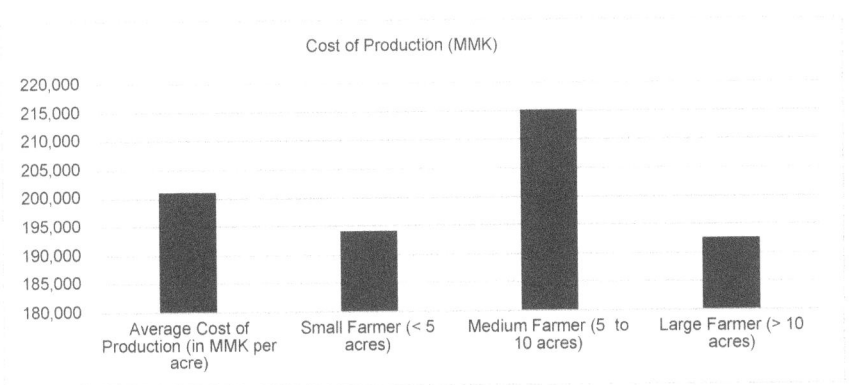

FIGURE 6.6
Cost of Production by Farm Size (MMK per acre)

Source: Producer survey conducted between December 2019 and February 2020.

for optimal production. The cost of production for medium-sized farmers is just over 10 per cent higher than for smallholders. Because they have better access to finance, they can rent farm machinery and buy fertilizers. Large farmers are also cost-efficient; they reduce their operational costs by using large machines, often their own.

In southern Shan State, the cost of cultivation mainly involves the cost of labour required for land preparation and sowing. Farm workers are from local areas and additional workers are needed each harvest season. The daily rate for farm work is around MMK5,000 (US$3.40),[6] slightly higher than Myanmar's legal minimum wage of MMK4,800 (as of January 2020).[7] Some maize plantations in Nyaung Shwe township hire seasonal workers for the harvest season; they are paid on a monthly basis at a cost of MMK100,000 per month per worker including accommodation and meals. The owner of a large farm in Nyaung Shwe township experimented by using large machines for land preparation and medium-sized combine harvesters. He reported that using machinery had halved his labour costs and increased productivity. See Figure 6.7. Unlike this farmer-entrepreneur, many large farmers cannot access farm machinery finance to buy their own equipment. Although they own large plots of more than 10 acres, they still use traditional farming methods and tend to produce lower yields per acre than small- and medium-sized farmers because they cannot hire enough seasonal workers to undertake farm activities such as weed

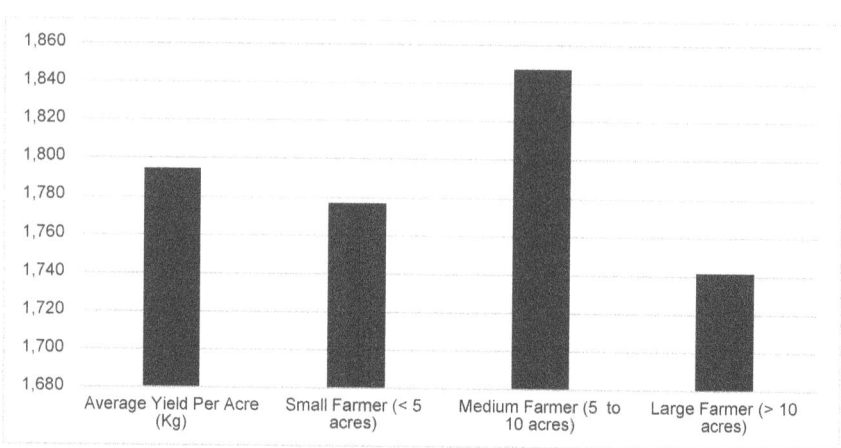

FIGURE 6.7
Productivity among Farmers (kg per acre)

Source: Producer survey in Shan State December 2019 to February 2020.

control and fertilizer application. For these farmers, as for many others, without ready access to affordable finance, farm mechanization remains a remote prospect.

As shown in Table 6.5, the average total variable cost (TVC) of maize farmers in the study area was MMK200,970 per acre, ranging from MMK93,450 to MMK302,980. At 58 per cent, labour and machinery accounted for the largest share of TVC, followed by farm inputs (28 per cent) and seeds (14 per cent). The weighted average selling price of maize in 2019 was MMK358 per *viss*, which was 25–30 per cent lower than that in 2018. Gross profit was only MMK192,727 per acre. In recent years, gross profit has been as high as 300 to 400 per cent of TVC depending on demand and trade control measures at the Myanmar-China border. The variation in sample farmers' gross profit was high depending on their yield, the amount of the crop sold, and the price they received.

For all farmers, the need for farm workers in the harvest season is very high. Workers are also required for postharvest activities, to sort, pack, weigh, carry and load maize onto trucks. Wages therefore constitute the most burdensome cost for farmers. Because of labour shortages in the area, it is hard to find available workers in the village, so farmers resort to labour-saving methods. Some leave the crops standing in the field

TABLE 6.5
Cost and Return Analysis for Average Farmer (per acre of production)

	Cost (MMK/acre)	TVC (% of total)
Seeds	28,136	14
Farm inputs	56,272	28
Labour and machinery	116,563	58
Total variable cost	200,970	100
Revenue	393,697	196
Gross profit	192,727	96

Note: US$1 = MMK1,480.
Source: Farmer survey in southern Shan State December 2019–February 2020.

for several weeks before harvesting the cobs, and others use sun-drying methods that need no labour at all. Most of the farmers in Taunggyi and Nyaung Shwe townships skip the drying process and sell wet maize to Mya Nadi, the largest maize dryer in the region. Some sun-dry their maize and sell it to local buyers.

Farmers are aware of the advantages of drying their maize before selling it, especially if the buyers are procuring maize for feed mills, which usually demand high-quality grain. Some farmers rent a small dryer from a local agent to dry their maize cobs immediately after harvest and store them properly before selling them. Some large farmers have their own small dryer, and usually dry cobs for other farmers as well. However, maize dried in small dryers is of inferior quality to that dried in large dryers; the cobs are not always dried evenly. Some buyers, particularly those buying for feed producers, do not like maize dried in small dryers. Although dried maize generally fetches a higher price than wet maize, most of the farmers surveyed would like to sell their maize crop as it is without drying it and would accept a lower price for high moisture content. They explained that the price incentive for drying their maize and waiting for a better market price is not sufficient, as the price difference between dried maize and maize with high moisture content is not substantial.

6.4.2.2 Traders

Most farmers sell their maize to village collectors, some of whom are also large farmers. They usually arrange credit with these buyers before land preparation begins. Some farmers wait until January and February before selling their maize to the local buyer who sends it to the Myanmar-China border area where maize fetches higher prices in those months. Less than 20 per cent of the farmers surveyed stated a preference for selling to township traders because doing entails having to harvest and deliver their maize by the dates set by these traders.

Farmers prefer to sell their maize to village collectors for the following reasons: (1) they rely on village collectors to supply them with seeds, credit and other farm inputs as they rarely go into town; (2) they can borrow emergency loans from collectors; (3) they have good long-lasting relationships with village collectors as they have the same roots; and (4) village collectors can arrange transport and pool collection times, saving farmers' transport costs. Village collectors sell the maize to township traders/agents, who then sell it locally to commercial poultry farms and feed factories or export it to China through border trade. Village collectors maximize their profits by putting a high mark-up on the inputs they loan to farmers, equivalent to a monthly interest rate of 3 per cent to 5 per cent. However, their repayment term is not fixed so farmers can pay the interest first and repay the entire loan in instalments.

Town traders usually purchase maize from village collectors or employ their own collectors in a few main maize-producing villages. Most of them sell their maize to buying agents from China at the Myanmar-China border. Some of them supply maize to contracted domestic feed mill factories such as CP, May Kha and Japfa Group. And a few of them have supply contracts with buyers for major feed mills in Yangon and Mandalay and are obligated to organize the delivery of maize from township market to destination. According to the focus group discussions with town traders, CP has the highest quality control standards and its buyers measure moisture content carefully. There have been a few instances when CP buyers rejected maize deliveries due to high moisture content. When this happens, town traders usually have to sell the maize elsewhere at a lower price and bear the additional transport costs.

Town traders usually keep their stock in storage facilities near Nyaung Shwe, a local trading town, and in the nearby Ayethaya Industrial Zone. They sell their products at the Myanmar-China border when the price is better than that offered by domestic feed processors. During the survey, most of the town traders in Taunggyi district arranged to sell and transport maize in 10-wheeler trucks to Naung Cho, a town in northern Shan State.

The town is located at a major intersection on the Mandalay-Muse highway, where big traders buy maize grown in southern Shan State and transport it to the border town of Muse. Many town traders in Taunggyi do not sell directly to Chinese buyers and have never attempted to sell directly in the Muse border trade zone. They are ill-informed about border trade, and usually take the price offered by buyers from northern Shan State.

In the past five years or so, farmers have also sold maize to buying agents from Thailand, who transport maize to the Tachilek-Mae Sai border trade zone. For the last three years, however, Chinese buyers have offered much higher prices. The consensus among traders was that China is the most important market. Moreover, they claimed that transport costs to China are cheaper and that it is easier to find trucks. This is because Taunggyi is the biggest import destination in Myanmar for consumer goods from China and truck companies offer to transport maize to the border at affordable prices. Traders also reported that the quality specifications set by Myanmar feed processors are far more stringent than those of border traders and Chinese buyers. In this respect, traders preferred exporting maize to China through border trade over supplying domestic feed millers.

During the survey, town traders or buyers were found in Taunggyi, Nyaung Shwe, Pindaya and Hsiseng. In Taunggyi, the buyers, who mostly run home-based storage facilities (called *pwe yone* in Burmese), buy not only maize but also other crops (e.g., soybeans, sesame and garlic) from nearby villages and small towns. But now that local buyers are operating at the village level, very few farmers sell their produce in Taunggyi. In Nyaung Shwe there are seed and fertilizer shops (e.g., Shwe Inn Lay and Cho Taraphu) and collectors who buy maize. In Yawk Sawk, many maize buyers buy maize from farmers and transport it to Muse. Farmers can get loans from buyers at the beginning of the maize season and in return sell their maize to those buyers. The interest rate is normally high at around 5 per cent to 10 per cent. Farmers do not mind paying the interest rates as they can still make a profit.

Shan State government recently exhorted town traders to become members of the Commodities Exchange Centre (CEC) in Taunggyi, under the umbrella association of the Union of Myanmar Federation of Chambers of Commerce and Industry (UMFCCI). In 2017, the new office of Shan State UMFCCI was opened in Taunggyi to coordinate traders in the wake of frequent border closures. UMFCCI is a non-profit association with a volunteer membership to facilitate agricultural product transactions, especially for pulses, maize, beans and oilseeds. Under UMFCCI, there are some subsector crop associations such as the Beans, Pulses and Sesame Seeds Merchants Association, Potatoes Growers Association, Fruit and Vegetable Growers Association, Culinary Commodity Association, and Orchard Association. Maize traders are also members of the Beans, Pulses and Sesame Seeds Merchants Association.

Most major traders who export goods to China live in Shan State, though a few are located in Yangon as members of the Yangon Bayintnaung CEC, which has more than 3,000 members. Yangon wholesalers used to buy and sell maize outside the CEC. Only a few Yangon-based exporters export maize to regional markets, mainly through normal trade. The main issue facing these maize exporters wanting to tap regional and other high-end markets is pre-export quality assurance inspection to ensure that fresh produce is free of microbial contamination, pesticide residues that exceed legal limits, aflatoxins, and so on. Samples have to be sent to Thailand for testing, which takes time and is expensive. Moreover, the price of maize in Myanmar is less competitive than in other countries. A few exporters are engaged in exporting maize to the Philippines, Vietnam and sometimes to other destinations in Asia such as Indonesia and South Korea. A Yangon-based SGS testing, inspection and certification company and Overseas Merchandise Inspection Co. Ltd. provide quality assurance and certification for those exporters, particularly for exports to the Philippines. In this case, the export operations for China are all handled in Shan State.

6.4.2.3 Processors

Maize processing mainly involves feed factories that produce poultry feed or fish food. Most of the feed factories are foreign-owned, and a few locally owned feed businesses such as Maykha and Myanadi are establishing joint ventures with foreign investors. CP Group of Thailand plays a dominant role in collecting maize from farmers as it has been operating in the area for more than a decade. Although feed factories pay higher prices than Chinese buyers or local traders, they often set stringent quality requirements. Moreover, compared to other buyers, these factories can buy only a fraction of production volume and they tend to deal only with medium and large farmers on a long-term basis.

- *Charoen Pokphand (CP)*, a Thailand-based company, dominates the poultry value chain in Myanmar and is therefore influential in shaping domestic maize demand. Most poultry farmers buy feed from CP so that they can get the necessary certification to sell live birds; when their birds are ready to sell, they simply inform CP and CP collects and buys them at market price. Even so, weak linkages between maize farmers and poultry farmers characterize maize supply. CP Livestock has factories in Yangon and Mandalay industrial zones. Most of the town traders in Taunggyi district are vertically integrated into CP's business model and they are also active across the poultry and other livestock sectors. CP accounts for about 40 per cent to 45 per cent of the poultry product market in Myanmar. It also has modern purchase systems, uses strict quality control procedures and has processing plants certified with ISO (International Organization for Standardization).
- *Japfa Comfeed Indonesia*, an agrifood company based in Jakarta, in 2015, established a joint venture with Maykha, a local dryer/feed processor located in Myaung Taka Industrial Zone, Yangon Region. It is vertically integrated with maize and livestock market operators and has set up buying facilities in Shan State. Japfa is reportedly establishing a new feed mill; however, its operations have been expanding slowly. It is currently estimated to supply 20 per cent to 25 per cent of Myanmar's feed market.
- *De Heus* is a Netherlands-based global feed mill. It has been implementing a maize and livestock value chain development project called Sustainable and Affordable Poultry for All in partnership with Fresh Studio and other partners with support from the government of New Zealand. De Heus has an office in Taunggyi township, southern Shan State.
- *Tet Chaung* poultry farm and feed company is located in Taunggyi township but is active across the country. Tet Chaung accounts for about 5 per cent of Myanmar's animal feed market.
- *Sunjin*, an early-stage South Korean investment firm based in Mingaladon Industrial Zone, Yangon, has been aggressively paying good prices for maize; however, few traders in southern Shan State knew about this company. Sunjin offers smart ICT farming solutions and specializes in pig and poultry farming.

6.4.2.4 Storage Facilities and Owners

Farmers in Hsihseng would like to store at least one-third of the maize they produce. However, most of them have to sell their maize immediately after harvest to repay loans and there are no storage facilities in the village. On average, they sell about half of their maize at harvest time. For drying, farmers simply leave the crops standing in the field and harvest them when they want to sell. In Nyaung Shwe township, especially in Hmawbee and Sagar villages, farmers have more capacity to store their crops. They sell about 30 per cent of their maize at harvest time and store the rest. Several large farmers were interested in taking out long-term loans to build storage facilities in the main maize-farming communities and a few would also like to buy small dryers.

Given storage constraints, farmers have a tough time deciding how to allocate their harvested crop between sale, consumption, storage and seed (Table 6.6). These decision patterns differ from one area to another depending on the availability of storage facilities or access to markets. For instance, farmers in Hopong often wanted to sell their crops because the storage facilities in their area are inadequate while farmers in Nyaung Shwe tended to store them as they have sufficient storage facilities as well as better access to Taunggyi Industry Zone where several large buyers and animal feed factories are located.

6.4.3 Challenges of Maize Trade with a Focus on China

6.4.3.1 Non-tariff Measures

As most agricultural products are exported to China through the land border crossing in northern Myanmar, it is important to review the

TABLE 6.6
Farmers' Decisions on Harvested Maize

Region	Sell at Harvest (%)	Home Consumption (%)	Storage (%)	Keep for Seed (%)	Total
Hsihseng	50	0	50	0	100
Nyaung Shwe	30	0	70	0	100
Hopong	70	0	30	0	100

regulatory environment surrounding border trade. On the Myanmar side, traders must hold official export licences and pay withholding tax to ship commodities across the border. These procedures are the same as for normal trade via ship from Yangon port to other export destinations. Therefore, the majority of maize exports to China are legal trade for Myanmar. On the Chinese side, the border authorities apply strict SPS measures on Myanmar's agricultural exports in addition to import quota restrictions on certain grains such as rice. Table 6.7 lists the 220 NTMs imposed by China on Myanmar's maize exports (HS Code 1005).

However, the actual enforcement of these NTMs at the Myanmar-China border is questionable. Traditionally, almost all maize exports went through informal trade channels until 2017, when agricultural commodities were not subject to Chinese SPS measures or quota control. This motivated a large number of small traders and SMEs to boost the supply of maize across the border and it also stimulated a huge expansion of maize production in southern Shan State. Beginning in 2018, the official trade channels enforced stricter NTMs, but farmers could not comply with these measures. Then, the traditional practices of informal border trade soon began to creep back. Informal trade by nature cannot manage bulky volumes and large logistics operations and associated high transaction costs. Consequently, the farmgate prices for Shan farmers have been suppressed for two consecutive years. That said, at the time of the study, a small fraction of imports was being managed by specialized Chinese agribusinesses that have administrative permits to promote contract farming under China's opium-substitution programme in northern Shan State. Many farmers in Shan State have tried to fill these official quotas. Such arrangements, however, were being phased out and it seemed that only informal border trade arrangements were available to Myanmar exporters.

6.4.3.2 Informal Trade and Its Implications

In examining UN Comtrade statistics, the study found large discrepancies, especially for developing countries. Discrepancy partly arises because exports are usually reported on a free on board basis and imports are reported on the costs, insurance and freight basis, leading to the reported import value being higher than the reported export value. In the case of Myanmar-China border trade, the methodology suggested that large trade discrepancy has less to do with the basis of recording than with the

TABLE 6.7
NTMs Imposed by China on Maize (HS 1005) Imports from Myanmar

Type of NTM (in Force)	NTM Subcategory	Number
Export-related measures		*59*
	P13	2
	P14	2
	P15	2
	P161	3
	P162	8
	P163	4
	P169	10
	P19	5
	P31	1
	P32	2
	P33	6
	P39	13
	P51	1
Preshipment inspection		*2*
	C3	2
Other measures		*11*
	H19	1
	N	8
	O	2
Price control measures		*2*
	F69	1
	F71	1
Quantity control measures		*13*
	E1	11
	E611	1
	E621	1
Sanitary and phytosanitary measures		*56*
	A11	1
	A14	4
	A15	2
	A19	2
	A21	1
	A31	4
	A33	3
	A41	1
	A49	2
	A59	1

	A63	3
	A64	5
	A81	1
	A82	3
	A83	5
	A84	6
	A851	1
	A86	10
	A89	1
Technical barriers to trade		77
	B19	3
	B21	1
	B22	2
	B31	13
	B33	1
	B49	2
	B7	9
	B81	3
	B82	5
	B83	14
	B84	10
	B851	4
	B852	3
	B853	2
	B89	5

Source: UNCTAD Integrated Trade Intelligence Portal: http://i-tip.unctad.org/

underreporting of commodity flows across the border. The study found that Myanmar customs accounted for maize using the correct classification and there seemed to be no misclassification on the China side either.

As Table 6.8 illustrates, the reported trade statistics from Myanmar and China are highly inconsistent for maize as for many other primary agricultural products exported through land-based border trade. For maize trade, China's highest reported imports were in 2017 whereas Myanmar's highest reported exports were in 2015. The study also found that China's trade statistics on many agricultural imports from Myanmar, such as rice, mung beans and fishery products, appear to be proportionally inconsistent with Myanmar's trade statistics. China's highest reported imports (in volume and value) between 2014 and 2017 do not coincide with the highest reported exports (in volume and value) from Myanmar.

TABLE 6.8
Discrepancies in Maize Trade Statistics between Myanmar and China

Year	Myanmar Export Data		China Import Data		Discrepancy Ratio (M/C)*	
	Volume (kg)	Value (US$)	Volume (kg)	Value (US$)	Vol M/ Vol C	Val M/ Val C
2014	1,189,013,459	354,248,764	41,016,864	11,241,751	29	32
2015	1,498,169,885	359,994,167	48,282,580	12,496,537	31	29
2016	275,057,480	220,902,510	77,416,848	17,855,197	4	12
2017	1,490,292,300	285,026,125	93,051,000	24,413,875	16	12

Note: Import data for 2018 is unavailable; * values rounded to the nearest whole number.

Table 6.8 reports substantial discrepancies in Myanmar-China trade.[8] Despite data limitations, Myanmar's trade discrepancies with China are six times those of comparator countries. When looking at the evolution of China-Myanmar trade, discrepancies in trade value increased considerably in 2014–15, driven by China reporting its lowest ever trade statistics with Myanmar.

Such large discrepancies indicate either systematic underreporting in China or over-reporting in Myanmar. Anecdotal evidence suggests that the source of the problem lies in Chinese border customs, where officials often do not recognize Myanmar exports and instead redirect them through informal channels. Meanwhile, maize export prices received by Myanmar from China and the rest-of-world markets appear to be diverging, as Figure 6.8 illustrates. Export prices received from China are declining at a faster rate than other markets in the world, suggesting an asymmetrical trade relationship between Myanmar and China. The caveat here is that Myanmar's export of maize to other markets than China is rather small and trade unit prices are based on reported volumes and value statistics, thus no realized market prices are shown.

For Myanmar, the reported maize trade price with China spiked in 2016, then dropped to levels lower than in previous years. Although information on the price trend for Lao maize exports to China is limited, the price has increased considerably over the past ten years. Thus, despite the non-availability of data, the regional dynamics of the increasing concentration of maize exports to China, declining terms of trade and subsequent lower prices suggest that the export prices of Lao maize are also declining.

FIGURE 6.8
Comparison of Myanmar's FOB Prices of Maize ($/ton) to Different Markets

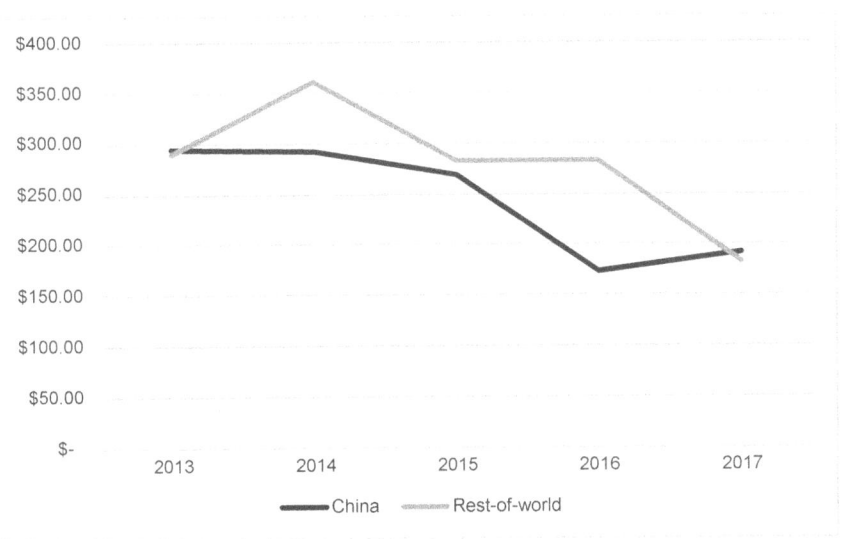

A tentative analysis of statistical discrepancies between Myanmar's and China's official trade data reveals that the margin for cereals, including maize, is one of the highest. Table 6.8 summarizes discrepancies between the trade statistics of China and Myanmar. Whereas Myanmar's statistics cover almost all of its commodity exports traded across the border, China's statistics report only a fraction of Myanmar's figures. The magnitude of discrepancies in maize trade, from four to thirty-one times, suggests that the fluid conditions of border control (reflected in official records) affect maize more than any other agricultural commodity. In fact, Chinese border authorities have already taken steps to selectively apply NTMs, either allowing or blocking imports in accordance with domestic supply and demand in Yunnan province. These latest regulatory actions and subsequent price fluctuations have had negative effects on farmers' incomes.

Official Myanmar data reveals a continuing decline in the terms of trade whereby Myanmar's export receipts are decreasing even though trade volumes have remained stable over the years. This suggests that maize exports to China not only face an uncertain future due to China's stricter border controls but also face a fall in value. On both counts, quality upgrading is imperative given the need to meet Chinese import standards towards formalizing informal export trade and to increase the value-added to Myanmar's raw materials. This situation requires urgent attention from both policymakers and development partners because farmers and traders themselves cannot upgrade the production system.

6.4.3.3 Impact on Domestic Value Chains

In recent years, Myanmar farmers have faced many challenges and watched their yields decline due to adverse weather conditions, unaffordability of good quality inputs, scarcity of labour and limited or no access to finance.

A key challenge facing smallholders in Shan State is market volatility, though the maize price in general has risen. The price of maize collapsed in 2016 following China's announcement of its new maize policy, which removed all controls on cheaper foreign imports. However, the maize price regained ground in 2017 and 2018 until the tightening of regulations at the Myanmar-China border in November 2018 barring imports of major agricultural commodities into China. At the time, none of the traders or local Myanmar trade officials fully understood the nature of border closures, whether they were permanent or temporary, but it is clear that the impacts of such bans were devastating for all stakeholders in Myanmar. Due to these uncertainties in the border trade zone, maize prices on the global market were highly volatile, exacerbating an already difficult situation for Myanmar farmers.

In this regard, the pathways for escaping from the monopsonist market power of China are clear. First, the government should promote investment that unlocks opportunities for smallholders to upgrade their production system and supports value chain integration through improved quality, reduced risk and increased resilience. International feed companies have recently entered the maize market, and these may provide alternative linkages with regional value chains away from China. Here government policy is key, and government commitment to improving quality assurance infrastructure, from seed research to laboratory accreditation, needs to be prioritized. At the same time, the government needs to act quickly and negotiate the dismantling of discriminatory regulatory measures with Chinese authorities to smooth cross-border trade. Yet neither the government nor the private sector has any understanding of what happens on the other side of the Myanmar-China border—no senior officials or major business players fully understand what it takes for China to act upon agricultural trade across the border. More focused research and data collection is urgently needed to fill this gap.

The same is true for an entrepreneur's private initiative in southern Shan State, which involved a vertically integrated maize plantation scheme for like-minded farmers to pool their land by allowing the entrepreneur to provide good-quality seeds, farm machinery for land preparation and harvesting, drying facilities and a minimum guaranteed price for the crop. Although this initiative was immensely helpful to the farmers, the sudden closure of Chinese border trade and price drop left the entrepreneur with big losses. The government should perhaps consider providing some support to ease the financial burden of such entrepreneurs so that they can continue supporting farmers.

6.5 CONCLUSION AND POLICY IMPLICATIONS

At this juncture, the maize sector faces the tremendous challenges of sustaining export growth due to its dependency on China as the single export destination and formalizing the activities of informal traders due to the government's inability to seize the potential of cross-border trade. The study finds that the root causes of these challenges are the outdated production and processing systems along the value chain and government policy that fails to support private sector value chain upgrading initiatives. The study also found that many farmers and traders have acted individually to invest in drying facilities so that they can improve the quality of their products and sell to processors instead of informal traders at the border. However, these initiatives cannot be scaled up due to a lack of access to finance for substantial infrastructure investments in processing and storage. On the other hand, the government can learn from the successful upgrading of Myanmar's pulses sector despite its dependency on the single market of India. Value chain transformation can unlock the full potential of Myanmar's maize value chain.

Maize is a strong candidate for achieving the second wave of value chain transformation in Myanmar, although it will require more active public support, particularly in breeding and agronomic research. As foreign-based private seed companies often invest heavily in developing hybrid maize varieties, their presence in the country suggests a hopeful scenario. Public research in plant breeding and agronomy that can support smallholders is therefore critical as good quality reliable seeds are a key cost driver of their production system. Moreover, clean seed supplies and a seed certification system will require ramped-up government capacity in this area.

Diversification into high-value export markets requires the government to encourage foreign direct investment in the processing sector, such as the feed industry, which in turn would support the developing poultry and livestock breeding industry. This would increase liquidity at peak marketing times and provide stronger incentives to achieve quality assurance standards. To ensure fair competition between local traders and processors, the former should have access to bank credit and export guarantee services. Exploring access to new international markets may well require diplomatic involvement, especially in the case of the ASEAN market, to support private sector overtures and efforts at expanding quantities and value-added in maize exports to importing economies such as the Philippines, Indonesia and Vietnam. Under the prevailing conditions of the near-total dependency of southern Shan State on maize production and border trade with China, it is important that the government adopts a long-term strategy of improving market access and facilitating agricultural transformation. Here quality improvement to meet the official trade standards set by the government of China is key. In this regard, Myanmar can seek aid-for-trade technical assistance from China to help improve quality assurance infrastructure and trade facilitation capacity to comply with statutory customs clearance at the Myanmar-China border.

In Shan State, due to poor transport and logistics infrastructure, farmers cannot sell their crops directly to final users. Throughout the value chain, dryers and warehouses are important infrastructures for farmers as they can improve the quality of their crops and reduce storage losses. Although farming communities are investing in dryers and warehouses, smallholders in remote villages have extremely limited access to postharvest services and facilities. Perhaps the government should support these communities with special loans to invest in postharvest storage and drying facilities.

Product improvement is urgently needed, particularly if border trade with China is to be normalized; and the government of Myanmar needs to take an in-depth look at where and how they can offer support to key stakeholders on both sides of cross-border trade. At the same time, the government should also pay attention to upgrading the national quality assurance infrastructure so that Myanmar exporters can diversify into other markets.

On production levels, the government can also improve extension services, strengthen agricultural research, provide adequate credit, and enforce quality standards and certification requirements for the benefit of smallholders who are struggling at the bottom of the value chain. Such transformation is already promised in the latest declaration of the government, the Myanmar Sustainable Development Plan. The timely and effective implementation of this plan can achieve all the opportunities cited in this report.

This study serves as the first step towards investigating the dynamics of an important value chain in Myanmar, which has the potential to diversify both the livelihood options of smallholders and the export destinations of the country. Given the atmosphere of recent market shocks and lacklustre policy environments, the study recommends further investigations or engagements with key stakeholders to improve value chain development strategies. Each of the following proposals warrants consideration:

- Encourage joint research by Myanmar and Chinese experts or research institutions on the cross-border value chains of major agricultural commodities in order to understand fully the key drivers of these value chains and the perspectives of all actors on both sides of the border.
- Advocate for value chain development strategy as the core element of achieving poverty reduction and sustainable development goals through agriculture and rural development policies under the auspices of the Ministry of Agriculture, Livestock and Irrigation.
- Integrate subsectoral maize strategies into the existing framework for the National Export Strategy on Beans, Pulses and Oilseeds sector undertaken by the Ministry of Commerce.
- Study public-private partnership models that could facilitate effective collaboration between government agencies, private companies and smallholders in Myanmar.
- Study digital agricultural solutions and technology/ICT adoption along value chains with a focus on supporting smallholders and farmers to maximize their gains from participating in regional and global value chains.

These recommendations need an overall framework for upgrading the maize value chain throughout Myanmar. As the assessment of NTMs in trade with China reveals, in the long run, it would be in Myanmar's best interests to improve quality standards and compliance with international trade regulations, especially with partners such as China. Such a drive could also benefit the underlying strategy of diversifying export destinations in the best interests of Myanmar stakeholders. On the other hand, the maize value chain in Myanmar, particularly that in southern Shan State and the focus of this study, faces several constraints. It is not sufficient for the government to leave the matter in the hands of private entities and market forces, as overcoming NTMs requires the government to take an active role in supporting smallholders while facilitating exporters and processors to achieve higher export quality. The government should therefore proactively coordinate various stakeholders to concentrate on a few attainable short-term goals such as quality improvements to meet the market demands of China while taking a step-by-step approach to integrating bilateral trade into regional and global value chains.

APPENDIX 6.1

Various Documentation and Procedural Requirements for Trade with China

Application for a phytosanitary certificate for export consignment:
1. Application form
2. Submission of a representative sample of goods to be exported (1 kg/100 tonnes)
3. Fumigation certificate
4. Authorization letter for representative (if one has been assigned) to transact company business
5. Authorization letter for pre-shipment application
6. Legal forest products certificate (specification/measurement/packing list)
7. Laboratory diagnosis of pests and diseases in accordance with importing country requirements (if any)

Phytosanitary certificate issuance procedure:
1. Application form
2. Fumigated representative sample for inspection
3. Visual inspection
4. No live pests in representative sample and goods meet importing country requirements—phytosanitary certificate issued
5. Live pests in representative sample—goods rejected

Application for import certificates for imported commodities:
1. Application form
2. Sample for lab test (0.005 per cent to 0.01 per cent of the commodity for disease test, pesticide residue test and fruit fly test) as needed
3. Phytosanitary certificate (country of origin)
4. Pest list from country of origin
5. Seed certification letter (for growing seeds, bulbs, plants)
6. Forest certification letter (for growing forest plants)
7. Sugarcane certification letter (for growing sugarcane)
8. Perennial crop certification letter (for growing perennial crops)
9. Health certificate, or fit for human or animal consumption certificate, or good agricultural practices certificate

10. Authorization letter for representative (if one has been assigned) to transact company business
11. Copy of certificate of incorporation

Import certificate issuance procedure
1. Application form submitted along with representative sample, list of related pests, and phytosanitary certificate from country of origin
2. Laboratory inspection
3. No pests found in representative sample—import certificate issued
4. Pests found in representative sample
    - Non-quarantine pests—treatment required
    - Quarantine pests—goods destroyed or rejected upon import

APPENDIX 6.2

More Statistics on Trade between China and Myanmar

TABLE 6.A1
Myanmar's Top Export Commodities to China in 2017

HS Code	Commodity	Trade Value (US$)
2711	Petroleum gases and other gaseous hydrocarbons	1,305,967,228
1701	Cane or beet sugar and chemically pure sucrose, solid form	811,359,078
1006	Rice	572,528,549
7103	Precious (excluding diamond) and semi-precious stones (jade)	343,522,467
7202	Ferro-alloys	320,009,071
1005	Maize	285,026,125
2710	Petroleum oils and oils from bituminous minerals, not crude	278,699,790
7403	Copper; refined and copper alloys, unwrought	233,149,837
0713	Vegetables, leguminous; shelled, skinned or split, dried	176,713,855
4001	Natural rubber in primary forms or in plates, sheets or strip	159,306,263
1207	Oilseeds and oleaginous fruits	124,437,988
0807	Melons (including watermelons) and papayas, fresh	101,012,459
1202	Groundnuts, not roasted or otherwise cooked	70,180,718
0803	Bananas, including plantains, fresh or dried	68,200,213
0306	Crustaceans in shell or not, live, fresh, chilled, frozen	64,799,467

Source: UN Comtrade, retrieved from comtrade.un.org

FIGURE 6.A1
Myanmar's Maize Exports (thousand tonnes), 2003–4 to 2017–18

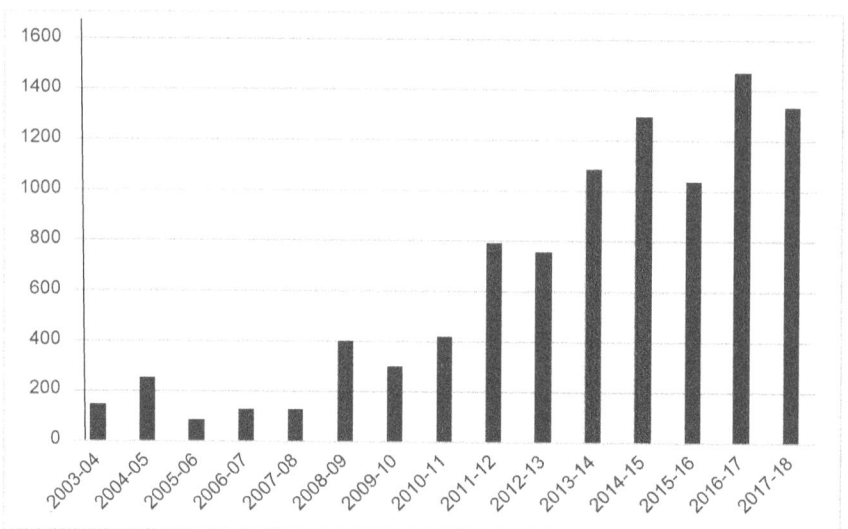

Source: Ministry of Commerce (2019).

Notes

1. Interview with senior trade official, Yangon, December 2018.
2. https://comtrade.un.org/data/
3. Southern Shan State does not have land borders with China, Laos and Thailand, unlike eastern and northern Shan State. In the latter two subregions, Chinese and Thai contractors finance large plantations, which are automatically guaranteed transfer of goods across the border, while farmers get land rental fees and wages. In southern Shan State, smallholders manage their own production, link up with local traders or processors, and export their products through trading posts in border towns. This study focuses on the challenges and opportunities of independent maize farmers and their struggles in trading with China.
4. The survey was not conducted in northern Shan State due to ongoing armed conflict in the area. Maize is grown in northern Shan State, but mostly on large plantations under a few connected firms or local chiefs.
5. Current data is not available; however, anecdotal accounts suggest that large land concessions were suspended in 2014.
6. The exchange rate at the time of survey was US$1 to MMK1,480.
7. https://wageindicator.org/salary/minimum-wage/myanmar
8. Trade volume and value discrepancies were calculated using the UN Comtrade database. Thus, analysis of specific regional partners was based on the availability of data for the observed period.

References

Aldaz-Carroll, Enrique, and Ly Sodeth. 2014. *Cambodia Economic Update: Clear Skies*. Washington, DC: World Bank Group. http://documents.worldbank.org/curated/en/964851468020720928/Cambodia-economic-update-Clear-skies

Ajmani, Manmeet, Pramod Kumar Joshi, Renjini Vr, and Devesh Roy. 2018. *Market Integration with ASEAN and Beyond: The Case of Myanmar*. IFPRIS Discussion Paper 01773. Washington, DC: International Food Policy Research Institute. http://ebrary.ifpri.org/cdm/singleitem/collection/p15738coll2/id/132974

Akibode, Comlanvi Sitou, and Mywish Maredia. 2011. "Global and Regional Trends in Production, Trade and Consumption of Food Legume Crops". No. 136293, Staff Paper Series, East Lasin, MI: Michigan State University.

Anderson, Kym, and Signe Nelgen. 2012. "Trade Barrier Volatility and Agricultural Price Stabilization". *World Development* 40, no. 1: 36–48.

APEC Business Advisory Council. 2016. *Non-Tariff Barriers in Agriculture and Food Trade in APEC: Business Perspectives on Impacts and Solutions*. Los Angeles, CA: University of Southern California, Marshall School of Business.

Asian Development Bank. 2013. *Key Indicators for Asia and the Pacific 2013*. 44th

Edition. Economic Transformation: Where To, How, and How Fast? Mandaluyong City: ADB.

Aung, Swe Mon. 2018. "Myanmar Beans and Pulses Update 2018". GAIN Report BM 8021. Yangon: USDA Foreign Agricultural Service.

Bernet, Thomas, Graham Thiele, and Thomas Zschocke, eds. 2006. *Participatory Market Chain Approach (PMCA): User Guide*. Lima, Peru: International Potato Centre. http://cipotato.org/publications/pdf/003296.pdf

Cadot, Olivier, and Julien Gourdon. 2015. *NTMs, Preferential Trade Agreements, and Prices: New Evidence*. CEP II Working Paper No 2015-01. http://www.cepii.fr/PDF_PUB/wp/2015/wp2015-01.pdf

Cambridge Economic Policy Associates. 2016. *Global Agriculture and Food Security Program (GAFSP): Private Sector Window: Agribusiness Country Diagnostic – Myanmar*. http://documents.worldbank.org/curated/en/541101490092426376/Agri business-country-diagnostic-Myanmar

Das, Sanchita Basu. 2018. "Do the Economic Ties between ASEAN and China Affect Their Strategic Partnership". *ISEAS Perspective*, no. 2018/32, 21 June 2018.

Disdier, Anne-Célia, Lionel Fontagné, and Mondher Mimouni. 2008. "The Impact of Regulations on Agricultural Trade: Evidence from the SPS and TBT Agreements". *American Journal of Agricultural Economics* 90, no. 2: 336–50.

Durufle, Gilles, Pierre Fabre, and Jean-Michel Yung. 1988. *The Social and Economic Effects of Development Projects: Evaluation Manual*. Paris: Ministry of Cooperation.

Egashira, K., and A.A. Than. 2006. "Cropping Characteristics in Myanmar with Some Case Studies in Shan State and Mandalay Division". *Journal of Faculty of Agriculture of Kyushu University* 51, no. 2: 373–82.

FAO and OECD. 2011. *Price Volatility in Food and Agricultural Markets: Policy Responses*. http://www.fao.org/fileadmin/templates/est/Volatility/Interagency_Report_to_the_G20_on_Food_Price_Volatility.pdf

Fujita, Koichi, and Ikuko Okomoto. 2006. *Agricultural Policies and Development of Myanmar's Agricultural Sector*. Discussion Paper No. 63. Chiba, Japan: Institute of Developing Economies.

Gereffi, Gary. 1999. "International Trade and Industrial Upgrading in the Apparel Commodity Chain". *Journal of International Economics* 48, no. 1: 37–70.

Gibbon, Peter. 2001. "Upgrading Primary Production: A Global Commodity Chain Approach". *World Development* 29, no. 2: 345–64.

Haggblade, Steven, Duncan Boughton, L. Seng Kham, and Myo Thaung. 2014. *Winds of Change: A Rapid Appraisal of Four Pulse Value Chains in Myanmar*. Yangon: Michigan State University and Myanmar Resource Development Institute/Centre for Economic and Social Development.

Hamanaka, Shintaro, and Romana Domingo. 2012. *Measuring Commodity-Level Trade Costs in Asia: The Basis for Effective Trade Facilitation Policies in the Region*. ADB Working Paper Series on Regional Economic Integration No. 95. Manila: ADB.

Hasan, Mohammad Maruf, Jiang Hai Cheng, and Li Xuan. 2014. "CAFTA: China-ASEAN Free Trade Area, Implications on Trade and Development". *Journal of Economics and Sustainable Development* 5, no. 15: 48–55.

Henson, Spencer, and John Humphrey. 2010. "Understanding the Complexities of Private Standards in Global Agri-Food Chains as they Impact Developing Countries". *Journal of Development Studies* 46, no. 9: 1628–46.

Henson, Spencer, and Rupert Loader. 2001. "Barriers to Agricultural Exports from Developing Countries: The Role of Sanitary and Phytosanitary Requirements". *World Development* 29, no. 1: 85–102.

Herghelegiu, Cristina. 2017. "The Political Economy of Non-Tariff Measures". *World Economy* 41, no. 11: 262–86.

Ing, Lily Yan, Olivier Cadot, and Janine Walz. 2016. "Transparency in Non-tariff Measures: An International Comparison". *ERIA Discussion Papers* DP-2016-23. Jakarta: ERIA.

Jaeger, P-M. L. 1998. *The Indian Market for East African Pigeon Peas*. London: Technoserve.

Jaffee, Stephen. 2003. *Malawi's Tobacco Sector: Standing on One Strong Leg Is Better Than on None*. Africa Region Working Paper Series No. 55. Washington, DC: World Bank.

Jongwanich, Jutathip 2009. *Impact of Food Safety Standards on Processed Food Exports from Developing Countries*. ADB Economics Working Paper Series 154. Manila: Asian Development Bank.

Kaplinsky, Raphael, and Mike Morris. 2001. *A Handbook for Value Chain Research*. Brighton: Institute of Development Studies, University of Sussex.

Kee, Huia Looi, Alessandro Nicita, and Marcelo Olarreaga. 2009. "Estimating Trade Restrictiveness Indices". *Economic Journal* 119, no. 534: 172–99.

Khin Than Nwe. 2008. *Plant Breeding and Related Biotechnology Capacity in Myanmar*. Yezin: Global Partnership Initiative for Plant Breeding Capacity Building and Global Crop Diversity Trust.

Kyaw Mying. 2013. "Pulses Production and Export in Myanmar". Presentation at the Agri Trade, Investment and Technology Global Summit 2013, Inya Lake Hotel, Yangon, 19 June 2013.

Kyaw Myint. 2014a. "Pulses Market Information", Bi-Weekly Report 1 (1, 5). Yangon: E-Trade Market Information Service 1.

———. 2014b. Weekly Market Information on Agricultural Commodities 2 (5). Yangon: E-Trade Market Information Service.

M4P. 2008. *Making Value Chains Work Better for the Poor: A Toolbook for Practitioners of Value Chain Analysis*. Version 3. Phnom Penh: UK Department for International Development.

Maertens, Miet, and Johan Swinnen. 2009. "Trade, Standards, and Poverty: Evidence from Senegal". *World Development* 37, no. 1: 161–78.

Maskus, Keith, E., Tsunehiro Otsuki, and John S. Wilson. 2005. *The Cost of Compliance with Product Standards for Firms in Developing Countries: An Econometric Study*. World Bank Policy Research Working Paper. No. 3590. Washington, DC: World Bank.

Ministry of Agriculture and Irrigation. 2000. *Agricultural Marketing in Myanmar*. Yangon: MOAI and FAO.

———. 2013. *Report of Myanmar Census of Agriculture 2010*. Yangon: MOAI and FAO.

———. 2014. *Myanmar Agriculture in Brief*. https://themimu.info/sites/themimu.info/files/assessment_file_attachments/Myanmar_Agriculture_in_Brief_-_GoM_2014.pdf.

———. 2018. *Myanmar Agriculture Development Strategy and Investment Plan (2018–19 ~ 2022–23)*.

Ministry of Commerce and International Trade Centre. 2015. *National Export Strategy 2015–2019*, various sectoral reports.

Ministry of Commerce. 2018. *Myanmar Trade News*. Nay Pyi Taw, various reports.

Myanmar Development Resources Institute/Michigan State University (MSU/MDRI). 2013. *An Agricultural Sector and Food Security Diagnostic for Myanmar*. Yangon: MDRI.

Nay Pyi Taw: The Government of the Republic of the Union of Myanmar, Ministry of Agriculture, Livestock and Irrigation.

Oh Yoon Ah. 2017. "China's Economic Ties with Southeast Asia". *World Economy Brief* 7, no. 18: Seoul: Korea Institute for Economic Policy.

Okamoto, Ikuko. 2008. *Economic Disparity in Rural Myanmar: Transformation under Market Liberalization*. Singapore: NUS Press.

Ramachandran, Sudha. 2020. "The China-Myanmar Economic Corridor: Delays Ahead". *China Brief* 20, no. 7. https://jamestown.org/program/the-china-myanmar-economic-corridor-delays-ahead/

Roy, Devesh, Pramod Kumar Joshi, and Raj Chandra, eds. 2017. *Pulses for Nutrition in India: Changing Patterns to Farm to Fork*. Washington, DC: International Food Policy Research Institute. https://doi.org/10.2499/9780896292567

Santeramo, Fabio Gaetano, and Emilia Lamonac. 2018. "The Effects of Non-Tariff Measures on Agri-Food Trade: A Review and Meta-Analysis of Empirical Evidence". *Journal of Agricultural Economics* 70, no. 30: 595–617. https://doi.org/10.1111/1477-9552.12316

Save the Children. 2013. *A Nutritional and Food Security Assessment of the Dry Zone of Myanmar in June and July 2013*. Yangon: Save the Children, WFP and Ministry of Livestock, Fisheries and Rural Development.

Tothova, Monika. 2011. "Main Challenges of Price Volatility in Agricultural Commodity Markets". In *Methods to Analyse Agricultural Commodity Price Volatility*, edited by Isabelle Piot-Lepetit and Robert M'Barek, pp. 13–29. Springer: New York.

UNCTAD (United Nations Conference on Trade and Development). 2013. *Non-tariff Measures to Trade:Economic and Policy Issues for Developing Countries.* Geneva: UNCTAD.

———. 2019a. *International Classification of Non-tariff Measures: 2019 Version.* New York: UNCTAD.

———. 2020. *Towards a New Trade Policy on Market Access for Myanmar: Identifying a Positive Agenda Among Challenges and Opportunities.* Draft manuscript.

UNIDO (United Nations Industrial Development Organization). 2011. *Pro-Poor Value Chain Development: 25 Guiding Questions for Designing and Implementing Agroindustry Projects.* Vienna: UNIDO.

USDA (United States Department of Agriculture). 2018a. *Myanmar Beans and Pulses Update.* Yangon, Myanmar: USDA Foreign Agriculture Service.

———. 2018b. *Union of Burma: Grain and Feed Annual Report 2018.* Global Agriculture Information Network, GAIN Report Number BM 8003. Washington, DC: USDA.

Woods, Kevin. 2015. *CP Maize Contract Farming in Shan State, Myanmar: A Regional Case of a Place-based Corporate Agro-Feed System.* BICAS Working Paper 14. https://www.eur.nl/sites/corporate/files/BICAS_WP_14-Woods.pdf

World Bank. 2018. *Myanmar Economic Monitor: Navigating Risks.* Washington, DC: World Bank.

WTO (World Trade Organization). 2012. *World Trade Report 2012. Trade and Public Policies: A Closer Look at Non-Tariff Measures in the 21st Century.* Geneva: WTO.

———. 2013. "Lamy: Together, We Have Strengthened the WTO as the Global Trade Body". News Items, 24 July 2013. https://www.wto.org/english/news_e/news13_e/gc_rpt_24jul13_e.htm

Yang Jun and Chunlai Chen. 2008. "The Economic Impact of the ASEAN-China Free Trade Area: A Computational Analysis with Special Emphasis on Agriculture". In *Agriculture and Food Security in China: What Effect WTO Accession and Regional Trade Arrangements?* edited by Chunlai Chen and Ron Duncan, pp. 372–407. Canberra: ANU E Press and Asia Pacific Press.

Zhang Huaqi and Kevin Chen. 2019. *Assessing Agricultural Trade Comparative Advantage of Myanmar and Its Main Competitors: Findings from UN Comtrade.* IFPRI Discussion Paper 1823. Washington, DC: International Food Policy Research Institute.

7

AGRICULTURAL EXPORTS FROM VIETNAM TO CHINA
A Value Chain Analysis of Dragon Fruit and Coffee

Nguyen Thang, Pham Minh Thai, Vu Hoang Dat and Vu Thi Van Ngoc

7.1 INTRODUCTION

China is the second-largest export destination for Vietnam's exports, with total export value increasing tenfold from around US$2 billion in 2000 to nearly US$22 billion in 2016, of which agricultural products accounted for 35 per cent. Total import-export turnover between the two countries increased from US$71.9 billion in 2016 to US$93.6 billion in 2017. The total value of Vietnam's trade with China amounted to 22 per cent of the value of its total trade with the world. More importantly, the ratio of Vietnam's trade with China to its total trade has been steadily increasing, with agricultural exports playing a significant role in overall export growth. China's market share of Vietnam's exports rose from about 6 per cent to 7 per cent between 2002 and 2008 to 26 per cent in 2017. This increase in

China's share of exports reflects an increase in Vietnam's major agricultural exports in particular and export products in general.

The total value of agricultural products exported from Vietnam to China grew significantly from US$3.8 billion in 2014 to US$4.5 billion in 2016. Rice, fresh fruit and coffee are Vietnam's top three exports by value. The value of rice exports remained relatively stable at around US$700 million throughout 2014–16, whereas the value of fresh fruit exports fluctuated, peaking at US$811 million in 2015 from US$627 million in 2014 then declining to US$533 million in 2016 (Atlas of Economic Complexity 2018). However, the value of fresh fruit exports was still vastly higher than that of coffee exports, which in 2014 stood at US$90 million.

Of special interest to Vietnam is the growing demand from China's expanding middle class[1] for fresh fruit and coffee. Between 2012 and 2015, the total value of Vietnam's fresh fruit exports to China almost doubled, from US$442 million to US$861 million. In 2017, China imported about US$2.5 billion worth of fresh tropical fruit from Vietnam, representing an increase of 179 per cent since 2011 (Kubo and Sakata 2018). This surge in fruit exports coincided with an equally remarkable surge in Vietnam's coffee exports to China, which in 2016 reached US$330.1 million, a heady 226 per cent increase in just two years. This reflects the fast-paced evolution of the Chinese coffee market, where total annual consumption is expected to reach around 500,000 tonnes by 2030.

Rice, fresh fruit and coffee were the three highest-value agricultural products exported from Vietnam to China between 2014 and 2016. China is and is likely to remain the biggest importer of Vietnamese rice due to growing demand. Consequently, much of the value chain literature in Vietnam has focused on economic analyses of the rice export value chain (Vo and Nguyen 2011; Dao, Hoang and Thai 2014; Nguyen and Dinh 2015; CIEM 2017). The dynamics of the rice value chain have therefore been carefully examined and well documented. So, as important as rice exports are to the Vietnamese economy, another rice value chain analysis would add little value to national agricultural research. Hence, we selected coffee and dragon fruit for value chain analysis.

With its long land border with China and numerous border gates,[2] Vietnam is well positioned to boost dragon fruit and coffee exports to the Chinese market, taking advantage of the relatively short transit time and distance. The two countries also have agreements on specific types of border trade for border residents. Border trade in agricultural products, which accounts for a significant proportion of total cross-border trade, has therefore been relatively specific. However, since early 2019, China has tightened cross-border trade for border firms and residents and imposed strict requirements for tracking product sources and packing houses.[3] In the face of tightening policy, Vietnam has only been able to export products that are officially allowed into China and has difficulty exporting many other agricultural products such as citrus fruits, durian, avocados, pineapples, and fresh and processed cassava.

The value chains of coffee and dragon fruit in Vietnam have been explored in various studies and reports; however, those studies focus more on characterizing the main value chain actors rather than analysing chain dynamics. Hanh and Diem (2017), for instance, use the ValueLinks and M4P (market for the poor) value chain approaches to describe the characteristics of farmers, traders and processors in the coffee value chain in the Central Highlands. The study identifies several weaknesses that need to be overcome in order to add value to Vietnam's coffee sector and improve the performance of the coffee value chain in general. Yet, the study neglected the impact of non-tariff measures (NTMs) on chain actors. Regarding dragon fruit, Nguyen Thoa, Nguyen Minh and Nguyen Thuy (2018) compiled a comprehensive manual on exporting dragon fruit to the Chinese market. The manual presents a structured analysis of the strengths and weaknesses of the value chain actors, and, to help Vietnamese dragon fruit farmers and exporters, details the processes and requirements for exporting agricultural products to China. Although the document provides a summary of the regulations, it stops short of analysing their impact on value chain actors. Addressing this knowledge gap is the focus of our research study, which sets out to contribute to improving the efficiency of dragon and coffee value chains in Vietnam.

The main research question guiding this study is how actors in the value chains of dragon fruit and coffee from Vietnam to China cope with the tightness of the management control over planting area codes and packaging facility codes, as well as the rules of origin requirements, from China. To answer the question, the study first identifies the key actors in Vietnam's dragon fruit and coffee value chains, and the bottlenecks hindering the country's export of these products to China. Second, the study examines exporters' perspectives of the effects of Chinese sanitary and phytosanitary (SPS) measures and technical barriers to trade (TBT) on Vietnam's coffee and dragon fruit exports to China. To that end, we collected data from primary and secondary sources to map and build insight into the value chains of coffee and dragon fruit in Vietnam, and to understand how TBT and SPS measures affect different actors involved in those value chains with China.

The remainder of the paper is organized as follows. Section 7.2 provides an overview of Vietnam's production and export of dragon fruit and coffee. Section 7.3 describes the methodology and data, and section 7.4 presents the main findings and discusses the value chain analysis of coffee and dragon fruit export from Vietnam to China. Section 7.5 concludes with policy implications and options.

7.2 BACKGROUND

Over the past thirty years of its comprehensive reform programme (1986–2016), Vietnam's GDP grew by an annual average rate of 6.5 per cent, more than double the world average growth rate of 2.8 per cent. GDP growth from 2000 to 2010 was even higher at 7.0 per cent, then fell slightly to 5.9 per cent between 2011 and 2016. There are many reasons for Vietnam's successful economic performance, and it is impossible not to mention the role that agriculture has played in delivering it. Although agriculture's share in GDP is slowly contracting, as of 2016 the sector contributed almost one-fifth of total GDP and employed nearly half of the workforce (Table 7.1). With about 70 per cent of the population living in rural areas, agriculture remains an important source of income. The sector also serves as a vital buffer in times of economic crisis when laid-off or displaced workers return to agriculture for their livelihoods and survival.

Although agricultural exports as a share of total export value have been declining, they still account for nearly one-fifth of the country's total exports. More importantly, the total value of agricultural exports from Vietnam to China increased markedly from US$1.1 billion in 2006–10 to nearly US$3.8 billion in 2011–16. The share of agricultural exports from Vietnam to China in total export value has also increased steadily, from 9.4 per cent in 2010 to 16.8 per cent in 2016.

7.2.1 Overview of Coffee Production and Export in Vietnam

The coffee tree was first introduced into the central region of Vietnam by missionaries in 1857, specifically, in Quang Binh and Quang Tri provinces.

TABLE 7.1
Contribution of Agriculture to the National Economy

Indicators	2000–5	2006–10	2011–16
GDP (annual growth %)	7.2	7.0	5.9
Agriculture value added (annual growth %)	4.0	3.1	2.8
Industry value added (annual growth %)	9.8	8.1	6.8
Services value added (annual growth %)	6.7	7.7	6.5
Economic structure			
% share of agriculture in GDP	22.7	20.8	18.6
% share of industry in GDP	39.0	40.9	36.9
% share of services in GDP	38.3	38.3	41.1
Employment share by sector (%)			
Agriculture	60.9	52.7	46.0
Industry	15.8	16.7	25.2
Services	23.3	20.3	28.9
Total exports (US$ million)	19,767	53,400	132,967
Agricultural exports (US$ million)	4,967	12,066	24,117
% share of agriculture export to total exports	25.13	22.60	18.14
Value of agricultural exports to China (US$ million)	—	1,129	3,782

Source: Author's compilation using data from the General Statistics Office of Vietnam (various years).

Coffee has been grown on the fertile basalt soils of the Central Highlands since 1920–25 but has only been grown commercially since the mid-1990s. Vietnam's coffee plantation area increased gradually from 10,700 ha in 1945 to around 150,000 ha in 1995, then expanded rapidly to around 500,000 ha by 2000. After receding slightly in the early 2000s, the coffee area reached 657,000 ha by 2018.

Two main species of coffee are cultivated in Vietnam, Robusta (accounting for 90 per cent of total production) and Arabica. The Central Highlands is the country's coffee capital, producing 90 per cent of the total yield. Twenty-one per cent (or 126,000 ha) of the coffee cultivation area was planted twenty to twenty-five years ago. These cultivation areas need to be replanted and rejuvenated as ageing coffee trees are the main cause of slow productivity growth.

The average annual coffee yield in Vietnam from 2013 to 2018 was around 2.3 tonnes per ha (Table 7.2). Replanted areas, however, produce much higher yields of 4 to 6 tonnes per ha, and those planted with new varieties of coffee yield as much as 8 tonnes per ha. Vietnam's coffee

TABLE 7.2
Coffee Production in Vietnam, 2013–18

	2013	2014	2015	2016	2017	2018
Area (million ha)	635.0	641.7	640.0	645.4	664.1	680.0
Yield (tonnes per ha)	2.2	2.2	2.2	2.3	2.3	2.5
Production (million tonnes)	1.4	1.4	1.4	1.5	1.5	1.7

Source: IPSARD (2019).

production increased 21.4 per cent between 2013 and 2018, from 1.4 million tonnes to 1.7 million tonnes.

Vietnam is the second-largest producer and exporter of coffee in the world (after Brazil) and currently exports green coffee to over eighty countries and territories. In export value, Vietnam retained the second top spot in the period 2013–18, accounting for 10.2 per cent of the world's coffee exports in 2018. By early 2019, Vietnam accounted for about 14 per cent of the market share and contributed 10.4 per cent of the value of world coffee exports (VNA 2019). Figure 7.1 illustrates the top eleven markets, which combined account for 80 per cent of the value of coffee exported from Vietnam.

Among the top importers of Vietnamese coffee, China sits in 11th place. As shown in Table 7.3, China's imports of Vietnamese coffee increased sharply between 2015 and 2016, from 29,380 tonnes to 46,110 tonnes, then declined almost as sharply to just over 28,030 tonnes (US$84.8 million in value) in 2017. Although most of the coffee exported from Vietnam to the world market is in the form of raw beans, it currently exports many processed coffee products to China.

Processed coffee products, instant coffee, 3-in-1 coffee, unroasted Robusta, and unpacked decaffeinated coffee constituted almost 60 per cent of Vietnam's total coffee export volume to China in 2017 and just over one-third in 2018 (Table 7.3). The export value of processed coffee accounted for 74 per cent of total coffee export value to China in 2017, and just over half of the total export value in 2018.

Table 7.4 presents information on the volume and value of coffee exported to China through the main border gates of Lang Son and Lao Cai and the seaport of Ho Chi Minh City. This data was collected by the research team during the consultation interview. It shows that the Chinese coffee market is mainly driven by instant coffee products. The

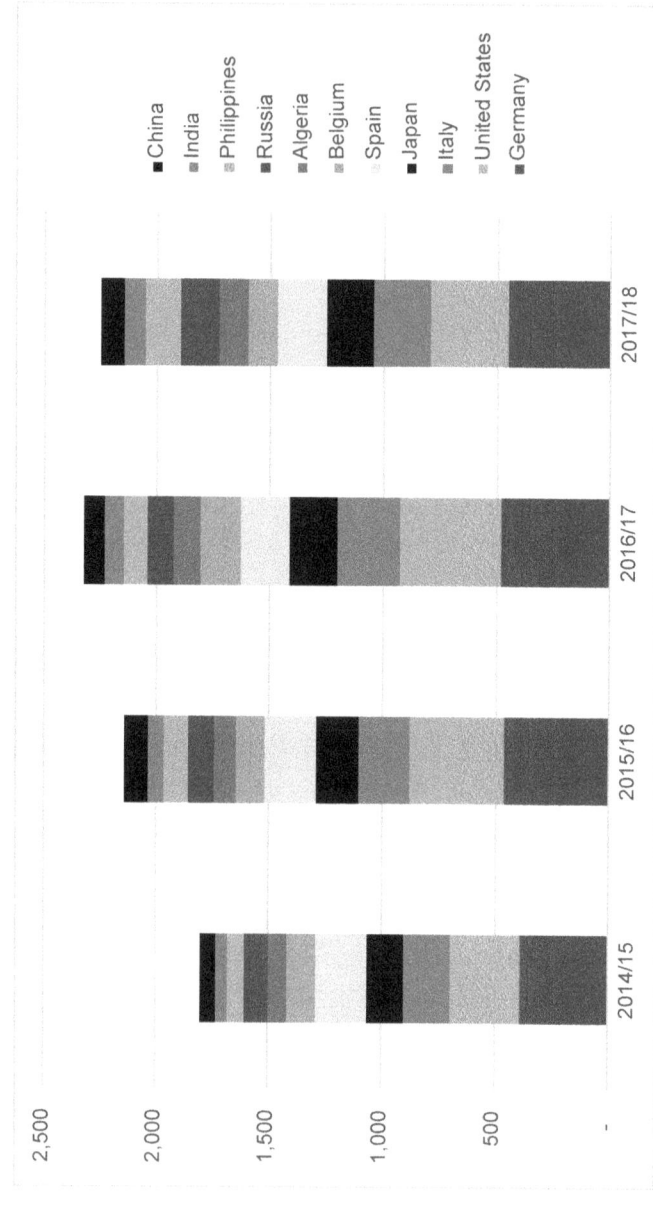

FIGURE 7.1
Top Destinations for Vietnam's Coffee Exports (US$ million)

Source: VICOFA (2018).

TABLE 7.3
Vietnam's Total Coffee Exports to China, 2015–18

	All kinds of coffee		Processed coffee	
Year	Volume (thousand tonnes)	Value (US$ thousand)	Volume (thousand tonnes)	Value (US$ thousand)
2015	29.38	73,553.46	11.90	44,604.26
2016	46.11	106,332.49	9.84	36,383.75
2017	28.03	84,836.30	16.75	62,427.13
2018	44.28	109,540.27	16.24	57,275.52

Source: VICOFA (2018).

TABLE 7.4
Coffee Exported through Lang Son and Lao Cai border Gates and Ho Chi Minh City, 2017–19

	2017		2018		2019 (Jan–Jun)	
Border gate	Volume (tonnes)	Value (US$ thousand)	Volume (tonnes)	Value (US$ thousand)	Volume (tonnes)	Value (US$ thousand)
Lang Son	N/A	N/A	3,657	2,629.00	N/A	N/A
Lao Cai (coffee beans)	3,669	5,986.24	2,343	2,801.71	250	451.43
Lao Cai (instant coffee)	3,042	12,571.98	8,451	30,900.56	1,862	7,295.58
Ho Chi Minh City	N/A	741,788.00	N/A	N/A	N/A	N/A

Source: Lang Son and Lao Cai Customs Offices (2019).

most popular of these is 3-in-1, which contains sugar, coffee, whitening and flavouring (Uyen 2017). Indeed, as of 2013, instant coffee accounted for 99 per cent of coffee retail sales in China (ICO 2015). In general, the growing popularity of branded coffee shops and the rapid evolution of coffee culture in China is also driving roast and ground coffee market growth. With the number of coffee shops in China estimated at 0.14 million by the end of 2018 (Statista 2020), trade sales of coffee have been increasing faster than retail sales. As incomes increase, consumers tend to buy more premium products. Accordingly, albeit still a niche market in China, retail sales of ground coffee have shown the most dynamic growth overall. In 2016, with a 48.46 per cent share of China's total coffee imports, Vietnam was the largest supplier of coffee to the Chinese market. Conversely, the unit price of Vietnamese coffee was the second lowest (after Myanmar) among 17 coffee-exporting countries, and even 9.87 per cent lower than it was in 2015.

In sum, coffee consumption in China is growing. Its large market promises growth potential for Vietnamese coffee exports.

7.2.2 Overview of Dragon Fruit Production and Export in Vietnam

Dragon fruit belongs to the climbing cactus family and is known by many other names. The name dragon fruit, by which it is most popularly known, is derived from the shape of the trees and fruits which are said to resemble a dragon, a symbol that has deep cultural significance in many Asian countries. Ninety-five per cent of the dragon fruit grown in Vietnam are white-fleshed with red skin, and red-fleshed fruit with red skin makes up the other 5 per cent. The natural dragon fruit growing season (the on-season) is from April to September and accounts for about 47 per cent of dragon fruit production. The off-season, when artificial lighting is used at night, is from October to March and accounts for about 53 per cent of dragon fruit production.

Vietnam has the largest area and output of dragon fruit in Asia and is the leading dragon fruit exporter in the world. The dragon fruit cultivation area has expanded tenfold over the last two decades, from 5,512 ha in 2000 to 55,419 ha in 2018 (Phan 2019). Output growth in recent years has been outstanding, rising from 614,346 tonnes in 2014 to 1.7 million tonnes in 2018 (Phan 2019), an increase of 74.9 per cent.[4] In 2017, dragon fruit exports reached 1.5 million tonnes, about US$1,000 million in value (Phuc 2018).

Dragon fruit is grown throughout Vietnam in almost all provinces, but large-scale cultivation areas are concentrated in the south-eastern provinces of Binh Thuan, Tien Giang and Long An. These three provinces alone account for 92 per cent of the total dragon fruit area and 96 per cent of total production. The value of Vietnam's dragon fruit exports has increased dramatically over the last decade, from US$59 million in 2010 to US$1,126 million in 2018 (Figure 7.2).

Vietnam exports dragon fruit to forty different countries and territories, including difficult markets such as the United States, Italy, Japan and Singapore, and is penetrating new markets such as India, New Zealand,

FIGURE 7.2
Export Value of Dragon Fruit (US$ million), 2003–18

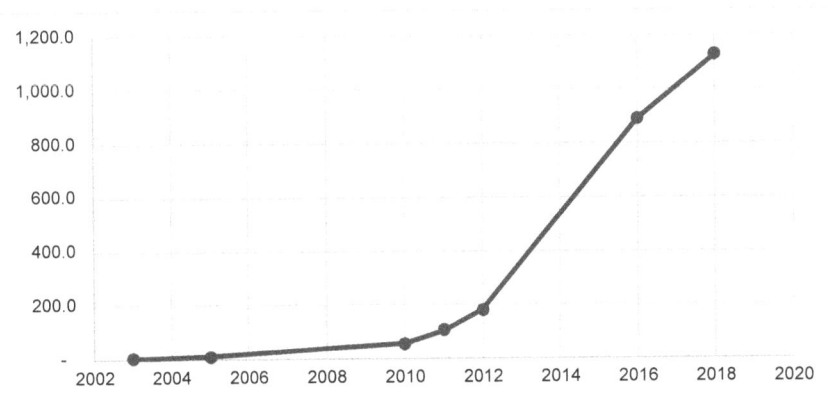

Sources: Luong (2013); Nguyen Thoa, Nguyen Minh, and Nguyen Thuy (2018)

Australia and Chile. However, China is still the largest market for Vietnam's dragon fruit both in volume and value (Figure 7.3). The share of Vietnam's total dragon fruit exports by value to China increased 18 percentage points between 2014 and 2018, from 73 per cent to 91 per cent.

Although dragon fruit is one of the eight fruits officially exported from Vietnam to China, the main dragon fruit export channel is cross-border trade. According to current regulations in Vietnam, dragon fruit is zero-rated for VAT[5] and export tax.[6] Dragon fruit exporters therefore pay customs fees only,[7] which apply to both official trade and cross-border trade, including the commercial trade of border residents.

The convenience of delivery and simplified payment procedures, which satisfy the needs of small-scale establishments and household businesses, means that cross-border trade remains steady. Since 2016, dragon fruit exports have entered China through three border gates: Tan Thanh (Lang Son, Vietnam)–Po Chai (Guangxi, China); Kim Thanh (Lao Cai, Vietnam)–Ha Khau (Yunnan, China); Thanh Thuy (Ha Giang, Vietnam)–Thien Bao (Yunnan, China). In addition, China has created favourable conditions to promote the import of Vietnamese fruits and other agricultural products through Mong Cai (Quang Ninh, Vietnam)–Dong Hung (Guangxi, China) border gate.

FIGURE 7.3
Distribution of Dragon Fruit Exports by Market Destination (per cent), 2014–18

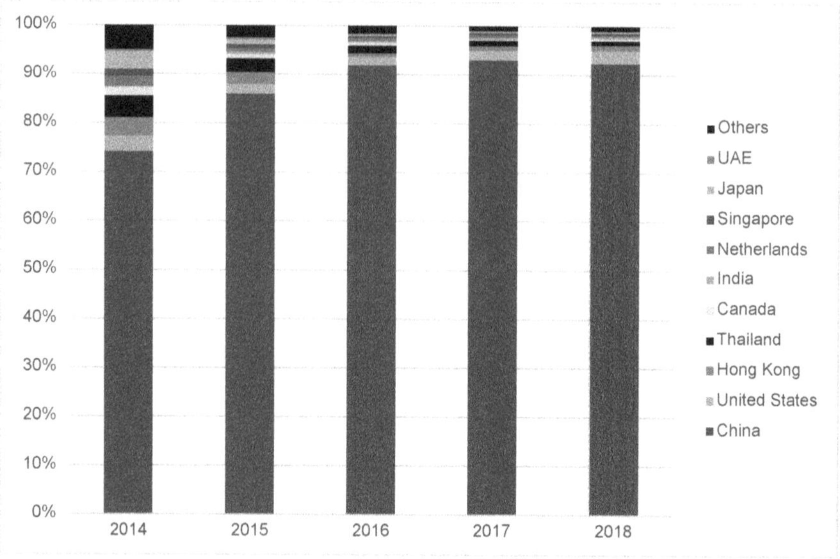

Source: Agro Processing and Market Development Authority (2019).

TABLE 7.5
Exports of Dragon Fruit via Lang Son, Lao Cai and Ha Giang, 2017–19

Border gate	2017		2018		2019 (Jan–Jun)	
	Volume (thousand tonnes)	Value (US$ thousand)	Volume (thousand tonnes)	Value (US$ thousand)	Volume (thousand tonnes)	Value (US$ thousand)
Lang Son	—	—	1,020.04	676,489.38	—	—
Lao Cai	264.51	151,649.77	669.13	414,168.67	400.79	244,563.92
Ha Giang	324.03	—	217.94	—	92.21	—

Source: Lang Son and Lao Cai customs offices (2019).

Data from the Lao Cai customs office shows that both the volume and the value of dragon fruit exported from Vietnam to China continue to increase (Table 7.5). Specifically, the volume of dragon fruit exported through the Lao Cai international border gate increased 153 per cent between 2017 and 2018 (equivalent to a 173 per cent increase in export value).

7.3 DATA AND METHOD

7.3.1 Data

The main source of data for this study comes from qualitative field surveys. The field surveys entailed in-depth interviews with key informants at different levels of government, from national departments and agencies to local authorities, processing and export companies, as well as farmers, traders, transporters and sales agents (Table 7.6).[8] The field surveys were implemented in five provinces: Lao Cai, Lang Son, Dak Lak, Long An and Binh Thuan. Different actors, the interactions among them and with stakeholders and experts, were also observed (Table 7.6). This provided a framework to understand the institutional relationships between different actors in the chain. The research team's interactions with farmers and exporters helped us to understand various problems related to production and export activities.

In addition to primary data, secondary data and information gathered from a comprehensive literature review were also explored. Secondary data was collected from, but not limited to, the Vietnam General Statistical Office, Vietnam Coffee and Cocoa Association, Ministry of Industry and Commerce, Ministry of Agricultural and Rural Development, and the Department of Agricultural and Rural Development in Binh Thuan and Dak Lak provinces.

TABLE 7.6
Summary of Qualitative Interviews

Key informants	Dak Lak	Binh Thuan	Lang Son	Ha Noi	Lao Cai	HCM City	Long An	Total
Officials, experts	16	14	9	10	8	10	9	76
Farmers	17	15	—	—	—	—	7	39
Traders	14	4	—	—	—	—	—	18
Businesses and associations	12	9	—	2	4	5	5	37
Total	59	42	9	12	12	15	21	170

Source: Authors' compilation.

7.3.2 Methodology

Value chain analysis (VCA) is an approach that analyses a production unit or a process from input suppliers to final buyers, and the interactions among all actors along the chain. Bellu (2013, p. 1) defines VCA as "the assessment of a portion of an economic system where upstream agents in the production and distribution processes are linked to downstream partners by technical, economic, territorial, institutional and social relationships". More importantly, VCA is an analytical method that analyses different actors and their functions in the chain to identify the bottlenecks and weaknesses for interventions to upgrade or improve underperforming chain actors.

There are no fixed rules for carrying out VCA (Kaplinsky and Morris 2001). Depending on the purpose, scope, scale, time and resources, either qualitative or quantitative or a combination of qualitative and quantitative methods can be used. An array of research tools is available for VCA, such as participant observations, semi-structured interviews, focus group discussions, structured questionnaires, market mapping, input-output accounting, econometrics, general computable equilibrium modelling and global commodity chain analysis. All of these tools and approaches can be used to measure and identify the power balance among actors along the chain (Faße, Grote and Winter 2009).

Using semi-structured interviews and focus group discussions, this research set out to examine the value chain of two agricultural products exported to China from Vietnam. Coffee and dragon fruit were selected as case studies.

The study combines descriptive statistics and qualitative VCA approaches and uses both primary and secondary data to take stock of the TBT and SPS measures imposed by China on agricultural imports from Vietnam, to identify bottlenecks if any, and to map the main value chain actors involved in exporting agricultural products to China.

First, we mapped the value chain by identifying the main actors and the interactions among them. Second, we identified the risks, constraints and needs of these actors. Third, we evaluated the chain by calculating the production costs, revenues and profit margins of the main actors in the chain. Finally, based on results from the previous analysis, we identified potential interventions or upgrading opportunities for each actor along the chain.

Information, feedback and insights gleaned from a consultation meeting, in-depth interviews with key informants, focus group discussions with main actors, and a validation meeting allowed us to achieve our research goals. First, a consultation meeting with key informants from national (ministries, associations) to local level (people's committees, departments) allowed us to draw a general picture of the value chain with the names of the main actors. Second, although to a large extent in-depth interviews and focus group discussions involve predetermined conversations, questions and insights arose during the discussions. These discussions helped the research team gain a sound understanding of the opportunities and challenges facing different value chain actors. Finally, the validation meeting enabled the research team to synthesize information gathered from consultations, in-depth interviews and focus group discussions. In the validation meeting, representatives of the value chain actors met and discussed issues directly with each other, taking advantage of the opportunity to exchange and share views on the common problems they are facing.

7.4 FINDINGS

7.4.1 Coffee Value Chain Analysis

7.4.1.1 Coffee Value Chain Mapping

Figure 7.4 depicts the coffee value chain in Vietnam and all actors involved, from input suppliers to final consumers. After buying fertilizers and pesticides from input suppliers, coffee farmers tend coffee trees throughout the season. Postharvest products are mostly sold to purchasing agents (60 per cent) and primary processing companies (30 per cent). The remaining 10 per cent is sold directly to final processing companies. Purchasing agents, after sorting the beans, also mostly sell directly to coffee import-export companies (65 per cent), and the rest is sold to preliminary and final processing enterprises. Preliminary processing enterprises buy coffee beans from farmers and buying agents, then sell the processed product mainly to import-export enterprises (80 per cent). The majority (90 per cent) of Vietnam's coffee is exported and 10 per cent goes to domestic markets.

Summarized below, the main actors engaged in the coffee value chain are fertilizer and plant protection product suppliers, farmers, traders, exporters and cooperatives.

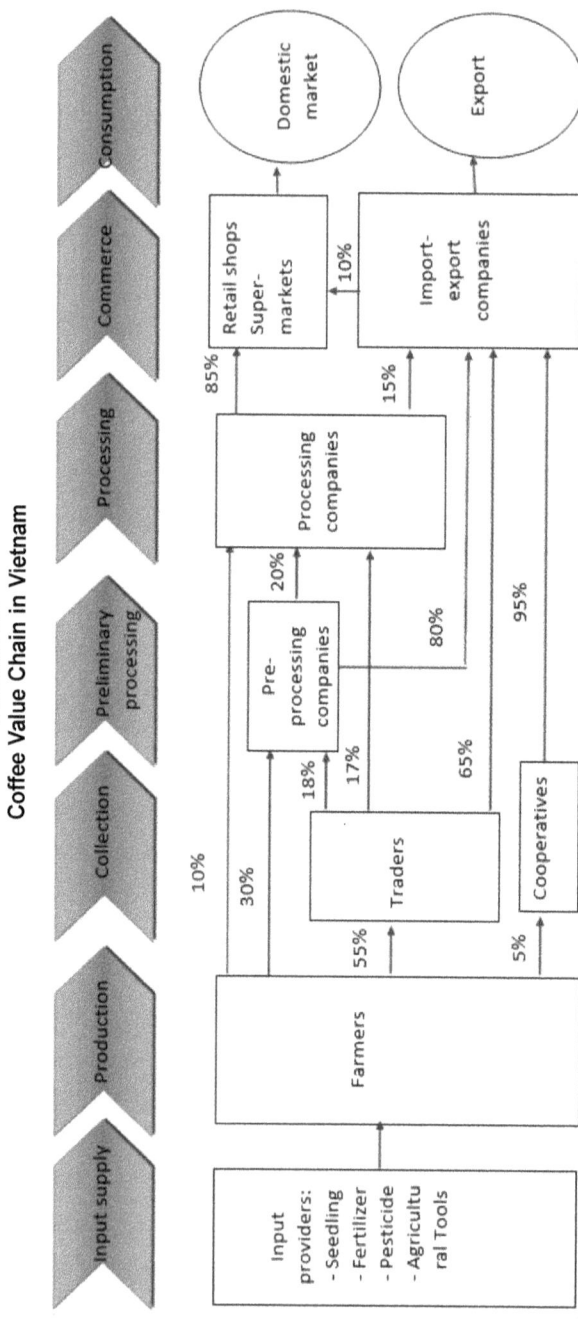

FIGURE 7.4
Coffee Value Chain in Vietnam

Source: Compiled by the authors using survey data.

Fertilizer and plant protection product suppliers: The main suppliers of fertilizer and pesticide inputs to coffee farmers are the buying agents who work through local traders. Farmers typically buy fertilizers and pesticides before and during the coffee growing season. There are two methods of payment, cash or credit, though most farmers depend on loans to buy inputs. They go through agents to collect manure for fertilizer and then pay for it after harvest. Commune-level agents generally buy fertilizer and pesticides from large dealers in district towns or provincial cities. Some deal directly with commercial input producers and then sell fertilizers and pesticides to coffee farmers. They sell inputs for slightly more than the purchase price, after accounting for loading and unloading costs.

Coffee farmers: Sixty-three per cent of coffee farmers have less than 1 ha of farmland, and only 10 per cent have 2.0 to 5.0 ha. The remainder (27 per cent) have more than 5.0 ha. The coffee-growing season starts in January and ends in December of the same calendar year.

Coffee processing usually starts at the farm level. There are two types of processing methods, wet and dry. The technique used depends on the facilities available in the coffee-growing region and the modernity and efficiency of the infrastructure. Coffee is harvested in the dry season when the sun is shining all day. Most farmers therefore opt for the dry method, which entails drying coffee cherries on a cement floor (or even clay ground).

Most farmers buy farm inputs on consignment basis: they deposit coffee with an agent (or trader) and receive advance payment in return. When the coffee price is favourable or when they need money, farmers go to the agent or trader to negotiate the price and receive the balance of their money. This deposit system has many advantages for farmers as they can optimize the use of their coffee storage area, but it also carries several risks. For example, agents could take all the coffee and flee, or farmers might have to accept a lower-than-expected price as they cannot sell deposited coffee to other agents.

Coffee traders: Traders, who collect coffee from farmers and sell it to processing and export companies, play a vital role in the coffee value chain. Most of them serve as input suppliers and therefore have close relationships with farmers. However, their most significant contribution to the coffee value chain is as logistics service providers (Truc and Hanh 2017). The flexibility of traders' activities allows them to buy and deliver inputs to farmers in remote areas. Traders have the advantage of being local and have transport facilities and warehouses spread throughout the coffee growing area. The shortcomings are that traders can manipulate prices and supply. This can slow the flow of goods and also obstruct the flow of transparent information.

For more than 90 per cent of farmers, traders are the sole source of market information and their single buyer of coffee beans. Thus, almost 95 per cent of coffee production is sold to traders. In the Central Highlands, traders include local private collection agents and coffee company agents.

Coffee exporters: Vietnam currently has about 150 coffee export enterprises, and more than 3,000 agents engage in buying coffee. The number of foreign enterprises investing in Vietnam's coffee industry is not large (20 per cent of total export enterprises), but they account for a 40 per cent share of the country's total coffee export volume. The majority of coffee exports are shipped via sea freight. Export firms buy green coffee from farmers, agents and other businesses, and then grade the beans according to quality. After being polished and packaged in accordance with buyers' requirements, the coffee beans are transported to Cat Lai seaport in Ho Chi Minh City for export (mostly f.o.b. price). The price at which businesses buy and sell coffee depends on London or New York coffee futures market prices.

Coffee cooperatives: According to the Department of Economic Cooperation and Rural Development, in the Central Highland provinces, several agricultural cooperatives specialize in coffee production and business. These cooperatives have been good role models for sustainable coffee development, particularly in mobilizing farmers to commit to growing coffee according to international standards such as UTZ Certified,[9] 4C Code of Conduct[10] and Fairtrade.[11] Currently, coffee production on around 297,000 ha meets international standards, producing an output of over 600,000 tonnes of certified green coffee. Cooperatives have collaborated with enterprises, gradually built their brands and penetrated foreign markets, prevented traders from squeezing prices, stabilized output, created good incomes for cooperative members and improved the standard of living for coffee farmers. For example, with the support of Dak Man Vietnam Co. Ltd., Ea Kiet Agricultural and Cooperative Agricultural Cooperative (Cong Bang cooperative) has applied for Fairtrade coffee certification. What makes coffee-producing households feel secure about participating in cooperatives is not having to worry about finding a buyer for their coffee beans, contributing to increased household incomes. The coffee beans produced by cooperative members are exported to European markets through the World Fair Trade Organization. In sum, good cooperatives are considered the "bridges" for sustainable coffee development in Vietnam.

7.4.1.2 Challenges in the Coffee Value Chain

Vietnamese coffee farmers currently face many challenges such as ageing coffee trees, poor soil fertility, overuse of inorganic fertilizers and especially coffee price volatility.

Ageing coffee trees: The coffee trees on around 126,000 ha (21 per cent of the total area) are more than twenty-five years old, well past peak productivity (VICOFA 2018). Efforts are being made through government projects to plant new coffee trees, though replacing all non-productive trees will require more concerted effort. Planting new trees requires considerable investment by farmers, as they do not bear fruit for the first three years. Farmers therefore usually replant just part of their coffee plantation at a time so as to manage costs and maintain production output and thus sustain their standard of living.

Poor soil fertility and overuse of inorganic fertilizers: As suitable areas were exploited to grow as much coffee as possible, chemical/inorganic fertilizers were generally overused to increase or even simply maintain yields. Excessive use of chemical fertilizers to improve productivity has led to serious soil degradation, nutritional imbalance and reduction of soil organic matter. This has culminated in a vicious cycle of low productivity, higher chemical fertilizer application rates, declining soil fertility and lower productivity.

Inaccessible formal credit: Most family and/or small-scale coffee farmers borrow from relatives, friends and agents because such informal credit is usually readily available. Although commercial banks offer formal credit, it is difficult for farmers to access it as the loan process requires collateral (usually a certificate of land use rights). This is a major problem, inhibiting much-needed investment in productivity improvement.

Low and fluctuating coffee prices: Coffee farmers in the Central Highlands have low bargaining power over the coffee price as they are highly dependent on local traders and enterprises. They have limited access to information about quality issues and standards. Almost all interviewed farmers reported not knowing where their produce ends up nor what price it fetches on end markets. Most of them sell their produce to agents with whom they have long-established close relationships and trust. Their weak bargaining power means they have little influence over the price they sell their produce for, or the prices they pay input suppliers for seeds/seedlings, fertilizers and pesticides. Consequently, most coffee farmers think that the biggest challenge for them is coffee price volatility. The situation of traders is not much better because they set the price based on that generated by wholesalers, though they usually make some profit. Although Vietnamese farmers can access the internet to check the coffee price traded on the London stock exchange, such a price is just a reference when selling their coffee beans.

7.4.2 Dragon Fruit Value Chain Analysis

7.4.2.1 Dragon Fruit Value Chain Mapping

In general, Vietnam's dragon fruit supply chain is relatively simple, being mainly constituted of traditional distribution channels that involve many intermediaries between growers and consumers. Trading between farmers, input suppliers and collectors is mainly done through verbal agreement rather than written contract, resulting in unsustainable trading relationships in which most producers are price takers. This is one of the shortcomings stymying the competitiveness of Vietnamese dragon fruit in the world market.

About 15–20 per cent of total dragon fruit production is destined for domestic consumption. The remaining 80–85 per cent is exported, of which 10 per cent goes through official trade channels and 70–75 per cent through cross-border trade conducted by border residents (Thoa, Minh, and Thuy 2018).

As Figure 7.5 shows, the main distribution channel for dragon fruit is traders (95 per cent). Dragon fruit farmers sell their produce from their garden or the local collection point to a collector, who grades the fruit and transports it to a larger collection point for local businesses or

Agricultural Exports from Vietnam to China

FIGURE 7.5
Dragon Fruit Value Chain in Vietnam

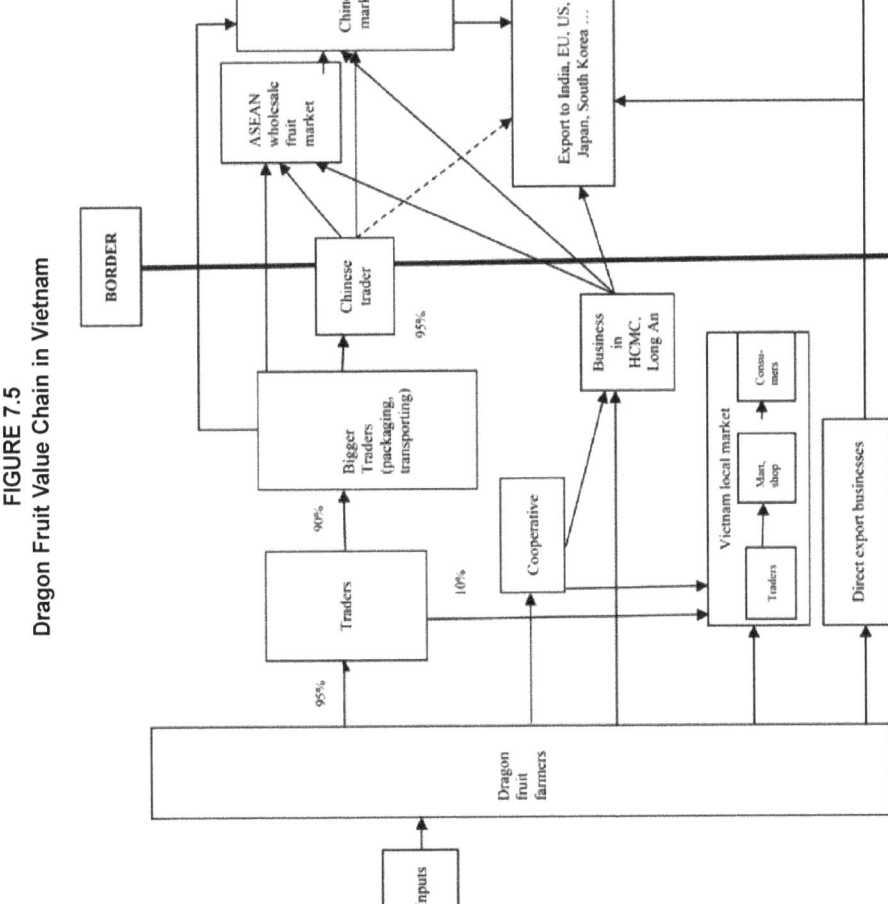

Source: Compiled by authors using field survey data.

wholesalers. Dragon fruits are then sorted, processed and packaged for export or domestic markets.

Another distribution channel is producer cooperatives, which enable smallholder farmers to participate in modern value chains: some farmers join a cooperative to develop their products to reach a wider customer base or to gain direct access to export markets. However, this channel is quite short though showing a growing trend.

The main actors in the coffee value chain are fertilizer and plant protection suppliers, farmers, traders, exporters and cooperatives, as elaborated below.

Fertilizer and Plant Protection Product Suppliers
Farm input suppliers are plentiful, diversified, distributed throughout the production areas and able to meet growers' demands in a timely manner. The relationships between suppliers and dragon fruit farmers are mainly acquaintanceships. Households that are regular customers of input suppliers can obtain pesticides and fertilizers in advance and pay later. However, the pesticides, growth stimulants and fertilizers sold by many store agents are of unknown origin and inferior quality. Furthermore, the retail prices of agrochemicals are often inconsistent, affecting productivity and product quality and, ultimately, can increase production costs.

Dragon Fruit Farmers
Dragon fruit farmers can be divided into two groups: smallholder farm households and large commercial farmers. The former account for 90 per cent of dragon fruit producers in Vietnam. The average land area planted for dragon fruit by farmers in this group is 0.5 to 0.6 ha. These households cannot expand their production due to a lack of capital and limited farmland. They have weak purchasing power and are usually price takers. They are also bound by the payment conditions and production quotas set by traders and do not have a pre-processing point. If they do not sell the whole crop at once, they harvest the fruit using wheelbarrows and then pack it into plastic trays ready for traders to collect and transport by truck. Farmers also transport dragon fruit from their garden to the local collector/wholesaler collection point by motorbike or tricycle.

In contrast, commercial dragon fruit farmers usually cultivate a large area of over 10 ha. They grow and sell their products to customers or export them directly. These farmers often build their own processing zone for quality grading, packaging and storage that meet international export standards.

Regarding trading relations, transactions and agreements between farmers and traders are done via telephone or in person. Depending on their relationship or need (to sell or to buy), the seller actively contacts the buyer, or vice versa, to negotiate and agree on the price and the form of delivery. After contacting farmers, buyers visit the farm/garden to inspect and evaluate the crop (colour, size, weight, scales or ears of the fruit, slugs, fungal diseases, insect damage). After agreeing on the price and method of calculation, the buyer makes an advance payment. The buyer usually pays the balance to the farmer in cash before the shipment is delivered.

Economic analysis, after deducting all costs, reveals that dragon fruit growers suffer a loss of US$0.02 per kg in the main season, but can earn about US$0.17 per kg in the off-season (equivalent to about US$3,441 per ha). However, this calculation is based on the assumption that farmers hire workers for all stages of tree care, from sowing seeds and planting tree seedlings to harvesting ripe fruit; in fact, farmers do much of the work themselves. The negative profit margin in the main season, therefore, does not fully reflect the actual situation. Moreover, the margin depends on the dragon fruit price at the time of harvest. The price in the main season is usually significantly lower than in the off-season, so farmers are less motivated to tend their dragon fruit in the main season than in the off-season. Therefore, production costs in the main season are significantly lower, equal to about one-third of costs in the off-season, and output per hectare is half that in the off-season.[12]

Dragon Fruit Traders

Traders play a crucial role in Vietnam's dragon fruit value chain. Most traders buy dragon fruit from farmers and resell to export enterprises in their province.[13] Although there is no signed document, the relationship between firms and traders is quite tight. To ensure sufficient supplies of dragon fruit, each enterprise has a network of traders specializing in purchasing produce. This network covers the whole dragon fruit production area. Enterprises notify traders of the purchase price, quality and quantity needed on the day. Traders buy dragon fruit from farmers and deliver the fruit to enterprises on a commission basis. The rate of commission depends on familiarity built over time and timely provision of dragon fruit in sufficient quantity and of satisfactory quality. In addition, traders receive a markup when they buy dragon fruit at a lower price than they sell it for. They also gain the difference in the volume/weight of dragon fruit (via depreciation rate, the weight difference of packaging). There are many cases where these traders deliberately withhold dragon fruit from the market, increasing virtual prices, leading to a virtual hot phenomenon in the market. As a result, they can sell dragon fruit at a higher price to make more profit. Traders and "Chinese enterprises" control the prices of dragon fruit, which can sometimes rise and fall many times in one day, causing traders and Vietnamese businesses to struggle.[14] Consequently, many Vietnamese enterprises have to sell or sublet their packing facilities to Chinese enterprises.

Generally, traders make a profit in both on-season and off-season, and the profit (US$0.05 per kg) from trading dragon fruit in the off-season is higher than in the on-season (US$0.03 per kg). This means that, unlike farmers, traders do not face the risk of crop loss. Traders are merely intermediaries between farmers and wholesalers, so they can always on balance ensure some profit for themselves. However, due to the cash payment method for farmers, traders also have to pay in advance before collecting payment from wholesalers, and they may be at risk at this stage if the wholesaler refuses to buy or defers payment, or even flees without paying traders.[15]

Dragon Fruit Exporters

Dragon fruit export enterprises are mostly located in the provinces and are registered as businesses under Vietnam's Enterprise Law. However, the survey results show that up to 90 per cent of enterprises exporting dragon fruit are registered by Vietnamese business owners but leased to Chinese traders. Thus, in essence, the group of individuals who have the authority and power to make decisions about trading activities and the purchase price of dragon fruit are Chinese businesspeople.

Because export enterprises purchase dragon fruit through traders, most of them do not control the quality and safety of produce during growing and harvesting. Pesticide residue amounts and the traceability of dragon fruit are not guaranteed. Overcoming the consequences if a shipment is found to violate pesticide residue limits is challenging. To reduce risk, some large enterprises have their own dragon fruit farms or buy fruit directly from farmers. This allows them to control quality from sowing to harvesting (including the types and quantities of pesticides used). Export enterprises often have relatively modern means of transport (refrigerated trucks), which is vital to preserving the quality of dragon fruit during and after transportation.

Whereas the costs of farmers and traders are very different between the main crop and the off-season, the season makes no difference to the costs of export enterprises. This is mainly because exporters apply the same treatment to dragon fruit on both on- and off-seasons. In general, export enterprises make more profit per kilogram of dragon fruit than traders and farmers in both seasons. The profit of the main dragon fruit crop is US$0.8 per kg and the off-season profit is US$0.17 per kg.[16] Thus, it can be said that in the dragon fruit value chain, farmers are the lowest profit earners and dragon fruit export enterprises are the highest profit earners, especially in the off-season.

Dragon Fruit Cooperatives

Given that most farmers have a small dragon fruit growing area, they produce spontaneously based on their own experience. Moreover, farmers rely heavily on traders to sell their dragon fruit, so they are often the price takers. Cooperatives were established to overcome this situation with the aim of standardizing production practices among members, for example, through the adoption of VietGAP[17] and GlobalGAP.[18]

Cooperatives can amass enough produce to supply export enterprises directly and thereby circumvent traders and other intermediaries. In this sense, cooperatives play a vital role as a bridge between small-scale farmers and export businesses. Cooperatives still face some difficulties such as the limited capacity of staff, members and facilities, passive marketing and commercial information sharing, inability to promote the primary export market, and lack of linkages to reduce input costs by buying fertilizers and pesticides in bulk.

7.4.2.2 Dragon Fruit Export Challenges: Cross-Border Trading Risks in Exporting to China

Dragon fruit is mostly exported from Vietnam to China via cross-border trade or the commercial trade of border residents in specified areas near the border. This poses many challenges and risks for Vietnamese exporters in general and dragon fruit farmers in particular.

Briefly, for dragon fruit exported to China by official trade channels, Vietnamese enterprises (or individuals) sign contracts to export dragon fruit to partners in China under the signed agreement (or commitment) between the two countries following international practice.

Although cross-border trade[19] is limited to border residents of both Vietnam and China, it is the primary channel through which dragon fruit reaches Chinese markets. This is mainly because official trade[20] is subject to higher import costs (VAT, other technical control fees), whereas the cost of cross-border trade is much lower (zero per cent VAT, no control fee).

Cross-border trade in dragon fruit is characterized by low product quality, low selling price, loose trade relations and exposure to many risks. Passive trade relations lead to forced price taking and erratic price swings. Lack of linkages coupled with unstable market conditions create waves of irrational psychology and unstable trade relations. Moreover, the market is dominated by Chinese traders. Most of the dragon fruit procured by Chinese traders through cross-border trade has Chinese language information labels. Furthermore, most commercial activities between Vietnamese farmers/traders and Chinese traders are not backed by written contracts, which could hurt Vietnamese partners. For instance, lack of a financial contract means there is no legal basis for settlement should a dispute arise. Instead, the cost will fall on farmers and small-scale/individual Vietnamese traders. The risk of insolvency, for example, through loss of part or all of the dragon fruit value, is the most harmful. In other words, exporting in the form of cross-border trade means that Vietnamese enterprises (or individuals) export dragon fruit to China without a foreign trade contract, invoice or payment document. Only declaration papers and the cross-border fee are required. However, they are subject to taxes, stringent quality inspection, animal and plant quarantine inspection, and food safety and standards checks by domestic specialized management agencies before customs clearance. Although the procedures are simpler and transport costs lower, cross-border trade is unstable and risky because once the dragon fruit consignment has cleared customs it cannot be brought back to Vietnam.

To sum up, Vietnam's dragon fruit exports are heavily dependent on cross-border trade, which is not sustainable. Further, export via cross-border trade always carries risk because the contracts between buyers and sellers are not legally binding. Despite these problems, most dragon fruit continues to be traded and exported from Vietnam to China in this way. With new import regulations and processes imposed by China heightening these difficulties, Vietnamese dragon fruit farmers are likely to confront more complex challenges in exporting their products to China.

7.4.3 Non-tariff Measures

The non-tariff measures (NTMs) encompass seven categories, namely technical barriers to trade (TBT), export-related measures (EXP), sanitary and phytosanitary (SPS) measures, quality control measures (QC), preshipment inspection (INSP), price control measures (PC) and other measures (OTH). However, this section focuses on SPS and TBT measures.

7.4.3.1 SPS and TBT System in Vietnam: Overview and Challenges

Vietnam has in place an SPS monitoring system from the central to the local level as a focal point for the Ministry of Agricultural and Rural Development. Many legal documents have been issued, but the weakest aspect of this system is poor implementation (Adachi 2017; GIZ 2017). Vietnamese authorities have issued an array of legal documents related to food safety. For example, about 400 documents have been promulgated by the government and ministries and more than 1,000 documents issued by local authorities (Adachi 2017). Such a large number of legal documents causes many overlaps and dissipates focus, leading to a heterogeneous SPS information system. "As a result, of a heterogeneous SPS information system, small household farmers, who cultivate the majority of the land, are having difficulties in collecting data from export destinations" (GIZ 2017, p. 13). That leads to food safety violations and environmental impacts, and such breaches can constrain the ability of Vietnamese businesses to export and reduce the value of Vietnamese agricultural product exports to the world.

Vietnam's SPS office is beset by three important issues that need to be addressed. First, SPS notices from China for exporting goods from Vietnam are in Chinese, with only a one-page summary in English. Yet, the SPS office has no funding and no translator to translate the content from Chinese to Vietnamese. Second, the awareness of Vietnamese enterprises and farmers about SPS-related issues is not high. Often businesses only go to the SPS office when they encounter an operational problem. Although farmers and businesses have been fully informed about these regulations, they only perform well when meeting the requirements for the first batch of exports. After that, they typically fail to adhere fully to the correct process. This way of doing business harms farmers and enterprises in the long term. Third, the SPS office rarely receives feedback from ministries and therefore does not always have enough information to fulfil its tasks.

Related to the TBT system, the Regulation on the Organization and Operation of the Network of Notification and Enquiry Agencies and the Interdisciplinary Committee on Technical Barriers to Trade in Vietnam was promulgated on 24 November 2017. The Ministry of Science and Technology organizes and manages the operation of Vietnam's TBT network. One of the main functions of this network is implementing Vietnam's notification obligations and TBT inquiry obligations in implementing TBT-related international treaties. Furthermore, it has to support the community to increase awareness and advise businesses on TBT-related issues. In most provinces, the TBT office operates professionally and effectively. For example, the Binh Thuan Provincial Department of Standards and Quality has issued forty-seven TBT bulletins in Binh Thuan province and updated them to June 2019.[21] These newsletters have fairly up-to-date and detailed information on the latest TBT regulations from WTO member countries so that businesses and citizens can grasp the updates.

Although it was set up from central to local levels, Vietnam's TBT office has encountered operational difficulties and shortcomings. First, according to regulations, the Department of Quality and Measurement Standards comes under the management of the Ministry of Science and Technology (MOST). Meanwhile, TBT activities involve many import and export activities that are managed by the Ministry of Industry and Trade (MOIT). Therefore, provincial TBT inquiry points can only answer enterprises' questions related to goods regulated by MOST and must forward other issues to the national TBT office. This leads to overlap and inefficiency in TBT activities in the provinces. Another shortcoming is that the negotiation of import and export issues is carried out by MOIT, but issues related to quality standards come under the management of MOST. The lack of adequate coordination between the two ministries makes negotiating terms and conditions especially challenging. Third, regarding the TBT segment, the most pressing issue is that the national TBT office was established by MOST under the General Department of Standards and Quality. This means that the national TBT office is subordinate to the ministerial level, but in terms of TBT-related expertise, the national TBT office is of a higher level. The resultant lack of coordination creates problems. In other words, requesting information from other ministries is complicated. That the national TBT office has insufficient information leads to a lack of information for provincial TBT points. Finally, in theory, if enterprises need any information about the array of TBTs, they only need to reach the provincial TBT points. However, as mentioned above, the response to TBT information has not been effectively implemented.

7.4.3.2 SPS and TBT Measures Imposed by China on Agricultural Products: Overview

According to the most recent UNCTAD data, updated on 24 February 2021, China has imposed a total of 5,685 NTMs on agricultural product imports from all trading partners, of which TBT and SPS measures account for 69.9 per cent and 10.3 per cent, respectively.

TBT Measures Imposed by China in General
Of the 100 TBT measures imposed by China on its bilateral trade partners, only twenty-five concern fruit exports to China. For example, measure B31 (labelling requirements) affects China's imports of blueberries, walnuts and avocados from Chile, pears from Taiwan, mangoes from India, rose apples from Thailand, bananas from Sri Lanka, apples and pears from the United States, mangoes from Pakistan, and pineapples from Costa Rica.[22]

Vietnam faces only one TBT measure, namely TNM code B7 (product quality or performance requirements) on rice (including brown rice, milled rice and broken rice), effective 24 June 2016.[23] To date, China has not imposed TBT measures on its imports of dragon fruit (HS 08109092) and coffee (HS 09012110) from Vietnam.

Out of the 3,954 TBT measures applicable to all China's trading partners, only twenty-nine are related to HS 08 codes (edible fruit and nuts, peel of citrus fruit or melons) and HS 09 codes (coffee, tea, maté and spices). These measures apply to agricultural products generally imported into China, and then dragon fruit and coffee from Vietnam will follow instructions from these general measures.

SPS Measures Imposed by China in General
Out of a total of 1,054 SPS measures imposed by China on its bilateral trade partners, 351 concern products with HS 08 and HS 09 codes. For example, measures A51, A61 and A64 regulate China's imports of persimmon from New Zealand; blueberries and walnuts from Chile; apples and pears from the United States; pears and grapes from Taiwan; avocados and citrus fruits

from Peru; pineapples from Costa Rica; rice from Japan; bananas from Sri Lanka; rose apples, pomegranates, pineapples, ginseng, bananas, passion fruit, coconuts, longans and durian from Thailand; and grapes from South Korea. However, there are no specific measures for Vietnam's coffee and dragon fruit exported to China.[24]

Among the 588 SPS measures that China has applied to all trading partners, only twenty-nine apply to products with HS 08 and HS 09 codes and only eleven are related to dragon fruit and coffee from Vietnam.[25]

In sum, among the ten SPS and TBT measures imposed by China on Vietnamese products, there is only one TBT measure for rice and nine SPS measures for various products, as follows: code A11 for poultry and poultry products (effective 14 January 2004), codes A83, A851, A69, A53, A64, A11 and A19 for rice (effective 24 June 2016) and code A83 for live cattle semen and embryos (effective 25 October 2006). There are no specific SPS or TBT measures for dragon fruit and coffee. This means that the UNCTAD NTM database does not provide detailed information on SPS and TBT measures for the two selected Vietnamese products—coffee and dragon fruit. Therefore, the mapping of existing SPS and TBT measures imposed by China on imports of dragon fruit and coffee from Vietnam relied on the information gleaned from in-depth interviews with representatives from the Ministry of Agriculture and Rural Development, Ministry of Industry and Commerce, Lao Cai and Lang Son customs offices, and export enterprises.

7.4.3.3 SPS and TBT Measures Imposed by China on Coffee Exports to China

Vietnam's coffee exports to China have been on an upward trend in recent years, but most of the coffee exports have been in soluble form for domestic consumption or coffee beans for re-export to other countries. Coffee is mainly exported from Vietnam to China through exploiting support policies applicable to border residents' cross-border trade (i.e., without written contract), and there is relatively little official trade. Vietnam's exports to China using China Certificate of Origin Form E are subject to 5 per cent import duty and 13 per cent VAT, which must be paid immediately. Specifically, exports of roasted ground coffee to China are subject to the same rates of import duty and VAT, whereas exports of instant coffee are subject to zero per cent import duty and 13 per cent VAT. Further, the majority of Chinese coffee importers defer payment until 2 to 3 months after receipt.

Agricultural Exports from Vietnam to China

During the fieldwork and review of previous studies, very few separate regulations on SPS and TBT related to Vietnamese coffee products entering China were noted. Generally, China's standards for compulsory labelling and product quality are also increasing. All goods circulating on Chinese territory must be labelled with information in Chinese. China's National Health and Quality Quarantine Agency requires foodstuffs to be affixed with stamps and food safety certificates before being exported or imported. Pictures and labels are only affixed with the approval of the Chinese State Quarantine Department of Exports and Imports. Importers bear the cost of labelling. Recently, China has started managing and licensing Vietnamese businesses that are eligible to export agricultural products to China as per the list of registrations, and this list must be approved by a competent Chinese authority. This is applied to all agricultural products including coffee and dragon fruit.

7.4.3.4 SPS and TBT Measures Imposed by China on Dragon Fruit Exports to China

China's increasing demand for evidence of traceability activities in production is making it more challenging to export agricultural products. To meet China's food safety and plant quarantine regulations, dragon fruit exporters must register the planting area codes and places with Chinese customs. Products imported into China must be labelled with the place (plantation) of origin, comply with China's technical specifications for packaging and food hygiene standards, and not contain harmful insects. In particular, there have been changes in the monitoring of imports of fruits and vegetables into the country. From 1 October 2019, food products imported into China must have a food safety certificate issued by the competent authority of the exporting country. From 1 January 2019, Chinese customs offices must check the quarantine certificates for fruit and vegetables imported from Vietnam along with the registered name and the packing code. Products that originate from gardens and packing facilities registered with Vietnamese authorities and recognized by the General Department of Customs of China are coded. If appropriate, quarantine clearance is approved. If the goods originate from non-registered growers or packing facilities, they are prohibited from entering China.

China's new requirements demand that all agricultural and aquatic products imported into China be packed and labelled with traceability information. Packaging and labelling must follow Chinese legal provisions, and National Technical Code requirements are mandatory for bilateral trade and related agreements. The packaging and labelling requirements for dragon fruit are as follows:

1. Label must be affixed detailing the type of fruit, planting area, packaging unit/exporter name or code
2. Fruit packaging materials must be brand new, clean and hygienic
3. Non-toxic net sacks, not natural straw or other water-absorbent materials, must be used for packing
4. Permitted packaging materials include cartons, cowhide and plastic boxes
5. Packaging must be pre-printed with the origin traceability label, which must be affixed to the fruit or pasted/printed on the outside of the box
6. Traceability information must be understandable, and information must be in Chinese and English.

These new requirements for packaging and traceability mainly affect fruit exporters. To comply with these regulations, exporters have to pay additional registration fees, print traceability stamps, and equip packing houses with cartons and fruit baskets. In addition, China has applied another TBT measure by appointing certain border crossings and ports for importing Vietnamese agricultural products. They are Pingxiang, Dongxing, Thuy Khau, and Long Bang border gates; Fangchenggang and Qinzhou seaports; and Guilin Liangjiang international airport.

Finally, other TBT measures through increased requirements for agricultural products imported into China have increased processing costs and customs clearance time. Specifically, at the checkpoints, China has built irradiation centres and requires imported fruit to be irradiated. Fruit from Vietnam must be transferred to Chinese vehicles to be irradiated, loaded onto conveyor belts for irradiation, and then loaded onto transport vehicles. Again, this increases customs clearance time and increases export costs.

In sum, the tightening of regulations on quarantine, traceability, packaging design and packaging specifications for agricultural products exported to China has increased costs as well as transit time for exports of Vietnamese agricultural products.

7.5 CONCLUSIONS AND POLICY IMPLICATIONS

Using information gathered from semi-structured interviews and focus group discussions, this study tries to identify how actors in the value chains of dragon fruit and coffee from Vietnam to China are coping with the tightening of Chinese SPS and TBT measures. The main findings show that farmers are in the weakest position vis-à-vis other actors in both value chains in having to accept both the purchase price of inputs and the selling price of outputs, yet they have no effective countermeasure except to hope for a higher selling price. Dragon fruit farmers and coffee growers depend heavily on traders to sell their products. Moreover, they face problems caused by severe diseases affecting the productivity of coffee trees and dragon fruit trees. The most challenging issue for farmers is market price volatility. While coffee prices depend heavily on world market prices, dragon fruit prices depend almost entirely on the Chinese market, the destination of 90 per cent of Vietnam's total dragon fruit production. Traders, who collect coffee or dragon fruit from farmers and sell to processing and export companies, play a vital role in the respective value chains. Traders also face price risks, and they also have no effective countermeasures. Even exporters face similar difficulties when they rely heavily on prices and major export markets. Although there have been many efforts to diversify export markets, these measures are just the beginning and there needs to be more concerted effort to implement them in the long term.

Furthermore, this study also finds that Vietnam already has an SPS and TBT monitoring system from the central to the local level and many legal documents have been issued, yet the weakest point of this system is poor implementation. Food safety violation both constrains the ability of Vietnamese farmers to export and reduces the value of Vietnamese agricultural exports. Dragon fruit export standards to China compared to other markets such as Japan, South Korea, the United States and Europe are still relatively lenient. This led to farmers abusing plant protection drugs and growth stimulants to produce bigger, heavier and better-looking dragon fruits to export to China. Therefore, as China tightens its quality control and plant quarantine rules, substantial losses could accrue to Vietnamese farmers. The overuse of pesticides and growth stimulants is not only detrimental to the environment but also harmful to the health of farmers and consumers. Meanwhile, the capacity for food safety inspection of fruits consumed domestically is far from adequate as the relevant Vietnamese agencies have not developed an adequate handling and management regime.

China's enforcement of stricter import requirements such as planting area codes, packing facility codes, food safety inspection certificates, and plant quarantine will present real challenges to Vietnamese farmers in the short run. Such requirements from China's side are not new, and they conform to international practices. These regulations have existed, but China has not enforced them adequately before. Strict requirements on SPS and TBT measures from China will be an excellent opportunity for Vietnamese producers and exporters to improve the quality of their products in the long term.

Finally, cross-border trade, which is the major export channel for dragon fruit to China, poses many challenges and risks for Vietnamese exporters and farmers.

Based on the findings, the following recommendations merit consideration.

For Short and Medium Term
- Strengthen the application of VietGAP and GlobalGAP standards to fully meet the increasingly strict quarantine regulations associated with exporting agricultural products to China.
- Improve the capacity and awareness of regulatory agencies, businesses and farmers to satisfy the technical regulations and quarantine requirements demanded by China. There should be measures to educate farmers about safe production processes.
- Have policies to mitigate the negative effects of the monopsony of Chinese traders, by controlling collection activities at production sites and cooperating with Chinese authorities to create a level playing field for all traders regardless of their nationality.
- Encourage farmers to improve their farming practices such as better planting techniques, good-quality planting materials, irrigation, better pest control, packaging and storage. A very simple practice that farmers can apply is keeping good records. By keeping track of labour and inputs on the farm, farmers can better understand their costs of production and calculate their selling prices more precisely.
- Build a system of adequately large warehouses to store coffee after harvest when the price is lowest. Only by building such warehouses can Vietnam reduce its dependence on world prices.

For Long Term
- The government should change its food safety approach from final food safety inspection to monitoring all stages along the entire production chain. Establishing a manager-business-producer cooperation mechanism to ensure safety in the whole supply chain is another critical activity that must be undertaken.
- Export enterprises should gradually shift to doing business in the form of formal trade rather than cross-border trade to minimize price squeeze or other risks in payment.
- The state must have policies in place to continue supporting the development of the agricultural cooperative model.
- Farmers should have vertical relationships with other actors in the value chain. Contract farming is a form of vertical cooperation that has proved very effective and has been further developed recently. Accordingly, processing enterprises, purchasing agents and export enterprises sign contracts with farmers to produce a certain quantity of products of specific quality within specific time limits and for a set price. In vertical relationships, large companies often provide farmers with quality inputs at reasonable prices, access to credit, technical support and equipment.
- Besides maintaining traditional markets, Vietnam should step up marketing and trade promotion activities to diversify the country's export base for coffee and dragon fruit, thereby reducing dependence on the Chinese market.
- Vietnam should also equip and install deep processing technologies to diversify dragon fruit (e.g., dragon fruit wine, dried dragon fruit) and coffee products. Deep processing adds value to raw agricultural products and reduces dependence on the harvest season.

Notes

1. "Estimates of the size of China's middle class vary depending on the definition. China's National Bureau of Statistics puts the figure at nearly 400 million, less than a third of the population, by defining a middle-class household as one making 25,000 yuan (US$3,640) to 250,000 (US$36,400) yuan a year—a fairly low threshold. Nevertheless, in a 2015 report, UBS Investment Bank and PricewaterhouseCoopers narrowed it to 109 million Chinese with a wealth of between US$50,000 and US$500,000—a relatively high standard"(Zhou 2018, p. 2).

2. Vietnam and China share a 1,450km border with eight international border gates, thirteen main border gates, and many auxiliary border gates as well as border markets.
3. Information provided by officials of various government line departments responsible for agricultural exports such as the Department of Agricultural Processing and the Sanitary and Phytosanitary Office, which come under the Ministry of Agriculture and Rural Development, during a workshop at the Centre for Analysis and Forecasting, Vietnam Academy of Social Sciences, 25 September 2019.
4. http://ap.fftc.agnet.org/ap_db.php?id=1038
5. Circular No. 219/2013/TT-BTC dated 31 December 2013, guiding the implementation of the Law on Value Added Tax, and Decree No. 209/2013/ND-CP dated 18 December 2013 detailing and guiding the implementation of some articles of Value Added Tax Law; dragon fruit exports are not subject to VAT.
6. Circular No. 164/2013/TT-BTC dated 15 November 2013 of the Ministry of Finance stipulates that organizations and dragon fruit export enterprises must declare the code of the export product (0810.90.92) and sets export tax at 0 per cent.
7. Circular No. 172/2010/ TT-BTC dated 2 November 2010 of the Ministry of Finance provides guidance on collection rates, collection regimes, remittance, and management and use of customs fees.
8. Detailed information on the site selection process will be provided by the author upon request via phamminhthai80@gmail.com
9. "UTZ is the benchmark for the sustainable production of coffee, tea (including rooibos and herbal teas) and cocoa.... UTZ certified products have been sourced in a way that is better for producers and the environment" (https://utz.org/what-we-offer/certification/products-we-certify/).
10. In the words of the 4C Association, "The 4C Code of Conduct includes baseline requirements for the sustainable production, processing and trading of coffee and eliminates unacceptable practices. The code facilitates a dynamic improvement process by providing guidance for and commitment to continuous improvement" (https://www.coffeehabitat.com/2011/01/4c-code-of-conduct-marginal-standards-for-corporate-coffee/#:~:text=The%204C%20Association%20states%3A%20%E2%80%9CThe,and%20commitment%20to%20continuous%20improvement.%E2%80%9D).
11. As stated on the homepage of the Fairtrade website, "Fairtrade changes the way trade works through better prices, decent working conditions and a fairer deal for farmers and workers in developing countries" (https://www.fairtrade.net/about/what-is-fairtrade).
12. Detailed table calculation will be provided by the author upon request via phamminhthai80@gmail.com

13. Sometimes traders transport dragon fruit to the northern provinces where they sell it directly to Chinese customers in the border area or to export businesses in the border provinces.
14. Vietnamese enterprises are registered by Vietnamese directors under Vietnamese names, yet Chinese businesspeople rent these enterprises. So, the real activities of these enterprises are under the control of Chinese businesses.
15. Detailed table calculation will be provided by the author upon request via phamminhthai80@gmail.com
16. Detailed table calculation will be provided by the author upon request via phamminhthai80@gmail.com
17. VietGAP (Vietnamese good agricultural practices) details the regulations on good agricultural production practices for agricultural and fishery products in Vietnam; including principles, orders and procedures to guide organizations and individuals to produce, harvest and prepare products in a way that ensures food safety, improves product quality, ensures social welfare, ensures producer and consumer health, protects the environment and ensures product traceability.
18. GlobalGAP is a trademark and set of standards (technical measures) for good agricultural practices developed to voluntarily apply to the production, harvesting and post-harvest handling of agricultural products (including crop cultivation, animal husbandry and aquaculture). GlobalGAP has 252 criteria: 36 mandatory 100 per cent compliance criteria, 127 mandatory 95 per cent compliance criteria, and 89 recommendations.
19. Chinese residents living within 20 km of the Chinese side of the Vietnam-China border are exempt from import duty and VAT when trading or exchanging goods as long as transactions do not exceed RMB8,000/person/day. They must, however, abide by the inspection and supervision of the local customs office and fill in customs declaration forms for imported/exported goods. They are entitled to resell those goods to Chinese enterprises. Similarly, Vietnamese policy exempts border residents from import tax on goods below the value of VND2 million/person/day. The number of transactions is limited to four per month. The aim of the policy is to support and improve socio-economic conditions for people living in the border areas. An unforeseen consequence is that the policy has created conditions for Chinese traders to procure Vietnamese dragon fruit through border residents without having to pay tax.
20. Official trade in dragon fruit products is carefully monitored by specialized agencies for quality, food safety and hygiene. All procedures must be completed and taxes paid in full before customs clearance. Dragon fruit exported to the Chinese market through the official channel are transported through the border gates in large quantities.
21. https://chicuctdcbinhthuan.gov.vn/News/hoatdongtbt/banintbt/2019/06/768.aspx

22. A detailed list will be provided by the author upon request via phamminhthai80@gmail.com
23. Article 4 "Food safety requirements: Imported Vietnamese rice should be in line with China's relevant laws and regulations and meet the national food safety requirements."
24. A detailed list will be provided by the author upon request via phamminhthai80@gmail.com
25. A detailed list will be provided by the author upon request via phamminhthai80@gmail.com

References

Adachi Aya. 2017. *Sanitary and Phytosanitary (SPS) Measures: Status Report on Agricultural Trade between Cambodia, the Lao PDR, Viet Nam and China*. Bonn: GIZ.

Agro Processing and Market Development Authority. 2019. Documents prepared for the working session between the research team and the Division of Crop Market Development, Ministry of Agriculture and Rural Development of Vietnam.

Atlas of Economic Complexity. 2018. "What Did China Import from Vietnam in 2014?". http://atlas.cid.harvard.edu/explore/?country=43&partner=239&product=undefined&productClass=HS&startYear=2000&target=Partner&tradeDirection=import&year=2014

Bellù, Lorenzo Giovanni. 2013. *Value Chain Analysis for Policy Making: Methodological Guidelines and Country Cases for a Quantitative Approach*. EASYPol Series 129. Rome: FAO.

CIEM (Central Institute for Economic Management). 2017. *Institutional Review of the Rice Value Chain*. Hanoi: CIEM.

Dao The Anh, Hoang Thanh Tung, and Thai Van Tinh. 2014. *Developing the Mekong Delta Rice Value Chain and Vietnamese Rice Brand*. Hanoi: Centre for Agrarian Systems Research and Development.

Faße, Anja, Ulrike Grote, and Etti Winter. 2009. *Value Chain Analysis Methodologies in the Context of Environment and Trade Research*. Discussion Paper No. 429. Hannover: Leibniz University Hannover.

GIZ (German Society for International Cooperation). 2017. "Exporting Agricultural Goods to China: Challenges and Opportunities of Sanitary and Phytosanitary (SPS) Measures". Proceedings of Regional Workshop on SPS, Beijing, China, 6–7 December 2017. Bonn: GIZ.

ICO (International Coffee Organization). 2015. "Coffee in China". 115th Session, 28 September – 2 October 2015, Milan, Italy.

IPSARD (*Institute of Policy and Strategy for Agriculture and Rural Development*). 2019. "Report of Coffee Industry". Documents prepared for the working session between the research team and the Institute of Agricultural Strategy and Rural Development.

Kaplinsky, Raphael, and Mike Morris. 2001. *A Handbook for Value Chain Research*. Brighton: Institute of Development Studies. www.ids.ac.uk/ids/global/pdfs/Vch Nov 01.pdf

Kubo Koji, and Sakata Shozo. 2018. "Impact of China's Increasing Demand for Agro Produce on Agricultural Production in the Mekong Region". BRC Research Report No. 21. Bangkok: Bangkok Research Centre, IDE-JETRO.

Lang Son and Lao Cai Customs Offices. 2019. Documents prepared for the working session between the research team and the Lang Son and Lao Cai customs offices.

Luong Ngoc Trung Lap. 2013. "Demand Trend, Market, Price Development and Promotional Requirements for Dragon Fruit". Presentation to the International Symposium on Superfruits: Myth or Truth? Ho Chi Minh City, Vietnam, 1–3 July 2013.

Nguyen Bao Thoa, Nguyen Thi Hong Minh, and Nguyen Thi Minh Thuy. 2018. *Guide for Exporting Dragon Fruit to China*. Decentralized Trade Support Services for Strengthening the International Competitiveness of Vietnamese Small and Medium-sized Enterprises Program. Hanoi: Vietnam Trade Promotion Agency and GIZ.

Nguyen Duc Thanh and Dinh Tuan Minh. 2015. *Vietnam's Rice Market: Reform to Integrate, Market Approach*. Hanoi: Hong Duc Publishing House.

Nguyen Thi Thuy Hanh and Mai Thi Thuy Diem. 2017. "Describing the Coffee Value Chain in the Central Highlands of Vietnam". *Australasian Agribusiness Perspectives* 20, no. 5: 1442–6951.

Phan Thi Thu Hien. 2019. "The Dragon Fruit Export Challenge and Experiences in Vietnam". Food and Fertilizer Technology Centre Agricultural Policy Platform, 18 October 2019. https://ap.fftc.org.tw/article/1598

Phuc Hau. 2018. "13,000 Tons of Dragon Fruits Exported to China a Day". *Saigon Online*, 10 October 2018. https://sggpnews.org.vn/national/13000-tons-of-dragon-fruits-exported-to-china-a-day-78102.html

Statista. 2020. "Number of Cafes in China from 2007 to 2016 with Estimates until 2018". https://www.statista.com/statistics/872181/number-of-cafes-in-china/#: ~:text=This%20statistic%20shows%20the%20number,around%20 140%2C902%20cafes%20in%202018

Truc, Phan Thi Thanh, and Hanh, Nguyen Thi Thuy. 2017, "The Linkage Between Actors Coffee Value Chain in the Central Highland of Vietnam". *Science and Technology Magazine*, Danang University No. 2 (111)/2017.

Uyen To. 2017 "Vietnamese Coffee Wants to Conquer the Chinese Market". https://vietnambiz.vn/ca-phe-viet-muon-chinh-phuc-thi-truong-trung-quoc-18328.htm

VICOFA (Vietnam Coffee and Cocoa Association). 2018. "Coffee Annual Report 2017/2018 and Orientation for the year 2018/19".

VNA (Vietnam News Agency). 2019. "Vietnam Targets Higher Coffee Quality, Value". *Vietnam News Agency,* 18 March 2019. https://en.vietnamplus.vn/vietnam-targets-higher-coffee-quality-value/148447.vnp

Vo Thi Thanh Loc and Nguyen Phu Son. 2011. "Value Chain Analysis of Rice Product in the Mekong Delta". *Can Tho University Journal of Science* 19: 96–108.

Zhou Xin 2018. "The Question Mark Hanging over China's 400 Million-strong Middle Class: Burdened by Rising Costs, Debt and Worries about the Future, Will They Vanish or Thrive?". *South China Morning Post*, 12 October 2018.

INDEX

A
Agricultural Cooperatives, 93
Agricultural Development Strategy, 164
air freight, 84, 88–89
APEC Business Advisory Council, 208
AQSIQ (Administration of Quality Supervision, Inspection and Quarantine), 96, 100, 174–75, 191–92, 194–97, 199, 201
Armo, 228
ASEAN (Association of Southeast Asian Nations), 18–19, 30, 40, 48, 51, 60, 109–10, 205, 244
ASEAN-China Free Trade Area, 59, 110
ASEAN Economic Community (AEC), 4
ASEAN Master Plan on Connectivity, 19
ASEAN Trade in Goods Agreement, 174
Australia, 42, 148, 265
Automated System for Customs Data, 109
AVE (ad-valorem equivalent), 211–12
Avian influenza, 224
Awba (Syngenta), seed company, 227
Ayethaya Industrial Zone, 215, 232
AyeyawadyChao Phraya-Mekong Economic Cooperation Strategy, 19

B
Bank for Agriculture, 93
Beans, Pulses and Sesame Seeds Merchants Association, 234
Belt and Road Initiative, 7, 18, 30, 42, 44, 48–49, 57
border trade, 209, 213, 216, 224, 226, 230, 232–33, 237, 239, 242–44, 257
see also cross-border trade
brick-and-mortar stores, 82

C
Cambodia
  agricultural economy, 111
  cassava, and, 114, 118–28, 137–48, 158
  exports, 113
  GDP growth, 2
  population, 110
  sugarcane, and, 115, 128–48, 153–57, 159
Cambodia Development Resource Institute (CDRI), 9
Cambodia Industrial Development Policy, 109

Cambodia Trade Integration Strategy, 109, 121–22, 146
cassava, 9–10, 13–14, 60, 64–70, 73–78, 84, 85, 92–94, 118–28, 137–48, 158
global value chain, 152
Catalogue of Fresh Fruit Types and Export Countries/Regions, 51
Cavendish banana value chain, 192–95
Centre for Analysis and Forecasting of the Vietnam Academy of Social Sciences (CAF-VASS), 10
Centre for Economic and Social Development (CESD), 9
CGCOC Group, 7
China
  agricultural sector, 25–39
  border with Vietnam, 290
  documentation requirements for trade, 247–48
  economic growth, 31–34
  Five-Year Plan, 7, 32, 34, 44
  food security policy, 23
  free trade agreement, 30, 51
  GDP growth, 2
  labour force, 27–29
  Lancang-Mekong countries, trade with, 40–48
  middle class, 257, 289
  non-tariff measures, imposed by, 95–100, 135–36
  outward foreign direct investment, 40–44
  population, 6, 22–23, 34
  trade partners, 4, 10, 30, 55, 205
  trade statistics, discrepancies in, 239–42, 249–51
China-ASEAN cooperation framework, 7
China-ASEAN Free Trade Agreement (FTA), 108

China Certificate of Origin, 284
China Certification and Inspection Company, 192
China Communist Party, 24
China Inspection and Quarantine, 194
China Inspection Co., Ltd, 88
China International Import Expo, 49
China-Japan-South Korea Free Trade Zone, 48
China Oil and Foodstuffs Corporation (COFCO), 175–77, 179–80, 190
"Chinese enterprises", 278
Chinese entrepreneurs, 87
"Chinese impact, the", 182
Chinese State Quarantine Department of Exports and Imports, 285
CITIC Construction, 7
climate change, 85–86, 101, 213
CLMV-T, 4–8, 14–15, 17–19
  see also GMS
coffee
  value chain, and, 269–74
  Vietnam, and, 257–64, 269–74, 284, 287
"Collaborative Farming", 92
Commercialization of Rice and Vegetables Value Chains in Lao PDR: Status and Prospects, 170
Committee on World Food Security, 17
Commodities Exchange Centre (CEC), 233–34
Common Agricultural Policy, 66
Confederation of Thai Durian Orchardists, 86, 102
Cong Bang cooperative, *see* Ea Kiet Agricultural and Cooperative Agricultural Cooperative
contract farming, 11, 16–17, 19, 109, 166–67, 175–76, 190, 195, 198, 207, 237, 289

Index

COVID-19 pandemic, 5–6
CP (Chaoroen Pokphand), 218, 223, 227, 235
CP Group of Thailand, 234
CP Livestock, 232, 235
cross-border trade, 14, 18, 57, 114, 117, 120–21, 148–49, 206, 208–9, 213, 216, 241–45, 251, 258, 265, 274, 279–80, 284, 288–89
  see also border trade
Cross-Border Transport Agreement (CBTA), 19, 91, 104, 197
Culinary Commodity Association, 234

D
Dak Man Vietnam Co. Ltd, 272
De Heus, 235
deforestation, 166
Dehus, 218
Department of Agricultural and Rural Development, 267
Department of Agricultural Extension (DOAE), 86
Department of Agricultural Processing, 290
Department of Agricultural Research, 227
Department of Agricultural Statistics, 220
Department of Agriculture, 81, 96, 99, 104, 214–15
Department of Consumer Affairs, 215
Department of Economic Cooperation and Rural Development, 272
Department of Foreign Trade (DFT), 84, 98
Department of Highways, 94
Department of Import and Export, 174
Department of Industry and Handicraft, 191

Department of Land Use Statistics, 216
Department of Quality and Measurement Standards, 282
Department of Standards and Quality, 282
Department of Trade, 215
Department of Trade and Production Promotion, 180
Diamond Star, 228
disease epidemic, 14, 85, 93, 98, 101–2, 105, 150, 158, 226, 247, 277, 287
drying yard, 80–81
durian
  non-tariff measures on, 95–97
  Thailand, and, 61–64, 73–92
  value chain, and, 73–92
Durian Exporter Registration, 95

E
Ea Kiet Agricultural and Cooperative Agricultural Cooperative, 272
East-West Economic Corridor, 105
e-commerce, 73
economic land concessions (ELCs), 109, 128, 130–32
  see also land concession
Economic Research Institute for Industry and Trade (ERIIT), 9, 183
economic sanction, 9, 205
Enterprise Law, 278
environmental issues, 94
epidemic, see disease epidemic
European Union, 60, 66, 205, 210, 212
export tax, 265, 290
exporters, 8–10, 15, 54, 60, 64, 76, 78, 80–82, 84, 88, 91, 94–97, 99–100, 103, 111, 115, 117–18, 128, 136, 138, 144–46, 148, 150, 167–69, 172, 174–75, 181, 188, 190, 192, 194–95,

197, 200–1, 208, 210, 212, 216, 234, 237, 245–46, 258, 261, 264–65, 267, 269, 272, 276, 278–79, 285–88

F
Facebook, 226
Fairtrade, 272, 290
farm debt, 85, 93, 101
farm gate price, 61, 63, 93, 178, 180, 213
farm law, 218
farm machinery, 229–30, 243
farm service provider, 128, 130–31, 135, 153
farmers, 4, 11–13, 22, 27–29, 61, 64, 66, 71, 76–77, 80–81, 92–94, 101–2, 105, 109, 115, 117–18, 120–22, 126–28, 147, 149, 158, 166–68, 170–73, 175, 178–79, 190, 194–96, 198, 207, 209, 213–18, 222, 224, 226–37, 241–45, 251, 258, 267, 269, 271–74, 276–81, 287–89
fertilizer, 115, 118, 125, 131, 173, 175, 178, 182–84, 186, 226, 228–30, 233, 269, 271, 273–74, 276, 279
filière approach, 216
focus group discussions (FGDs), 117, 120, 122, 126, 133, 214, 287
food safety, 19, 138, 144, 168, 175, 188, 191–92, 194, 200, 212, 280–81, 285, 287–89, 291–92
Food Safety Cooperation Forum, 19
Food Safety Law, 192
formal credit, 273
4C Code of Conduct, 272, 290
free market economy, 25
free trade zone, 19, 56
freight, types of, 88–89
Fresh Studio, 235
Fruit and Vegetable Exporter Registration, 95

Fruit and Vegetable Growers Association, 234

G
GAP (good agricultural practices), 95–97, 101–2, 104–5, 174
General Administration of Customs China (GACC), 96–97, 100, 174, 179, 191, 196–97, 201
General Administration of Quality Supervision, Inspection and Quarantine of China, 51
General Agreement on Tariffs and Trade, 30
General Department of Customs of China, 285
generalized system of preference, 108
GlobalGAP, 279, 288, 291
GMP (good manufacturing practices), 95–97, 101, 104–5, 174, 191
GMS Cross-Border Transport Agreement (CBTA), 104
GMS (Greater Mekong Subregion), 1–8, 13, 18–19, 59, 91, 103, 197, 205
  population, 1, 3
  see also CLMV-T
GMS Programme, 4, 19
GMS Regional Investment Framework, 18
Golden Tiger, seed company, 227
growth stimulant, 276, 287

H
herbicide, 118, 183, 186, 194
Hoang Anh Gia Lai (HAGL) Group, 182, 183–84
Hong Kong, 42, 88, 138, 224, 266
human capital, 16
hypermarket, 82

Index

I
IFAD, 17
importers, 14, 66, 76, 78, 80–82, 88, 98–100, 112, 128, 130, 146, 148, 179, 184, 190, 192, 194, 196, 210, 213, 257, 261, 284–85
Indo-China Development Partners (IDP) rice mill, 170, 174, 175, 177–80, 190, 195
Indonesia, 42, 64, 66, 234–35, 244
informal credit, 273
Interdisciplinary Committee on Technical Barriers to Trade in Vietnam, 282
International Trade Centre, 170
ISO 9001 standard, 171, 201, 235

J
Japfa Comfeed Indonesia, 235
Japfa Group, 218, 232
JD.com, 84
Jiang Nan Fresh Fruit and Vegetable Wholesale Market, 82
Jiangong Agriculture, 182
Jingdong online store, 201

K
key informant interviews (KIIs), 117, 126, 132–33

L
labour shortage, 87
Lamy, Pascal, 210
Lancang-Mekong Cooperation, 4
Lancang-Mekong countries, 23–24
 China's trade in, 40–48
LancangMekong River Dialogue and Cooperation, 7
land concession, 11, 13, 109, 183, 186, 188, 194–95, 198, 220, 251
 see also economic land concessions (ELCs)
land freight, 88–91, 93–94
Lao Bureau of Statistics, 170
Laos
 cash crops in, 165–66
 Cavendish banana, and, 165, 167, 169–70, 182–95
 GDP growth, 2
 minimum wage in, 12, 183
 rice, and, 169–81, 191–92
Legal Guide on Contract Farming, 17
Li Keqiang, 7
Likert scale, 188
London stock exchange, 274
LS Company, 184, 192

M
M4P (market for the poor), 258
Making Value Chains Work Better for the Poor: A Toolbook for Practitioners of Value Chain Analysis, 216
Malaysia, 9, 42, 88, 206, 224
Mangkone Trading, 184, 187–88, 192
market competition, 88
May Kha, 232, 234–35
microfinance institutions (MFIs), 118, 120
migrant workers, 85, 87
Mingaladon Industrial Zone, 235
minimum wage, 12, 183, 229
Ministry of Agricultural and Rural Development, 267, 281, 284, 290
Ministry of Agriculture, 37, 43, 191
Ministry of Agriculture and Cooperatives (MOAC), 96, 100
Ministry of Agriculture and Forestry, 170, 193
Ministry of Agriculture, Forestry and Fisheries (MAFF), 114

Ministry of Agriculture, Livestock and Irrigation, 214, 220, 245
Ministry of Commerce, 45, 78, 84, 98, 100, 133, 145, 191
Ministry of Health, 192
Ministry of Industry and Commerce, 170, 180, 267, 284
Ministry of Industry and Trade (MOIT), 282
Ministry of Planning and Investment, 170
Ministry of Science and Technology (MOST), 282
most favoured nation, 108
MOU (memorandum of understanding), 84
Mya Nadi, maize dryer, 231, 234
Myanmar
  crop areas in, 219–20
  exports, 206
  GDP growth, 2
  maize, and, 206–9, 216–46
  minimum wage, 229
  natural gas, and, 206–7
  population, 223
  trade statistics, discrepancies in, 239–42, 249–51
Myanmar Investment Commission, 215–16
Myanmar Pulses Beans and Sesame Seeds Merchants Association, 215
Myanmar Sustainable Development Plan, 245
Myaung Taka Industrial Zone, 235

N

National Bureau of Agricultural Commodity and Food Standards, 71
National Bureau of Statistics of China, 24
National Health and Quality Quarantine Agency, 285
National Institute of Statistics, 110
National Technical Code, 286
New Economic Mechanism, 164
Northeastern Tapioca Trade Association, 71
North-South Economic Corridor, 105
NTMs (non-tariff measures), 5, 6, 8, 14–15, 18–19, 60, 70, 110, 112, 117, 135–36, 138–49, 166–69, 190–91, 194, 197, 206–12, 214, 216–17, 236–38, 241, 246, 258, 281, 283–84
  agricultural trade, and, 210–12
  cassava trade, on, 97–100
  definition, 210
  durian exports, on, 95–97

O

ODM (original design manufacturer), 78
OECD, 8
OECD-FAO Guidance for Responsible Agricultural Supply Chains, 17
OEM (original equipment manufacturer), 78
Office of Agricultural Economics, 71
Office of Agricultural Research and Development, 97
Office of the Prime Minister, 86
offline distribution channels, 84
online platforms, 84
Opium Replacement Programme, 165
Orchard Association, 234
Overseas Merchandise Inspection Co. Ltd, 234

P

packing houses, 78–79, 87, 104–5
Pagoda, greengrocer chain, 84

Index 301

Pakistan, 30, 42, 283
Partnership Training Institute
    Network, 19
pellet factories, 81
pesticide, 115, 125, 183, 186, 194,
    228, 234, 247, 269, 271, 274, 276,
    278–79, 287
Phnom Penh Sugar Co. Ltd, 130–31,
    133
Plant Quarantine Act, 95
plantation workers, 183, 186
Porter, Michael E., 170
Porter's value chain, 71, 115, 170,
    184–86
Potatoes Growers Association, 234
poverty, 2–3, 5, 12, 165, 188, 206, 245
price volatility, 212–14, 218, 287
Principles for Responsible
    Agricultural Investment, 17
Principles for Responsible
    Investments in Agriculture
    and Food Systems (CFS-RAI
    Principles), 17
processors, 73, 76–78, 80, 84, 92–95,
    103, 115, 117, 122, 133, 145–46,
    158, 168, 175, 179, 190, 215, 224,
    232–35, 243, 244, 246, 251, 258
producer associations, 16
Project for Agricultural Development
    and Economic Empowerment,
    111
protectionism, 32, 47
protectionist policy, 44
Provincial Committee on the Price of
    Goods and Service, 98
public-private partnership, 18
purchasing power, 59, 276

Q
Q Mark, 96
QR code, 103

R
RCA (revealed comparative
    advantage), 6–7, 38, 160
Regional Comprehensive Economic
    Partnership, 7, 48, 56, 59
Regulation on the Organization
    and Operation of the Network
    of Notification and Enquiry
    Agencies, 282
Report on Development of China's
    Outward Investment 2018, 24
rice value chain, 172–81, 191–92
road-rail transport, 84
road-water transport, 84
Rui Feng, 130–31
Rural Economic Research Centre,
    36–37
Russia, 42–44, 138, 262

S
sea freight, 88–89, 272
seed distributors, 227–28
seed research stations, 173
Siem Reap Action Plan, 19
Singapore, 30, 42, 224, 264, 266
Sino-US economic trade, *see* US-
    China trade
small- and medium-sized enterprises
    (SMEs), 147–49
smart farm project, 102
specialty store, 82
spot market, 8
SPS Information Management System
    database, 210
SPS (sanitary and phytosanitary),
    14–15, 17, 60, 70, 95–98, 110, 136,
    138–39, 145, 148, 180, 191–92, 195,
    200, 208–12, 237–39, 258, 268,
    281–85, 287–88, 290
Standardization Administration of
    China, 191

starch factory, 81
State Administration for Industry and Commerce, 194
State Food and Drug Administration, 194
Strategy for Promoting Safe and Environment-Friendly Agro-based Value Chains in the GMS, 19
street hawker, 82
street vendor, 82
sugarcane, and Cambodia, 115, 128–48, 153–57, 159
Sunjin, investment firm, 235
supermarket, 82
Sustainable and Affordable Poultry for All, 235

T
Taunggyi Chamber of Commerce, 215
Taunggyi Industry Zone, 236
Taunggyi University, 216
technical barriers to trade (TBT), 14, 17, 70, 110, 136, 138–39, 145, 148, 191, 208–12, 239, 258, 268, 281–88
see also trade barrier
Tet Chaung, poultry farm, 235
Thai Durian Institute, 86, 102
Thailand, 42
   cassava, and, 64–70, 73–78, 84–85, 92–94
   downstream, 76, 81–82, 84–85, 87, 94, 105
   durian, and, 61–64, 73–92
   exports, 9
   GDP growth, 2
   midstream, 76, 78, 82, 85, 87, 93
   upstream, 76–78, 82, 85–86, 92
Thailand Development Research Institute (TDRI), 9

T-mall, 84
TOWS analysis, 171
trade barrier, 30, 51, 110, 167
   see also technical barriers to trade (TBT)
Trade Facilitation Agreement, 56
trade preferential status, 108
traders, 76, 80–84, 111–12, 114–15, 120–21, 126, 190, 208–9, 213–18, 224, 226–27, 231–35, 237, 242–44, 251, 258, 267, 269, 271–72, 274, 276–80, 287–88, 291
traditional retailers, 82–84
transporters, 76–78, 80, 115, 128, 153, 267
TVC (total variable cost), 230
Twelve-Point Action Plan for Trade Facilitation and Investment, 109

U
UN Comtrade database, 24, 208, 214, 237, 249, 251
UNCTAD, 17, 136, 139, 283–84
UNIDROIT, 17
unilateralism, 32, 47
Union of Myanmar Federation of Chambers of Commerce and Industry (UMFCCI), 233–34
United Nations Industrial Development Organization (UNIDO), 71
United States, 32, 39–40, 42, 44, 47–48, 60, 103, 205, 262, 264, 266, 283, 287
United States Department of Agriculture (USDA), 224
US–China trade, 5, 32, 37, 39, 44, 47, 49
UTZ Certified, 272, 290

V

value chain
  cassava, and, 73–78, 84–85, 92–94, 118–28, 158
  Cavendish banana, 192–95
  coffee, 269–74
  definition, 268
  downstream, 76, 81–82, 84–85, 87, 94, 105, 133
  dragon fruit, 274–80
  durian, and, 73–92
  GMS countries, in, 7–13
  maize, and, 216–36
  midstream, 76, 78, 82, 85, 87, 93, 218
  rice, 172–81, 191–92
  upstream, 76–78, 82, 85–86, 92
ValueLinks, 258
Vanida rice mill, 170, 174–76, 178–80, 190
VAT (Value Added Tax), 265, 280, 284, 290–91
VFV (vacant, fallow and virgin) land, 218, 220
Viber, 226
VietGAP (Vietnamese good agricultural practices), 279, 288, 291
Vietnam
  border with China, 290
  coffee, and, 257–64, 269–74, 284, 287
  dragon fruit, and, 257–60, 264–67, 274–80, 284–87, 291
  exports, 256–57
  GDP growth, 2, 259, 260
Vietnam-China border, 290–91
Vietnam Coffee and Cocoa Association, 267
Vietnam General Statistical Office, 267

W

wholesalers, 73, 76, 82, 84, 168, 173, 181, 196–97, 234, 274, 276, 278
World Bank, 2, 17–18, 169–70
World Education, 169
World Integrated Trade Solution database, 24
WTO (World Trade Organization), 4, 8, 15, 17, 26–27, 30, 38, 56, 109–10, 174, 209–10, 273, 282

X

Xi Jinping, 48
Xuanye Company, 170, 174–76, 179–80, 190, 192, 195, 201

Y

Yellow Field International, 130–31

www.ingramcontent.com/pod-product-compliance
Lightning Source LLC
Chambersburg PA
CBHW040212020526
44111CB00050B/2942